This study contributes to debate about the portraits of Paul in Acts and his epistles by considering Paul's Miletus speech (Acts 20.18b–35) and identifies and compares major themes in Luke and Paul's views of Christian leadership. Comparisons with Jesus' speeches in Luke show how Lukan the speech is and, with 1 Thessalonians, how Pauline it is.

The speech calls the Ephesian elders to service after Paul's departure to Jerusalem, focusing on: faithful fulfilment of leadership responsibility; suffering; attitudes to wealth and work; and the death of Jesus. Paul models Christian leadership for the elders.

Parallels in Luke highlight his view of Christian leadership – modelled by Jesus and taught to his disciples, and modelled by Paul and taught to the elders. Study of 1 Thessalonians identifies a remarkably similar portrait of Christian leadership. The Miletus speech is close in thought, presentation and vocabulary to an early, indubitably Pauline letter.

An ordained priest and former chaplain to the Bishop of St Albans, **Steve Walton** is Lecturer in Greek and New Testament Studies at the London Bible College. Author of *A Call to Live: Vocation for Everyone* (1994) and numerous articles, he is a member of the British New Testament Society, the Society for Biblical Literature, and the Tyndale Fellowship for Biblical and Theological Research.

SOCIETY FOR NEW TESTAMENT STUDIES

MONOGRAPH SERIES

General Editor: Richard Bauckham

108

LEADERSHIP AND LIFESTYLE

Leadership and Lifestyle

The portrait of Paul in the Miletus speech
and 1 Thessalonians

STEVE WALTON

London Bible College

CAMBRIDGE
UNIVERSITY PRESS

PUBLISHED BY THE PRESS SYNDICATE OF THE UNIVERSITY OF CAMBRIDGE
The Pitt Building, Trumpington Street, Cambridge, United Kingdom

CAMBRIDGE UNIVERSITY PRESS
The Edinburgh Building, Cambridge CB2 2RU, UK
40 West 20th Street, New York, NY 10011–4211, USA
10 Stamford Road, Oakleigh, Melbourne 3166, Australia
Ruiz de Alarcón 13, 28014 Madrid, Spain

First published 2000

Printed in the United Kingdom at the University Press, Cambridge

Typeface Times Roman 10/12pt   *System* 3b2 [CE]

A catalogue record for this book is available from the British Library

Library of Congress Cataloguing in Publication data
Walton, Steve, Dr.
Leadership and lifestyle: the portrait of Paul in the Miletus speech
and 1 Thessalonians / Steve Walton.
    p.   cm.
Originally presented as the author's thesis (doctoral) – University of
Sheffield, 1997.
Includes bibliographical references and indexes.
ISBN 0 521 78006 3 (hardback)
1. Bible. N.T. Acts XX, 18–35 – Criticism, interpretation, etc.
2. Bible. N.T. Thessalonians, 1st – Criticism, interpretation, etc.
3. Paul, the Apostle, Saint.
4. Leadership – Biblical teaching.   I. Title.
BS2625.2.W25   2000
225.9′2–dc21   99–051378

ISBN 0 521 78006 3 hardback

In memory of
Ruby Walton and Colin Hemer

CONTENTS

ACKNOWLEDGEMENTS

This is a revised version of a PhD thesis submitted to the University of Sheffield in 1997. Scholarship combines individual effort and collective support, and I am acutely aware that without the latter this monograph would never have seen the light of day.

First and foremost I thank my successive supervisors, Dr (now Professor) Andrew Lincoln and Dr Loveday Alexander. In quite different ways they provided stimulation, critical challenge and warm encouragement, along with fine personal examples of scholarship. Their patience in helping me shape my ideas has been exemplary. I am deeply grateful to them both.

Next are those who helped me in my first steps in NT studies at Cambridge, particularly the Revd Prof. C. F. D. Moule, who kindly supervised both an essay and an undergraduate dissertation which kindled my interest in the area which this study discusses, the Revd Dr R. T. France and the Very Revd Dr N. T. Wright.

I have had excellent help from the university libraries of Cambridge, Sheffield and Nottingham, the library of St John's College, Nottingham and, particularly, Tyndale House, Cambridge, where I have very much appreciated the readiness of successive staff to help. The atmosphere and facilities there are beyond praise.

Grants from Tyndale House Council and the St Aidan's College Charity were a considerable help at key stages of the work, as was financial assistance in the latter stages from St John's College, Nottingham.

My examiners, Dr John T. Squires and Dr Loveday Alexander, provided helpful and stimulating comment and challenge, and this published version attempts to meet some of their valuable observations and criticisms. I regret that the stimulating works of Joseph A. Fitzmyer (*The Acts of the Apostles: A New Translation and Commentary*, AB 31, New York, Doubleday, 1998) and Stanley E. Porter (*The Paul of Acts: Essays in Literary Criticism, Rhetoric and*

Theology, WUNT 115, Tübingen, Mohr Siebeck, 1999) appeared too late for me to interact with them in this book.

I owe a great deal to the encouragement and support of colleagues and friends over the period of this research, particularly those at the Church Pastoral Aid Society, the Rt Revd John B. Taylor (whose Chaplain I had the privilege to be), and colleagues and students at St John's College, Nottingham. Graham and Jackie Cray, and Janet Henderson and Dave Challoner generously provided a *pied à terre* in Cambridge at critical stages of the work. My mother, Cynthia Walton, and my wife, Ali Walton have been particularly important. Without these people, this book would still be no more than a nice idea. I cannot repay their support, but I do express my heartfelt thanks.

I am also very grateful to Professor Richard Bauckham, the series editor, and the Syndics of the Cambridge University Press for accepting this monograph for publication, and to the excellent staff of the Press for their work in preparing it for publication, not least Jocelyn Pye, my copy-editor, and Kevin Taylor, my editor.

Finally, two particular people have provided me with examples of thoughtful godliness: my aunt, Ruby Walton, and Dr Colin Hemer. Sadly, neither has lived to see this book, but both were profoundly influential upon me. In gratitude to God, this book is dedicated to their memory.

ABBREVIATIONS

Abbreviations (apart from those listed below) are those in the *Instructions for Contributors* of the *Journal of Biblical Literature*, to be found on the SBL Web site (http://www.sbl-site.org/scripts/SBL/Publications/handbook/SBL-pubs-JBL-inst.html).

A1CS   The Book of Acts in its First-Century Setting

EDNT   Balz, Horst and Schneider, Gerhard (eds.), *Exegetical Dictionary of the New Testament*, 3 vols., ET of *Exegetisches Wörterbuch zum Neuen Testament* (translators: Medendorp, John W. and Stott, Douglas W.), Grand Rapids: Eerdmans, 1990–3.

NA[27]   Aland, Barbara, Aland, Kurt, Karavidopoulos, Johannes, Martini, Carlo M. and Metzger, Bruce M. (eds.), *Novum Testamentum Graece,* 27th edition, Stuttgart: Deutsche Bibelgesellschaft, 1993.

NIBC   New International Biblical Commentary

NIDNTT   Brown, Colin (ed.), *The New International Dictionary of New Testament Theology*, 3 vols., Exeter: Paternoster Press, 1975–8.

SIG[3]   Dittenberger, W. (ed.), *Sylloge Inscriptionum Graecarum*, 4 vols., 3rd edition, Leipzig: S. Hirzelium, 1915–24.

TNT   McHardy, W. D. (ed.), *The Translator's New Testament*, London: British and Foreign Bible Society, 1973.

UBS[3]   Aland, Kurt, Black, Matthew, Martini, Carlo M., Metzger, Bruce M. and Wikgren, Allen (eds.), *The Greek New Testament,* 3rd (corrected) edition, Stuttgart: United Bible Societies, 1983.

UBS⁴   Aland, Barbara, Aland, Kurt, Karavidopoulos,
          Johannes, Martini, Carlo M. and Metzger, Bruce M.
          (eds.), *The Greek New Testament,* 4th revised edition,
          Stuttgart: Deutsche Bibelgesellschaft/United Bible
          Societies, 1994.
v.l.   *varia lectio* (variant reading)

1

WHY STUDY THE MILETUS SPEECH?

The study of the portrait of Paul in Acts has a long history; it has been investigated by virtually every modern scholar who has written substantially on Acts. Two particular issues gave rise to this study: how far the portraits of Paul in Acts and the Pauline epistles are compatible, and what knowledge Luke[1] has of the Pauline epistles. In both of these debates Paul's Miletus speech (Acts 20.18b–35) is pivotal.

On the one hand, it is the only Pauline speech in Acts given to a Christian community – in other words, it is addressed to an 'epistle-like' situation, by contrast with other Pauline speeches, which are evangelistic or apologetic. It is therefore a key 'test case' for the compatibility of the two portraits of Paul, for it offers the opportunity to compare Luke's and Paul's dealings with Christians and, in particular, the understandings of Christian leadership which are presented.

On the other hand, the speech's language and ideas are widely recognised as paralleling the language and ideas of the Pauline epistles. This raises the question of the relationship between the speech and the epistles: are the epistles the source for the speech, directly or indirectly, or is Luke utilising independent Pauline tradition or composing freely?

In order to orientate ourselves, we shall consider the state of play in these debates and highlight the contribution which studying the Miletus speech can make to them. We shall also briefly survey previous work on the speech, to learn positively from the work of other scholars, as well as to identify their blind spots and failings.

---

[1] I use 'Luke' throughout to denote the author of the Third Gospel and Acts, without presupposing anything further about him (beyond his gender – see Alexander, 'Luke's Preface', p. 2 n. 2).

1.1   The Paul of Acts / Paul of the epistles debate

1.1.1   Three schools of thought

Recent study of the relative values of Acts and the epistles as sources for the study of Paul – both his life and his thought – can be divided roughly into the 'schools' enumerated by Mattill.[2] They are not necessarily mutually exclusive: Mattill notes that some scholars seem to shift between one and another.[3] Nevertheless, they form useful broad categories to outline the debate. In each case Mattill considers the areas of general description; the method used to distinguish tradition from redaction; Paul's *cursus vitae*; the supernatural; practices and principles; and Paul's doctrine.[4]

First is the 'One Paul View of the School of Historical Research',[5] represented by scholars such as Rackham, Gasque and Bruce.[6] This 'school' sees only one Paul in Acts and epistles, and finds consistency with regard to the views of the law, the Jewish-Gentile problem, divine calling and adaptability to different kinds of people and situations. Proponents of this approach see the linguistic uniformity of Acts as a barrier to any separation of sources, and believe that the so-called 'we' sections[7] derive from Luke having been Paul's travel-companion.

The 'Lopsided Paul View of the School of Restrained Criticism'[8] is the second group, represented by scholars such as Munck, Harnack and Mattill himself.[9] This group believes that, while there is no absolute divergence between the two portraits of Paul, a

---

[2]   Mattill, 'Value of Acts'.

[3]   Mattill, 'Value of Acts', pp. 77 n. 1, 83 n. 10.

[4]   Mattill considers four 'schools', although the fourth includes only van Manen, whose views have not been followed in recent scholarship (e.g. he regards all of the Pauline corpus as pseudepigraphic) and are not germane to our topic. See Mattill, 'Value of Acts', pp. 95–7; van Manen, 'Paul'.

[5]   Mattill, 'Value of Acts', pp. 77–83.

[6]   Rackham, *Acts*; Gasque, 'Speeches of Acts'; Bruce, *Acts* (2nd edn); Bruce, 'Speeches: Thirty Years After' (but see n. 9 below).

[7]   That is, the parts of the book narrated in the first person plural, namely Acts 16.10–17; 20.5–15; 21.1–18; 27.1–28.16. For brief discussion from the perspective of this 'school', see Bruce, *Acts* (3rd edn), pp. 40f.

[8]   Mattill, 'Value of Acts', pp. 83–7.

[9]   Munck, *Acts*; Harnack, *Acts*, esp. pp. 231–8; Mattill, 'Purpose of Acts'. Mattill, 'Value of Acts', p. 77 n. 1 also suggests that the later Bruce belongs to this group, citing Bruce, 'Paul of Acts'. We might add Bruce's subsequent work, particularly Bruce, 'Acts: Historical Record?', in which he seems to go further towards a 'lopsided Paul' position.

portrait of Paul emerging from either Acts or epistles alone would be lop-sided. Acts fills out gaps left by the epistles and the epistles may balance the one-sidedness of Acts. This 'school' holds that written sources lie behind the early parts of Acts, a consequence of the belief that Luke used Mark's Gospel as a source plus the evidence of Luke 1.1–4 (especially the work of 'the many', verse 1). In the 'we' sections Luke is composing freely in describing events in which he took part – he continues to be seen as Paul's travel-companion. This is why the (Pauline) speeches are not seen as free inventions of Luke, for Luke had heard Paul speak and understood him enough to present his thought reasonably accurately.

The third view is the 'Two-Paul View of the School of Creative Edification',[10] represented by Dibelius, Vielhauer, Haenchen and Conzelmann.[11] These scholars see the Paul of the (authentic) Pauline epistles (at least, Romans, 1 and 2 Corinthians and Galatians) as the historical Paul. The portrait to be found in Acts is the work of an admirer of Paul looking from some distance, both chronologically and theologically. Acts is only to be depended upon when it is corroborated by the epistles. Luke is not Paul's travel-companion,[12] but an 'edifier' of the church of his day – which means that the primary significance of Acts is not as an historical record: 'it is above all a *religious* book that we are dealing with. [Luke] is trying to show the powers of the Christian spirit with which the persons in his narrative are charged, and which he wishes to make live in his readers.'[13] The portrait of Paul thus created is virtually fictional. Miracles and events involving the supernatural are regarded as unhistorical, on the grounds that they are incredible. The speeches are seen as free compositions by the author. Haenchen's commentary is a brilliant exposition of Acts from this perspective.[14]

1.1.2   Vielhauer and Haenchen

It is the debate between these views that is of interest for our study. In particular, Vielhauer continues to be cited as having shown that

[10]   Mattill, 'Value of Acts', pp. 88–95.
[11]   Dibelius, *Studies in Acts*; Vielhauer, 'Paulinism of Acts'; Haenchen, *Acts*; Conzelmann, *Theology of St Luke*; Conzelmann, *Acts*.
[12]   With the exception of Dibelius, *Studies in Acts*, p. 95 n. 4.
[13]   Dibelius, *Fresh Approach*, p. 265 (italics his).
[14]   Haenchen, *Acts*.

the theology of Paul in Acts is incompatible with that found in his letters.[15] His article, in combination with Haenchen's arguments on the subject in his commentary,[16] set the agenda for scholarly study of the portrait of Paul in Acts for a generation. We shall therefore summarise their arguments before looking at the responses that resulted.

Vielhauer's important essay appeared in 1950, and its influence was increased by an English translation in 1966. Vielhauer argues that the Paul of Acts is at variance with the Paul of the epistles at four significant theological points.

First, the Paul of Acts shows a natural theology closer to the later apologists than the real Paul.[17] Vielhauer contrasts the Areopagus speech (Acts 17.22–31) with Romans 1.18–32. He believes the speech offers a positive view of pagan religion as a *praeparatio evangelica* – Acts 17.28f implies people may find God on the basis of human kinship to the deity.[18] The tone of the Areopagus speech is enlightenment, not accusation – by contrast with Romans 1, where mention of 'natural' knowledge of God appears in the context of God's wrath.[19] The natural theology functions differently in the two contexts – in Athens it is seen positively and can be built on by Paul, whereas in Romans its sole purpose is to show that people are responsible for their actions.

Second, Vielhauer sees the Paul of Acts as having a positive view of the Jewish law, whereas the real Paul waged an anti-Jewish polemic against the law.[20] Vielhauer believes eight points show the Lukan Paul's loyalty to the law: his missionary method of beginning with the synagogue in each place; his submission to the Jerusalem authorities; his circumcision of Timothy (Acts 16.3); his spreading of the apostolic decree (Acts 16.4); his assumption of a

[15] Vielhauer, 'Paulinism of Acts'. Haenchen, *Acts*, p. 48 implies that Vielhauer's article marks the opening of a new chapter in study of Acts. Vielhauer's influence can be seen in Ziesler, *Pauline Christianity*, pp. 133–6, who repeats most of the ideas of Vielhauer's article (without acknowledgement).

[16] Haenchen, *Acts*, pp. 112–16.

[17] Vielhauer, 'Paulinism of Acts', pp. 34–7.

[18] Vielhauer argues in dependence upon Dibelius' analysis of the Areopagus speech, which posits a Stoic origin for many of the speech's key ideas (Dibelius, *Studies in Acts*, pp. 26–77, originally published in German in 1939). Dibelius' work is in turn dependent on Norden, *Agnostos Theos* (Dibelius, *Studies in Acts*, p. 28 n. 27). For critique of Vielhauer and Dibelius, see Gempf, 'Historical and Literary Appropriateness', pp. 111–34; Gempf, 'Athens, Paul at'.

[19] Vielhauer, 'Paulinism of Acts', p. 36, citing Rom. 1.18, 20, 21.

[20] Vielhauer, 'Paulinism of Acts', pp. 37–43.

vow (Acts 18.18); his journeys to Jerusalem for festivals (Acts 18.21; 20.16); his participation in a Nazirite vow (Acts 21.18–28); and his stress on being a Pharisee when on trial (Acts 23.6; 26.5). By contrast, the historical Paul believed that in Christ he was free from the Jewish law. He could therefore accommodate himself to Jewish practices at times (1 Cor. 9.19–23), while being unbending when the substance of the gospel was at stake (e.g. Gal. 2). Vielhauer cannot accept that the Paul who wrote Galatians 5.2–6 could have circumcised Timothy, for to be circumcised must have allowed saving significance to the law. Even in Acts 13.38f, which Vielhauer sees as the only place where Luke's Paul speaks thematically on the law's significance, there are contrasts with the real Paul: justification is equated with the forgiveness of sins, something that Paul never does; forgiveness derives from Jesus' messiahship, based on the resurrection, rather than coming from the death of Jesus; and justification is partial, being *'also* by faith'.[21] This misrepresentation of Paul results from Luke's Gentile origins, which meant that he had never experienced the law as a means of salvation, and so he did not grasp the Pauline antithesis of law and Christ.

Third, Vielhauer sees Christological differences between Paul in Acts and Paul in the epistles.[22] He sees Acts 13.13–43; 26.22f as the only extended Pauline statements on Christology in the book, both made before Jews. There, Paul asserts that Jesus is the Messiah, using scriptural proof-texts in support. Vielhauer sees the obvious Pauline parallels (Rom. 1.3f; 1 Cor. 15.3f) as pre-Pauline formulae[23] which therefore display neither Luke's nor Paul's Christology, but that of the earliest congregations. Likewise, the Christological statements of Acts 13.16–37; 26.22f are the views of the earliest congregations, and neither Pauline nor Lukan. Lukan Christology is 'adoptionistic', whereas Pauline Christology is metaphysical.

Fourth, Vielhauer sees the Lukan Paul's eschatology as different from the real Paul's. Paul himself expected an imminent parousia;

---

[21] Vielhauer, 'Paulinism of Acts', p. 42 (italics his).

[22] Vielhauer, 'Paulinism of Acts', pp. 43–5.

[23] Vielhauer, 'Paulinism of Acts', p. 44 n. 32 cites Bultmann, *Theology*, vol. 1, p. 49 in support of the assertion that Rom. 1.3f is non-Pauline. But Bultmann offers no arguments! (Cf., *contra*, Wright, 'Messiah and People of God', pp. 51–5.) Vielhauer, 'Paulinism of Acts', pp. 43f observes that Paul states 1 Cor. 15.3f to be tradition from the earliest congregation, in agreement with Jeremias, *Eucharistic Words*, pp. 101–3 and, more recently, Fee, *1 Corinthians*, p. 718.

this motivated his work and determined his relationship with the world (1 Cor. 7.29ff). He never speaks of the 'age to come', since the fullness of time is already here. By contrast the Lukan Paul presents Luke's own eschatology, which expects the parousia in the distant future and replaces the imminent expectation by a theology of history 'as a continuous redemptive process'.[24] This is why Luke writes a history of the early church at all – those who are expecting the end of the world any moment do not write their own history![25]

Haenchen accepts Vielhauer's points[26] and adds further discrepancies. First, Luke's Paul is a great miracle-worker (Acts 13.6–12; 14.8–10, 19f; 20.7–12; 28.3–6), whereas the real Paul's exploits were so unexceptional that his opponents could deny that he performed miracles.[27] Second, the Paul of Acts is an outstanding orator, but the real Paul was a feeble and unimpressive speaker (2 Cor. 10.10). Third, Luke did not accept Paul's claim to be an apostle; for Luke, only the Twelve were apostles, for they alone were witnesses to the ministry, teaching, death and resurrection of Jesus.[28] Fourth, Haenchen contrasts Luke's portrayal of the risen Jesus eating and drinking with the disciples and Paul's belief that Jesus was no longer flesh and blood (1 Cor. 15.50).[29] Luke's image of the risen Jesus was the kind required for a later generation, when eyewitnesses were no longer available and the threats of gnostic docetism and Jewish or pagan scepticism appeared.

1.1.3   Responses to Vielhauer and Haenchen

Responses may conveniently be considered as methodological or evidential. There have been responses on particular points, notably

---

[24] Vielhauer, 'Paulinism of Acts', p. 47.

[25] The outlines of an understanding of Luke as a proponent of nascent *Frühkatholizismus* can here be seen, and are developed more fully by Conzelmann, *Theology of St Luke*; Käsemann, *NT Questions*, pp. 21f, 236 n. 1; Dunn, *Unity and Diversity*, pp. 341–66 (esp. 346–9, 352–8, 362).

[26] Haenchen, *Acts*, pp. 48f.

[27] Haenchen, *Acts*, pp. 113f sees this as the background to 2 Cor. 12.12.

[28] Haenchen, *Acts*, p. 114 n. 5 sees the use of 'apostles' of Paul and Barnabas (Acts 14.4, 14) as irrelevant, since they are envoys from Antioch. But Wilson, *Gentiles*, pp. 113–20 (esp. 116f) argues cogently that Luke used the term 'apostles' both as a shorthand for the Twelve and for a wider group of apostles, including Paul and Barnabas – a group recognised by Paul as apostles too (e.g. Rom. 16.7; Gal. 1.1; 1 Cor. 9.6; 15.5); cf. Clark, 'Role of the Apostles', esp. pp. 182–90.

[29] Haenchen, *Acts*, pp. 114f.

Vielhauer's four contrasts,[30] but these are not particularly relevant to our theme.

Methodological responses

Critics of Vielhauer and Haenchen cite problems caused by the nature and paucity of material at our disposal in considering the 'theologies' of Luke and Paul. Luke's account is selective and episodic, impressionistic rather than integrated, and linked together by generalising summaries or an itinerary.[31] In Acts, we have only three recorded missionary sermons of Paul, which can only be summaries.[32] Hengel asserts that to see Luke primarily as a 'theologian' is to err:

> The radical 'redactional-critical' approach so popular today, which sees Luke above all as a freely inventive theologian, mistakes his real purpose, namely that as a Christian 'historian' he sets out to report the events of the past that provided the foundation for the faith and its extension. He does not set out primarily to present his own 'theology'.[33]

Further, Paul's role in Luke's writings is not primarily as a theologian, but 'as the missionary, the charismatic and the founder

---

[30] On natural theology, see Ellis, *Luke*, pp. 45f; Gärtner, *Areopagus Speech*; Gasque, *History of the Criticism*, pp. 213f, 288, 290; Bruce, 'Paul of Acts', 301–3; Marshall, *Acts* (NT Guides), pp. 96f. On the law, see Gasque, 'Book of Acts and History', p. 66 n. 39; Marshall, *Acts* (NT Guides), p. 97. (The debate over Paul's understanding of the law has moved on considerably in the light of the 'new perspective'. For discussion, see Cranfield, *Romans,* vol. II, pp. 845–62; Sanders, *Paul, Law and Jewish*; Dunn, *Jesus, Paul and the Law*, esp. pp. 183–214; Wright, *Climax*, esp. p. 208.) On Christology, see Ellis, *Luke*, p. 46; Marshall, *Acts* (NT Guides), p. 62; Moule, 'Christology of Acts', pp. 171, 182. On eschatology, see Hengel, *Acts and the History*, p. 59; Ellis, *Luke*, pp. 48–50; Munck, *Paul and the Salvation*, pp. 36–55; Borgen, 'Paul to Luke'; Wenham, *Paul*, pp. 297–304; Maddox, *Purpose of Luke-Acts*, pp. 115–32; Moore, *Parousia in the NT*.

[31] Davies, *Gospel and Land*, p. 285.

[32] Barclay, 'Comparison', p. 165. Marshall, *Acts* (TNTC), p. 41 argues forcefully that the speeches were never meant to be seen as verbatim reports, since: (a) it would only take a few minutes to read each one, whereas Luke indicates that Paul spoke at length (Acts 20.7!); (b) it is unlikely that audiences remembered what early Christian preachers said, or that the preachers themselves kept records; (c) at times it is evident that Luke is summarising by the variant forms of the same speech that are reported (e.g. the message of the angel to Cornelius: Acts 10.4–6, 31f); (d) on some occasions it is impossible for Luke to have known what was said, such as Festus and Agrippa's private conversation (Acts 25.13–22; 26.30–2).

[33] Hengel, *Acts and the History*, pp. 67f.

of communities'.[34] Therefore the nature of Acts as a source is not easily conducive to reading off Paul's theology as Luke understands it.

On the other hand, Hengel rightly notices what a limited knowledge of Paul's preaching the epistles provide.[35] Moreover, the epistles are occasional documents responding to particular situations, rather than full expositions of Paul's thought.[36]

In the light of the paucity of material, Gasque argues for caution, comparing the knowledge of Paul available from such limited sources with the picture of Augustine or Luther or Barth which a similarly limited range of source material would give us.[37]

The alleged contrast between history and edification is a second target for critics. Haenchen, Gasque observes, alleges that Luke has no concern for historical accuracy, but rather is concerned to edify the church.[38] Gasque properly asks whether the two are mutually exclusive. Haenchen confuses two issues: first, the distinction between aiming at history or edification; and second, measuring how accurately a writer records history. Hemer stresses that sweeping statements that ancient historians felt free to be creative are too strong, for 'at least some of the ancients were moved by a lively concern for historical accuracy'.[39]

Bruce suggests that differences between the 'two Pauls' may be those which would be expected between a portrait by another and a self-portrait.[40] Marshall argues in a related vein that the differences may be explicable by the dissimilar interests and audiences of the writers – Luke's concerns focusing on the evangelistic mission of Paul and his relation with Jewish Christians, and Paul's on problems in emerging new churches and freedom from the law for Gentile Christians.[41]

[34] Hengel, *Between Jesus and Paul*, p. 110.
[35] Hengel, *Acts and the History*, p. 43.
[36] Jervell, *Unknown Paul*, pp. 52f; Hemer and Gempf, *Book of Acts*, p. 246.
[37] Gasque, *History of the Criticism*, p. 289.
[38] Gasque, *History of the Criticism*, p. 246, citing Haenchen, 'Acts as Source Material', p. 278. It is inaccurate of Gasque, *History of the Criticism*, pp. 206f to describe Dibelius as pre-judging the question of historicity. Rather, Dibelius appears to shelve the question (e.g. Dibelius, *Studies in Acts*, p. 184). It is Dibelius' successors, such as Haenchen, who assume that Dibelius has shown that certain events were unhistorical, e.g. Haenchen, *Acts*, p. 590 on the Miletus speech. Cf. Gempf, 'Historical and Literary Appropriateness', pp. 70f.
[39] Hemer and Gempf, *Book of Acts*, p. 69.
[40] Bruce, 'Paul of Acts', 282; see also § 2.5 on Acts' categorisation as 'secondary'.
[41] Marshall, *Acts* (TNTC), p. 43 n. 4. Cf. Marshall, *Acts* (NT Guides), p. 96 for a later re-statement; cf. Nolland, *Luke 1–9:20*, p. xxxvi.

Then, Gasque argues that Haenchen is antipathetic to Luke's theology (as Haenchen understands it).[42] In particular Gasque believes that Haenchen reads Lukan theology in Acts through (Haenchen's own) existentialist Lutheran spectacles, with the result that Luke comes off second best to Paul. Gasque criticises Haenchen and Vielhauer for misrepresenting both Luke and Paul, since they present Luke as the father of *Frühkatholizismus* and Paul as a great existentialist Lutheran.

A final methodological criticism is that the comparison made is the wrong one. It is *prima facie* likely that Paul's preaching outside the Christian community would be different from his teaching within that community.[43] Accordingly, it is mistaken to compare the theology of Paul in his speeches in Acts as a whole with that in his epistles as a whole.

Jervell[44] develops this point in arguing that the historical Paul may well have agreed on much with the generality of early Christians, but that we only see hints of this in the epistles, because of their (often) polemical content. He criticises Vielhauer for his reliance on Paul's ideas, seen separately from his actions, as his source for Paul's beliefs. Jervell finds hints in the epistles of a Jewish-Christian Paul who lived in accordance with the law (e.g. 1 Cor. 9.19–21), and argues that this is the Paul of the oral tradition which lies behind the Paul of Acts. Accordingly, he claims, we need to look carefully in both epistles and Acts for a Paul who is in agreement with other Christians, rather than polarise the two.

Evidential responses

A number of scholars point to similarities in the two portraits of Paul, notably Bruce. He observes a number of 'undesigned coincidences' between the two, including biographical and similar information[45] and, more significantly for our discussion, the impression of Paul given by the two sources.[46] Bruce draws attention to Paul's self-support (Acts 18.3; 20.34; 1 Thess. 2.9; 2 Thess. 3.7f; 1 Cor. 9.18); his policy of going first to Jews and then to Gentiles (Acts 13.46; Rom. 1.16; 2.9f); his adaptability (in Acts to Jew and

---

[42] Gasque, *History of the Criticism*, p. 246.
[43] Barclay, 'Comparison', p. 175; Marshall, *Luke: Historian and Theologian*, p. 291; Bruce, *Speeches in Acts*, p. 26.
[44] Jervell, *Unknown Paul*, pp. 52–76.
[45] Bruce, 'Paul of Acts', 285–93.   [46] Bruce, 'Paul of Acts', 293–8.

Gentile, learned and unlearned, Athenians and Sanhedrin, cf. 1 Cor. 9.19–23), which explains why Paul at times lives as a Jew among Jews (e.g. Acts 18.18; 21.23ff). Bruce argues that the circumcision of Timothy (Acts 16.3) does not contradict Paul's hostility to circumcision (e.g. Gal. 5.3), for in Galatians Paul takes issue with the view that circumcision is necessary for salvation, while seeing circumcision *of itself* as a matter of indifference (Gal. 5.6; 6.15). Hengel, likewise, argues that if he had refused to circumcise Timothy, Paul would have been seen as supporting apostasy and synagogue doors would close to him. Therefore it is feasible that Paul did circumcise Timothy.[47]

A second criticism relates to speeches. Vielhauer and Haenchen build their study of the speeches on the work of Dibelius.[48] Dibelius focuses on the literary artistry of Luke in the speeches, continually asking the question, 'What did *Luke* intend to put across by this speech?'[49] His approach is predicated on two axioms: that the speeches in their present form are the work of Luke;[50] and that the question whether the speeches were delivered is irrelevant. At times he appears to assume that a speech cannot be a summary of what was said, but without discussing his reasons for this axiom.

Criticisms of Dibelius have been legion. His view of the role of speeches in the ancient historians has been challenged.[51] Gasque and Hemer argue that the evidence contradicts Dibelius' assertion that ancient historians uniformly invented speeches for historical figures where source material was lacking; they reply partly by producing claimed counter-examples, and partly by claiming that the interpretation of a key passage in Thucydides (1.22.1) offered by Dibelius is mistaken.[52]

Gasque also offers evidence that Luke did not freely compose speeches.[53] Gasque sees a contrast between the speeches in Acts

[47] Hengel, *Acts and the History*, p. 64.

[48] Vielhauer, 'Paulinism of Acts', p. 33 n. 1; Haenchen, *Acts*, pp. 34–7, 39–41.

[49] e.g. Dibelius, *Studies in Acts*, p. 144, writing about ancient historians, asserts: 'What seems to the author his most important obligation is not ... establishing what speech was actually made; to him, it is rather that of introducing speeches into the structure in a way which will be relevant to his purpose.'

[50] Dibelius, *Studies in Acts*, p. 3.

[51] Gasque, 'Speeches of Acts', pp. 242–6; Gasque, 'Book of Acts and History', pp. 59–61; Hemer, 'Luke the Historian', pp. 29–34; Hemer and Gempf, *Book of Acts*, pp. 63–100. For critical discussion of Gasque's arguments in the light of study of Graeco-Roman historical writing, see Gempf, 'Public Speaking', esp. pp. 295f.

[52] On the Thucydides passage, cf. Porter, 'Thucydides 1.22.1'.

[53] Gasque, 'Book of Acts and History', pp. 61–3.

and those in 'obviously inferior Greek historians', such as Josephus. He cites Ehrhardt's observation[54] that there are obvious occasions in Acts where Luke could have inserted a speech (e.g. after 5.21 and 28.6[55]) but chose not to do so, proposing that the lack of a speech at such points results from the author's lack of knowledge of a speech on that occasion. Gasque believes that the Third Gospel's use of Mark provides evidence of the author's method: there, he does not freely invent speeches of Jesus. Therefore the possibility should be considered that in Acts Luke works similarly.

Gasque regards the linguistic and theological diversity of the speeches in Acts as significant. As one example, he refers to the speeches of Stephen, Peter, and Paul in Athens and Miletus, concurring with Moule that there are varying Christologies within these speeches.[56] This suggests that Luke has not uniformly imposed his own theology on the speeches, and that they cannot be read simply as expressions of Luke's own view.

Jervell believes that Luke had access to traditions about the apostles and early churches in composing Acts.[57] He finds places in the Pauline epistles where Paul shows that the formation of an already existing church is part of the missionary proclamation of the gospel in another place (e.g. Rom. 1.8; 1 Thess. 1.8ff; 2 Cor. 3.1–3).[58] He further identifies allusions to stories about the life of a congregation being used in paraenesis and paraclesis (e.g. 1 Thess. 3.6; 2 Thess. 1.3ff).[59] Finally, Jervell finds the Jerusalem church being used by Paul as a model for other churches (e.g. 1 Thess. 2.14; Rom. 15.6–28).[60] Jervell concludes that conditions favoured the formation and preservation of traditions about the apostles and their churches.[61]

Such scholars also seek to provide an historical framework for Luke's writing on the basis of the evidence available, with the limited aim of undercutting claims that Acts is entirely unhistorical. For example, Hemer cites Ramsay's work,[62] which shows Luke's

---

[54] Ehrhardt, *Framework*, p. 88.
[55] Mis-cited by Ehrhardt as 28.16, a mistake reproduced in Gasque, 'Book of Acts and History', p. 62.
[56] Moule, 'Christology of Acts', esp. pp. 166–72.
[57] Jervell, *Luke and the People of God*, pp. 19–39.
[58] Jervell, *Luke and the People of God*, pp. 23–8.
[59] Jervell, *Luke and the People of God*, pp. 28–30.
[60] Jervell, *Luke and the People of God*, pp. 32f.
[61] Jervell, *Luke and the People of God*, p. 36.
[62] Hemer, 'Luke the Historian', 36–9, citing Ramsay, *St Paul*; cf. Barrett, *Acts*, vol. II, p. cxiv, providing a similar list of features represented accurately by Luke.

accuracy on small points of administrative and geographical detail – Hemer sees this as suggesting that it is likely that Luke is reporting first hand, particularly because the library resources available to modern scholars writing historical novels (for example) were not freely available to ancient writers.

Similarly, after his own extensive discussion of a considerable number of points of contact between Acts and external evidence, Hemer affirms that he is not seeking 'to *prove* the historicity of Acts',[63] but believes that the accuracy on detail which Luke demonstrates is an important factor in an estimation of Luke as a writer.

1.1.4   The relevance of the Miletus speech

Paul's speech at Miletus is central to this discussion, for it contains a number of parallels of vocabulary with the Pauline epistles. Indeed, Dodd asserts that this implies either that Luke used the epistles (which he regards as unlikely) or that he used reminiscences of a genuine Pauline speech.[64]

The Miletus speech occurs within a 'we' section of Acts[65] and is the only speech of Paul to occur within such a section. Bruce therefore believes the author was present and suggests that Luke may have taken shorthand notes.[66] At least, the 'we' sections have

---

[63] Hemer and Gempf, *Book of Acts*, p. 219 (italics his).

[64] Dodd, *Apostolic Preaching*, p. 32. For verse-by-verse lists of parallels, see, e.g., Rackham, *Acts*, pp. 389–96; Bruce, *Acts* (3rd edn), pp. 429–37; Conzelmann, *Acts*, pp. 173–6; Johnson, *Acts*, pp. 360–6.

[65] Although 20.18–38 itself is in the third person. The first person plural is found in 20.6–15; 21.1–18. Nonetheless, the first person plural in 20.15, recording the arrival in Miletus, implies that 20.18–38 should be seen as part of the 'we' section, *contra* Barrett, *Acts,* vol. II, p. xxvi.

[66] Bruce, *Acts* (2nd edn), p. 377. Haenchen, *Acts*, p. 590 can only respond with an exclamation mark to this suggestion, but Bruce, 'Speeches: Thirty Years After', p. 63 argues that shorthand was not unknown in the first century and that Luke is the kind of man who would use it. For evidence of shorthand in our period see Milne (ed.), *Greek Shorthand Manuals*, p. 1; Kenyon, 'Tachygraphy'. Both cite Diogenes Laertius 2.48 (concerning Xenophon (4th century BC) being the first to represent spoken words using signs (ὑποσημειωσαμένος τὰ λεγόμενα)); Plutarch *Cato Minor* 23.3 (attributing the introduction of shorthand in Rome to Cicero in 63 BC); Cicero *Letters to Atticus* 13.32 (3 June 45 BC, where Cicero suggests that Atticus might not have understood what he wrote concerning the ten legates, because he wrote it διὰ σημείων; the use of the Greek term in a Latin author Milne and Kenyon understand to mean that the Greek shorthand system preceded the Latin).

been understood as indicating a source used by Luke which goes back to eyewitness testimony.[67]

Further, the Miletus speech echoes the theology of Paul. Most notably, verse 28 contains the most explicit reference to the redemptive significance of the death of Jesus in Acts. Moule claims not only that the theology of Paul is heard at this point, but also that the situation is like that of a Pauline letter – Paul is 'recalling an already evangelized community to its deepest insights'.[68]

The audience of the speech is also significant. Moule argues that it is likely that Paul would speak differently to a non-Christian audience by comparison with addressing those who were already Christians. This is why the Miletus speech is pivotal for the comparison of the two portraits of Paul, for it is the only occasion in Acts where Paul speaks to Christians: all the other Pauline speeches are evangelistic.[69]

Haenchen is quite dismissive of the possibility that the Paul of the Miletus speech may be similar to the Paul of the epistles, claiming, 'Dibelius finally proved the speech to be Luke's work and evaluated it.'[70] However, Dibelius himself carefully differentiates the task of examining the artistry of Luke in writing the speech and the question of the origins of the speech. On the latter, he asserts that we cannot know whether Paul spoke at Miletus or what he said there.[71] Thus Dibelius side-steps the question of the historicity of the speech and the portrait of Paul it offers.

So the Miletus speech provides a significant test case for the Vielhauer-Haenchen thesis that the 'two Pauls' are at variance theologically. If the Paul of the speech proves to be quite different from the Paul of the epistles, their thesis may be well grounded; if not, questions are raised against it.

[67] *Pace* Robbins, 'By Land', pp. 215–43. For critique see Porter, 'We Passages', esp. pp. 554–8; Hemer, 'First Person Narrative'.

[68] Moule, 'Christology of Acts', p. 171. The first proponent of the similarity of the situation at Miletus to the Pauline epistles seems to be Tholuck, 'Reden'.

[69] Moule, 'Christology of Acts', p. 173. He further observes that there are a small number of occasions within the epistles (where Paul is undoubtedly addressing professing Christians) where Paul recalls his initial evangelistic message (he cites 1 Thess. 1.10; Rom. 1.3f; 1 Cor. 15.1ff), and it is notable that these summaries approximate to the 'bare κήρυγμα of the Acts'.

[70] Haenchen, *Acts*, p. 590.

[71] Dibelius, *Studies in Acts*, p. 158.

1.2   Luke's knowledge of the Pauline epistles

A related debate concerns whether Luke knew and used the Pauline epistles in writing Acts. The 'Tübingen school' of the last century believed that Luke was writing Acts in the second century to reconcile the Petrine and Pauline versions of Christianity, and therefore assumed that Luke had access to the epistles.[72]

Subsequent research tended to react against this axiom as part and parcel of the reaction against the Tübingen reconstruction of early Christianity.[73] It was left to Enslin in 1938 to re-open the question.[74] More recent work has divided on this issue, with some arguing that Luke knew the epistles, but did not utilise them in writing Acts; some that Luke knew and used the epistles; and some that Luke did not know the epistles at all. We shall briefly summarise the main lines of argument before indicating the relevance of the Miletus speech.

1.2.1   The case for no knowledge

The case for Luke not having known the letters hinges on three arguments.[75] First, if Luke had known the letters, he would surely have used them in writing Acts. Scholars believe it is incredible that Luke, having such a rich source at his disposal, would decline to use it.[76]

Second, there is no hint in Acts that Paul wrote letters. But if Luke had known that Paul wrote letters, even if Luke had no access to them, he would have mentioned that fact in Acts, not least because Paul's letters were acknowledged to be 'weighty and strong' (2 Cor. 10.10).

Third, Luke provides quotations from letters elsewhere in Acts (e.g. 15.23–9; 23.26–30). This shows that he had no *a priori* objection to letters as such. If he had access to Pauline epistles, there were natural opportunities within the narrative to quote

---

[72] For a helpful summary of the 'Tübingen school', see Gasque, *History of the Criticism*, pp. 21–54.

[73] Thus Emmet and Windisch in Foakes Jackson and Lake, *Beginnings*, vol. I, pp. 297, 308 (arguing respectively for and against the identification of Luke as the travel-companion of Paul) both agree that Luke did not know the Pauline epistles.

[74] Enslin, '"Luke" and Paul'.

[75] e.g. Enslin, 'Once Again', p. 253; Walker, 'Acts and the Pauline Corpus', p. 3.

[76] e.g. Zahn, *Introduction*, vol. III, p. 119.

them. The lack of such quotations demonstrates that Luke did not have such access.

Thus the case for Luke's lack of knowledge of the epistles is put.[77] This argument is combined by some with the view that Luke was the travel-companion of Paul. Some of these scholars then argue that Luke knew Paul so well that he would not need to use the epistles, which makes the case one for having knowledge, but not using it.[78] Others also hold that Luke never knew Paul.[79]

1.2.2 The case for knowledge

Enslin, Knox and Walker argue that Luke had access to the Pauline epistles.[80] Enslin and Walker hold that Luke used the letters, whereas Knox believes that Luke preferred to use independent traditions, because of the association of Paul with schism in Luke's day.[81] Three arguments favour Luke knowing and using the letters.

First, it is mistaken to claim that Luke would not have modified and transformed his sources. On the basis of the freedom with which he believes Luke handles Matthew and Mark,[82] Enslin

---

[77] e.g. Bruce, *Book of Acts* (revised edn), p. 15; Conzelmann, *Acts*, p. xxxiii; Haenchen, *Acts*, pp. 125f; Hemer and Gempf, *Book of Acts*, p. 245; Hengel, *Acts and the History*, pp. 38, 66; Longenecker, 'Acts', pp. 237f; Maddox, *Purpose of Luke-Acts*, p. 68; Marshall, *Acts* (TNTC), p. 48.

[78] e.g. Bruce, *Commentary on Acts*, p. 25 n. 30. He appears to have changed his mind on the grounds for this view, while continuing to hold that Luke was Paul's travel-companion, in Bruce, *Acts* (3rd edn), p. 53. Hengel, *Acts and the History*, p. 66 suggests that the reason for Luke's lack of knowledge of the letters is that, by the time he began travelling with Paul, almost all of the letters (save Philippians and Philemon) were already written. Marshall, *Acts* (TNTC), p. 48 n. 1 suggests that the epistles are not mentioned because Luke's concerns were with the progress of the gospel, rather than the internal problems of Paul's churches – thus the crisis in Corinth, known to us from the epistles, receives no mention in Acts. Walaskay, *Acts*, pp. 4, 190 argues that Luke can show a deep understanding of Pauline theology, particularly in the Miletus speech, but he has internalised Paul's teaching, rather than simply quoting the letters (which Walaskay thinks Luke knew).

[79] e.g. Conzelmann, *Acts*, p. xxxiii.

[80] Enslin, '"Luke" and Paul'; Enslin, 'Once Again'; Enslin, *Reapproaching Paul*, pp. 25f; Enslin, 'Luke, the Literary Physician'; Knox, 'Acts and Pauline Letter Corpus'; Walker, 'Acts and the Pauline Corpus'.

[81] Knox, 'Acts and Pauline Letter Corpus', pp. 281–6; cf. Schmithals, *Apostelgeschichte*, pp. 15f, arguing that Luke saw the epistles as suspect because of their use by hyper-Pauline false teachers, against whom Luke was directing a polemic.

[82] Enslin, '"Luke" and Paul', pp. 82f, Enslin, 'Once Again', p. 256. Enslin rejects the existence of Q.

claims that Luke handled the Pauline epistles with liberty, amending their information at various points.

Second, examples of Luke using the letters are proposed: the destinations visited by Paul in Acts are either destinations for the epistles, or places mentioned in the epistles;[83] 1 Corinthians 15 is the source for the appearance to Simon (Luke 24.34) and the period of time after the resurrection during which Jesus was seen (Acts 13.30f);[84] some unusual vocabulary is shared by Acts and the Paulines;[85] Paul's escape from Damascus (Acts 9.23–5; 2 Cor. 11.32f);[86] the Jerusalem Council (Acts 15.1ff; Gal. 2.1–10, 11–14);[87] the (fictional) presence of Paul at Stephen's stoning;[88] the visit to Corinth (Acts 18.1–17; 1 Cor. 1);[89] Paul's change of plans (Rom. 15.31; 2 Cor. 1.15ff);[90] the circumcision of Timothy (Acts 16.1–3; Gal. 2.3–5).[91]

Third, Luke did not mention Paul's letter-writing because he tones down controversy within the church in Acts – and the epistles are full of controversy.

1.2.3   Responses to the case for knowledge

Barrett acknowledges that Luke could have had an apologetic motivation which led him to minimise church conflicts, but argues that Luke could have made selective use of the epistles.[92] Barrett rejects the argument that Acts is late enough for Paul to need recovering from the clutches of heretics. His proposal is that Luke

---

[83] Enslin, '"Luke" and Paul', pp. 84f; Enslin, 'Once Again', pp. 258–60; Lindemann, *Paulus in ältesten Christentum*, p. 165. Thiering, 'Acts as Art', pp. 185f argues that the places where Paul is persecuted in Acts are all mentioned in the epistles. But Alexander, 'Narrative Maps' shows that Acts includes many places not mentioned in the epistles.
[84] Enslin, '"Luke" and Paul', pp. 86f; Enslin, 'Once Again', pp. 260f.
[85] Πορθεῖν in Acts 9.21; Gal. 1.13, 23 (the only NT uses); the instrumentality of angels, and the verbal similarity of Acts 7.53 and Gal. 3.19f; similarities between Acts 22.3; Gal. 1.14 and Acts 11.30; Gal. 2.10 (Enslin, '"Luke" and Paul', pp. 87f; Enslin, 'Once Again', p. 262).
[86] Enslin, '"Luke" and Paul', pp. 88f; Enslin, 'Once Again', p. 263.
[87] Enslin, '"Luke" and Paul', pp. 89; Enslin, 'Once Again', p. 263 believes Acts 15 to be dependent on Gal. 2.11–14. Walker, 'Acts and the Pauline Corpus', pp. 11f prefers Gal. 2.1–10.
[88] Enslin, '"Luke" and Paul', p. 89; Enslin, 'Once Again', p. 264.
[89] Enslin, '"Luke" and Paul', pp. 89f; Enslin, 'Once Again', pp. 264f.
[90] Enslin, 'Once Again', pp. 266f.
[91] Walker, 'Acts and the Pauline Corpus', p. 11.
[92] Barrett, 'Acts and the Pauline Corpus'. For example, the collection is mentioned relatively little in the letters, so Luke could have used those letters selectively.

knew of Paul, although not personally, and knew that Paul wrote letters, but did not have access to any. In favour of this Barrett argues: Paul's epistles were not regarded as 'canon' at the time of the writing of Acts – some were lost and others may have been deliberately suppressed – and therefore they were not carefully preserved; Acts is early enough for this view, for there are no traces of *Frühkatholizismus* within Acts; it is unlikely that Luke knew Paul personally; and the 'we document' used by Luke was most likely a bare itinerary, rather than a diary including references to letters.

Lüdemann is similarly critical of the arguments for use of the epistles by Luke. He accepts that there are genuine parallels between Acts and the epistles at a number of the points noted, but concludes that Luke has independent traditions from the Pauline mission territories, without specifying how Luke obtained them.[93]

1.2.4   The relevance of the Miletus speech

The Miletus speech is central to this discussion, for it is acknowledged on all sides to be the speech in Acts with most points of contact with the Pauline epistles.[94]

Schulze and Soltau seek to demonstrate by synoptic tables that the speech is derived from 1 Thessalonians.[95] More recently, Aejmelaeus has argued for the dependence of the Miletus speech on 1 Thessalonians (and other Paulines) on the basis of a detailed redaction-critical study of the speech, concluding that every verse of the speech contains possible connections with the Pauline letters.[96] We shall consider Aejmelaeus' arguments following our discussion of possible parallels between the speech and 1 Thessalonians,[97] but for now we note that the relationship between the material in the speech and 1 Thessalonians is potentially significant for the question whether Luke knew the Paulines.

1.3   Review of previous work on the speech

To provide orientation for our detailed study, and to help identify potentially helpful (and unhelpful) approaches to the study of the

[93] Lüdemann, *Apostelgeschichte*, pp. 8f.
[94] e.g. Gardner, 'Speeches of Paul', p. 401 notes that 'the speech ... at Miletus has the best claim of all to be historic ... we find in the address constant parallels, to the Epistles'.
[95] Schulze, 'Unterlagen'; Soltau, 'Herkunft'.
[96] Aejmelaeus, *Rezeption*.   [97] See §7.2.2.

Miletus speech, we shall review previous work on the speech, before outlining our own plan. In broad terms study of the speech has progressed from a focus on Pauline tradition in the speech to considering Lukan composition (using tools from source and redaction criticism). More recently there have been a number of generic and structural studies, and most recently narrative and rhetorical analyses.

1.3.1 Pauline tradition

One stream of scholarship focuses on the speech as evidence for Pauline thought, and therefore looks to the epistles as a basis for interpreting the speech. Tholuck suggests that the Miletus speech is the only speech in Acts which really parallels the epistles, since it alone is pastoral in nature.[98] Gardner,[99] Dodd[100] and Rackham[101] typify this approach in the first half of this century, agreeing that Luke does not know the Paulines, and therefore regarding the parallels as suggesting that the speech derives from independent Pauline tradition.

In the post-war era, a significant group continues to regard the Miletus speech as derived from non-epistolary Pauline tradition, from Bruce (writing first in 1943) to Hemer (1989). Such scholars agree that the wording of the speech is Lukan, while holding that it reflects Pauline thought and usage.

Bruce is representative;[102] he cites extensive parallels with the epistles, combined with Luke's lack of knowledge of the epistles, as evidence for the authenticity of the speech. When criticised[103] Bruce rarely offers direct critique in response, preferring to give a positive case for his own views.[104] Hemer offers a more extensive study,

---

[98] Tholuck, 'Reden', p. 312: 'So markierte Charakterzüge tragen die paulinischen Briefe, daß es nicht schwer fällt, denselben Mann anderswo wieder zu erkennen.' (The Pauline letters have such marked characteristics that it is not difficult to recognise the same man [writing] in other places.) See also Foakes Jackson and Lake, *Beginnings*, vol. IV, p. 259.

[99] Gardner, 'Speeches of Paul', pp. 401–4, although allowing that there are non-Pauline elements, such as the use of ἐπίσκοπος (Acts 20.28).

[100] Dodd, *Apostolic Preaching*, pp. 32f.   [101] Rackham, *Acts*, p. 384.

[102] Bruce, *Book of Acts* (revised edn), pp. 387–95; *Acts* (3rd edn), pp. 429–37. Others include: Marshall, *Acts* (TNTC), p. 330; Longenecker, 'Acts', p. 511; Williams, *Acts* (GNC), p. 347; Neil, *Acts*, p. 213.

[103] e.g. Haenchen, *Acts*, p. 590.

[104] 'He [*sc.* Haenchen] seems, moreover, to assume that if Dibelius has argued for a case, the case is thereby established' (Bruce, 'Acts Today', p. 44) is an exception.

focused on historical questions.[105] He sees the speech as a précis of a Pauline speech, and claims extensive parallels of language, biographical information and theology with the epistles.[106]

In sum, these scholars focus on the Pauline connections of the Miletus speech, see independent Pauline tradition lying behind the speech, and generally identify Luke as Paul's travel-companion. Luke's creative role is limited to working with the material provided by these traditions. He handles the material conservatively, although the final form of the speech bears the marks of Lukan style.

1.3.2   Lukan composition

A second group of scholars focuses on Luke's creative role in composing the Miletus speech.

The speech derived from the epistles

The oldest suggestion of this type sees the speech as derived directly from the epistles.

Schulze is the first to raise this idea; he sets out a synoptic comparison of the Miletus speech and the epistles.[107] He finds extensive verbal parallels, particularly with 1 Thessalonians, but also with other Paulines. He concludes that the influence must run from the epistles to Luke and that 1 Thessalonians is the *Grundlage* for the Miletus speech. Soltau sees 1 Thessalonians 2–4 as the most significant source for the speech, but he also regards the Miletus speech as paralleling material from 1 Thessalonians 5, Ephesians, Romans and 1 and 2 Timothy (without necessarily suggesting that Luke was using these other letters).[108] Both scholars seem to believe that to exhibit a parallel is to demonstrate dependence. However, at most they give examples of parallels without necessarily offering a cogent explanation.

Style criticism

With the work of Dibelius a new era in Acts scholarship begins.[109] Dibelius believes that in Acts Luke had the scope to exercise a

[105] Hemer, 'Ephesian Elders'.   [106] Hemer, 'Ephesian Elders', p. 82 n. 18.
[107] Schulze, 'Unterlagen'. His presentation of his case is not helped by his use of his own (somewhat idiosyncratic) German translation of the texts.
[108] Soltau, 'Herkunft', 133–5.
[109] Dibelius, *Studies in Acts* brings together work published in German between 1923 and 1949.

creativity which he did not exercise in writing his Gospel. This leads to Dibelius's *Stilkritik*, which focuses on the literary method of Luke.[110] Dibelius tries to trace the traditions with which Luke worked and then to examine how Luke utilised this material, using a form-critical approach not dissimilar to that applied to the Gospels. He thus develops tools which form the basis of (later) redaction criticism. In his research historical questions are by and large not raised.

When Dibelius considers the Miletus speech[111] he notes its importance for the narrative of Acts, particularly that it is Paul's last speech as a free man. Thus a key function of the speech is that, like a will, it is providing for the future.[112] It is the nature of such a speech, Dibelius believes, to contain apologetic such as verses 20, 26f, 31, 33f. This apologetic is aimed not at the elders of Ephesus, who would scarcely have needed such persuasion, but at church leaders of Luke's day. Dibelius sidelines the question of the speech's authenticity and argues that only by this means can Paul's mention of his death (Acts 20.23–5) be understood correctly, that is in terms of its significance for Luke's narrative.[113] He concludes that the speech is located in the only place where it could go, at the end of Paul's public ministry and at the point of Paul laying down his missionary work in the east. The speech serves as Paul's testament to the church of Luke's day.[114]

Conzelmann and Haenchen develop Dibelius' analysis. Both assume that Dibelius has shown that Luke created the speech virtually *ex nihilo*.

Conzelmann[115] sees the key function of the speech as marking the close of Paul's missionary activity, and a subsidiary function as edifying the church of Luke's day. The second function is accom-

---

[110] Dibelius, *Studies in Acts*, pp. 1–25 outlines this method.

[111] Dibelius, *Studies in Acts*, pp. 155–8.

[112] Dibelius, *Studies in Acts*, p. 155 n. 42 cites Peregrinus' farewell speech as an example (Lucian, *The Passing of Peregrinus* 32).

[113] Dibelius, *Studies in Acts*, p. 158 n. 46 believes Paul was dead when Luke wrote.

[114] Conzelmann, *Acts*, p. 174 n. 17 refers to Dibelius and Conzelmann, *Pastoral Epistles*, p. 121, who compares 2 Tim. 4.7 ('I have completed my course', using the same language as Acts 20.24) with Virgil *Aeneid* 4.653: 'I have lived and accomplished the course which fortune appointed.' However, as Houlden, *Pastoral Epistles*, p. 133 notes, the relationship between the Pastorals and the Miletus speech could be one of several possibilities: 'genuine Pauline speech and writing; coincidental use of the same imagery; our writer's [*sc.* the author of the Pastorals] use of a crucial Pauline speech in Acts; the incorporation by the writer of Acts of what he took to be a vivid Pauline image.' See further § 6.2.

[115] Conzelmann, *Acts*, pp. 172–6.

plished by Luke 'reading back' a later, idealised portrait of Paul into the apostolic age, and by Luke's use of conventional themes from the 'farewell speech' genre. Conzelmann sees the speech as unhistorical because the institution of elders in the Pauline churches (Acts 20.17) is assumed, along with a concept of ecclesiastical office from a later period (notably the use of ἐπίσκοπος in conjunction with reference to false doctrine, Acts 20.28).

Haenchen[116] regards the speech as Luke's testimony to Paul, partly because there would have been no need for Paul to defend himself before the Ephesian elders. Luke thus offers, at the last point in Acts where Paul speaks as a free man, an idealised portrait of Paul for later Christians to follow. The motif of Paul's innocence should be seen as an attempt to distance Paul (as the representative of the valid church) from the capture of the Asian churches by Gnosticism after his death.

A further important theme for understanding the speech is the 'prophecies of suffering'. Haenchen believes that because Luke has made it clear that Paul is to be martyred (Acts 20.25), he can disregard that fact for the remainder of Acts. This explains the victorious note running through the trials and journeys that follow.

Overall, Conzelmann and Haenchen develop Dibelius' approach along lines which are doubtful of the value of Luke's narrative as an historical record, especially at this point. They use Dibelius' analysis mainly to draw conclusions about Luke's own concerns and the issues of Luke's day, thus 'mirror-reading'[117] Acts. Conzelmann and Haenchen thereby initiate redaction-critical studies, which see a burgeoning of work on the Miletus speech.

Redaction criticism

Redaction critics approach the Miletus speech asking why Luke composed the speech as he did. They posit various degrees of freedom exercised by Luke in composing the speech, dependent on their estimate of the likelihood that Luke had access to traditions about Paul at this point in Acts, and treat the speech as a window into issues faced by the church of Luke's day.

Klein discusses the Miletus speech as an example of Paul's relationships with the young churches.[118] He believes that Luke

---

[116] Haenchen, *Acts*, pp. 589–98.   [117] See p. 144.
[118] Klein, *Die zwölf Apostel*, pp. 178–84.

subordinates Paul to the Jerusalem Christian authorities because Luke is trying to rescue Paul from associations with second-century Gnostics.[119] He regards this speech as theologically important, since it is the only address to Christian office-bearers in Acts. There is a principle of 'apostolic succession' at work (verse 32), evidenced by the use of παρατιθέναι. Paul is equipping the elders with authority as church leaders because he himself is about to leave the scene, and is thus providing for the church to be safeguarded as the authorised bearer of the tradition.[120] Klein thus places Luke in the *frühkatholisch* period of early Christianity, concerned with the safeguarding of the faith through a succession of office-bearers.[121]

Hanson[122] believes that in other speeches in Acts there is a pattern which suggests that Luke is working on traditional material. However, the Miletus speech lacks this pattern, which suggests that it was composed by Luke: 'it fits the occasion in a dramatic and literary sense, that is, not in an historical one'.[123] While Hanson admits the presence of Pauline language in the speech (in verses 18–21, 24f, 32, 34), he is clear that the 'fit' of the speech to the 'farewell' situation (which Hanson views as Paul saying farewell to his whole work around the Aegean) means that it should be treated as a Lukan creation.

Budesheim proposes that Acts 20.18–35; 22.1–21 are two parts of one speech, which Luke has edited.[124] Luke has made the narrative of the departing one's life (which should be part of a farewell speech) a separate speech (22.1–21). The likely *Sitz im Leben* of the material is a hellenistic Jewish Christian community, and the Miletus speech derives from an appeal to the name of Paul in the original speech, an appeal which could have been to Gentile non-Christians or to Jewish Christians.

Barrett[125] recognises the importance of the Miletus speech for the debate about the portrait of Paul in Acts. He views this address as displaying the relationship between the time of Paul and the time of Luke. The Miletus speech presents Paul as 'the chief and

---

[119] See summary and critique in Rohde, *Rediscovering*, pp. 219–29; Haenchen, *Acts*, pp. 122–8.

[120] Klein, *Die zwölf Apostel*, p. 180. Schürmann, 'Testament des Paulus' similarly believes that Luke presents Paul as providing, through 'Paradosis und Amt' ('tradition and office'), for the preservation of the church from Gnosticism.

[121] For response, see p. 196.

[122] Hanson, *Acts*, pp. 202–6.   [123] Hanson, *Acts*, p. 202.

[124] Budesheim, 'Paul's *Abschiedsrede*'.

[125] Barrett, 'Paul's Address' and now Barrett, *Acts,* vol. II, pp. 961–84.

exemplary evangelist and pastor, who instructs the new generation in their duties'.[126] Luke is rounding out a portrait in which, through speeches, he has already presented Paul as a missionary to Jews and Gentiles.

Barrett takes the considerable number of echoes of the epistles to imply that Luke used 'general Pauline tradition' in composing the speech.[127] He believes that Luke has 'read back' into Paul his own, later beliefs. He concludes, 'the general picture of Paul that is presented is in harmony with that which can be deduced from the letters'.[128] However, the provision for the role of the elders lacks any evangelistic imperative or, indeed, arrangements for succession. Paul is presented as opposed to a paid ministry, which is at variance with Paul's ostensible views in the epistles.[129] The purpose of the passage for Luke is the transfer of the apostolic task to Luke's (post-apostolic) time.

Lambrecht begins by considering the structure of the speech.[130] He helpfully reviews previous work and identifies features to consider in seeking a structure for the speech. The formal structure produced leads him to suggest that the key focus of the speech is paraenetic: Paul's past conduct is presented as a model to be followed, rather than as apologetic for Paul's actions.

Lambrecht goes on to consider the relation of tradition and redaction in the speech.[131] He argues that the speech is not directly dependent upon the epistles, but that Luke shows knowledge of biographical traditions about Paul; Luke is using 'universally admitted Christian tradition' to emphasise Paul's orthodoxy. Lambrecht concludes that the Miletus speech must be considered 'in the light of Luke's conceptions and theology'.[132] Luke is using Paul to urge the church of his day to be alert to the dangers of internal false teachers (verse 30) and external 'fierce wolves' (verse 29), and to encourage proper care for the weak (verses 33ff).

Prast argues that continuity is crucial for the speech, which seeks a continuity of spiritual authority, rather than a continuity of

[126] Barrett, 'Paul's Address', p. 108.
[127] As does Jervell, *Apostelgeschichte*, pp. 515f.
[128] Barrett, 'Paul's Address', p. 117.
[129] Barrett, 'Paul's Address', p. 118, citing 1 Cor. 9 (although Barrett notes that Paul denies that he received money from the Corinthians).
[130] Lambrecht, 'Paul's Farewell-address', pp. 314–18.
[131] Lambrecht, 'Paul's Farewell-address', pp. 319–28.
[132] Lambrecht, 'Paul's Farewell-address', p. 328.

authority based on office.[133] Prast offers six reasons for seeing the speech as a Lukan composition:[134] (1) an historical doubt that Paul would give such a speech at Miletus, rather than Ephesus; (2) the speech, although sandwiched between two 'we' sections (Acts 20.5–15; 21.1–18), is in the third person, which implies that the author was not present; (3) the speech seems to show a closed, homogeneous conception of leadership; (4) the vocabulary of the speech is strongly Lukan, which implies that the speech is not based on a source; (5) some themes have little or no Pauline parallel (such as the division between apostolic and post-apostolic times implied by ἄφιξις, the beginnings of the hardening of the Pauline gospel into a tradition, the development of elder-bishops, the background of the church which is envisaged, and the clear knowledge of the death of Paul); and (6) the *Gattung* of the speech as an *Abschiedsrede* suggests that it is a Lukan composition, since a truly Pauline speech would not reflect the concerns of this *Gattung* so clearly.

Prast treats the speech as a Lukan composition, drawing parallels with Acts 14.21–3[135] and passages from Luke (especially 12.35–48; 17.7–10; 22.24–7).[136] He also considers parallels with the Pauline epistles, but does not see these parallels as indicating that Luke used the letters.

During a four-year period Roloff, Schmithals, Schneider and Weiser all published redactionally oriented commentaries on Acts. Roloff[137] believes that Luke is using traditions about Paul, although the language and style of the speech is Lukan and the ecclesiastical situation is that of a later time. Accepting the consensus view that the speech is an *Abschiedsrede*, Roloff suggests particularly that verse 24 can only be understood if Paul is dead at the time of writing.

Schmithals also sees the speech as a farewell, believing that Luke uses the speech to address issues of his own day;[138] the false teachers attacked in the speech (verse 29) are in reality later hyper-Paulinists. Schmithals claims that the issues addressed by the speech and the Pastoral epistles are those raised by gnostic teachers who were introducing dualistic ideas and mythological speculations

[133] Prast, *Presbyter und Evangelium*, p. 205.
[134] Prast, *Presbyter und Evangelium*, pp. 30–6.
[135] Prast, *Presbyter und Evangelium*, pp. 212–22.
[136] Prast, *Presbyter und Evangelium*, pp. 228–59.
[137] Roloff, *Apostelgeschichte*, pp. 300–7.
[138] Schmithals, *Apostelgeschichte*, pp. 186–91.

into the churches of Luke's time. Luke used Paul-sources for the speech similar to those used by the composer of the Pastorals, with the same purpose.[139] Specifically, Schmithals proposes that the speech's basis in tradition is found in verses 18b, 19a, 25a, 26–32.[140]

Schneider's massive and erudite commentary seeks to come to a balance between views of Acts as primarily theological or primarily historical. Schneider believes that Luke was never a companion of Paul and had not read any of his letters, but that he was using Pauline tradition in composing the Miletus speech.[141] He identifies numerous parallels with the Pauline corpus, drawing on all the letters attributed to Paul except Philemon.[142] Schneider sees the speech as an *Abschiedsrede*, a type of speech not found earlier in Acts, although Luke's Jesus has such a speech (Luke 22.21–38).[143]

Weiser likewise sees the speech as an *Abschiedsrede* which Luke presents to his church at the end of the first century.[144] The style of the speech is strongly Lukan, and the flow of thought is confused; hence the speech is a Lukan creation, although there are elements of Pauline tradition worked into the speech.[145]

Lüdemann aims to distinguish tradition and redaction at every point in Acts,[146] and assumes that Luke did not know the Pauline letters, but did have access to Pauline tradition.[147] He doubts whether a meeting between Paul and the Ephesian elders ever took place because of extensive Lukan 'linguistic peculiarities'.[148] Lüdemann believes Luke composed a testament from the Paul of Acts to Luke's own church using some Pauline tradition. Overall Lüdemann is pessimistic about the amount of Pauline tradition which is present in the speech.

Aejmelaeus, in contrast to others, is confident that he can identify the Pauline tradition used by Luke in composing the speech.[149] He meticulously analyses the speech for Lukan and Pauline vocabulary

---

[139] Cf. Schmithals, 'Apg 20,17–38', a detailed comparison of the speech and the Pastorals.
[140] For critique, see Lüdemann, *Acts*, p. 229.
[141] Schneider, *Apostelgeschichte*, vol. II, pp. 41–5, 293.
[142] Schneider, *Apostelgeschichte*, vol. II, pp. 294–9.
[143] Schneider, *Apostelgeschichte*, vol. II, p. 293 n. 4.
[144] Weiser, *Apostelgeschichte*, vol. II, pp. 567, 569.
[145] Weiser, *Apostelgeschichte*, vol. II, pp. 571f.
[146] Lüdemann, *Acts*, esp. pp. 1–18.
[147] Lüdemann, *Acts*, pp. 7–9.
[148] Lüdemann, *Acts*, pp. 226f.
[149] Aejmelaeus, *Rezeption*; see § 7.2.2 for critique.

using statistical methods,[150] and argues that the Pauline parallels are derived from Luke's knowledge of the Pauline letters. Aejmelaeus detects parallels of the sequence of material as well as coincident vocabulary or the use of synonyms. He also believes that Luke, writing early in the second century, uses 1 Clement as a source.[151] Aejmelaeus argues a cumulative case for the use of the Pauline letters by Luke, rather than depending on one particular parallel. He sees differences of vocabulary between the Paulines and the speech reflecting differences between Paul's and Luke's situations.

Lövestam believes the background to the Miletus speech is Ezekiel 33–4. The introduction of the shepherd motif in Acts 20.28ff is the spur to Lövestam's thinking, for he claims that this motif is neither Lukan (for it does not appear elsewhere in Acts) nor Pauline.[152] He sees Paul/Luke reapplying Ezekiel's teaching to a new situation.[153] He concludes that the speech's main focus is the shepherding work of the elders with whom Paul speaks.

Donelson's interest is in the sources of Acts, and he writes to test a hypothesis that local cult histories form a source for Luke's writing.[154] He proposes that the Miletus speech and 2 Timothy use a local tradition from Ephesus that Paul gave a testamentary address to the church elders, handing them particular responsibilities and giving them authority to carry those tasks out.[155] He identifies five features of the Miletus speech which significantly modify the standard testamentary form in the direction of the later heterodoxy–orthodoxy debates:[156] the presentation of Paul as a paradigm to be imitated, especially in his faithfulness under persecution; Paul handing over control to the elders; Paul predicting the coming of 'wolves'; Paul promising the elders that God will equip and sustain them, and will reward them in the future life; and the imminence of Paul's death. The memory of a Pauline testament has been shaped by contemporary debates in the Ephesian church, and

---

[150] Aejmelaeus, *Rezeption*, pp. 89–95, especially the table on pp. 90f.

[151] Aejmelaeus, *Rezeption*, pp. 175–83.

[152] Lövestam, 'Paul's Address' in dependence upon Dupont, *Discours de Milet*, pp. 145–9.

[153] Lövestam, 'Paul's Address', p. 5; he never answers the question whether the reapplication of the Ezekiel material is the work of Paul or Luke or someone else. Williams, *Commentary on Acts*, pp. 233f (and others) previously noted the 'shepherd' motif and the Ezekiel parallels.

[154] Donelson, 'Cult Histories', pp. 1–10.

[155] Donelson, 'Cult Histories', p. 11.

[156] Donelson, 'Cult Histories', pp. 14f.

Luke has used it in that form in Acts.[157] Nevertheless, Donelson is not sanguine about recovering the original form of the tradition about Paul's testament, since Luke grafted the material so seamlessly into his own garment.[158]

There is a clear consensus among redaction-critical scholars that Luke is addressing the issues of his own day through an ostensibly Pauline speech. They therefore interpret the speech in the context of the issues they believe to be 'live' in Luke's day, such as hyper-Paulinism or Gnosticism. There are, of course, inherent dangers in this approach, for our only source of knowledge of the situation in Luke's day is Luke-Acts (which may lead to circularity of argument), and it is a presupposition that Luke's writing reflects only the conditions of his day (whereas it may reflect more earlier times).

1.3.3   Farewell speech as genre

The approach of many studies is that the Miletus speech fits into a 'farewell speech' genre which would have been recognised by Luke's readers.[159] Dupont's analysis is typical.

He draws attention to farewell discourses which are significant backgrounds to the Miletus speech:[160] OT examples (particularly 1 Sam. 12; 1 Macc. 2.49–70), intertestamental Jewish examples (especially the Testaments of the Twelve Patriarchs and the farewell speeches in Jubilees) and NT examples (notably Luke 22.24–38; John 13–17; the Pastorals; 2 Peter). He concludes that the Miletus speech fits this genre, and has the character of a pastoral testament of Paul as the great founder of the churches. His exegesis of the speech focuses on this theme. Luke, Dupont believes,[161] seeks to pass on the Pauline tradition to his generation, and this makes it less than straightforward to decide where Luke is using Pauline tradition and where he is building on traditional material.

Dupont does not enumerate the characteristics of this genre; this

---

[157] Donelson, 'Cult Histories', pp. 18f.

[158] Grafting is a method of joining two pieces of knitted fabric so that it appears that they have been knitted as a whole (Norbury and Agutter, *Encyclopaedia of Knitting*, pp. 66f). I owe both metaphor and reference to the Revd Gillian Cooper.

[159] See fuller discussion, § 3.2.

[160] Dupont, *Discours de Milet*, pp. 11–21.

[161] As does Schille, *Apostelgeschichte*, pp. 401ff, who sees Luke as being at a 'nodal point' in the post-Pauline period.

task is left to others, particularly Munck,[162] Michel[163] (who focus on Jewish examples) and Kurz (also discussing Graeco-Roman examples).[164]

1.3.4   Structural studies

Study of the speech includes considerable debate over its structure.[165] At this stage it will suffice to note three particular studies. Exum and Talbert propose a structure for the speech as chiastic, focusing on verse 25, which is the centre of their chiasmus.[166]

Dupont catalogues the variety of views (including changes in his own view),[167] before seeking criteria for a structural analysis. He identifies: the Greek sentences; the repetitions; and the progression of thought.[168]

Kilgallen also reviews suggested structures[169] before proposing a fresh approach based on the use of key Greek causal terms. He sees words such as γάρ (verse 27), διότι (verse 26), καί (verse 30) and διό (verse 31) as determinative for structure, since these words indicate ideas or sentences which are subordinate to others, either as justification for or result of a statement.

1.3.5   An attempt to re-set the agenda

Gempf seeks to move beyond the polarisation in previous discussion, because he doubts whether the debate over 'accuracy' versus 'invention' in the Acts speeches can ever be answered with the data at our disposal.[170] He therefore outlines key criteria which might help in evaluating the historical faithfulness of a speech, that is, how 'in tune' with the situation and the speaker the speech seems.

Regarding the Miletus speech,[171] Gempf notices that criteria for

[162] Munck, 'Discours d'adieu'.
[163] Michel, *Abschiedsrede*; discussion in § 3.2.1.
[164] Kurz, 'Luke 22:14–38': he provides a helpful table of features and their occurrences in various Graeco-Roman speeches, pp. 262f.
[165] See § 3.3.
[166] Exum and Talbert, 'Structure'; discussion in § 3.3.2.
[167] Dupont, 'Construction'; the review is on pp. 424–9.
[168] Dupont, 'Construction', pp. 429–45; cf. Lambrecht, 'Paul's Farewell-address', pp. 314–17.
[169] Kilgallen, 'Paul's Speech': the review covers pp. 112–14; see discussion, pp. 68–9.
[170] Gempf, 'Public Speaking', esp. pp. 298–303.
[171] Gempf, 'Historical and Literary Appropriateness', pp. 268–340.

a 'farewell' spill out from the speech into the narrative, such as calling the hearers together. Hence the Miletus speech should be considered as part of an *Abschiedsszene*. Two factors suggest that the speech shows literary and historical appropriateness: the likeness of the Paul of this speech to the Paul of the letters; and the probability that Luke is here answering the questions, 'How did Paul preach to Christians?' and 'How did Paul view his approaching death?'[172] Nevertheless, Gempf is pessimistic about recovering the Pauline tradition used by Luke, because of 'the nature and completeness of Luke's redaction'.[173]

1.3.6 Narrative-critical approaches

An important trend in recent biblical study is the use of narrative criticism,[174] and this approach has found application to Acts. The focus is on the final form of the text; rather than seeking 'seams' and other signs of the sources from which Luke composed Acts, narrative critics look for the flow of the story and the unity of the text. In the case of passages within Acts, narrative critics seek parallels of wording or actions (both similar and contrasting) in both Luke and Acts, in line with the parallelism between different characters in Acts and in Luke-Acts.[175]

Tannehill sees the speech as an example of the widespread Lukan device of previews and reviews.[176] Paul is reviewing his past ministry and previewing events yet to come. These two themes are intertwined in the speech, which makes its structure more complicated than some have supposed. Within the speech Tannehill sees literary devices at work, particularly the use of repeated words (or synonyms) in the two halves of the speech. More widely, there are links with Luke's Jesus.[177]

Johnson observes numerous parallels between the Miletus speech and the Pauline letters.[178] He identifies parallels with the travel narrative in Luke's Gospel in the repeated use of the name

---

[172] Gempf, 'Historical and Literary Appropriateness', pp. 334–9.

[173] Gempf, 'Historical and Literary Appropriateness', p. 339.

[174] For a valuable introduction, see Powell, *Narrative Criticism*.

[175] e.g. Johnson, *Literary Function of Possessions*, pp. 38–69.

[176] Tannehill, *Narrative Unity*, vol. II, p. 252 (cf. Tannehill, *Narrative Unity*, vol. I, p. 21); similarly Spencer, *Acts*, pp. 192–6.

[177] Tannehill, *Narrative Unity*, vol. II, pp. 255–61; see also Spencer, *Acts*, pp. 195f.

[178] Johnson, *Acts*, pp. 360–6.

'Jerusalem'. On a number of points of detail he draws attention to words in the speech used by Luke most (or alone) of NT writers. Johnson sees a parallel with the Lukan Last Supper discourse (Luke 22.24–38),[179] also a farewell speech. But the note which Johnson sounds most strongly is Luke's ability to compose a speech fitting for Paul, using Pauline language and themes.[180]

Neyrey outlines parallels between the Miletus speech and the Lukan Jesus' farewell discourse (Luke 22.14–38) in context, content and function.[181] Concerning context, a journey to Jerusalem is involved (Jesus is already there; Paul is on the way there), both Paul and Jesus are constrained by the divine 'must' (δεῖ), there are plots by the Jews against both, and both give their farewell speech to their favourite disciples and associates. Concerning content, both are farewell speeches and therefore contain predictions of death and of attacks on the disciples, both urge ideal behaviour, both provide for succession, and both contain protestations of innocence. Neyrey proposes a number of verbal and thematic links between the two speeches – and the function of the speeches is similar, focused on the proper succession of authorised leadership in the church.

A number of the connections proposed by narrative-critical scholars are suggestive, and will be taken up in chapter 4 in our study of the speech in relation to Luke's Gospel.

1.3.7   Rhetorical-critical approaches

Rhetorical criticism has recently revived,[182] and this has led some to examine the speeches of Acts from the perspective of ancient rhetoric.

Kennedy, a classicist, uses the ancient rhetorical groupings of deliberative, judicial or epideictic to classify speeches. He sees the Miletus speech as an epideictic form with a future orientation, for 'the apostle's major concern throughout is with the future'.[183] Thus, Kennedy sees the discussion of Paul's past ministry as concerned with how Paul will be perceived in the future.

Alexander's doctoral thesis is the most thorough rhetorical study of the Miletus speech, being oriented towards literary and rheto-

---

[179] Johnson, *Luke*, pp. 344–9.   [180] Johnson, *Acts*, p. 367.
[181] Neyrey, *Passion according to Luke*, pp. 43–8.
[182] See my brief review of research, Walton, 'Rhetorical Criticism'.
[183] Kennedy, *NT Interpretation*, p. 133.

rical issues.[184] He considers the address in the context of Jewish and Graeco-Roman farewell discourses, finding significant parallels in both cases.[185]

Alexander considers rhetorical topics in the Miletus speech and the Pauline letters, and stresses that the narrative framework of the speech (Acts 20.17–18a, 36–8) is part of the rhetorical unit. He concludes that the speech is epideictic, for Paul is re-calling the elders to things they know, rather than offering new advice.

Alexander's comparison with the Pauline letters focuses on rhetorical topics, particularly the appeal to the knowledge of the audience, Paul's present and future conduct, the admonition to proper conduct in the face of opposition, and the commendation to God and his word.[186] In each case he identifies extensive parallels with the Pauline corpus. There are also elements in the narrative framework which are paralleled in the Paulines: the epistolary prescript, and prayer requests and reports.[187]

Finally, Alexander studies style, invention and arrangement. By considering rhetorical arrangement he seeks to decide the structure of the speech – although he is finally doubtful that a clear-cut structure can be identified.[188] However, he is clear that the speech reflects the exigencies of Paul's situation as Acts presents it. Alexander then refers to classical authors to identify styles of presentation and argument used.[189]

Alexander concludes that the Graeco-Roman farewell speeches offer a better 'form' for the speech than the Jewish examples, since the Graeco-Roman examples do not always end with the death of the speaker.[190]

Watson applies Kennedy's method of rhetorical criticism to the Miletus speech. Watson sees the speech as a farewell address from the epideictic species.[191] Having identified the rhetorical unit as Acts 20.18b–35, Watson works through the speech picking out examples of ancient rhetorical topics and forms of argumentation.

[184] Alexander, 'Paul's Final Exhortation', pp. 1–43.
[185] Alexander, 'Paul's Final Exhortation', pp. 73f (Jewish), 114–22 (Graeco-Roman).
[186] Alexander, 'Paul's Final Exhortation', pp. 159–216.
[187] Alexander, 'Paul's Final Exhortation', pp. 217–29.
[188] Alexander, 'Paul's Final Exhortation', pp. 261–72.
[189] Alexander, 'Paul's Final Exhortation', pp. 284–329.
[190] Alexander, 'Paul's Final Exhortation', pp. 340–2.
[191] Watson, 'Paul's Speech', pp. 184–91; so also Soards, *Speeches in Acts*, pp. 104–8.

The speech follows a classical epideictic pattern: *exordium* (verses 18b–24), *probatio* (verses 25–31), and *peroratio* (verses 32–5), surrounded by an historical preface (verses 17–18a) and a narrative summary (verses 36–8).[192] Watson notes a number of places where the Pauline letters parallel points in the speech, while making it clear that he regards the speech as a Lukan creation using the device of *prosopopoeia*.[193]

Witherington[194] discusses the speech from a 'socio-rhetorical' perspective, and argues that Watson's classification is mistaken. He identifies verses 18–21 as *narratio*, verses 22–5 as concerning Paul's future, verses 26–30 as applying Paul's example to the elders, and verses 31–5 as *peroratio*.[195] He believes that the speech overall is deliberative, since its focus is on the elders' future conduct. Paul is being held up as a model for imitation. He agrees that the speech should be regarded as a farewell address, but rejects the idea that Paul must be dead by the time Luke writes.[196] Witherington also draws attention to the Pauline parallels in the speech;[197] he believes that the speech is derived from a Pauline tradition of a speech at Miletus, and has been written up by Luke in his own style.

1.4   Orientation of this study

After such a survey, the reader might be wondering what else can be said about the Miletus speech. What perspectives and orientation does this study have to offer?

This monograph aims to contribute to the debate about the Paul of Acts and the Paul of the epistles by considering a key case study, the Miletus speech. Past scholarly work suggests that within the speech there is evidence of both Lukan composition and Pauline language and concepts. A key question is the balance of these two elements. Dupont states this acutely:

> It is necessary to illuminate the text by reference, on the one hand, to similar expressions and ideas which we meet elsewhere in Luke's two volumes and, on the other hand, to that which Paul writes in his letters.[198]

[192] Watson, 'Paul's Speech', pp. 193–208.
[193] Watson, 'Paul's Speech', p. 208.
[194] Witherington, *Acts*, pp. 610–27.
[195] Witherington, *Acts*, pp. 613f.
[196] Witherington, *Acts*, pp. 613, 618–20.
[197] Witherington, *Acts*, p. 610.
[198] Dupont, *Discours de Milet*, p. 30 (my translation).

While this has been attempted before by point-by-point comparisons with the Pauline corpus as a whole (however many authentic letters that is thought to contain), no previous attempt has been made to compare the speech as a whole with a single Pauline letter as a whole. This is the approach taken here.[199] What follows is an outline of the structure of this book, so that readers are aware of the key lines of argument.

Our first task is to understand the speech as Luke presents it. This will be attempted in two stages. First (chapter 3), we shall study the speech in its immediate context (Acts 20.17–38), considering its genre, seeking its structure, analysing its contents and development of ideas, and identifying key themes. Second (chapter 4), we shall consider the place of the speech in Luke-Acts and seek whole speeches by Jesus which parallel the Miletus speech, as well as seeking parallels to particular points in the speech. This will allow us to state Luke's understanding of the speech. In turn, it may throw light on issues raised by the speech.

Turning to Paul, we shall examine 1 Thessalonians for parallels to the Miletus speech (chapter 5). We shall first move from the Miletus speech to 1 Thessalonians, to see whether the key themes of the speech are present in the letter. Then we shall reverse the comparison, and ask if there are other themes and ideas in 1 Thessalonians which are present in the speech.

This two-way process should help us to compare the thought of the speech and the letter, and permit us to weigh the relative Lukan and Pauline contributions to the speech, as well as to ask what knowledge of the Pauline letters (if any) Luke might have. Thus the detailed work of chapters 3–5 forms the heart of the argument.

A natural question which arises is whether other letters from the Pauline corpus might also provide significant parallels with the Miletus speech, particularly from the so-called 'deutero-Paulines'. We shall examine two cases where close links have been claimed, namely Ephesians and 2 Timothy (chapter 6), asking particularly how close the parallels with these letters are, and whether the Miletus speech is closer to these (deutero-)Paulines or to the indubitably Pauline 1 Thessalonians.

Our conclusion (chapter 7) will summarise our results, consider some issues arising from our study, and identify areas for further research.

---

[199] § 2.5.1 offers reasons for this limitation.

2

ARE PARALLELS IN THE EYE OF THE BEHOLDER?

2.1   Introduction

What constitutes a valid parallel? This question has been debated often in biblical scholarship, famously provoking Sandmel's warning that a parallel does not necessarily imply dependence of one upon the other, or of both upon a common source.[1] This chapter will explore issues raised by this exercise and outline our approach.

We shall notice the widely recognised use of parallelism by Luke and discuss what kind of 'unity' the Gospel and Acts might have. Then we shall consider criteria for parallels, and outline how we shall seek parallels within the Lukan *Doppelwerk*, including some consideration of the strategy for listening to the texts which is involved. Finally, we shall consider the application of this method to parallels between Acts and 1 Thessalonians, offering an explanation of our limitation to one letter (rather than a wider Pauline letter-group), and discussing the application of criteria for parallels to this comparison.

2.2   Parallelism in Luke-Acts

We shall not repeat the work of a number of competent surveys of the history of research of this topic.[2] Rather, we shall briefly discuss three key approaches to parallels within Luke-Acts – those of Rackham, Goulder and Talbert[3] – to show that parallelism in the Lukan writings is widely recognised.

---

[1] Sandmel, 'Parallelomania'; cf. the helpful survey and methodological proposals for history-of-religions parallel study in Donaldson, 'Parallels', esp. 193–204.

[2] e.g. Praeder, 'Parallelisms in Luke-Acts'; Gasque, *History of the Criticism*; Clark, 'Parallel Lives', pp. 44–52.

[3] Other examples include: Schneckenburger, *Über den Zweck*; Morgenthaler, *Die*

2.2.1 Rackham

Rackham is not the first to remark on the parallels within Acts, but he works the parallels out in considerable detail and presents them with particular clarity.[4] He sees a 'general parallel' between Luke and Acts, including a common period of waiting (Luke 1–2; Acts 1), a baptism by the Spirit (Luke 3; Acts 2), a time of active ministry and a 'passion' – a time of suffering – which takes up an apparently disproportionate amount of the two books. Each book ends with a time of 'victorious but quiet preparation'.

Rackham identifies a similar parallel between Acts 1–12 and 13–28. Both begin with a particular appearance of the Holy Spirit (2.1–4; 13.1–3) which leads into a time of preaching, suffering and opposition (2.14–9.43; 13.4–19.41), and both close with the departure of the chief actor via suffering to deliverance (Acts 12; 20–6). Further, each section focuses on a particular character – Peter (chapters 1–12) or Paul (chapters 13–28) and the two mirror each other's actions, as follows:[5]

	Peter	*Paul*
new name after conversion	?Luke 5.8 (cf. John 1.42)	13.9
equipping of Spirit	2.1–4 (baptised)	13.1–3 (set apart)
accusations about them and their solemn 'forth-speaking'	2.13f (drunk)	26.24f (mad)
gospel for Jews	2	13
healing of a lame man which brings trouble	3.1ff	14.8ff
silver and gold	3.6	20.33
arrested in temple and brought before Sanhedrin	4.1ff; 5.25ff	21.27ff; 23
filled with Spirit	4.8	13.9
fear upon all	5.5, 11 (sin of Ananias and Sapphira)	19.17 (Ephesus)

lukanische Geschichtsschreibung; Flender, *St Luke*, pp. 8–35; Thiering, 'Acts as Art'; Stolle, *Der Zeuge als Angeklagter*; Mattill, 'Jesus-Paul Parallels'; Radl, *Paulus und Jesus*; Petersen, *Literary Criticism*, pp. 83–6; Trompf, *Idea of Historical Recurrence*, pp. 116–78; Muhlack, *Die Parallelen*; O'Toole, 'Parallels'; Moessner, 'The Christ Must Suffer'; Green, 'Internal Repetition in Luke-Acts'; Clark, 'Parallel Lives'.

[4] Rackham, *Acts*, pp. xlvii–xlix.
[5] Based on Rackham, *Acts*, p. xlviii: references listed are those given by Rackham; where the reference is in *italics* he does not give the relevant references.

	Peter	*Paul*
signs and wonders by their hands	2.43; 4.30; 5.12	14.3
miracles	5.15f (Peter's shadow)	19.11f (Paul's skin)
jealousy of Jews	5.17	13.45
Gamaliel and Gallio's policies	5.34–9	18.14–17
a beating follows	5.40	18.17 (cf. 16.22)
ordinations	6.6 (the seven)	14.23 (presbyters)
laying on of hands for gift of Spirit	8.17f	19.6
speaking in tongues	10.46	19.6
denouncing of people	8.20ff (Simon Magus)	13.9ff (Bar-Jesus)
healing of sick lying on beds	*9.32–35 (Aeneas)*	*28.8 (Publius' father)*
raising dead (use of 'alive')	9.36–41 (Dorcas)	20.7–12 (Eutychus)
converts with Latin names	Cornelius	Sergius Paulus
Caesarea and centurions	*10.1 (Cornelius there)*	*27.1 (in care of centurion Julius there)*
stories told three times, involving a voice from heaven at midday	10.9–16,28;11.5–10	9.1–9;22.6f;26.12f
visions in the above stories	10.3 (Cornelius)	9.10 (Ananias)
worshipped	10.25 (Cornelius)	14.13 (Lycaonians)
falling at feet	10.25 (Cornelius)	16.29 (Philippian jailer)
Jewish–Christian opposition	11.3	15.1–5
defences	once	several
Agrippas[6]	*12 (Agrippa I arrests Peter)*	*25.13ff (Agrippa II hears Paul)*
miraculous deliverance from jail[7]	12.6ff	16.25ff
angelic help	12.7	27.23
earth-shaking events following prayer	4.24–31	16.25f

[6] This 'parallel' is less than persuasive; the former Herod Agrippa is not called 'Agrippa', but Ἡρῴδης ὁ βασιλεύς (12.1) and the latter is not called 'Herod', but Ἀγρίππας ὁ βασιλεύς (25.13).

[7] Rackham, *Acts*, p. xlviii lists other detailed parallels between the two stories.

Rackham believes that the common apostolate of the two leads to similar experiences – and he suggests that the Christian life generally has this common pattern because it is modelled on the life of Jesus.

Rackham's work proves influential on subsequent scholarship, for Luke's use of parallelism is widely recognised,[8] while later critics also feel free to disagree with Rackham on detail.

2.2.2 Goulder

Goulder believes that Acts is cyclical because Jesus' life, especially his death and resurrection, forms a type of the church's life.[9] He acknowledges a debt to Rackham, whom he regards as 'a typologist before his time'.[10] Goulder's theory is similar to Rackham's proposal about the pattern of the Christian life, although Goulder regards it as a construct of Luke, whereas Rackham sees it as 'arising from the facts'. Goulder concludes that Luke depicts the story of the church as a re-run of the story of Jesus.

Goulder builds on the widely canvassed view that Luke parallels the journeys of Jesus and Paul to Jerusalem. He suggests that there are three 'passion predictions' for each man (Luke 9.22, 44; 18.31f; Acts 20.23; 21.4, 10f). He also notes that Luke does not include the accusation that Jesus would destroy the temple (Mark 14.58) in his Gospel, but in Acts (21.28), where it is the cause of Paul being arrested.[11] Further, the crowd's verdict in both cases is, 'Away with him.'[12] The shipwreck and deliverance of Paul he sees as paralleling the death and resurrection of Jesus.[13] His overall plan of the parallel is given in the table on p. 38:[14]

[8] Mattill, 'Jesus-Paul Parallels', pp. 15, 20.

[9] Goulder, *Type and History*, esp. chs. 1–4.

[10] Goulder, *Type and History*, p. 34 n. 1.

[11] He claims this point is in dependence on Bruce, *Acts* (2nd edn), p. 224, but it is difficult to see how Bruce supports his (valid) point. Goulder, *Type and History*, p. 35 also claims that both Jesus and Paul are accused of defiling the temple, but without a supporting reference concerning Jesus.

[12] Αἶρε τοῦτον (Luke 23.18, Luke alone); αἶρε αὐτόν (Acts 21.36); αἶρε ... τὸν τοιοῦτον (Acts 22.22).

[13] Goulder, *Type and History*, pp. 36–41.

[14] Goulder, *Type and History*, p. 61.

chapter(s)	Gospel	chapter(s)	Acts
1–2	incarnation	1	ascension
3	Jesus baptised in water	2	church baptised in Spirit
4	Jesus' κήρυγμα rejected in *patris* attempt to do away with Jesus	3–5	church's κήρυγμα rejected in Jerusalem attempt to do away with apostles
4.31–9	Galilean ministry		(parallels distributed)
9.10	feeding of 5000	6	feeding of widows
9.28	three see Jesus in glory	7.55	Stephen sees Jesus in glory
9.51	Samaritan village	8	Philip in Samaria
10	mission of seventy	6–8	mission of seven
10–13	first half of journey: condemnation of Israel	8–13	church leaving Israel behind, turning to Gentiles
13.31	Herod's intention to kill Jesus	12	Herod's attempt to kill Peter
14–18	second half of journey: gospel of the outcast	13–20	Gospel to the Gentiles
9–19	Jesus' long journey to Jerusalem	19–21	Paul's journey to Jerusalem
20–3	Jesus' passion, and four trials	21–6	Paul's passion, and four trials
23	Jesus' death	27	Paul's 'death'
24	Jesus' resurrection Jesus' ascension	28	Paul's 'resurrection' Paul's arrival at Rome

As well as Jesus–Paul parallels, Goulder sees Jesus–Stephen parallels, Jesus–Peter parallels, and Jesus–Twelve parallels.[15] He believes Luke uses a 'death and resurrection' type derived from Jesus, upon which Luke then models his presentation of the body of Christ, the church – drawn from Paul's understanding of the church as Christ's body (Rom. 12; 1 Cor. 12).[16] Luke re-shapes the material he derived from Mark around this skeleton.[17]

Goulder briefly discusses criteria for parallels – an advance on Rackham – and offers three 'safeguards'.[18] First, there is a need to

---

[15] Goulder, *Type and History*, pp. 42–6.
[16] Goulder, *Type and History*, p. 52.
[17] Goulder, *Type and History*, p. 61 n. 1.
[18] Goulder, *Type and History*, p. 10.

find 'catenas' of correspondences; second, the Greek words used should agree between type and antitype – and the rarer the words the better; third, there should be a persuasive reason for the author to construct such a parallel scheme.

2.2.3 Talbert

Talbert also builds on the work of Rackham[19] and others. He calls his approach 'architecture analysis'. He seeks structural similarities between Luke and Acts and between sections within each book, looking for correspondences at large-scale level and in detail.

He begins by focusing on parallels between Luke and Acts, both of content and of sequence[20] – although some of his parallels lack coincidence of vocabulary and exist only at the level of general content.[21] He goes on to claim that the parallels he observes are the result of Luke's editorial activity,[22] although conceding that this is harder to argue in Acts, since we lack extant sources.

He finds a second group of parallels between Acts 1–12 and 13–28, again suggesting that Luke has engineered the parallels.[23] Talbert also identifies parallels within the Gospel, especially between Luke 9.1–48 and 22.7–23.16.[24] He compares the Gospel with Luke's putative sources (Mark, Q and L) and contends that Luke deliberately modifies his sources to produce parallelism.

Talbert sees smaller-scale parallels, too, and proposes that the beginnings of Luke and Acts each include balancing series of people and events. Acts 1.12–4.23 parallels 4.24–5.42,[25] and Luke 4.16–7.17 parallels 7.18–8.56.[26] Luke 1.5–38 and 1.57–2.52 are both two-part cycles of seven panels within each cycle, each section having internal parallelism between the two cycles.[27] A similar pattern exists in Luke 3.1–4.15, where John and Jesus are balanced against each other.[28]

---

[19] Talbert, *Literary Patterns*, pp. 15, 30 n. 5.
[20] Talbert, *Literary Patterns*, pp. 15–18.
[21] e.g. Talbert, *Literary Patterns*, p. 17 proposes that Luke 19.45–8; Acts 21.26 should be seen as parallel, since both Jesus and Paul enter the temple and have 'a friendly attitude toward it'.
[22] Talbert, *Literary Patterns*, pp. 18–23.
[23] Talbert, *Literary Patterns*, pp. 23–6.
[24] Talbert, *Literary Patterns*, pp. 26–9.
[25] Talbert, *Literary Patterns*, pp. 35–9.
[26] Talbert, *Literary Patterns*, pp. 39–43.
[27] Talbert, *Literary Patterns*, pp. 44f.
[28] Talbert, *Literary Patterns*, pp. 45–8.

Talbert sees such construction techniques as derived from classical culture, although he also draws attention to parallelism in Hebrew poetry – which he believes stems from a deep-seated feature of Near-Eastern thought. Talbert goes further than Rackham and Goulder in seeing parallelism as a near all-pervasive Lukan architectural principle. Later scholars have not generally been persuaded by Talbert, suspecting that at times the parallels are in his eyes alone.[29] Talbert never offers criteria by which parallels are to be recognised, apparently assuming that they will be clear to all.

2.2.4   Conclusion

These three scholars are representative of approaches to parallels in Luke-Acts over the last century, and form the tip of a very large iceberg of agreement that Luke writes using parallelism as a conscious literary technique to structure his material, at both macro- and micro-level. We may take it that the search for parallels is a legitimate exercise, but the great need is for adequate criteria for valid parallels. Granted that there is an inevitable subjectivity in reading a text – for readers contribute to the 'meaning' of texts – safeguards are required to ensure that the author is not entirely sidelined.

2.3   What kind of unity have Luke and Acts?

A key to the study of parallels in Luke's two books is the modern consensus that Luke and Acts are two parts of one work, and not merely two books from the same hand. This finds classic expression in Cadbury's work;[30] he is the father of the hyphenation of the two books as 'Luke-Acts'. Until recently the unity of the two books was taken as read in scholarship,[31] to the extent that Johnson writes on

[29] e.g. Minear, review of Talbert, *Literary Patterns*, 85f: 'I find the study to be an excellent example of industrious and ingenious parallelomania. So many instances are cited of the architectural symmetries that I became more sceptical of them all. Each thesis is driven so hard, is buttressed by such a vast army of footnotes, as to increase doubts concerning both method and conclusions.'

[30] Cadbury, *Making of Luke-Acts.*

[31] e.g. Barrett, *Luke the Historian*; Keck and Martyn (eds.), *Studies in Luke-Acts*; Marshall, *Luke: Historian and Theologian*; Talbert, *Literary Patterns*; Radl, *Paulus und Jesus*; Schneider, 'Zur Bedeutung'; Talbert (ed.), *Perspectives*; Tiede, *Prophecy and History*; Maddox, *Purpose of Luke-Acts*; Tannehill, *Narrative Unity*, vols. I and II; Tyson, *Death of Jesus*; Brawley, *Luke-Acts and the Jews*; Esler, *Community and*

'Luke-Acts, *Book* of' (italics mine) in the *Anchor Bible Dictionary*.[32] However, a challenge comes from Parsons and Pervo,[33] who wish to re-state the relationship of the two books. We shall briefly summarise their challenge, and outline the kind of unity between the two books assumed in this study.

Parsons and Pervo examine the unity of Luke and Acts at the levels of authorship, canon, genre, narrative and theology. They have no argument with shared authorship,[34] but contend that scholarship has too quickly assumed that authorial unity necessarily implies other kinds of unity.

The canonical disunity of the two books is problematic for the consensus view, they argue,[35] for there is no extant canonical list or NT manuscript in which Luke and Acts are adjacent. The compilers of the canon located Luke's Gospel with other generically similar books, and Luke stands alone in providing a volume about the life of the followers of Jesus after his departure. Thus, a key question is why Luke chose to write Acts at all, given that what he was doing was probably *sui generis*.[36]

In considering this question, the lack of generic unity is a stumbling block, for the two works are not from the same literary genre.[37] They see little to be gained by pressing generic unity – even if an ancient model analogous to Luke and Acts could be found (which they doubt) – and much to be lost in failing to hear the two books separately, with their differences and individualities. The danger is that one of the two books is subordinated to the other in reading.[38]

The more crucial parts of their argument are the two chapters on narrative unity and theological unity, for these are the kinds of unity most assumed – and most important – in recent scholarship. Regarding narrative unity, while not denying that there are

Gospel; Sanders, *Jews in Luke-Acts*; Johnson, 'Luke-Acts'; Kurz, *Reading Luke-Acts*; Squires, *Plan of God in Luke-Acts*.
[32] Johnson, 'Luke-Acts'.
[33] Parsons and Pervo, *Rethinking the Unity*.
[34] Parsons and Pervo, *Rethinking the Unity*, pp. 7f, 116; *contra* the linguistic arguments of Clark, *Acts*; Argyle, 'Greek' (on which see the critique of Beck, 'Common Authorship').
[35] Parsons and Pervo, *Rethinking the Unity*, pp. 8–13, 116–19.
[36] Parsons and Pervo, *Rethinking the Unity*, p. 86.
[37] Parsons and Pervo, *Rethinking the Unity*, pp. 25–37, *contra* Aune, *Literary Environment*, pp. 77–157.
[38] Parsons and Pervo, *Rethinking the Unity*, p. 120.

elements of literary and narrative unity (including parallels[39]), they assert that the differences between Luke and Acts are in danger of being submerged in a sea of unity. They see Tannehill's approaches to the two books as evidence for diversity:[40] he studies the Gospel thematically, frequently drawing together material on a topic from different parts of the Gospel, but takes Acts passage by passage consecutively.[41]

Concerning theological unity, they note that interest in Lukan theology grew up with redaction criticism, and they have no quarrel in principle with the search for a Lukan theology. But redaction criticism in Acts is much harder than in the Gospel, for the sources are not available for inspection. The result is that Acts is effectively treated as secondary in seeking Luke's theology. Further, they believe that the unity of Lukan theology has more often been assumed than demonstrated; an example is the shift in Christology from the Gospel to Acts, where (in Bultmann's phrase) the proclaimer becomes the proclaimed.[42] So although they welcome the quest for theological unity,[43] they see methodological difficulties in it.

A number of responses can be made to these points,[44] but here we simply note that Parsons and Pervo raise important questions for the consensus position. We may summarise our view of unity in three affirmations. First, the author of the two books is the same person – one mind is behind the Gospel and Acts.

Second, this author draws attention to the links between Acts and the Gospel by the introduction of Acts (esp. 1.1). Luke points back to his πρῶτον λόγον, which must refer to the Gospel.

---

[39] Parsons and Pervo, *Rethinking the Unity*, pp. 57–9.

[40] Parsons and Pervo, *Rethinking the Unity*, pp. 48, 123 n. 21.

[41] Tannehill, *Narrative Unity*, vol. I, esp. chs. 3–7 (although note now his commentary Tannehill, *Luke*); Tannehill, *Narrative Unity*, vol. II.

[42] Parsons and Pervo, *Rethinking the Unity*, p. 86, drawing upon Bultmann, *Theology*, vol. I, pp. 33–7.

[43] Parsons and Pervo, *Rethinking the Unity*, p. 23.

[44] See Marshall, 'Acts and the "Former Treatise"', who ably surveys views of the relationship between Luke and Acts and argues for a strong view of unity on the basis of: (i) the prologues; (ii) evidence that the Gospel has been redacted in the light of material in Acts; (iii) the ending of the Gospel, which implies that the Gospel was published as a first part. Marshall, '"Israel" and the Story of Salvation' explores the question of theological unity, and argues that there are unifying themes to the two books: Jesus himself; the role of apostles and witnesses; the kingdom and the Messiah; discipleship; and salvation for all people. (I am grateful to Prof. Marshall for a copy of the latter paper, presented to the Synoptic Evangelists' seminar of the British NT Conference, September 1995.)

Alexander argues, on the basis of parallels with ancient 'scientific' treatises, that a recapitulation of this kind need not imply the kind of close literary relationship assumed in contemporary scholarship.[45] Marshall responds that recapitulation is used where works are closely connected, and observes that thematic similarities and chronological closeness between Luke and Acts make it highly probable that Luke viewed the two as strongly linked.[46] Accordingly, Marshall sees Luke 1.1–4 as referring to the whole of the *Doppelwerk*.[47]

It is not necessary to resolve this debate here: significant for our purposes is the undoubted reference back to the Gospel, which means that Luke is writing his second book with an awareness (to which he deliberately draws Theophilus' attention) of his former book. Indeed, he goes on to write that his former book described 'everything which Jesus *began* to do and teach' (1.1), and the use of ἤρξατο is no Semitic redundancy, but implies that Acts describes the continuing ministry of Jesus through his Spirit and the church.[48] Barrett is thus correct to observe that the introduction to Acts (1.1–14) points the reader to the book which follows, and indicates the continuity between the Gospel and Acts.[49]

Third, in the light of this back-reference we take seriously the possibility of links from Acts to Luke's Gospel, including verbal echoes and parallels. For Luke to refer back in this way suggests that he wishes to show how events in the Gospel continue into Acts – for example, both Jesus and his apostles heal (e.g. Luke 5.17–26; Acts 3.1–10[50]). In similar manner, prophecies made in the Gospel are fulfilled in Acts (e.g. Luke 21.12–15 predicts tribulation for Jesus' followers and Acts 4.3–5, 14; 5.17–42 fulfil this[51]). The quest for parallels in Luke's writing is legitimated by the hints which

[45] Alexander, *Preface to Luke*, pp. 145f; more fully, Alexander, 'Preface to Acts', pp. 76–82.

[46] Marshall, 'Acts and the "Former Treatise"', esp. pp. 172f (responding to Alexander, *Preface to Luke*); cf. Marshall, review of Alexander, *Preface to Luke*.

[47] So also Bruce, *Acts* (3rd edn), p. 97.

[48] With Bruce, *Acts* (3rd edn), p. 98; Longenecker, 'Acts', p. 49 (who compares Acts 11.15); Barrett, *Acts*, vol. I, pp. 66f; Johnson, *Acts*, p. 24 (comparing Luke 3.23; Acts 1.22); Rackham, *Acts*, p. 4; Marshall, *Acts* (TNTC), p. 56; *contra* Conzelmann, *Acts*, p. 3; Haenchen, *Acts*, p. 137 n. 4.

[49] Barrett, *Acts*, vol. I, p. 63.

[50] The echo of ἔγειρε καί in Acts 3.6 (cf. Luke 5.23) may be a result of a scribe (or, if the reading is original, Luke) emphasising the similarity of the two stories (discussion in Metzger, *Textual Commentary* (1st edn), p. 307). Either way, the connection is close.

[51] Cf. Johnson, *Luke*, p. 322.

Luke himself has given. Hence we seek internal connections in the narrative with a view to a greater understanding of the significance both of specific parts and, in the light of the relationships of the parts, of the whole.[52]

2.4   A hierarchy of connections

In light of the above, seven points are significant in our detailed discussions in the subsequent chapters.[53] The first four form a hierarchy, from those most encouraging of seeing parallels (the first) to the more debatable (the third and fourth). In the nature of the case, the connections are mostly at the level of discourse, that is, the way Luke constructs the narrative, rather than story, the content of the narrative.[54]

First, the repetition of a key word or phrase from another part of the same work may be important in grasping the fuller significance of the passage in question. Coincidence of Luke's lexical choices should alert us to connections of potential value. It is, of course, possible that these are mere coincidences, and we shall therefore need to consider the actual use of the words. For example, Clark observes that εὐαγγέλιον is found only twice in Acts (15.7; 20.24), once spoken by Peter and once by Paul. He rightly suggests that it would be unwise to use this as a major plank in an argument for Peter-Paul parallelism, since the nature of the occasions is so different.[55] On the other hand, the use of αἷμα in Luke 22.20; Acts 20.28 may be a legitimate parallel, since it is a rare use of the word in a redemptive context in the Lukan corpus.[56]

In seeking verbal echoes, we shall be alert to the use of cognate forms, for it would be over-precise to seek only (e.g.) nouns where it is a noun we are considering – the use of a verbal or adjectival form may be of significance. Likewise, the use of compound verbs may echo the simple form, given Luke's proclivity for compound verbs.[57] For example, the repetition of words from the μαρτύρεω word-group in Luke 21.13 and Acts 20.21, 24 raises the possibility that the passages are linked.[58]

---

[52] Tannehill, *Narrative Unity*, vol. I, p. 3.

[53] Cf. Clark, 'Parallel Lives', pp. 52–7, offering a not dissimilar account, although his categories are different.

[54] For this distinction, see Powell, *Narrative Criticism*, pp. 23–34 (esp. 23).

[55] Clark, 'Parallel Lives', p. 53 n. 119.   [56] See § 4.2.3.

[57] Plummer, *Luke*, pp. liif; cf. p. 110 n. 66.   [58] See § 4.4.

It is clearly possible to argue too much from such coincidences of vocabulary, and a certain amount of caution is necessary. We shall seek *significant* words, rather than the repetition of common particles and the like. Where coincidences of vocabulary also represent uses of rare words (or unusual collocations) – either rare in Luke-Acts or used only or mainly by Luke in the NT – the presumption of connection is thereby strengthened.[59]

The second link we shall seek is in the use of synonyms.[60] Many ideas are not tied to only one form of verbal expression; the same idea may be present where the vocabulary differs. Luke has a penchant for synonyms,[61] which suggests he may vary language while working with similar ideas. As with more exact parallels of vocabulary, we shall also consider cognate and compound forms of synonyms.

Third, we shall seek conceptual parallels where synonyms are not present. This is a more subtle method of showing that an idea is shared. The material of the speech may be re-applied to fresh circumstances or needs – or the speech may include material which offers a renewed understanding of teaching from Luke's Jesus for a new situation or context. There may be stories of a character which exemplify a particular point from the Miletus address – or the speech may contain words which epitomise an action found elsewhere in the Gospel or Acts. These links will often be more debatable than connections of coincident vocabulary or synonyms, but they are nonetheless important.

A fourth level of connection is in style of argumentation, where Luke's Paul uses methods or structures of teaching similarly to other characters in the narrative. If there are places where the Miletus speech argues in the same manner as other speeches or teaching, a connection may be present.

Fifth, clustering of parallels to the Miletus speech (found using the four approaches above) in another speech or narrative section

[59] So also Goulder, *Type and History*, p. 10.

[60] Blomberg, 'Midrash, Chiasmus', pp. 233, 260f observes the danger of taking this too far for OT passages thought to be behind the structuring of the 'central section' of Luke (9.51–20.18), and produces a list of 'coincidental parallels' between Luke 1.14.37 and Pss. 1–10. It is not parallels of vocabulary that are in use here, but, in debate with Evans, Drury and Goulder, parallels of ideas.

[61] Ropes, 'Observation on Style', pp. 301–3 observes that Luke varies words in the same context (e.g. four different verbs for 'enter' in Acts 3.1, 2, 3, 8) and in different contexts (e.g. compare λαλούντων ... τὰ μεγαλεῖα τοῦ θεοῦ, Acts 2.11, and μεγαλυνόντων τὸν θεόν, Acts 10.46). Cadbury, 'Four Features', pp. 88–97 lists numerous examples.

suggests that we should see these links as especially significant. It also assists in reducing the chance that the parallels are merely in the eye of the beholder. Structure of argumentation (our fourth point) is a special case of this wider point, for the presence of a speech organised to persuade – whether the audience in Miletus or Luke's later audience – opens the possibility that Luke organises another speech or section similarly. Further, the discovery of sequences of parallels in groups, especially when extensive, provides a strong argument for intentional parallelism. An observable sequential parallel should not be seen as a *sine qua non* of genuine parallelism – more subtle methods of showing parallelism exist, and Luke may at times have been constrained by historical sequence[62] – but it would provide a particularly persuasive example.

Sixth, our quest for parallels will require sensitivity to questions of genre. We shall need to consider the generic classification of the Miletus speech, and then ask whether any clusters of parallels can be attributed to generic considerations, or may be more specifically linked to the particular situation or context.

Finally, in reading Luke's Gospel we shall look for evidence that Luke has provided a particular emphasis or slant to the text by synoptic comparisons with Matthew and Mark. If material parallel to the Miletus address shows signs of being either Lukan redaction or from Lukan *Sondergut*, that will add to the expectation that Luke has something particular to communicate – and thereby it will increase the probability of an intended parallel with the speech where other signals are present. In pursuing this search we assume the still-dominant hypothesis of Markan priority, and that Luke and Matthew draw on a common stream of tradition (which may be written, oral or some combination of the two) usually known as Q.[63]

In working this way, we are seeking connections which might be

[62] Cf. Barrett, *John*, p. 43, who sees a common sequence of events in John and Mark, and argues that this shows that John has used Mark: but his list includes the sequence of the departure for Jerusalem, the entry into Jerusalem, the last supper, the arrest, the passion and the resurrection, a sequence which it is hard to imagine coming in another order – and it is at such points that John and Mark were, surely, constrained by historical sequence. See criticisms in Morris, *Studies in Fourth Gospel*, p. 17 (responding to the earlier edition of Barrett's commentary, which contains the same argument as the 1978 edition).

[63] For recent statements of the case for this position, see Stein, *Synoptic Problem*; Evans, 'Source, Form and Redaction Criticism', pp. 19–27; Sanders and Davies, *Studying the Synoptic*, pp. 51–67 (pp. 68–119 consider evidence which is more problematic for this theory and outline alternative theories).

noted on second, third or fourth hearing[64] of the text.[65] This strategy, we believe, is one which Luke wished his readers/hearers to adopt, since it seems likely that books of the length and complexity of Luke and Acts were intended as manuals of instruction for Christian people, so that they might learn and develop in their faith (Luke 1.1–4[66]). Of necessity this involves hearing the book more than once and reflecting on the listening process – with the result that parallels begin to be noticed on second, third, fourth and subsequent hearings, as well as some being signalled so clearly that they would stand out first time through.[67]

In pursuing this quest, we shall be helped to see how Lukan the Miletus speech appears to be. Strong evidence for parallels to the address within Luke-Acts would suggest that Luke's hand is particularly evident in the final form of the speech.

2.5   Acts and the Pauline parallels

The other side of our study is to consider how Pauline the Miletus speech is. We discuss below why we shall read 1 Thessalonians alongside the speech;[68] our purpose here is to consider why we limit our search to one letter, and what criteria for parallels will assist us in reading the letter alongside the speech.

It is a commonplace of scholarship to categorise the (authentic) Pauline letters as 'primary' and Acts as 'secondary' when studying the history and thought of the earliest Christians.[69] From one perspective, this distinction is unexceptionable, for it distinguishes material 'from the horse's mouth' and that from others; however, in some hands the primary/secondary distinction is elevated into a statement of historical reliability in principle, on the assumption

[64] The kinds of parallels signalled by common vocabulary, or by words or phrases which echo other words or phrases, will be those which are *heard*, for ancient reading was normally aloud (e.g. Acts 8.30). The NT documents should therefore be seen as having an oral quality. See further Walton, 'Rhetorical Criticism', pp. 6, 8 n. 53 (and the literature there cited); Downing, 'Theophilus's First Reading', pp. 91f; Gempf, 'Public Speaking', esp. pp. 260–4; Alexander, 'Living Voice'; Dean, 'Grammar of Sound'.

[65] Cf. Tannehill, *Narrative Unity,* vol. I, p. 6.

[66] See Alexander, 'Luke's Preface', pp. 102–42, concluding that Luke's intended readership should not be seen as particularly highly educated or upper class.

[67] Cf. Gaventa, 'Towards a Theology', esp. pp. 149–52.   [68] § 5.1.1.

[69] e.g. Longenecker, *Paul,* pp. 14f; Lüdemann, *Paul,* pp. 289f; Jewett, *Dating Paul's Life,* p. 23; Bruce, *Paul,* pp. 16f; Hengel, *Acts and the History,* p. 38; Fitzmyer, 'Pauline Letters', pp. 82f.

that primary sources must be more dependable. Thus Knox asserts, 'of our two sources [*sc.* for the life of Paul], the letters of Paul are obviously and incomparably the more trustworthy'.[70]

But it is a gratuitous assumption that Paul's letters are more 'objective' than something else. The distorting effect of polemics can cause the presentation of information or opinions in a slanted form (e.g. Paul's language about his opponents in Galatians or Philippians), and we need therefore to allow for such distortions in reconstructing the circumstances of a document. Riesner rightly asserts that we can speak 'nur von einer *relativen* Priorität der Paulus-Briefe vor den chronologischen Angaben der Apostel-geschichte' ('only of a *relative* priority of the Pauline letters over the chronological information from Acts').[71] Similarly, Lüdemann observes, 'Paul did not write as a historian either. His statements require critical consideration, due weight being given to the circumstances in which he wrote and to the literary genre of his statements.'[72] Thus both sets of data require critical reading.

2.5.1   Why focus on one letter?

So why limit ourselves to one letter, rather than considering a wider range of Pauline letters? To answer this question we shall consider both drawbacks of the traditional approach – comparing the speech with a wider range of letters – and also some advantages of focusing on one letter in our comparison.

One drawback is that there is no widespread agreement on which letters can be regarded as authentically Pauline. While Romans, 1 and 2 Corinthians, Galatians and 1 Thessalonians would be accepted by most scholars, the question then becomes where to stop. Should Philippians be included? The majority view is probably that it is Pauline. What about 2 Thessalonians, Ephesians or Colossians? Scholarship is much more divided there. And the Pastorals? The majority view is against them being Pauline. What this shows is that there is no agreed database of authentic Pauline letters for scholars to use for purposes of comparison. Working with one (universally accepted) Pauline letter has the advantage

---

[70] Knox, *Chapters*, p. 18; cf. Jewett, *Dating Paul's Life*, p. 23: 'These data from the letters have *intrinsic superiority* over anything contained in Acts' (italics mine).

[71] Riesner, *Frühzeit*, p. 27 (italics his).

[72] Lüdemann, 'Chronology', p. 294; cf. Taylor, *Paul, Antioch and Jerusalem*, pp. 50f.

that we can be confident of the admissibility of our argument in scholarly debate.

A further drawback of working with several letters is that the results of such a comparison are inconclusive. To illustrate, both Barrett[73] and Witherington[74] draw attention to numerous clear parallels between the Miletus speech and the Pauline corpus, each observing that there are many parallels in the most widely accepted Paulines. Many of their parallels are common, but they draw different conclusions. Barrett allows that the general picture of Paul in the speech is in harmony with the epistles, but sees the Paulinisms as evidence of a later Paulinist composing a speech.[75] Witherington, on the other hand, asserts that there is nothing un-Pauline in the speech (although he concedes that the language can be more Lukan than Pauline), and concludes that the speech is Pauline, rather than Paulinist.[76] On the evidence of a range of Pauline letters it is difficult to see how we can decide between their two views, for the most that such a comparison of vocabulary and concepts can show is that in general terms the two portraits are compatible – which both scholars agree. Such a comparison only considers 'sound bites' from Paul's letters for comparison – but an author can be made to *appear* compatible with another person's summary of that author by selective use of the points of comparison, while being in fact incompatible (which is Barrett's view).

Thus our approach, comparing the Miletus speech with one Pauline letter, has advantages at key points over this traditional method. It will allow us to listen to a whole letter of Paul alongside a Pauline speech reported by Luke, and therefore will permit us to compare not just individual points of argument, but the way that arguments are assembled into a whole. It will open the possibility of seeing not just individual words as points of comparison, but how these words are grouped into larger complexes – seeing the nuances which they receive in particular contexts (and allowing us to see where synonyms are being used with the same effect). Comparing the speech with a complete letter will open the way to considering the conceptual worlds assembled by the two, and to look at them side by side.

The results of this study may be more meagre than might be

---

[73] Barrett, 'Paul's Address'.
[74] Witherington, *Acts*, pp. 610–27 (esp. 610f).
[75] Barrett, 'Paul's Address', esp. pp. 116f.
[76] Witherington, *Acts*, p. 611.

claimed after a study of the Miletus speech against all of the Pauline letters (however many there are supposed to be!). But our conclusions will be all the more firmly grounded by studying the two portraits this way – and will allow subsequent work on the speech to be built on a firm foundation of comparison. Those are real gains over against the possibility of unclarity or ambiguity arising from the more traditional approach. So how shall we go about our comparison with 1 Thessalonians?

2.5.2   The use of criteria

We clearly cannot apply criteria mathematically to prove parallelism; such a process would not be nuanced or subtle enough. The value of the criteria which follow is in assessing relative probabilities, for certainty is a chimera in our quest.

In broad terms similar criteria can be used in comparing the Miletus speech and 1 Thessalonians as in our search for parallels in Luke-Acts,[77] apart from our final two criteria, for there are no obvious synoptic comparisons to make in the case of the letter, and the speech and the letter are different in genre.

Thus we shall seek parallels of vocabulary first, with the same readiness to notice cognate words or the use of compounds. As with the Lukan parallels, we shall regard as particularly significant rare words or unusual collocations – rare both in NT use and in each individual author. We shall see as second in importance the use of synonyms (and their cognate and compound forms), since both Luke and Paul have favourite words for particular ideas, as well as because both authors can use various different words for an idea.

Third, we shall seek conceptual parallels where vocabulary differs. Possibilities include: an action epitomising teaching found in the other document; a piece of didactic material drawing out the significance of an action or event; or an event or piece of teaching re-interpreting or re-applying material found in the other source. These links are likely to be more debatable than those with clearer vocabulary or synonym links, but they should not be by-passed.

---

[77] Cf. Thompson, *Clothed with Christ*, pp. 28–36, discussing criteria for allusions to Jesus tradition in the Pauline letters, a parallel but not completely unrelated question. On that question, cf. Stanton, *Jesus of Nazareth*, pp. 86–110; Wenham, *Paul* (see p. 19 n. 37 for a list of recent key studies, and pp. 412–28 for an excellent bibliography).

Fourth, styles of argument are of importance. We shall consider whether the Paul of the Miletus speech seeks to persuade in similar manner to the Paul of 1 Thessalonians.

Fifth, if the parallels are 'clustered' in the one letter, and cover many of the major themes of the Miletus speech, that would be of interest, for it would present a portrait of Paul in the two sources using similar themes grouped together.

2.6   Conclusion

We have attempted to provide a framework for the thought and study in what follows. However, the value of this study should not stand or fall by the criteria alone, but by the coherence of the resulting picture of Luke's Paul, and his relation both to Luke's Jesus and to the Paul of 1 Thessalonians – along with the correspondence of these portraits to the realities of the texts. To that central task we now turn.

3

THE MILETUS SPEECH IN CONTEXT

3.1 Immediate context

The speech at Miletus falls into the so-called 'third missionary journey' of Paul (Acts 18.23–21.17), and within that section into the journey to Jerusalem. The intention of Paul to go to Jerusalem is noted in 19.21, following on a summary statement (19.20),[1] although the journey itself does not begin until 20.3. At that point, the intention is to go from 'Greece' (? = Corinth[2]) to Syria via Macedonia.

The journey develops as Paul visits Philippi (20.6), Troas (20.6–12), Assos (20.13), Mitylene (20.14) and Miletus (20.15). At Miletus Luke notes that 'Paul had decided to sail past Ephesus, so that he might not have to spend time in Asia; he was eager to be in Jerusalem, if possible, on the day of Pentecost' (20.16). This, in Luke's understanding, is why Paul then sends to Ephesus for the elders to come to Miletus and addresses them there, rather than going to Ephesus itself. The meeting with the elders then takes up 20.18–38, and the journey resumes, on to Cos, Rhodes and Patara (21.1), and then Syria (21.2–6). They then travel by ship along the coast to Ptolemais (21.7) and Caesarea (21.8–14), where several

---

[1] Some take 19.20 as a section-ending marker, by analogy with the statements in Acts 6.7; 9.31; 12.24; 16.5; 28.31; that would suggest that a new section begins at 19.21. E.g. Longenecker, 'Acts', pp. 233f, 499; Gooding, *True to the Faith*, p. 11; Filson, 'The Journey Motif', pp. 72f.

[2] This seems the likely place, given that Corinth was the most significant Pauline church established in Greece (i.e. Achaia) itself and Paul had expressed the intention to winter in Corinth (1 Cor. 16.5f); so Jewett, *Dating Paul's Life*, pp. 55, 58; Lüdemann, *Paul*, pp. 17, 155; Hemer and Gempf, *Book of Acts*, pp. 188, 258–60; Bruce, *Book of Acts* (revised edn), pp. 381f; Conzelmann, *Acts*, p. 167; Haenchen, *Acts*, p. 581; Fitzmyer, *Romans*, pp. 85f; Cranfield, *Romans,* vol. II, p. 12; Dunn, *Romans*, vol. I, p. xliv. (Fee, *1 Corinthians*, pp. 817f observes that 2 Cor. 1.15–2.4 suggests that Paul in the event did the opposite of his plans in 1 Cor. 16.5ff.)

days are spent. Finally, the group travels on to Jerusalem (21.15–17).

During the journey two motifs may be noted which will affect our understanding of the Miletus episode, namely the focus on Jerusalem and the sense of divine constraint.

The *focus on Jerusalem* is clear from the earliest stages of the journey in 19.21, and continues with the note of 20.16 mentioned above. Paul speaks of his sense of divine compulsion to go to Jerusalem at Miletus (20.22), and the church at Tyre attempts to dissuade him from going on to Jerusalem (21.4), as does the church at Caesarea (21.11f). Paul responds by repeating his intention to go (21.13), and the closing verses of the journey continue to mention the city by name (21.15, 17).[3]

The *sense of divine constraint* is also present from the beginning of the journey, with Paul resolving ἐν τῷ πνεύματι (19.21) to go to Jerusalem. It is further developed with the haste to get there for Pentecost (20.16), and mentioned again by Paul in the Miletus speech (20.22f: δεδεμένος ... τῷ πνεύματι[4]). This resolve even overcomes the churches' opposition to Paul travelling on (21.4f, 11–13). The church at Caesarea submits to the will of the Lord in the matter (21.14). The sense of divine constraint acts as a counterpoint to the theme of Paul's future suffering which also runs through these chapters (e.g. 20.23; 21.11, 13).

Lambrecht[5] suggests that a double shift of perspective occurs as the journey develops: from Rome to Jerusalem as Paul's destination (19.21) and from Jerusalem as the scene of the feast of Pentecost to Jerusalem as the place of Paul's sufferings. Certainly he is right to emphasise the focus on Jerusalem in the journey, along with the

---

[3] There are two different spellings of 'Jerusalem' in this section, as more widely in Acts: Ἰερουσαλήμ is used in 20.22; 21.11–13, and Ἱεροσόλυμα in 19.21; 20.16; 21.4, 15, 17. The variety of spelling has given rise to a number of explanations: see, e.g., De Young, *Jerusalem in the NT*, pp. 15–22; Elliott, 'Jerusalem' (both arguing that Ἰερουσαλήμ is used in Jewish or ecclesiastical contexts, or when Luke reports words from Palestinians in their home setting, and that Ἱεροσόλυμα is used for the city as a city within the Roman world); de la Potterie, 'Les deux noms' (suggesting that Luke uses Ἰερουσαλήμ for Jerusalem as the holy city, where Jesus accomplished his work of salvation, and where the apostles were based and Ἱεροσόλυμα in mission and diaspora contexts); Sylva, 'Ierousalēm and Hierosoluma' (proposing that Luke deliberately used the two terms unpredictably in order to convey his view that the city was 'holy Salem'); Ross, 'Spelling of Jerusalem' (arguing that the gradual increase in use of Ἱεροσόλυμα through Acts reflects Luke either forgetting, or deliberately choosing to ignore, his preference for the other form).

[4] See discussion, pp. 87f below.

[5] Lambrecht, 'Paul's Farewell-address', p. 308.

growing sense that Paul will suffer at Jerusalem, both of which have obvious parallels in the last journey of Jesus to Jerusalem in Luke's Gospel.[6] It is therefore possible that Luke is presenting Paul as one who follows his Master on the road to suffering in Jerusalem. This might be for a variety of purposes, such as Paul being presented as a model of Christian discipleship, or Luke stressing the continuity of Paul with Jesus. In either case the point could have a polemical thrust against opponents of Paul in Luke's day.

For Luke, therefore, this journey to Jerusalem has growing storm clouds around it: Paul is on his last journey to Jerusalem,[7] and for the remainder of Acts (from 21.27 onwards) he will be under arrest or imprisoned. The Miletus speech comes at a significant point in the narrative, and its importance stems partly from Paul's soon-to-follow loss of freedom.

A further question in this regard is how far the Miletus speech also comes as a watershed between the first- and second-generation church. Is Paul being presented here as handing the torch on to the second generation of Christian leaders? This raises the wider issue of why Luke places a farewell speech at *this* point in the narrative, rather than at the end of Acts.

Luke obviously regards the Miletus meeting as important, describing it very fully, while only giving a bare itinerary for the rest of the journey to Jerusalem. Compare this with the journey to Rome (Acts 27.1–28.16) – full of colour and incident, with vignettes of characters drawn with a few strokes of Luke's pen.[8] It is therefore the more significant that Luke spends 22 verses describing the meeting with the Ephesian elders, compared with only 31 verses on the remainder of the journey. Luke is saying by the sheer quantity of space given to the episode that it is important.[9] The key question in what follows will be why the meeting and the speech are important.

---

[6] Luke 9.51ff describes the last journey; the development of the thought that Jesus must go and suffer there can be seen from such passages as Luke 12.50; 13.22, 33–5; 17.11; 18.31–4; 20.9–18. See Blomberg, 'Midrash, Chiasmus'; Filson, 'The Journey Motif', pp. 70–2.

[7] Note particularly 20.25, 28 which set the Miletus speech in a 'farewell' context.

[8] e.g. the centurion Julius (27.1, 3, 11, 43f), the sailors (27.17–20, 27–32, 36–8), the soldiers on the ship (27.42), Publius (28.7–10), the believers at Puteoli (28.13b–14a), the believers from Rome (28.14b–15), the Jewish leaders in Rome (28.17, 23–5).

[9] As he does elsewhere, for example, by the space given to the conversion of Paul (Acts 9; 22 and 26) or the conversion of Cornelius (Acts 10–11).

3.2 Literary genre

Considerable amounts of scholarly ink have been spilled over the question of the genre of the Miletus speech, but with a remarkable degree of consensus that it should be regarded as a 'farewell speech' or 'testament'.[10] Two qualifying cautionary notes are entered, by Gempf and Hemer,[11] who respectively suggest that we ought to speak of an *Abschiedsszene* (not merely an *Abschiedsrede*), and warn against making the genre a Procrustean bed. We shall consider what qualifications of the genre identification might be necessary after reviewing the case for the consensus position. Discussion divides into two issues: is there an identifiable genre 'the farewell speech'; and does the Miletus speech belong to this genre?

3.2.1 Is there a genre 'farewell speech'?

Three scholars' work is used by many others in their analysis of the Miletus speech as a farewell speech: Michel, Munck and Stauffer.[12] Each has analysed speeches given on farewell occasions, particularly in the OT and other Jewish writings, seeking a description of a genre. Subsequently Alexander has offered an analysis of Graeco-Roman farewell speeches, taking up Talbert's complaint that Luke's writings should be seen in both the Graeco-Roman and the Jewish literary contexts.[13]

Before we can ask whether there is a genre of farewell speech, we need briefly to outline our understanding of literary genre. Genre can be thought of as an implicit contract between writer and reader which ideally allows a reader to share the expectations of the writer in order that good communication takes place. In practice, readers

[10] Alexander, 'Paul's Final Exhortation', pp. 135f; Lambrecht, 'Paul's Farewell-address', pp. 332f; Barrett, *Acts,* vol. II, pp. 963f; Kurz, *Farewell Addresses,* p. 33; Bruce, *Acts* (3rd edn), p. 429; Johnson, *Acts,* p. 366; Lüdemann, *Acts,* p. 227; Prast, *Presbyter und Evangelium,* p. 36; Michel, *Abschiedsrede,* pp. 68–71; Roloff, *Apostelgeschichte,* p. 302; Conzelmann, *Acts,* p. 173; Aejmelaeus, *Rezeption,* pp. 79–83; Budesheim, 'Paul's *Abschiedsrede*', pp. 25f; Dupont, *Discours de Milet,* pp. 11–21; Lövestam, 'Paul's Address', pp. 2f; Marshall, *Acts* (TNTC), pp. 328f; Munck, *Acts,* p. 205; Watson, 'Paul's Speech', p. 185; Tannehill, *Narrative Unity,* vol. II, p. 252.

[11] Gempf, 'Historical and Literary Appropriateness', p. 319; Hemer, 'Ephesian Elders', pp. 78f (esp. 79 n. 11).

[12] Michel, *Abschiedsrede,* esp. pp. 35–56; Munck, 'Discours d'adieu'; Stauffer, *NT Theology,* pp. 344–7; cf. Kolenkow and Collins, 'Testaments'.

[13] Alexander, 'Paul's Final Exhortation', pp. 76–134; Talbert, review of Michel, *Abschiedsrede.*

of a particular text will have their initial genre expectations modified and focused as they read the text. Thus there is a process of trial and error by which the readers narrow the field of possible genres to identify one particular genre to which the text belongs.[14]

The reader's developing grasp of the conventions used by the author includes understanding the literary structure, content and function. In seeking to define a genre we are looking for a combination of motifs and conventions which can be found across a range of examples, and which are well-defined enough to be recognisable when they recur in combination.

Of course, an author can break the bounds of a recognised genre and introduce novel elements or use it for a novel purpose.[15] Thus in this particular study we shall need to be alert to the possibility that one or more of the generally present markers of a 'farewell speech' genre might be absent from the Miletus speech, or that Luke may present 'classic' motifs or themes in an unusual or idiosyncratic way.

Michel suggests four criteria which are decisive in identifying a 'farewell speech' genre, namely: (1) the writing of the speeches arises from a well-defined common spiritual and religious milieu (in our case, in his view, the OT and Judaism); (2) each speech contains subjects or motifs which point naturally to a farewell situation; (3) there is no other genre which explains the blend of subjects/ motifs; (4) only subjects or motifs which recur regularly across the range of such speeches can be identified as typical of the genre.[16]

Jewish examples

There are numerous examples of speeches given on farewell occasions in the OT and later Jewish literature.[17] Michel's summary of

---

[14] Osborne, *Hermeneutical Spiral*, p. 150.

[15] The debate over how far the NT Gospels are like other contemporary literature and how far they are different from such literature – and which literature they should be compared with in any case – shows the importance of discussion of genre, for the conclusions reached influence the expectations we bring to reading the Gospels. See, e.g., Burridge, *What are the Gospels?* and Alexander, review of Burridge, *What are the Gospels?*.

[16] Michel, *Abschiedsrede*, pp. 47f.

[17] Michel, *Abschiedsrede*, pp. 36–47 briefly discusses Gen. 47.29–49.33; Deut. 31–3; Josh. 23.1–24.30; 1 Sam. 12.1–25; 1 Kgs 2.1–9; 1 Chr. 28–9; Tob. 14.3–11; 1 Macc. 2.49–70; Jub. 7.20–9; 20.1–10; 21.1–25; 22.7–30; 31.4–29; 36.1–18; 45.14f; various passages in T. 12 Patr.; T. Isaac; T. Abraham; Adam and Eve; Pseudo-Philo; As. Mos.; 4 Ezra 14.18ff; 2 Apoc. Bar. 31–4; 44–7; 2 Enoch 55; 57.1f; 58–66.

features of Jewish farewell speech is typical:[18] (1) nearness of death; (2) the gathering of the hearers; (3) future-oriented paraenetic sayings, often illustrated by an historical review; (4) a prophetic section; (5) self-defence of the dying person; (6) the naming of successor(s); (7) the blessing; (8) prayer; (9) final instructions; (10) directions concerning burial; (11) promise and oath made by the hearer(s); (12) farewell gestures, such as kissing and weeping; (13) the death, usually only briefly described. Michel goes on to observe, however:

> It is probable that, especially in shorter speeches, all of the motifs do not always appear; the proportions of the sections also changes. One should not expect [the authors] to be bound to a fixed plan in every case.[19]

Michel explains that motifs (1), (2), (3) and (13) occur in just about every example, that motifs (4), (5), (7), (10) and (12) come moderately often, and that the other motifs are less frequent, but still present in a significant number of examples. Equally, he observes that the sequence of the motifs is not rigidly fixed, although on the whole the sequence is roughly in the order listed above. In the light of this variety, Michel concludes that there are four elements which form the basic framework of a farewell speech: the introduction of the speaker; the assembling of the hearers; the exhortations and prophecies; and the closing (farewell gestures, death).

Nelson concurs with Michel's four elements, but warns that a speech should not be identified as a 'testament' to the neglect of its unique content and context.[20] For example, he points to examples of Jewish and Graeco-Roman farewell speeches which contain dialogue (Josh. 23–4; 1 Sam. 12.1–25; Socrates' farewell speech in *Phaedo*).[21] This observation underlines the variety of form, and suggests that the identifying features are found in the narrative framework as well as the speech. Of Michel's four elements, only the exhortations and prophecies belong in the speech proper; the

Stauffer, *NT Theology*, pp. 344–7; Munck, 'Discours d'adieu' list references from a similar range of literature.

[18] Michel, *Abschiedsrede*, pp. 48–53.
[19] Michel, *Abschiedsrede*, p. 54 (my translation).
[20] Nelson, 'Leadership and Discipleship', p. 113.
[21] Nelson, 'Leadership and Discipleship', pp. 122f.

other elements are part of the scene. It may be that exhortation is particularly characteristic of the Jewish examples.

The functions of a farewell speech can also be summarised, although with the same caveat, that the function of a particular speech depends on the context of the speech, both literary and cultural. Nevertheless, some key functions emerge from the examples: it supplies continuity between author and readers; it lends authority to a message by associating it with a valued past figure; it offers paraenesis to the readers concerning future conduct; it handles the matter of proper succession; and it can be apologetic for the views of the author.[22]

Graeco-Roman examples

A criticism of the approach typified by Michel has been that he considers only Jewish examples.[23] Kurz also considers Graeco-Roman examples, concluding that the Miletus speech is closer to the Jewish style than the Graeco-Roman.[24] The functions of a farewell address include the paraenetic, both within the story and for the readers of the story, and the historiographical. Under the latter Kurz includes justifying the transfer of authority, recalling the foundations of the community's teaching and practice, apologetic for the founders of the community, and future predictions (the last is missing from his Graeco-Roman examples).

Alexander adds a number of Graeco-Roman examples drawn from historical writers,[25] biographies[26] and philosophical litera-

[22] See Nelson, 'Leadership and Discipleship', pp. 113–16; Kurz, 'Luke 22:14–38', pp. 264–7; Spencer, *Acts*, p. 194.

[23] e.g. Talbert, review of Michel, *Abschiedsrede*.

[24] Kurz, 'Luke 22:14–38', pp. 252f, 257, 261.

[25] Herodotus *History* 3.1–38, 61–88 (5th-century-BC Greek: the speech is 3.64–6); Sallust, *The War with Jurgutha* 9–11 (1st-century-BC Latin); Tacitus, *Annals* 15.61ff (1st/2nd-century-AD Latin: but hardly a speech, since it only refers to a speech by Seneca which Tacitus says is recorded elsewhere); Herodian, *History of the Kingdom after Marcus* 1.3–5 (3rd-century-AD Greek: the speech is 1.3–4); Ammianus Marcellinus 25.3.1–23 (4th-century-AD Latin: the speech is 25.3.15–20, being the dying words of Emperor Julian, fatally wounded in battle with the Persians); discussed in Alexander, 'Paul's Final Exhortation', pp. 76–88.

[26] Xenophon, *Cyropaedia* 8.7.1–28 (5th/4th-century-BC Greek: the speech is 8.7.6–28); Tacitus, *Life of Agricola* 44f (1st-century-AD Latin: a farewell by Tacitus, Agricola's son-in-law, to Agricola, composed some years after the event, and not a farewell speech by the departing one); Plutarch (1st/2nd-century-AD Greek), *Parallel Lives: Pericles* 38.1ff (not a speech in the mouth of Pericles, but a description of the circumstances of his death with a few brief words); *Pompey* 77–9 (a description of the murder of Pompey, with few words from the man himself); *Caius Marius* 45.5–7

ture.[27] (Many of these texts are later than NT times.) He later turns to discuss the Graeco-Roman συντακτικός or speech of leave-taking, particularly as found in Menander Rhetor (430.10–434.9).[28]

Alexander's work leads him to a list of ten marks common to the scenes of farewell: (1) the imminence of separation, almost always because of the death of the speaker; (2) a reference to the permanence of separation; (3) a prior indication of the death of the speaker; (4) the presence of intimate acquaintances, giving a tone of intimacy to the scene; (5) the speaker summoning acquaintances; (6) the departing person's address; (7) an appeal to deity through prayer and/or sacrifice; (8) the grief of those left behind; (9) parting gestures; (10) the death of the speaker.

In the speech proper Alexander additionally identifies a number of recurring features: (a) self-references (e.g. acknowledgement of past mistakes, concern for the hearers, the speaker presented as an example, protestations of the speaker's innocence, affirmation of the speaker's courage and acceptance of his destiny); (b) concern for the hearers' future problems; (c) instructions for future conduct; (d) reminders of former teaching; (e) warnings of the results of keeping or neglecting the speaker's teaching; (f) an oath; (g) concern for succession (particularly in political examples); (h) words of consolation; (i) exhortations as to how the hearers should live in relation to the deity; (j) philosophical discussion (usually about death); (k) burial instructions; (l) specific final words.[29]

His study of Menander Rhetor's theoretical discussion of the συντακτικός produces a different structure, which may be due to

(a description of the circumstances of his final illness and death, with some reported speech); *Cato Minor* 66.3–70.6 (an outline of the circumstances of Cato's suicide, with some reported speech and a little direct speech from Cato, but no 'set piece' farewell speech); *Otho* 15.3–18.1 (a narrative of Otho's suicide, with a longer speech (15.3–6) and a few shorter words from Otho); discussed in Alexander, 'Paul's Final Exhortation', pp. 89–100.

[27] Plato, *Phaedo* (4th-century-BC Greek: a description of the final dialogue of Socrates before he committed suicide); Xenophon, *Memorabilia* 4.7.1–8.11 (5th/4th-century-BC Greek: summarises Socrates' virtues, and only alludes to his manner of death); Dio Chrysostom, *Oration* 30 (1st-century-AD Greek: a (possibly fictional) farewell discourse written by Charidemus for his father, brother and friends, and read after his death); Diogenes Laertius, *Lives of Eminent Philosophers* 10.15f, 17–22 (3rd-century-AD Greek: outlines the circumstances of Epicurus' death and records his will); discussed in Alexander, 'Paul's Final Exhortation', pp. 101–8.

[28] Alexander, 'Paul's Final Exhortation', pp. 123–34; the text (and an English translation) may conveniently be found in Russell and Wilson (eds.), *Menander Rhetor*, pp. 194–201.

[29] Alexander, 'Paul's Final Exhortation', pp. 109–14.

the fact that Menander Rhetor is thinking of a departure which does not involve the death of the speaker.[30] Menander Rhetor recommends three constituents: (1) acknowledging gratitude to the city which the speaker is leaving (430.30–431.6; 433.19–33), and expressing distress at leaving (431.6–10, 13–15); (2) directing attention to the destination and the reason for leaving (431.15–433.9); (3) prayer for those being left behind (432.22f; 433.10) and for the journey and possible return (431.27–9; 433.10–13).[31]

A distinctive feature of some of the Graeco-Roman speeches, according to Alexander, is that departure by ship is a significant component not found in the Jewish examples, which tend to focus upon departure by death.[32]

Conclusion

We may agree with the consensus view that farewell speeches were known and recognised in antiquity across a range of cultures, and that there is a degree of commonality between the examples considered. There is a *prima facie* case for utilising both Jewish and Graeco-Roman examples in examining the Miletus speech, for the speaker is presented by Luke as living within both cultures, as a Jew with Greek and Roman citizenship (e.g. Acts 16.38; 21.39; 22.25–8).[33] Nevertheless, we shall take the cautions of Hemer, Gempf and Nelson seriously, to ensure that we listen carefully to *this* text and do not import mistaken assumptions by classifying the speech as a 'farewell speech'.

[30] e.g., 'The orator should acknowledge his gratitude to the city from which he is returning' (430.30f) and 'let the second part of your speech contain a praise of the city which is your destination' (432.2f) imply that the orator expects to go on living.

[31] Discussion in Alexander, 'Paul's Final Exhortation', pp. 123–5.

[32] He cites Homer, *Odyssey* 13.64ff (8th-century-BC Greek: the farewell speech is 13.38–46, 59–62, but Odysseus expresses the hope of return, differing – naturally! – from farewells prior to death); Sophocles, *Philoctetes* 1450f, 1464f, 1469–71 (5th-century-BC Greek: here Philoctetes bids farewell to the island of Lemnos as he returns to Troy with Neptolemus); Virgil, *Aeneid* 4.381f, 393ff, 571ff (1st-century-BC Latin: Aeneas' farewell to Dido before leaving by ship, her response, pleading with him to stay, and Aeneas' call to the men to unfurl the sails and his prayer to the gods); Propertius, *Elegies* 3.21.11–15 (1st-century-BC Latin: a seemingly hypothetical voyage is proposed to forget Cynthia, the poet's love) (Alexander, 'Paul's Final Exhortation', p. 134). While departure by ship is a clear point of parallel with the Miletus speech (Acts 20.38), the hope of return in some cases is not, nor is the hypothetical nature of the journey.

[33] *Pace* Lentz, *Luke's Portrait*, this aspect of Paul's portrait is historically plausible; see Rapske, 'Pauline Imprisonment', esp. pp. 7–15, 119–68; Rapske, review of Lentz, *Luke's Portrait*.

3.2.2 Is the Miletus speech a 'farewell speech'?

The overwhelming consensus of scholarship is that the Miletus speech should be seen as a 'farewell speech'. This stems from both the occasion and the contents of the speech.

Occasion

Paul plainly states that the elders will never see him again (verse 25), and speaks of the time after he has departed (verse 29). Luke draws attention to the fact that the reactions of the elders are occasioned by these statements (verse 38).[34] The event has an unmistakable 'farewell' feeling about it.

Alexander sees the Miletus scene as having many elements found in the Graeco-Roman examples he discusses.[35] Specifically: (1) separation is imminent, verses 24, 29;[36] (2) separation will be permanent, verses 25, 38; (3) Paul has insight into his destiny, although it is not necessarily death which awaits him, verse 23; (4) Paul is well known to the elders, which brings a sense of intimacy to the scene, verses 18b, 20, 31, 34; (5) Paul sends for the hearers, verses 17–18a; (6) Paul delivers the speech, verses 18b-35 (which forms the major part of the scene); (7) they pray, verse 36; (8) those left grieve, verses 37f;[37] (9) they make parting gestures, verse 37.

Although caveats need to be entered concerning some of these identifications, in general it seems clear that we are viewing an *Abschiedsszene*.

Contents

The contents of the speech also correspond to the 'classic' form of a farewell speech.[38] Michel lists these correspondences:[39] (1) the announcement of death, verses 22–5;[40] (2) the calling of the circle

[34] Lövestam, 'Paul's Address', pp. 1, 3.

[35] Alexander, 'Paul's Final Exhortation', pp. 116–22. Bracketed numbers in the following paragraph correspond to Alexander's ten marks above.

[36] Alexander concedes that the speaker's death is not imminent in this instance, whereas he argues it is in the Graeco-Roman examples.

[37] Although it is unclear whether those left will survive after the speaker's death.

[38] Dupont, *Discours de Milet*, pp. 11–21; Kurz, *Farewell Addresses*, pp. 33–51; Munck, *Acts*, p. 205.

[39] Michel, *Abschiedsrede*, pp. 69f. Bracketed numbers here refer to Michel's thirteen elements of a farewell speech.

[40] Michel, *Abschiedsrede*, p. 69 argues that the combination of the Spirit's

of hearers, verse 17;[41] (3) paraenetic sayings, verses 28, 31, 35;[42] (4) prophetic utterances, verses 29f; (5) an account of Paul's former conduct, verses 18–21, 31, 33–5, and Paul's declaration of his innocence, verse 26; (6) succession of office, verse 28;[43] (7) wish for blessing, verse 32;[44] (8) prayer, verse 36; (12) farewell gestures, verse 37.[45]

Alexander similarly argues that there is a close correspondence between the topics of this speech and the elements found in Graeco-Roman farewell speeches. He notes:[46] (a) self-references: concerning positive relationships with the hearers, verses 18b–20, 27, 31; remarks which reveal the speaker's character, verses 18b–20, 24, 31, 33; the speaker presented as an example, verses 19ff, 31, 34f; protestations of innocence, verses 26f; affirmation of the speaker's courage and acceptance of his destiny, verses 22–4; (b) concern for the hearers' future problems, verses 29f; (c) instructions about future conduct, verses 28, 31, 35; (d) reminder of former teaching, verses 18b–20, 21, 25, 27, 31, 34, 35;[47] (g) concern for succession,

warning of suffering (v. 23) and Paul's statement that they will never see him again (v. 25) add up to foreknowledge of Paul's death. See § 3.4.3 and the next footnote.

[41] Michel, *Abschiedsrede*, p. 68. Michel sees this occasion as the handover to the next generation, and therefore sees the Ephesian elders as representative of the elders of *all* the churches; similarly Aejmelaeus, *Rezeption*, pp. 79, 84; Lövestam, 'Paul's Address', p. 1; Jervell, *Apostelgeschichte*, pp. 509, 511; Schürmann, 'Testament des Paulus', p. 312; Tragan, 'Destinaires', p. 797 (aimed at the elders of all the churches of Asia Minor). On the other hand, Marshall, *Acts* (TNTC), pp. 332f argues that v. 25 states only that Paul will not return to *Ephesus*, and Rom. 15.23 suggests that Paul intended to move to work in new areas. Thus, 'The case that Luke saw this speech as Paul's farewell address to all his mission churches . . . is not compelling' (333).

[42] Michel, *Abschiedsrede*, p. 69. Johnson, *Acts*, p. 367 proposes that 'the "Farewell Discourse" is in reality a kind of paraenetic discourse, in which the main point is the instruction of the listener in certain moral values'.

[43] Michel, *Abschiedsrede*, p. 70 concedes that there is no formal handover of office in v. 28, but argues that the statement that the Holy Spirit has made them overseers corresponds to the OT theme that God knows who the successor should be. This seems to be rather stretching a point. Cf. Barrett, *Acts*, vol. II, pp. xcvf, arguing that there can be no successors to the apostles and that we should speak of a concern for continuity rather than succession.

[44] Michel, *Abschiedsrede*, p. 70 suggests that v. 32 functions as a wish-prayer for God's blessing. Again, this seems to be stretching a point.

[45] Michel, *Abschiedsrede*, p. 70, referring to weeping, embracing and kissing (I here assume that v. 37 is misprinted as v. 17 in Michel's book).

[46] Alexander, 'Paul's Final Exhortation', pp. 118–22. Here, bracketed letters correspond to Alexander's points listed in § 3.2.1.

[47] Alexander, 'Paul's Final Exhortation', p. 120 draws attention to references to the hearers' knowledge and instructions to remember (vv. 18, 31, 34, 35), descriptions of the manner of Paul's ministry (vv. 18b–20, 27, 31, 34), mention of the content of Paul's teaching (vv. 21, 25, 27), and the use of the word of Jesus (v. 35).

by reminding the elders of their task, verses 17, 28, 32; (h) words of consolation, verses 22–4;[48] (i) the hearers' future life in relation to God, verse 32; (l) the words of Jesus as a specific final utterance, verse 35.

It is clear, however, that the συντακτικός of Menander Rhetor corresponds little with the Miletus speech, for none of the three emphases in that structure can easily be found in Paul's words.[49] Alexander acknowledges that the strongest link with the Miletus speech is the departure by ship, and claims that other classical examples show that there is a 'literary propriety' in a farewell discourse in the setting of a journey from one place to another.[50] This seems little more than a statement of the obvious.

Discussion

That the Miletus scene and speech contain significant features to be found in other farewells seems beyond cavil. But there are also items present in each scholar's list of classic features of a farewell scene/speech that are absent from the Miletus story. From Michel's list of features there are no directions concerning burial (10), promise and oath made by the hearers (11), or record of the death of the speaker (13). From Alexander's list of features it is again the death of the speaker (10) which is absent, although he does observe that some Graeco-Roman examples contain a departure by ship.[51] Likewise, from Alexander's list of features of the speech proper, several are not present in the Miletus speech: the consequences of keeping or neglecting the speaker's teaching (e), an oath (f), philosophical discussion (j) and burial instructions (k).

Further, a number of the farewell motifs which Michel and Alexander confidently identify in the Miletus speech do not appear to be the same as the 'standard' motifs, especially given that Paul (within the horizon of Acts) does not die.[52] Thus it is vital to listen

---

[48] Alexander, 'Paul's Final Exhortation', p. 121 argues that vv. 22–4 approach words of consolation, but if so they are somewhat indirect.

[49] As also argued in Alexander, 'Paul's Final Exhortation', pp. 132–4; Kennedy, *NT Interpretation*, pp. 76, 132f.

[50] Alexander, 'Paul's Final Exhortation', p. 134.

[51] As noted above, some such examples show the expectation of meeting again, esp. Homer, *Odyssey* 13.64ff.

[52] Lövestam, 'Paul's Address', p. 2 notes that Paul in Acts is not about to die, but will continue his journey to Jerusalem (v. 22). Gempf, 'Historical and Literary Appropriateness', p. 169 observes that the speech is at the end of a phase of Paul's life, namely his free missionary work, rather than the end of his life.

carefully to this particular speech, rather than force it into conformity with a pattern abstracted from elsewhere.

This point can be focused further, for there are features in the Miletus speech which fit its specific audience well. One function of the speech may be to fill out the picture of Paul's ministry in Ephesus (Acts 18.19–21; 19.1–20.1), which Luke presents as a centre of considerable success for Paul.

Luke emphasises Paul's time in Ephesus by devoting a significant amount of space to it (a period of more than two years, and likely close to three: 19.8, 10, 22), and informs his readers that 'all the residents of Asia, both Jews and Greeks, heard the word of the Lord' (19.10b). Luke signals, by slowing down narrative time and by this (rhetorically exaggerated) authorial comment, that Ephesus was a place where God was active through Paul's ministry. The sense that Luke regards Ephesus as a key place in Paul's mission is further reinforced by: reports of overcoming opposition in the synagogue (19.8f), from disease and evil spirits (19.11f), and from rioting crowds (19.21–41); believers abandoning magical practices (19.18f); and Luke's summary statement that 'the word of the Lord grew mightily and prevailed' (19.20).

A number of features of the Miletus speech refer back to the Ephesian ministry.[53] There are, most obviously, the references to the memory of the elders (verses 18b, 31, 34), but there are other links too. The length of Paul's stay (verse 31) recapitulates the information in 19.8–10, 22.[54] There are phrases in the Miletus speech which echo similar phrases in the Ephesian ministry passages, such as πίστιν εἰς τὸν κύριον ἡμῶν Ἰησοῦν (20.21, cf. ἵνα πιστεύσωσιν, τοῦτ' ἔστιν εἰς τὸν Ἰησοῦν, 19.4) and κηρύσσων τὴν βασιλείαν (20.25, cf. [τὰ] περὶ τῆς βασιλείας τοῦ θεοῦ, 19.8,

---

[53] Gempf, 'Historical and Literary Appropriateness', pp. 269f; Tannehill, Narrative Unity, vol. II, p. 258. There are, of course, features in the speech without antecedent in the account of the Ephesian ministry, such as the considerable 'gaps' which the reader must fill in. The mention of Paul's tears (20.19, 31) is such an example, where the reader must infer that Paul's ministry in Ephesus was not as plain sailing as a quick reading of Acts 19 might suggest. An alert reader will also wonder why there is no explanation why Paul delays a journey which Luke says he is in a hurry to complete (20.16), by sending for the elders. Gempf, 'Historical and Literary Appropriateness', pp. 270–2 discusses a number of possible historical explanations for this. Here we simply observe the literary phenomenon of the need for 'gap-filling'.

[54] Codex Bezae adds an explicit reference to the time in v. 18b, ὡς τριετίαν ἢ καὶ πλεῖον (= 'for about three years or more'), presumably a deduction from 19.8–10, 22 or from 20.31 (Johnson, Acts, p. 360; Metzger, Textual Commentary (1st edn), pp. 478f).

the only previous use in Acts of this phrase to summarise Paul's message;[55] κηρύσσει, 19.13[56]). Ἰουδαίοις τε καὶ Ἕλλησιν (20.21) recalls the description of Ἰουδαίους τε καὶ Ἕλληνας (19.10) hearing the word of the Lord. The idea that Paul is going to Jerusalem δεδεμένος ... τῷ πνεύματι (20.22) echoes Paul resolving ἐν τῷ πνεύματι (19.21) to go to Jerusalem.

An examination of the contents of the speech reveals Paul preparing the elders for problems to come (20.29f), and much of the content of the speech can be seen to meet this need, rather than the standard 'farewell' themes. The anticipation of future problems is certainly present in some farewell speeches, but the presence of this motif here may not be the result of the farewell nature of the occasion, but rather part of the Lukan Paul's foreboding about what will come – for he has already experienced persecution, not least in Ephesus (19.23–41), and he anticipates that his converts will face the same (cf. Luke 6.22; 21.12, 17).[57]

In sum, then, we may accept the designation 'farewell speech' for the Miletus speech as a working hypothesis, while not being sanguine that this identification in itself will get us much further in understanding this speech – not least because of the caveats entered above. To label a section of text as belonging to a certain genre incurs the risk of not looking carefully enough at the particularities of the text in its specific setting. We shall need to ask carefully how Luke has presented *this* speech; by doing this we shall move closer to a grasp of what Luke's Paul is saying and why.

---

[55] Tannehill, *Narrative Unity,* vol. II, p. 258. Although βασιλεία (τοῦ θεοῦ) is common in Luke's Gospel, it occurs much less frequently in Acts (8 times only). Two uses are βασιλεία alone (1.6; 20.25). In Acts it is found most frequently in Jewish contexts (1.3, 6; 19.8; 28.23, 31 – the uses in chs. 1, 28 may form an *inclusio* for the whole book) or amongst Christian groups (14.22; 20.25). Both groups may be assumed to have some understanding of what is essentially a Jewish concept (Tannehill, *Narrative Unity,* vol. II, pp. 351f).

[56] Κηρύσσω is used in Acts only 8 times, characteristically of Paul. His first act on becoming a follower of Jesus is to preach Jesus in the synagogues of Damascus (9.20), his Ephesian ministry is described as preaching (19.13; 20.25), and the final picture of him in Acts is preaching (28.31). The verb is also used of others – Moses (who is preached each sabbath, 15.21), John the Baptist (10.37), Philip (8.5) and Peter (10.42) – but the weight of emphasis is on Paul as preaching.

[57] Cf. Kilgallen, 'Paul's Speech', esp. 120f, suggesting that the farewell speech genre should not be allowed to dominate the exegesis of the speech, which he sees as focused on the forthcoming persecution which the Ephesian church will face.

3.3 Structure

The structure of the speech is important, for the proportions spent on different topics – and the place those topics have in the overall shape of the speech – significantly affect how the speech should be understood. Our discussion will give particular attention to the subdivisions of the speech.

Greek sentences	18–21	22f	24	25	26f	28	29f	31	32	33f	35
Marshall 2					|						
Bruce 3		|			|						
Michel 3			|		|						
Watson 3		|						|			
Rackham 3						|		|			
Boismard and Lamouille 4		|	|								|
Bruce, Haenchen, Longenecker, Kurz, Walaskay 4		|		|				|			
Conzelmann, Schneider, Soards, Jervell 4		|				|		|			
Witherington 4		|			|		|				
Munck 4		|			|			|			
Dibelius 5		|			|				|		|
Exum and Talbert 5	|		|		|		|				
Dupont 6		|		|			|		|	|	
Lambrecht, Gempf, Aejmelaeus 6		|		|	|				|	|	
Lüdemann 6		|		|		|			|	|	

The subdivision of the Miletus speech is much debated;[58] the above table shows how the various scholars do the subdividing. First we note the sentence divisions in Greek, and then where the various scholars place dividing markers. The number after each name is the number of sections produced by that scholar.[59]

---

[58] Although some scholars do not offer a structure for the speech, e.g. Johnson, *Acts*, pp. 359–68; Tannehill, *Narrative Unity*, vol. II, pp. 252ff (who discusses structure without making a definite proposal); Hemer, 'Ephesian Elders'. Kilgallen, 'Paul's Speech' discusses the structure extensively without finally proposing a clear subdivision; see discussion in § 3.3.1.

[59] Marshall, *Acts* (TNTC), p. 329; Bruce, *Acts* (2nd edn), p. 377; Michel, *Abschiedsrede*, p. 27; Watson, 'Paul's Speech'; Rackham, *Acts*, p. 385; Boismard and

There is evidently no consensus about the structure of the speech. Indeed, Barrett despairs of the possibility of a sensible analysis,[60] in similar vein to the verdict of Gardner, who writes of the 'faulty order of the speech, which has offended the commentators'.[61] However, this may be too pessimistic.

3.3.1 Markers of structure

Dupont[62] helpfully suggests that any analysis of the speech should take account of two factors, namely the literary structure and the content;[63] this idea will be pursued below. Four phenomena in the passage are suggestive as to structure, and each needs to be taken into account in producing an analysis. These are: the Greek sentence structure, the repetitions, the time references, and the shift in the subject of the content from Paul to the elders.[64]

Greek sentence structure

The sentence divisions have already been noted above, in the table of analyses, and we suggest that any analysis ought to take cognisance of them. While we do not know for certain the sentence division Luke intended (because the oldest manuscripts available are uncials, which are little – if at all – punctuated[65]), this at least shows how the structure was understood by early readers of Acts – and in this speech there are no differences in sentence breaks between the two main modern editions.[66]

Lamouille, *Les Actes III*, pp. 249–51; Bruce, *Book of Acts* (revised edn), pp. 389–95 (Bruce appears to change his mind in the revision of his commentary: hence there are two entries in the table for him); Haenchen, *Acts*, p. 595; Walaskay, *Acts*, pp. 189f; Longenecker, 'Acts', p. 512; Kurz, *Farewell Addresses*, pp. 33–51; Walaskay, *Acts*, pp. 189f; Conzelmann, *Acts*, p. 173; Schneider, *Apostelgeschichte*, p. 293; Soards, *Speeches in Acts*, p. 105; Jervell, *Apostelgeschichte*, pp. 508–16; Witherington, *Acts*, pp. 613f; Munck, *Acts*, pp. 203–5; Dibelius, *Studies in Acts*, p. 157; Exum and Talbert, 'Structure'; Dupont, 'Construction', p. 441; Lambrecht, 'Paul's Farewell-address', p. 318; Gempf, 'Historical and Literary Appropriateness', pp. 272–80; Aejmelaeus, *Rezeption*, pp. 84–8; Lüdemann, *Acts*, p. 226.

[60] Barrett, 'Paul's Address', esp. p. 110; Barrett, *Acts*, vol. II, p. 963.

[61] Gardner, 'Speeches of Paul', p. 403.

[62] Dupont, 'Construction', pp. 424–45.

[63] Conzelmann, *Acts*, p. 173; Bruce, *Acts* (2nd edn), p. 377; and Lüdemann, *Acts*, p. 226 see the importance of content for analysis.

[64] Cf. Lambrecht, 'Paul's Farewell-address', pp. 314–16.

[65] Metzger, *Text of the NT*, pp. 26f; Aland and Aland, *Text of NT*, p. 282.

[66] UBS[4] and NA[27].

Kilgallen's proposal[67] begins by observing the sentence structure and, within the sentences, the grammatical structure. He points to the key 'transition' words διότι (verse 26), γάρ (verse 27), καί (verse 30) and δίο (verse 31) as indicating which elements in the speech are grammatically dependent on others. Thus he argues that verses 25–7 form a unit with verse 25 as its main focus, since διότι (verse 26) indicates that verse 26 is dependent on verse 25 and γάρ (verse 27) indicates that verse 27 is a justification of verse 26. In similar manner, Kilgallen argues that verses 28–31 are a unit, with verse 28 as focus, since καί (verse 30) links verses 29 and 30, δίο (verse 31) shows that verse 31 is a conclusion from verses 29–30, and verse 31 parallels and reiterates verse 28.

Thus far Kilgallen's argument seems plausible, although it need not always follow that grammatical structure alone will indicate the central ideas of a text. He goes on to sketch the diagram of verses 25–31 below, which leads him to argue that verses 25, 28 are in parallel, implying that the reason for Paul's concern about the future (verse 28) is that he himself will be unavailable to help.

```
   25
           26
                   27
   28
           29–30
      31
```

It must be doubted whether Luke's readers would have noticed such a parallel, since Kilgallen's argument hinges on detailed study of a *written* text and comes to conclusions that he himself admits no one has noticed before, whereas the ancients seem to have noticed – and expected – clues to parallelism in a text which would be evident to someone *hearing* the text read aloud. If Luke intended such a parallel to be vital to comprehending the speech, he would be likely to have given a clearer aural signal.

What is surprising is that when Kilgallen goes on to examine the other parts of the speech, which lack the connectives which he uses in analysing verses 25–7 and 28–31, he puts on one side the structural markers provided by καὶ νῦν (verses 22, 25, 32), which is a grammatical signal of development in the speech – as may be πλὴν ὅτι (verse 23) and the strong adversative ἀλλ᾽ (verse 24), both

---

[67] Kilgallen, 'Paul's Speech'.

of which he also sidelines. This means that he has to use what he himself calls 'a rather subjective analysis'[68] for the other parts of the speech. The result is the structure below, which is more an analysis of the flow of thought than a formal structure:[69]

> 18b–21: My work has been such and
> 22–3: I now go to Jerusalem, warned
> 24: but I am ready to die for the Gospel
> 25: Note, I am never to see you again
> 26: So I tell you of my innocence
> 27: for I told you everything of God's plan
> 28: Watch out for yourselves and for the flock
> 29–30: there is danger from within and without
> 31: so watch
> 32: I leave you to God and to the word
> 33: I desired no one's gold
> 34: but rather supported myself and others
> 35: so support the weak, as I have done, as Jesus has urged.

Kilgallen's analysis is not without difficulties, but he identifies an important issue, that the grammar and sentence structure of the text are the bedrock of any structural analysis of the speech.

Repetitions

Four groups of phrases or words are repeated in the passage.

First, καὶ νῦν is used three times in the speech (verses 22, 25, 32),[70] and in each case this phrase leads on to a new point: the move on to Jerusalem (verse 22); Paul never seeing his hearers again (verse 25); and Paul committing the elders into God's care (verse 32).[71] Haenchen and Kurz[72] are surely right to notice this repetition as significant for the movement of the speech.

---

[68] Kilgallen, 'Paul's Speech', p. 116.

[69] Kilgallen, 'Paul's Speech', p. 119.

[70] As noted by Tannehill, *Narrative Unity*, vol. II, p. 253 – among numerous others.

[71] Other uses of καί νῦν in speeches in Acts are at key 'hinge' points in the speeches, usually moving from past event to present implications for action, e.g. 3.17; 5.38; 10.5; 13.11; 16.37; 22.16. Particularly interesting is 4.29, when the 'speech' is a prayer to God, and the same shift from past event to present action is taking place – but God is being asked to do the present action.

[72] Haenchen, *Acts*, p. 595; Kurz, *Farewell Addresses*, pp. 41, 43, 48; *contra* Conzelmann, *Acts*, p. 173.

Second, emphatic personal pronouns are used at six points in the speech. Paul uses ἐγώ of himself three times (verses 22, 25, 29), and ὑμεῖς (verses 18, 25) or αὐτοί (verse 34) of his hearers. In each case a point is being hammered home, and it is noteworthy that in verse 25 two emphatic personal pronouns coincide.

Third, there is the use of verbs of knowing. This has been noted by Dupont[73] as important for the movement of the speech. The speech begins and ends with the use of such verbs: ἐπίστασθε[74] (verse 18) and γινώσκετε (verse 34). Three times within the body of the speech the verb οἶδα is used (verses 22, 25, 29). Knowledge (or the lack of it, verse 22) is obviously an important commodity for this speech.

It is interesting how often these first three literary 'markers' coincide. All six uses of emphatic personal pronouns are close to verbs of knowing, and two of the uses of καὶ νῦν coincide with these places, as follows:

	καὶ νῦν	emphatic personal pronouns	verbs of knowing
verse 18	no	ὑμεῖς	ἐπίστασθε
verse 22	yes	ἐγώ	οἶδα[75]
verse 25	yes	ἐγώ, ὑμεῖς	οἶδα
verse 29	no	ἐγώ	οἶδα
verse 32	yes	no	no
verse 34	no	αὐτοί	γινώσκετε

The fourth group of repetitions are particular words which recur within the speech.[76] The idea that Paul has expounded 'the whole counsel of God' and not held back anything profitable is repeated using the same verbs in the same forms: ὑπεστειλάμην and ἀναγγεῖλαι (verses 20, 27). Δακρύα mark Paul's past ministry in Ephesus (verses 19, 31). Paul's apostolic ministry is characterised using διαμαρτύρομαι (verses 21, 24) and the message he proclaims is τῆς χάριτος τοῦ θεοῦ/αὐτοῦ (verses 24, 32). And, strikingly, the

---

[73] Dupont, 'Construction', p. 439; also Witherington, *Acts*, p. 416; Rackham, *Acts*, p. 389.
[74] A favourite word of Luke: of 14 NT uses, 9 are found in Acts. Luke uses it rhetorically to allow the speaker to refer to something already known (Acts 10.28; 15.7; 19.15, 25; 22.19; 24.10; 26.26) (*EDNT*, vol. I, p. 37).
[75] Codex Bezae and 𝔓⁴¹ (both Western witnesses) have γινώσκων instead of εἰδώς.
[76] Cf. Spencer, *Acts*, pp. 193f.

elders are to remember both Paul's example (verse 31) and the words of Jesus (verse 35), using μνημονεύω in both places.

These repetitions may be less significant for the structure of the speech than for the emphasis which they demonstrate; repetition may be because the idea is important, and the exegetical material below will consider this point. On the other hand, perhaps we should see these verbal repetitions as being more like the inter-woven colours in a tapestry, which may submerge for a time in the pattern and then reappear elsewhere, so that the eye notices the reappearance, but finds it difficult to trace the precise line from one to the other. Such an image is helpful as a way of understanding the whole speech, for it is the picture portrayed in the tapestry which provides the 'structure' – and the very complexity of the inter-weaving of the themes and words in the speech is suggestive as to why there is no scholarly consensus on the overall pattern, even though there are many structural signals.

Time references

Some time references have already been mentioned above, namely the uses of καὶ νῦν in verses 22, 25, 32. These mark points where implications for the future are drawn from earlier material in the speech, or new material is introduced which also looks towards the future. They are therefore significant for the structuring of the speech.

Change of subject

There is a shift in the speech at verse 28, where the subject changes from Paul to the elders and thenceforward they become the principal topic of discussion. Paul returns to his example in verses 31, 34, but by those points in the speech the focus has shifted from description of Paul's past activity to the use of Paul as an *exemplar* for the elders to follow.

These four phenomena are all important in considering the structure of the speech, along with the dictum of Dupont that a division should take account of both form and content.

3.3.2   Chiastic structure?

Two specific proposals for the structure of the speech merit

comment, those of Exum and Talbert, and Lambrecht. Both
suggest that the speech may have a chiastic structure.[77]

Exum and Talbert argue that the whole speech is chiastic.[78] The
particular significance of the chiasmus for them is that the central
section (verse 25) contains the key theme of the speech, that Paul's
hearers will never see him again. This point is underlined by Luke's
comment closing the scene (verses 36–8).

They claim that chiasmus is a recognised literary device used by
Luke elsewhere, citing the overall organisation of Luke-Acts, the
so-called 'central section' of the Gospel, and the miracles of Peter
and Paul in Acts. They therefore suggest that Luke is organising
the material chiastically here. In particular, they repeat the oft-
made suggestion that verse 21 is organised chiastically, which might
suggest that the primary need of the Jews to whom Paul has spoken
is 'faith in our Lord Jesus Christ', and the primary need of the
Gentiles is 'repentance toward God'.[79] Developing this point, they
consider that Luke is using the chiasmus in verse 21 to hint at a
wider use of the device in the speech. Their chiasmus is as follows:

> a: verses 18–21   Paul testifies to his witness
>   b: verses 22–4   foreboding: Paul in Jerusalem
>   c: verse 25   to be seen by them no more
>   b': verses 26–30   foreboding: false teachers from within
>   and without
> a': verses 31–5   Paul testifies to his witness

The dividing points of the first half of the speech are the uses of
καὶ νῦν ἰδού in verses 22 and 25, and in the second half of the
speech the repetitions of 'therefore' (διότι, verse 26; διό, verse 31).

While this analysis has points to commend it, questions need to
be raised about it. Notably, it seems arbitrary to use two of the
occurrences of καὶ νῦν in the speech as dividing markers and ignore
the third (verse 32), which might provide another natural division.
Further, the basis on which they proceed, of an assumed chiasmus
in verse 21, is at least questionable. Both repentance toward God
and faith in the Lord Jesus Christ were marks of *all* who joined the
Christian community, and there were not two different membership

---

[77] Tannehill, *Narrative Unity,* vol. II, p. 253 suggests that some of the repetitions
fall into a chiastic pattern, but does not draw conclusions about structure from this,
not least because his chiasmus only includes vv. 18–21, 24, 27, 31, 34.

[78] Exum and Talbert, 'Structure', 233–6.

[79] e.g. Dupont, *Discours de Milet*, pp. 82f; Stier, *Words of the Apostles*, pp. 319f.

requirements.[80] This can be seen particularly from the summaries of Paul's message in Acts, such as 17.30f, where the Athenians are called to repent because of who Jesus is, and 26.20, where no differentiation between Paul's message to Jews and to Gentiles can be seen. That is not to deny that preaching in specific situations would be contextualised and thus given a particular 'slant', but it is to deny a hermetically sealed division between the content of the message in Jewish and Gentile contexts. If a chiasmus is present, it is a literary device, but not a theological statement.

Moreover, Exum and Talbert's proposal appears artificial: apart from their title of 'foreboding', there is no obvious connection between their sections b and b′ in content, for verses 22–4 are to do with Paul's future and verses 26–30 with the Ephesian church's future, particularly the role of the elders.

Further, the assumption that a chiasmus focuses attention on its central section[81] is not necessarily correct. For example, Greek rhetors were advised to organise their material so that the key points came at the beginning and the end of a speech, so that the hearer would be grasped by the strength of the case at the beginning and be left with the key issues at the end, and therefore not remember any weaker points which came in between.[82] Thus, accepting Exum and Talbert's proposal on structure need not lead to accepting their conclusion that the statement in verse 25 is the heart of the speech.

Lambrecht's proposal is rather different, in that he suggests a double chiasmus, based on a major division of the speech at verse 28, where the shift from Paul talking about himself to Paul applying what he says to the elders occurs.[83]

This looks rather more well-founded in the four phenomena noted above, but does the chiastic structure stand up to examination? We may note several points.

First, the strength of this analysis is that it attempts to take seriously the content of the passage. Lambrecht tries to find

---

[80] Marshall, *Acts* (TNTC), p. 331, citing Rom. 1.16; 10.9–13. Barrett, 'Paul's Address', p. 112 also notes Rom. 10.9 in this connection. Strelan, *Paul, Artemis*, p. 267 n. 252 observes that Jews are called to repentance both in Luke (3.3; 5.22 (*sic*: presumably v. 32); 15.7; 24.47) and Acts (5.31).

[81] Cf. Lund, *Chiasmus in the NT*, pp. 40–4; Thomson, *Chiasmus*, pp. 43, 224–6.

[82] Cicero, *Rhetorica ad Herennium* 3.10.18 (advocating this approach); Quintilian 5.12.14 (discussing this approach).

[83] Lambrecht, 'Paul's Farewell-address', p. 318.

connections of content between his parallel sections, which are absent in Exum and Talbert's proposal.

> *I. Self defence and announcement (verses 18b–27)*
>   a: verses 18b–21   previous conduct (apology)
>   b: verses 22–5   announcement of departure and
>   future suffering
>   a': verses 26–7   previous conduct (apology)
> *II. Exhortations and farewell (verses 28–35)*
>   a: verses 28–31   warning: vigilance in the face of
>   imminent dangers (Paul's example)
>   b: verse 32   farewell
>   a': verses 33–5   warning: help for the weak (Paul's
>   example)

Second, however, it is doubtful whether verses 26f are a real *parallel* to verses 18b–21. Rather, they seem to develop further the points made in verses 18b–21. The use of διότι at the beginning of verse 26 underlines this point.

Third, it seems strained to see verses 28–31 as parallel to verses 33–5. Verses 28–31 discuss false teachers and the consequent need for good teaching from the elders, whereas verses 33–5 are to do with care for the poor, as Lambrecht himself notes.[84] Thus the only connection between them is Lambrecht's title of 'warning', which hardly describes the content of verses 33–5, for no warning is contained in those verses.

Finally, we should apply the caveat mentioned above, that even if a chiasmus is present, that need not imply that the central section is where the main emphasis lies. Overall, we therefore find Lambrecht's analysis, although a significant improvement on Exum and Talbert's approach, questionable.

3.3.3   A proposed structure

Is there a structure that would better reflect the four phenomena noted in § 3.3.1? In what follows we shall pursue the analogy offered above of seeing the speech like a tapestry. First we shall look at the speech from the perspective of its sequential arrangement, utilising the verbal clues of structure which we have noted, and then we shall consider the various 'colours' or major themes used in the tapestry and how they are woven into the speech.

---

[84] Lambrecht, 'Paul's Farewell-address', pp. 317f.

A preliminary sketch of the movement of the passage might look as follows:

> *Verses 18–21* form an introductory retrospect.
>
> *Verses 22–4* focus on the future of Paul in Jerusalem.
>
> *Verses 25–7* return to retrospect in the light of Paul's belief that he will never see the Ephesian elders again, and underline the claim that Paul has faithfully discharged his responsibility towards the elders.
>
> *Verses 28–31* call the elders to their (present and future) task in the light of dangers to come, and urge them to be alert.
>
> *Verses 32–5* re-focus the elders on the grace of God, which is able to uphold them, and finally hammer home the example of Paul for his hearers in terms of the elders' responsibility to care for the poor, underlined by a saying of Jesus.

The major division in the speech is at verse 28, the shift from Paul's description of himself in the past to consideration of the role of the elders in the future. The other divisions hinge on the καὶ νῦν markers (verses 22, 25, 32) and their coincidence with the use of emphatic personal pronouns and verbs of knowing (verses 22, 25).

3.4 Overview of contents

We therefore turn to consider the content and thread of thought of the speech section by section, following the structure outlined above. The section-by-section approach will allow us to see the main thread of the speech.

3.4.1 Verses 18–21: retrospect

The focus in this long sentence is on Paul's fulfilment of his task in the past, and this theme has three main aspects. First (verses 18b–19a) Paul reminds the elders of his past conduct and appeals to their knowledge of that conduct, which is marked by humility. Ταπεινοφροσύνη occurs only here in Acts; it is not common in the NT, occurring only seven times.[85] It does not occur in the LXX at

---

[85] Acts 20.19; Eph. 4.2; Phil. 2.3; Col. 2.18, 23; 3.12; 1 Pet. 5.5.

all; the cognates ταπεινοφρονέω and ταπεινόφρων only occur once each;[86] and the noun itself is very little attested, if at all, in pre-Christian literature.[87] Thus the noun ταπεινοφροσύνη, a combination of ταπεινός, 'lowly', and φρονέω, 'I think', may be a Christian coinage – or at least a word given an entirely different 'atmosphere' by its use by the earliest Christians, where it is contrasted (e.g. in Phil. 2.3) with ἐριθεία (seeking followers by means of gifts – hence ambition, rivalry[88]) and κενοδοξία (vanity, conceit, excessive ambition[89]).

Then (verse 19b) Paul refers to the hardship and suffering he endured in his ministry, characterised by tears and trials resulting from the plots of the Jews against him.[90] Grammatically, πάσης ταπεινοφροσύνης, δακρύων and πειρασμῶν are all dependent on the same μετά,[91] which suggests that Luke's Paul sees all three as results or concomitants of his 'serving the Lord'.

Paul then draws out the conclusion that he has faithfully fulfilled his responsibilities towards the church at Ephesus (verses 20–1).[92] He has taught them all that could profit them. He has taught them in every possible situation. He has taught both sides of the great racial and religious divide between Jews and Gentiles. The message he has taught is summarised as τὴν εἰς θεὸν μετάνοιαν καὶ πίστιν εἰς τὸν κύριον ἡμῶν Ἰησοῦν (verse 21).

Several key themes are introduced in this first sentence, rather like (to change our simile for the speech) the overture of a longer

---

[86]   Respectively Ps. 130.2; Prov. 29.23.

[87]   Thus Fee, *Philippians*, p. 187 n. 73. Lightfoot, *Philippians*, p. 109 notes that uses of ταπεινός in pre-Christian writers are mostly negative, using the word in the sense 'grovelling' or 'abject', e.g. Epictetus, *Discourses* 4.1.2: Τίς θέλει ζῶν ... ταπεινός; – Οὐδείς ('Who wishes to live ... abject? No-one'). See further *NIDNTT*, vol. II, pp. 259–64; BAGD, p. 804.

[88]   BAGD, p. 309 notes that the only pre-Christian attestation for this is in Aristotle with the sense of 'a self-seeking pursuit of political office by unfair means'.

[89]   BAGD, p. 427.

[90]   Dupont, *Discours de Milet*, p. 36 observes that the plots (ἐπίβουλαι) of 'the Jews' against Paul occur elsewhere in Acts (9.23f; 20.3; 21.27; 23.30; 24.19). Note also 23.27, which sets the context for 23.30 and clarifies that the plotters are 'the Jews'.

[91]   Thus Johnson, *Acts*, p. 360, who sees a distinction between the first two items, which refer to Paul's subjective inner attitudes, and the third, which refers to external pressures.

[92]   Conzelmann, *Acts*, p. 173 argues that this point is directed by Luke towards the advocates of 'gnostic' teaching which was being traced back to Paul in the church of Luke's day. See also Haenchen, *Acts*, p. 596; Barrett, 'Paul's Address', p. 111. But cf. Marshall, *Acts* (TNTC), p. 331: 'Such self-defence was typical of farewell discourses.'

piece of music. The links may be tabulated as follows. Some are precise verbal echoes and some use synonyms.[93]

ὑμεῖς ἐπίστασθε verse 18	αὐτοὶ γινώσκετε verse 34
τὸν πάντα χρόνον verse 18	τριετίαν νύκτα καὶ ἡμέραν verse 31
δουλεύων τῷ κυρίῳ verse 19	τὴν διακονίαν ἣν ἔλαβον παρὰ τοῦ κυρίου Ἰησοῦ verse 24; ὑπηρέτησαν verse 34
δακρύων verse 19	δακρύων verse 31
ἀπεστειλάμην ... τοῦ μὴ ἀναγγεῖλαι verse 20	ὑπεστειλάμην τοῦ μὴ ἀναγγεῖλαι verse 27
διαμαρτυρόμενος verse 21	διαμαρτύρεταί verse 23 διαμαρτύρασθαι verse 24

It is also noticeable that the last paragraph of the speech (verses 32–5) echoes a number of themes from this paragraph, especially Paul's exemplary lifestyle, which is derived from the words of the Lord Jesus himself (verse 35). This *inclusio*-type arrangement suggests that one of the major themes of the speech is Paul's ministry as an example to the elders for their ministry.[94]

3.4.2 Verses 22–4: the future of Paul in Jerusalem

The speech then turns towards the future of Paul,[95] a shift marked by καὶ νῦν ἰδού (verse 22). Paul is going to Jerusalem under the constraint of the Spirit,[96] knowing little of what is ahead, save that suffering for him is prophesied by the Spirit everywhere (verse 23).[97] The information that imprisonment is ahead adds to our knowledge of Paul's expectations.[98]

Paul's lack of detailed knowledge of the future does not produce any shirking from the way ahead, for he sees obedience to God as of greater importance than the preservation of his own life (verse 24).[99] This develops the point from verses 18b–21, that just as Paul

---

[93] Cf. Tannehill, *Narrative Unity,* vol. II, pp. 253f; Spencer, *Acts*, pp. 193.

[94] As also argued by Jervell, *Apostelgeschichte*, p. 509.

[95] Jervell, *Apostelgeschichte*, p. 510.

[96] § 3.5.2 discusses possible understandings of πνεῦμα (v. 25).

[97] Echoing Acts 19.21; further examples are to follow in 21.4, 11f, as are other uses of the δέω word group in 20.23; 21.13, 33; 22.29; 24.27 (Johnson, *Acts*, p. 361).

[98] Tannehill, *Narrative Unity,* vol. II, p. 254.

[99] Rapske, *Paul in Roman Custody*, pp. 403–7 argues that Paul's imprisonment will be part of his obedient witness, not least because 'Διαμαρτύρομαι followed by

has been faithful in the past in fulfilling his God-given task, so he will be in the future. Paul is not to be deflected by the prospect of suffering to come.

The message he proclaims is characterised as τὸ εὐαγγέλιον τῆς χάριτος τοῦ θεοῦ (verse 24).[100] This combination of εὐαγγέλιον and χάρις is unprecedented in Acts and the Pauline letters – the noun εὐαγγέλιον is rare in Acts, occurring only here and at 15.7.[101] Nevertheless, Haenchen believes that 'Luke wants to let a specifically Pauline catchword ring out'.[102] Barrett more cautiously claims, 'Luke uses words that are superficially Pauline, but improbably represent words that Paul actually used. They are significant as the ... deposit of Paulinism that permeated to the next generation.'[103] Perhaps we might be closest to the truth in simply observing that Luke here uses Pauline words, but not in a combination found in Paul's writings.

3.4.3   Verses 25–27: prospect and retrospect

With another καὶ νῦν verses 22–4 are drawn to a climax, further signalled by the introduction of ἰδού. Paul states plainly that the elders will never see him again (verse 25), now making the implications of the earlier hints of forthcoming suffering explicit. Haenchen[104] believes that there is a twofold note in the speech here: it is not merely that Paul will never be seen again by the elders of Ephesus, but that 'you *all*' will never see him again. In other words, Paul is taking leave of *all* the churches at this stage of Acts.[105] Barrett persuasively responds that the proximity of πάντες to ὑμᾶς suggests that the 'all' must be the Ephesian elders, although there may be a secondary reference to all of the churches.[106]

A number of scholars believe that verse 25, in combination with verse 38, signals that Luke knows that Paul is dead at the time of the writing of Acts,[107] in spite of hints in the Pastorals that Paul

---

λέγων [? misprint for λέγον] (Acts 20.23) suggests solemn testimony or witness *and carries no negative freighting*' (p. 406, italics mine).

[100] The Western manuscripts 𝔓[41vid] D, some Sahidic manuscripts and the Latin Father Lucifer add, clearly from v. 21, Ἰουδαίοις καὶ Ἕλλησιν.

[101] Although the verb εὐαγγελίζομαι is fairly frequent, occurring 15 times in Acts and 10 times in Luke, forming nearly half the NT uses (52 total). Of the remaining uses, 21 are in the Pauline corpus.

[102] Haenchen, *Acts*, p. 592.   [103] Barrett, 'Paul's Address', p. 112.
[104] Haenchen, *Acts*, p. 592.   [105] Cf. n. 41 above.
[106] Barrett, *Acts,* vol. II, p. 972.
[107] e.g. Conzelmann, *Acts*, p. 174; Hanson, *Acts*, pp. 203f; Haenchen, *Acts*, p. 592;

visited Ephesus at a later date (1 Tim. 1.3; 2 Tim. 1.15–18). The key question from our perspective is the character's knowledge within the 'world' of the narrative. We may identify two possibilities: that Luke's Paul knew of his forthcoming death, but did not know of its particular circumstances – thus locating the open-endedness of verses 22–5 in the detail; or that he was hoping to go on to evangelise other areas, but was ready for his plans to be curtailed by suffering and imprisonment.[108] The first possibility derives from Dibelius,[109] who believes that Luke knows of Paul's death but does not narrate it because he wants his book to end in triumph.

It is not really possible, on the evidence of the text, to decide between these two possibilities, but it is unlikely that Luke would deliberately provide an anachronistic and misleading reference of this kind if he knew that Paul did, in fact, visit Ephesus again. If Luke had known that Paul had re-visited, it is more likely that he would have phrased verse 25 along the lines of 'I don't believe it is likely that you will ever see my face again.' This suggests that Luke did not hint at Paul's return to the area either because he was writing before it took place or because he simply did not know about it. Deciding between these two options involves larger issues than can be addressed on the evidence of this passage alone. Nevertheless, we may conclude that verses 25, 38 need not be read as implying knowledge by Luke of Paul's death, but may reflect Paul's (and Luke's?) uncertainty about the future at this stage – the definite expectation is that Paul will not return to Ephesus, but it is possible that circumstances will change and that Paul may at a future time find himself again in Ephesus.

The look forward (verse 25) is immediately followed by a look back (verses 26f), reminding the elders again that Paul has faithfully discharged his responsibilities towards them, using the same

Brawley, *Luke-Acts and the Jews*, p. 25; Dibelius, *Studies in Acts*, p. 158 n. 46; Jervell, *Apostelgeschichte*, pp. 511, 515; Barrett, *Acts,* vol. II, p. 964.

[108] Gempf, 'Historical and Literary Appropriateness', pp. 290f. Cf. Witherington, *Acts*, pp. 618–20, suggesting that when Luke wishes to use a euphemism for 'death' he chooses ἔξοδος (Luke 9.31) rather than ἄφιξις (Acts 20.29). However, ἄφιξις is not found elsewhere in the NT (as Witherington notes), and ἔξοδος carries particular connotations of God's action in releasing the people from Egypt (which Luke sees as foreshadowing Jesus' death). More persuasive is Witherington's argument that ἄφιξις in other literature (he cites Josephus, *Ant.* 2.18; 4.315; Demosthenes *Ep.* 1.2; 3.39; cf. LSJ, p. 291) is *never* used metaphorically for a person's forthcoming death; similarly Barrett, *Acts,* vol. II, p. 978.

[109] Dibelius, *Studies in Acts*, p. 15; the second comes from Bruce, *Acts* (2nd edn), pp. 379f.

words in verse 27 as have already been used in verse 20. The look
back here is not simply a reminder, but serves to tell the elders that
Paul is *now* innocent (verse 26). The language of 'innocent of blood'
is reminiscent of the OT, particularly Ezekiel 33.5f, 8f.[110]

The summary of Paul's preaching as ἡ βουλή τοῦ θεοῦ (verse 27)
repeats language already used in Luke-Acts, and particularly in
Acts (Luke 7.30; Acts 2.23; 4.28; 5.38f; 13.36), although it is also
Pauline language (1 Cor. 4.5, but there of human plans; Eph.
1.11).[111] The idea that God has a purpose which he is carrying out
is a central emphasis of Acts,[112] for God is arguably *the* key actor
in the story of the Book of Acts: he directs the mission, especially
by the Spirit's work and words (e.g. 8.29, 39; 10.19; 11.15; 13.2;
15.28; 16.6[113]), and pushes out the boundaries into new ethnic
groups (10.19; 11.12, 15) or new geographical areas (16.9f). But the
use of βουλή in 20.27 does not immediately seem to refer to the
'plan' of God, but to the whole of God's will or mind[114] – a
complete message for all kinds of people, both Jews and Gentiles
(verse 21).[115] 'It is a responsibility to all that arises from a gospel
that offers salvation to all.'[116]

---

[110] Lövestam, 'Paul's Address', p. 3, who discusses other possible OT parallels.

[111] Barrett, 'Paul's Address', p. 113 also notes the five Pauline uses of βούλεσθαι
(1 Cor. 12.11; 2 Cor. 1.15, 17; Phil. 1.12; Phlm 13), the two uses of βουλεύεθαι in
2 Cor. 1.17, and the use of βούλημα in Rom. 9.19, while viewing the more frequent
use of these words in Luke-Acts (βούλεσθαι sixteen times, βουεύεθαι three times) as
indicating that this is Lukan language; for similar views see Squires, *Plan of God in
Luke-Acts*, p. 75 n. 198; Marshall, *Acts* (TNTC), p. 333. Cf. Gempf, 'Historical and
Literary Appropriateness', p. 293, who draws attention to the Judaizers' criticism of
Paul that he had not given his converts the '*whole* plan of God' in omitting
circumcision and keeping the law (Gal. 1.10; 2.6).

[112] Peterson, 'Motif of Fulfilment'; Dupont, *Discours de Milet*, pp. 122f.

[113] Shepherd, *Narrative Function*, pp. 186, 187, 199f, 204, 209f, 218, 221–3;
Turner, *Power from on High*, pp. 402f.

[114] Dupont, *Discours de Milet*, p. 123 remarks: 'Le mot βουλή n'est pas le
synonyme exact de θέλημα, mais il s'emploie d'une manière à peu près équivalente:
la volonté délibérée et réfléchie de Dieu ne concerne pas seulement le plan de salut
qu'il compte réaliser lui-même, mais aussi, et davantage encore, les conditions à
remplir par les hommes qui désirent avoir part aux bienfaits divins.' ('The word
βουλή is not an exact synonym of θέλημα, but it is used as a rough equivalent:
God's resolute and considered will does not only concern the plan of salvation,
which he purposes to achieve himself, but also, and even more, the conditions for
fulfilment by people who wish to have a part in the divine generosity.') Squires, *Plan
of God in Luke-Acts*, p. 26 n. 44 also sees βουλή as a reference to the message,
because of the parallel with 'the kingdom' in 20.25 (mis-cited as 20.55).

[115] Note the stress on πᾶς in this section (vv. 25, 26, 27).

[116] Tannehill, *Narrative Unity*, vol. II, p. 257.

3.4.4 Verses 28–31: a charge to the elders

Paul therefore calls the elders to their task in the light of their knowledge that they will no longer have him to lean upon. They are to take heed (verses 28, 31)[117] both of themselves and of the church, pictured using the common biblical image of a flock (verse 28: a metaphor used frequently for Israel), and they are to shepherd that flock.[118] Although this image is common in the Hebrew Bible and (therefore) the LXX, it is rare in Luke-Acts, where such a metaphorical use of the verb or the noun is only found here and at Luke 12.32, where the followers of Jesus are described as τό μικρὸν ποίμνιον.[119]

Two points develop the understanding of their need to keep watch: first, their task has been assigned to them by the Spirit,[120] and second, the church is of tremendous value to God, having been obtained with the price of the blood of God's own.[121] The explicit reference to the redemptive significance of the death of Jesus is rare in Luke-Acts.

Paul not only declares what the task of the elders is to be, but warns them of the dangers ahead – and this is why they must keep

[117] Cf. Luke 21.34; 12.1.

[118] See 1 Kings 20.27 (LXX 21.27); 22.17; Ps. 78.52 (LXX 77.52); Isa. 40.11; Jer. 13.17, 20; Ezek. 34.12, 31; Mic. 2.12; 4.8; 5.4 (LXX 5.3); Zech. 10.3, all using ποίμνιον in the LXX, the diminutive form of ποίμνη used in Acts 20.28a. Likewise, there is considerable use of ποιμαίνω in the LXX, the verb used in Acts 20.28b of the role of the elders. It is used of David or the king of Israel (2 Sam. 5.2 (cf. 1 Chr. 11.2); Ps. 78.71f (LXX 77.71f); Ezek. 34.10, 23), sometimes of the leaders of Israel (1 Sam. 7.7 (cf. 1 Chron. 17.6); Jer. 3.15; 6.18 (LXX: MT has עֵדָה, which BDB, p. 417 understands commonly to mean 'congregation', sometimes the whole congregation of Israel – but there is also a problem of textual corruption here, discussed in Bright, *Jeremiah*, p. 45; Thompson, *Jeremiah*, p. 259 n. 3); 23.2, 4), and, archetypally, of God himself (Ps 28.9 (LXX 27.9); 48.14 (LXX 47.15); 80.1 (LXX 79.2); Isa. 40.11; Hos. 13.5; Micah 7.14). For discussion of the shepherd and flock metaphors, see *NIDNTT*, vol. III, pp. 564–9.

[119] The metaphorical use is quite rare in the NT, found predominantly in the Johannine literature (John 10.2, 11f, 14, 16; 21.16; Rev. 7.17; 12.5; 19.5); as well as at Mark 6.34 (//Matt. 9.36); 14.27 (//Matt. 6.31, both quoting Zech. 13.7); Eph. 4.11; Heb. 13.20; 1 Pet. 2.25; 5.2f; Jude 12. Of these, only Acts 20.28; Eph. 4.11 and 1 Pet. 5.2f use the metaphor for church leaders, perhaps reflecting the relative reluctance to use the metaphor for the leaders of Israel in the Hebrew Bible (*NIDNTT*, vol. III, pp. 565f).

[120] It is unusual for it to be said in Acts that the Spirit appointed leaders: the only possible parallels are 6.3, 5; 13.2, and these are hardly the appointment of local church elders, as here. Indeed, Luke can state that elders were appointed without even mentioning the Spirit – e.g. it is Barnabas and Saul who do the appointing (14.23).

[121] See Excursus 1 on the text and translation of v. 28b.

watch. False teachers will come from outside (verse 29) and inside the church (verse 30).[122] Indeed, the speech states that false teachers will come from amongst the very elders to whom Paul speaks (verse 30).[123] These false teachers are imaged as 'grievous wolves', a particularly appropriate metaphor in the light of the 'flock' image for the church (verse 28, cf. Luke 10.3).[124]

This explicit warning against false teaching from within the church is unique in Acts[125] and is followed rapidly by Paul's repeated charge to the elders to be alert (verse 31) in the light of the dangers ahead.[126] This is underlined by another reference to Paul's example (verse 31) of persistence and sincerity in teaching the church at Ephesus, again noting that he missed no opportunity and used the time fully (cf. verses 20, 27).[127]

3.4.5   Verses 32–5: conclusion

Again the shift of focus is marked by καὶ νῦν (verse 32), and the farewell becomes quite explicit: Paul commits the elders to God and the word of his grace, which will empower them for their ministry as it has empowered him for his.

Τῷ λόγῳ τῆς χάριτος αὐτοῦ (verse 32) echoes τὸ εὐαγγέλιον τῆς χάριτο1 τοῦ θεοῦ (verse 24), and it seems likely that Luke intends his readers to notice the echo, particularly as the first 'readers' would have heard Acts read aloud. The phrase ὁ λόγος τῆς χάριτος αὐτοῦ has been used by Luke already (Acts 14.3, cf. Luke 4.22) and, although it sounds Pauline (since both λόγος and χάρις are favourite Pauline words[128]), the phrase itself is only found in

---

[122] Haenchen, *Acts*, p. 593; Marshall, *Acts* (TNTC), p. 334.

[123] Stier, *Words of the Apostles*, p. 330.

[124] For discussion, see Lampe, 'Grievous Wolves', esp. p. 256. Luke 10.3 is discussed in § 4.5.3 below.

[125] Hanson, *Acts*, p. 205. Klein, *Die zwölf Apostel*, pp. 180f suggests that Luke implies by this that the original epoch of peace in the church ended with Paul's death.

[126] Thus, although the vocabulary is different (προσέχετε, v. 28; γρηγορεῖτε v. 31), there is a 'chiastic' feel to this section, beginning and ending with an imperatival call to action. Cf. Johnson, *Acts*, p. 364; Dupont, *Discours de Milet*, p. 135: 'L'appel qui commence le v. 28, «Soyez attentifs», sera repris et précisé au v. 31: «Soyez vigilants».' ('The appeal which begins v. 28, "Be attentive", will be repeated and focused in v. 31, "Be vigilant."')

[127] Dupont, *Discours de Milet*, pp. 227f points to the motif of the appeal to the memory of the hearers in vv. 18, 31, 34, 35 – the last appeals to their memory of a word of Jesus rather than the example of Paul.

[128] e.g. λόγος (meaning the gospel message), 1 Cor. 1.18; 14.36; 15.2; 2 Cor. 2.17;

Luke's writings. As with ἡ ἐκκλησία τοῦ θεοῦ (verse 28), Luke is using Pauline ideas and themes, rather than precise formulae (although we clearly cannot be certain that Paul never used such a phrase).

The final note of the speech is the elders' conduct over financial affairs (verses 33–5). Paul is again held up as a model (verses 33f), especially in that he provided for his companions.[129] There is an interesting word-play between χρείαις at the beginning of the ὅτι clause in verse 34 and χεῖρες at the end of that clause – both in emphatic positions. Some suggest that the latter phrase would have been accompanied by an appropriate gesture,[130] which would be natural – as Luke's Paul shows elsewhere (Acts 13.16; 21.40; 26.1). Moreover, Paul in Acts works with his hands (Acts 18.3) when necessary.[131]

Therefore the elders are called to copy Paul, using the rare verb ὑποδείκνυμι (verse 35).[132] The other use of this verb in Acts (9.16) shows 'the Lord' speaking to Ananias about Saul as one to whom the Lord will 'example'[133] how much he must suffer. If Luke has this other use in mind in using the verb here, it suggests that Luke sees Paul as following the path of suffering exemplified by Jesus.

The verb ἀντιλαμβάνομαι is similarly rare,[134] having the sense 'help', 'come to the aid of'.[135] Bruce suggests that the 'weak' to be helped are 'those who were sick and unable to earn their own

5.19; Gal. 6.6; 1 Thess. 1.8; 2.13 (twice); χάρις, Rom. 3.24; 4.16; 5.2, 15, 20f; 6.14; 2 Cor. 4.15; 6.1; 8.9; Gal. 1.6, 15; 2.21. Cf. Aejmelaeus, *Rezeption*, pp. 156f.

[129] This reflects a similar concern in Samuel's farewell, 1 Sam. 12.3 (Bruce, *Book of Acts* (revised edn), p. 395; Conzelmann, *Acts*, p. 176; Kurz, *Farewell Addresses*, pp. 48f; Trites, *NT Concept of Witness*, p. 72; Barrett, *Acts,* vol. II, p. 982).

[130] Bruce, *Acts* (3rd edn), p. 436; Williams, *Commentary on Acts*, p. 235.

[131] Johnson, *Acts*, p. 365; Dupont, *Discours de Milet*, pp. 299f. The fact that he stops working in this way when Silas arrives (18.5) may be due to Silas bringing a gift from Philippi, for which Philippians is possibly the 'thank-you letter' (2 Cor. 11.9; Phil. 4.15) – but in any case this is not an explanation available within the horizon of Luke-Acts, and within that 'world' the reader has no insight into why Paul stops working; cf. Kaye, 'Silas', which deals with the Acts data. For discussion of the historical questions, see Bruce, *Acts* (3rd edn), pp. 374f, 392; Foakes Jackson and Lake, *Beginnings*, vol. IV, p. 224; Lake, *Earlier Epistles of St Paul*, pp. 73–5; Wainwright, 'Where Did Silas Go?' (the latter arguing that Silas had been to Galatia bearing Paul's letter to the Galatians).

[132] Found five times in Luke-Acts (Luke 3.7; 6.47; 12.5; Acts 9.16; 20.35) and only once otherwise in the NT (Matt. 3.7, which parallels Luke 3.7). Goulder, *Luke: New Paradigm*, p. 809 regards ὑποδεικνύειν-ὑμίν as a Lukanism.

[133] Johnson, *Acts*, p. 365 suggests 'drawing a pattern' (and hence 'providing an example') as the sense of the verb.

[134] Found three times in the NT (Luke 1.54; Acts 20.35; 1 Tim. 6.2).

[135] BAGD, p. 74.

living',[136] and this is the use of οἱ ἀσθενοῦντες in all other uses in Luke-Acts (Luke 4.40; 9.2[137]; Acts 9.37; 19.12).[138]

The elders should be self-supporting so that they too can care for others. Luke's Paul caps this by quoting an otherwise unknown saying of Jesus to drive home the last point. The saying is introduced by the emphatic personal pronoun αὐτός, drawing attention to the one who speaks: the picture of Paul with which the speech leaves its readers is one who wants the words of his Master to be remembered.

3.5   Themes

The speech flows from past to present to future, with regular references to Paul's example throughout. Four themes are specially worthy of note, and will be developed further when we compare the Miletus speech with other material in Luke-Acts and 1 Thessalonians: the faithful fulfilment of leadership responsibility, suffering, attitudes to wealth and work, and the death of Jesus.

3.5.1   Faithful fulfilment of leadership responsibility

This theme runs through the whole speech, for Paul is both setting out his track record and using that track record as the basis for urging the elders to fulfil their ministry.

Paul has carried out his task fully: this can be seen particularly from the numerous uses of πᾶς in the passage.[139] The presence of πᾶς underscores Paul's faithfulness in fulfilling his task: he has been consistent the whole time (verse 18); his work has been thoroughly humble (verse 19); he has proclaimed the whole purpose of God (verse 27) – to Jew and Gentile alike (verse 21);[140] his message produces an inheritance amongst all the sanctified (verse 32); therefore he is innocent of the blood of them all (verse 26); and in

[136] Bruce, *Acts* (3rd edn), p. 436. Marshall, *Acts* (TNTC), p. 336 notes the parallel with 1 Thess. 5.14, and asserts that the 'weak' in Acts 20.35 are the physically needy. Rackham, *Acts*, p. 396 n. 3 draws the same parallel, and offers a range of options for the meaning of 'the weak', including the weak in body, mind or spirit. See discussion of 1 Thess. 5.14 below, § 5.3.3.
[137] NA[27] and UBS[4] place the words τοὺς ἀσθενεῖς in square brackets, indicating the editors' doubts about its presence in the original; see Metzger, *Textual Commentary* (1st edn), pp. 146f.
[138] Johnson, *Acts*, p. 365.   [139] Rackham, *Acts*, p. 390.
[140] Tannehill, *Narrative Unity,* vol. II, p. 257 sees the two themes of the full message and the full range of humanity being included in the church as parallel.

everything he has given an example to follow (verse 35). Moreover, a result of his words that they *all* will never see him again (verse 25) is that he kneels with them all to pray (verse 36) and they all weep (verse 37). Thus the elders themselves are to be alert παντὶ τῷ ποιμνίῳ (verse 28), using the same theme word, πᾶς, to make the point. Their ministry is to be as unstinting and as complete as Paul's.

The fulfilment of Paul's responsibilities can also be seen through seven of the negatives in the passage. In three cases Paul is denying that he has omitted anything that he should have covered in his teaching (verses 20, 27 (two negatives in the Greek reinforce each other here), 31). Paul also asserts that his life is not reckoned as valuable to him compared to future obedience to God's will (verse 24).[141] Paul's warning about the wolves who will not spare the flock (verse 29) implies that, by contrast, he has spared the flock from the pain and punishment which the wolves will bring.[142] Paul also emphasises that he has not coveted ἀργυρίου ἢ χρυσίου ἢ ἱματισμοῦ οὐδενός (verse 33), again using a negative statement to make a positive point, which is then applied to the elders (verse 35).

The elders are told to imitate Paul several times in the speech, both explicitly and implicitly, by statements about their responsibilities which parallel statements about Paul's ministry. They are to keep alert, remembering how Paul kept alert night and day for three years (verse 31). They are to keep watch over themselves (verse 28) as Paul kept watch over himself (verses 18b–19). They are to keep watch over the flock (verse 28) as Paul kept watch over them (verses 20f, 26f). God's word of grace is available to equip them (verse 32) as it equipped Paul (verse 24). And Paul draws the speech to a close with an explicit reference to his example 'in all this' (verse 35) – an example which he derives from the Lord Jesus.

Throughout, the elders are being schooled in Pauline ministry as Luke conceives it, and thus being prepared for the exercise of their ministry after Paul loses his ability to travel freely and perhaps his

[141] Pfitzner, *Agon Motif*, p. 183 n. 2 notes the athletic metaphor used here in δρόμος, which is found elsewhere in the NT only at Acts 13.25; Phil. 2.16f; 2 Tim. 4.6f; see also Aejmelaeus, *Rezeption*, p. 120.

[142] Φείδομαι is used only here in Luke-Acts and it is found elsewhere in the NT only at Rom. 8.32; 11.21; 1 Cor. 7.28; 2 Cor. 1.23; 12.6; 13.2; 2 Pet. 2.4, 5. The uses in 2 Cor. 1.23; 13.2 are particularly close in sense to the idea found here. Johnson, *Acts*, p. 363 proposes 'have compassion' on the basis of use in the LXX. He cites Ps. 18.13 (*sic*: presumably v. 14 (= MT 19.14)); 71.13; Joel 2.17.

life itself. They are being urged to fulfil their leadership responsibility faithfully, just as Paul has his.[143]

The leaders of the Ephesian church are designated in three ways in this passage: πρεσβύτεροι (verse 17), ἐπίσκοποι (verse 28) and (by implication) ποιμένες (verses 28f, cf. Eph. 4.11). As is widely recognised,[144] Luke is unusual in using the first two terms for the same group.

Πρεσβύτεροι has already been employed by Luke for church leaders, mainly for those in Jerusalem.[145] However, Campbell proposes that πρεσβύτερος should not be seen as the title of an office in the NT, since it did not denote an office in the Jewish and Graeco-Roman worlds at the time, but rather was an 'imprecise title of honour for whatever leaders there may be'.[146] He further argues that ἐπίσκοπος should be seen as the title given to leaders of house churches, originally in Jerusalem, who could also (by reason of their seniority) be collectively described as οἱ πρεσβύτεροι.[147] Similarly in the description of 'the apostles and the elders' in Acts 15.22ff he suggests that καί should be seen as epexegetic, with the result that 'the elders' designates 'the whole Jerusalem leadership ... both the apostles and every person of importance in the church'.[148] We can thus see the use of οἱ πρεσβύτεροι in 20.17 in this light, i.e. that these ἐπίσκοποι (verse 28) of the Ephesian house churches are collectively the senior leadership of the church in Ephesus, and so are given the honorific designation οἱ πρεσβύτεροι τῆς ἐκκλησίας.[149] Thus the description of the one group by these two terms may reflect a situation which did not obtain in Luke's day, which implies that Luke did not read the church leadership titles of his own day back into apostolic times.[150]

---

[143] Spencer, *Acts*, p. 194 recognises this dimension of a 'farewell speech'.

[144] e.g. Conzelmann, *Acts*, p. 173; Haenchen, *Acts*, pp. 592f; Bruce, *Acts* (3rd edn), p. 433; Foakes Jackson and Lake, *Beginnings*, vol. IV, p. 259; Marshall, *Acts* (TNTC), pp. 333f; Johnson, *Acts*, p. 362; Michel, *Abschiedsrede*, pp. 91f; Barrett, *Acts*, vol. II, p. 975 (the latter acutely observing that using the two terms for the same people does not necessarily mean that the terms have the same meaning).

[145] Acts 11.30; 15.2, 4, 6, 22f; 16.4; 21.18. In each case the definite article is present, perhaps implying that these elders are *the* elders of the whole church.

[146] Campbell, *The Elders*, esp. chs. 2–3; the quotation is from p. 161.

[147] Campbell, *The Elders*, pp. 151–9; cf. Jervell, *Apostelgeschichte*, p. 512: 'Episkopos ist hier keine Amtsbezeichnung' ('Episkopos is not the title of an office here').

[148] Campbell, 'Elders of Jerusalem', esp. 526–8; the quotation is from 526.

[149] Campbell, *The Elders*, p. 172.

[150] Campbell, *The Elders*, pp. 173f, *contra* Barrett, *Acts*, vol. II, p. 966.

3.5.2 Suffering

Suffering recurs as a theme in the speech, particularly in the first half, both echoing material earlier in Acts and preparing for development of this theme later in Acts.

Luke presents Paul as referring back to his own past suffering (verse 19b) at the hands of the Jews,[151] a suffering that is almost inevitable for this one who faithfully proclaims the Christian gospel. Sanders claims that in Paul's speeches in Acts it is consistently 'the Jews' who oppose the Pauline mission (e.g. 13.46; 18.6; 28.28), and that they are presented as hardened to God's purpose and offer of salvation.[152] Sanders also points to elements in the narrative of Acts which show 'the Jews' opposing Paul (e.g. 26.2, 21).[153] Recently in Acts, we have read of Jewish opposition in Macedonia (20.3, using ἐπιβουλή,[154] as in 9.24; 20.19;[155] 23.30). However, the material is more mixed in its description of Jewish matters than Sanders allows, including a positive evaluation of Paul's Jewish heritage and statements of Paul's continuing Jewishness (e.g. 21.40–22.2; 22.3; 23.1, 6; 26.4–7; 28.19) alongside statements of the Jews' opposition to Paul and his gospel (e.g. 22.5; 25.24; 26.2, 21; 28.19).[156] Further, persecution and opposition can come from non-Jewish sources, not least in Ephesus (19.23–7[157]). Nevertheless, in the Miletus speech it is certainly past Jewish opposition to Paul which is meant, of which Acts gives ample examples.[158] Luke has prepared carefully for this reference.

Suffering awaits Paul in the future too (verse 23). The perfect

---

[151] Cf. the inclusion of εἰς πάντα πειρασμόν ('in every trial') in some Western manuscripts of 15.26 (Rackham, *Acts*, p. 389 n. 9). Metzger, *Textual Commentary* (1st edn), p. 437 notes that 'the gloss may be reminiscent of 20.19'.

[152] Sanders, *Jews in Luke-Acts*, p. 54.

[153] Sanders, *Jews in Luke-Acts*, pp. 79, 366 n. 241.

[154] Dupont, *Discours de Milet*, p. 36 notes that all four uses of ἐπιβουλή in Acts (which are the only NT uses) refer to Jewish plots against Paul.

[155] Johnson, *Acts*, p. 360.

[156] Weatherly, 'Jews in Luke-Acts', p. 111; Tyson, *Images of Judaism*, pp. 187–9; Brawley, *Luke-Acts and the Jews*, pp. 79–83, 157. For a fuller evaluation and critique of Sanders' views, see Weatherly, 'Jews in Luke-Acts'.

[157] Note also the response to Alexander when the crowd recognised him to be a Jew (19.33f), which implies that Paul's very Jewishness was a cause of opposition in Ephesus, as earlier in Philippi (16.20f) (in agreement with Brawley, *Luke-Acts and the Jews*, p. 80).

[158] e.g. Pisidian Antioch (13.45, but note 13.43), Iconium (14.2, but note 14.1), Lystra (14.19), Thessalonica (17.5, but note 17.4), Beroea (17.13, but note 17.11f) and Corinth (18.6, 12f, but note 18.8).

participle δεδεμένος[159] (verse 22) suggests an event antecedent to the main verb (πορεύομαι), a prior compelling towards suffering, which has continuing consequences in Paul's present sense of divine constraint.[160] A possible occasion is 19.21, the sense of which turns on the meaning of ἐν τῷ πνεύματι, which could be a reference to Paul's own resolve[161] or to the divine Spirit.[162] The latter seems more likely, not least because it is probable that the reference to the Holy Spirit's testimony through the urban churches in verse 23 explains in what sense Paul is 'bound'.[163]

Paul's witness, which is a suffering witness (θλίψεις, verse 23; cf. 9.15f), will be a prison witness[164] (δέσμα, verse 23; cf. 21.11, 13, 33; 22.29; 24.27). Indeed, the use of ὡς (verse 24, if this is the correct reading[165]) in the unusual (in the NT) sense of purpose[166] implies that Paul's purpose in not considering his life precious – in going to prison – is to complete the work God has given him to do.[167]

[159] Spencer, *Acts*, p. 195 suggestively contrasts the pre-Christian Saul's 'binding' of believers (Acts 9.2, 14, 21).

[160] Rapske, *Paul in Roman Custody*, p. 404; Williams, *Acts* (NIBC), p. 353. Barrett, 'Paul's Address', p. 112 considers that the 'binding' is explained in 20.23, in the mention of the Spirit's testimony that Paul will be bound. Cf. 21.11, which uses the verb δέω twice, for both literal and metaphorical binding.

[161] Cosgrove, 'Divine ΔΕΙ', p. 178, claiming the support of Foakes Jackson and Lake, *Beginnings*, vol. IV, p. 244; however, its authors Lake and Cadbury see this view as an 'alternative rendering' and prefer 'was inspired to purpose', although tentatively. Cosgrove argues that the referent of πνεῦμα (Acts 20.22) is to be distinguished from the full reference τὸ πνεῦμα τὸ ἅγιον (Acts 20.23). He claims that nowhere else in Acts is a first use of the simple πνεῦμα followed by the full τὸ πνεῦμα τὸ ἅγιον. (See following note for response.)

[162] Rapske, *Paul in Roman Custody*, p. 404, noticing the use of δεῖ as implying divine involvement. Cosgrove, 'Divine ΔΕΙ', p. 178 renders the last phrase of the verse as 'I must see Rome', but some reference to God's action seems more likely; Conzelmann, *Acts*, p. 164 points to the similar use of δεῖ in 23.11; 27.24. *Contra* Cosgrove (see preceding note), Haenchen, *Acts*, p. 591 n. 6 observes, 'We cannot require the author to use the full formula "the Holy Spirit" twice in immediate succession.' Likewise Prast, *Presbyter und Evangelium*, pp. 86f argues that Luke generally uses τὸ πνεῦμα in the same sense as other nearby uses, irrespective of whether that form precedes or follows the fuller and more specific use.

[163] Barrett, 'Paul's Address', p. 112; Shepherd, *Narrative Function*, pp. 233 n. 249; 231 n. 244; Jervell, *Apostelgeschichte*, p. 510.

[164] Rapske, *Paul in Roman Custody*, pp. 398–403, 404.

[165] Haenchen, *Acts*, p. 592; Bruce, *Acts* (3rd edn), p. 432 agree with the editors of UBS[4] and NA[27] in adopting this reading. The manuscript support is ancient and strong (𝔓[41, 74vid] ℵ* A B* C Ψ).

[166] Moule, *Idiom-Book*, p. 138 n. 1; Porter, *Idioms*, pp. 199, 232.

[167] Rapske, *Paul in Roman Custody*, pp. 406f argues that the references in 21.4, 10–14 do not contradict this divine compulsion. He proposes that 21.4 should be read as a condensed version of an incident similar to that found in 21.10–14, in which the expression 'through the Spirit' refers, like 20.22–4, to a 'motivationally

Paul's attitude to suffering is twofold: there is an implied patience and fortitude in his description in verse 19;[168] and he is utterly committed to seeing through the path of witness-through-imprisonment which awaits him as the Lord's purpose (verse 24). By implication the elders are to regard suffering similarly when they meet it, as Paul hints that they will (verses 29f). That is why they need to keep watch and stay alert (verses 28, 31).

3.5.3 The attitude to wealth and work

This third theme is developed both in terms of Paul's own conduct and in terms of his expectations of the elders.

Paul's attitude is held up as exemplary (verse 35). He covets nothing of anyone else's (ἐπιθυμέω[169], verse 33). This denial parallels Samuel's farewell (1 Sam. 12.3–5),[170] where he asks the congregation of Israel whether he has taken others' possessions and receives a denial in response – characteristically for an agriculturally based society, ox and ass are specified. Luke's Paul specifies other forms of wealth, more appropriate to the Graeco-Roman world: gold, silver and clothing. There are also possible parallels in the ideal portrait of a philosopher or orator.[171]

It is not often noticed[172] that there is an ironic contrast with the story of Paul's ministry in Ephesus here, for the issue that led to the riot was Paul taking away others' wealth (derived from silver shrines) through the preaching of the gospel (19.24–27a). Moreover, in Ephesus those who gave up magic practices burned books worth a considerable sum (reckoned in silver coins: 19.19). Further, there is a contrast between Paul's defence of the gospel, motivated

neutral' prophecy given by God to what awaits Paul in Jerusalem and Rome; the prophecy was then mistakenly interpreted by the believers in Tyre as meaning that Paul should not go to Jerusalem.

[168] Marshall, *Acts* (TNTC), p. 330.

[169] The only use of the verb in Acts, and reminiscent of Exod. 20.17 LXX (Johnson, *Acts*, p. 364; Agrell, *Work*, p. 219 n. 56). The verb ἐπιθυμέω can have a positive connotation (e.g. Luke 17.22; 22.15) as well as the negative sense it carries here (BAGD, p. 293).

[170] e.g. Dupont, *Discours de Milet*, pp. 286f; Barrett, 'Paul's Address', p. 116; Aejmelaeus, *Rezeption*, p. 166; Johnson, *Acts*, p. 365; Jervell, *Apostelgeschichte*, p. 514.

[171] Dio Chrysostom, *Orations* 32.9, 11 (who, while recognising that some Cynics bring philosophers into disrepute by 'hanging around on street-corners', nevertheless portrays good philosophers as not seeking wealth; see Johnson, *Acts*, p. 365); Aristotle, *Rhetoric* 1.9.6, 10f.

[172] Gooding, *True to the Faith*, p. 341; Spencer, *Acts*, p. 194 both hint at this idea.

by concern for his hearers' salvation (20.25f) and Demetrius' defence of his trade, motivated by money (19.24f).[173]

Paul is also exemplary in his financial independence from those to whom he ministers, to the extent that he provides for his companions' needs (verse 34). This results from Paul's manual work, which is only mentioned elsewhere in Acts at Corinth (18.3).[174] The use of κοπιάω (verse 35[175]) also hints at the physical tiredness which is involved in manual labour.

Alexander suggests that Greek culture generally despised manual work,[176] but asserts that the scientific writers (amongst whom she places Luke) 'speak of the *technitai* with deep respect'.[177] Accordingly, it is interesting, she observes, that Luke simply mentions Paul's manual work without further comment in 18.1–3.

Paul's financial independence means that he is also able to give financial help to those he serves (verse 35), particularly 'the weak'.[178] The reader of the remainder of Acts might think of 21.23f, 26, where Paul pays the hairdressing expenses of Jewish Christians who have taken a vow.

As we have seen, the example of Paul is then hammered home by reference to an otherwise unknown saying of Jesus (verse 35), reinforcing the point that care for the poor and needy is an important function of the elders in the Ephesian church.

It is interesting that the attitude to wealth and work is picked out from the many things that could have been said about the role of the elders in this speech and is given a significant amount of coverage.[179] Part of the elders' 'feeding' task (verse 28) is to be

[173] Gooding, *True to the Faith*, p. 357.

[174] Dupont, *Discours de Milet*, pp. 299f.

[175] The only use of the word in Acts; it is found twice in Luke (5.5; 12.27), both times connoting physical effort. The verb occurs 23 times in the NT and the cognate noun κόπος 18 times, both predominantly in Paul.

[176] In agreement with Hock, *Social Context*, pp. 34f, who suggests there were three *stigmata* attached to 'the trades': they were considered the work of slaves; they left no time to help the city or friends, or for personal development (which meant that artisans were seen as uneducated); and they were only useful in providing goods and services for the wealthy.

[177] Alexander, 'Luke's Preface', p. 70. She cites Plutarch, *Parallel Lives: Pericles* 2; *Marcellus* 14f as examples of the former point, and Galen, *De Comp. Med. Sec. Loc.* VI 1; Philo, *Belopoeica*, Th. 51.9ff as examples of the latter. Cf. Hock, *Social Context*, pp. 38–41, pointing to examples of philosophers found in workshops, especially Simon the shoemaker, who is presented as teaching while plying his trade (e.g. Pseudo-Socrates, *Epistles* 9.4; 11; 13.1 (text and translation in Malherbe, *Cynic Epistles*, pp. 246f, 248f, 250f)).

[178] See pp. 170–2.

[179] Cf. Wilson, *Luke and Pastoral Epistles*, p. 57.

literal feeding, on the basis of verses 33–5. This is particularly striking in the light of the spread of material on wealth, work and possessions in Acts, showing a marked concentration in chapters 1–8.[180] This material both builds on what has gone before in Paul's ministry (18.3) and anticipates what is to come, for he will pay the expenses of Jewish Christians taking a vow (21.24, 26), decline to offer a bribe (24.26), and live at his own expense in Rome (28.30), thus virtually point by point fulfilling the requirements he sets out here for the elders to emulate.

3.5.4   The death of Jesus

Although the death of Jesus is mentioned only once in the speech (verse 28), it is highly significant, because the topic is otherwise little mentioned explicitly in Acts. We argue[181] that the likeliest text in verse 28 is τοῦ ἰδίου and the likeliest translation 'of his own one'.

Explicit references to the redemptive significance of the death of Jesus in Luke-Acts are rare.[182] Indeed, it is sometimes suggested that Luke has no theology of the cross.[183] But Luke gives his understanding of the cross more by 'showing' than 'telling', that is, by the way he portrays the death of Jesus.[184] Further, the fact that

---

[180] Johnson, *Literary Function of Possessions*, pp. 29–32 identifies seven passages in chs. 1–8 (1.15–26; 2.41–7; 3.1–10; 4.32–7; 5.1–11; 6.1–7; 8.18–24), but only the following occurrences in chs. 9–28: 9.36; 10.2, 4, 31; 16.18f; 18.3; 19.24–7; 20.33–5; 21.24; 24.26; 28.30.

[181] Excursus 1.

[182] As Barrett, 'Theologia Crucis', esp. pp. 73f, notes. This makes it the more extraordinary that Haenchen, *Acts*, pp. 589–98 does not discuss this aspect of v. 28 at all.

[183] This claim is often traced to Creed, *Luke*, pp. lxxif: 'Most striking is the entire absence of a Pauline interpretation of the Cross ... There is indeed no *theologia crucis* beyond the affirmation that the Christ must suffer, since so the prophetic scriptures had foretold.' Creed draws attention particularly to the absence of a Lukan parallel to Mark 10.45, and the lack of a parallel to the statement that the cup at the Last Supper is 'the blood of the covenant poured out for many' (accepting the shorter text of Luke 22.19f). The claim is repeated and developed by Conzelmann, *Theology of St Luke*, pp. 199–202. Cf., *contra*, Stein, *Luke*, pp. 54f.

[184] e.g. the saying to the penitent thief (Luke 23.43 – unique to Luke), and the particular emphasis Luke places on the 'exchange' of Jesus and Barabbas (Luke 23.24f//Mark 15.5//Matt. 27.26). See further Sylva (ed.), *Reimaging the Death*; Fitzmyer, *Luke I–IX*, pp. 22f, 219–21; Carroll, Green, Van Voort, Marcus and Senior, *Death of Jesus*, pp. 228f. The latter suggest, 'It may be, however, that Jesus' atoning death is an idea of such common currency in the early church that Luke can allude to it glancingly without invoking it overtly' (p. 229). On the distinction between 'showing' and 'telling' as ways authors give their own perspective, see Booth, *Rhetoric of Fiction*, pp. 3–20.

the central sections of his *Doppelwerk* focus on the death (and resurrection) of Jesus implies that the cross is central to his thinking.[185] This makes the presence of such an explicit statement remarkable: particularly so because it comes in a section of the book attributed to Paul.[186] Grasping the meaning of the verse involves more than the textual and translation difficulty over τοῦ ἰδίου. Some discussion of both περιποιέομαι and αἷμα is necessary. Περιποιέομαι occurs in the LXX at 2 Sam. 12.3 (in conjunction with κτάομαι, a near-synonym); Isa. 43.21; Mal. 3.17 (using the noun περιποίησις) – in the latter two cases, significantly, it is used of God's acquisition of Israel as his people. The idea of God obtaining his people by purchase (but using κτάομαι rather than περιποιέομαι) is also found in Ps. 73.2 LXX (MT 74.2).[187] The meaning here should be seen as derived from this world of thought: through the price of the blood of his own one, God has come into possession of the church (cf. 1 Pet. 2.9).[188] Περιεποιήσατο is thus stronger than RSV's 'obtained', and we should prefer 'bought'.[189]

The mention of 'blood' is particularly significant because Luke does not use the term in his passion narrative. This suggests that in mentioning 'blood' here Luke intends his readers to realise that he is speaking of the death of Jesus as sacrificial.[190] This becomes more probable in the light of Luke 22.19f (assuming the longer text to be original[191]), for there the allusion to the Passover lamb is explicit. More than that, δίδωμι (Luke 22.19) can be used with

[185] Barrett, *Acts*, vol. II, p. 977.
[186] This is even noted by Schmiedel, 'Acts', p. 48, who holds that the theologies of Acts and epistles were almost totally at variance. He grants, 'Only in Acts 13.38f; 16.31; 20.28, do some really Pauline principles begin to make themselves heard.' Marshall, *Luke: Historian and Theologian*, pp. 173f accepts the judgement that the saying is 'traditional', but later adds, 'we should not underestimate its significance as a statement which represented his [*sc.* Luke's] own belief as well as Paul's' (Marshall, *Acts* (TNTC), p. 334). Bruce, *Acts* (3rd edn), p. 434 is quite confident that the saying is Pauline.
[187] Bruce, *Book of Acts* (revised edn), p. 393 n. 65; Marshall, *Acts* (TNTC), p. 334; Johnson, *Acts*, p. 363. See discussion of Ps. 73.2 LXX in Excursus 1 below.
[188] Richard, 'Jesus' Passion', p. 148 agrees that Acts 20.28 'shows clearly that Luke is acquainted with the expiatory tradition' [*sc.* of understanding the death of Jesus].
[189] Marshall, *Acts* (TNTC), p. 334; similarly Morris, *Apostolic Preaching*, p. 60, *contra* Dolfe, 'Greek Word of Blood', 68–70, who prefers 'preserved', on the ground that God was preserving his ἐκκλησία (i.e. Israel) which was in danger of perishing.
[190] Stein, *Luke*, p. 55.
[191] See Excursus 2.

sacrificial overtones (e.g. Exod. 30.14 LXX; Lev. 22.14 LXX; Luke 2.24; and, not least, Mark 10.45).

Grayston suggests that the thought here is 'more pastoral than theological',[192] in the light of the use of 'blood' in verse 26. We may agree that Luke has a pastoral intent in recording the speech – but it is an intent which is carried out through theological means. The last clause of verse 28 should not be seen as mere theological window-dressing, but evidence of a wider view of theology, and a theology of the death of Jesus particularly, to which Luke can allude.

---

[192] Grayston, *Dying, We Live*, p. 232.

EXCURSUS 1: THE TEXT AND TRANSLATION OF ACTS 20.28B

There are two interconnected issues in Acts 20.28b, the question of the correct reading and then the meaning of the reading adopted.

The correct reading

There are two significant variant readings in τὴν ἐκκλησίαν τοῦ θεοῦ, ἣν περιεποιήσατο διὰ τοῦ αἵματος τοῦ ἰδίου. First, some manuscripts read θεοῦ and some κυρίου;[1] and second, some manuscripts replace τοῦ αἵματος τοῦ ἰδίου with slightly different wording, particularly τοῦ ἰδίου αἵματος.

The external evidence is finely balanced on the first variant,[2] both readings being well supported by ancient manuscripts from different text types: θεοῦ has Alexandrian (ℵ B) and Western (614 vg) support, and κυρίου has Alexandrian (𝔓⁷⁴ A C* Ψ 33) and Western (D E 1739 Irenaeus^lat) support. The palaeographic use of abbreviations for θεοῦ (Θ͞Υ)and κυρίου (Κ͞Υ) means that the difference between the two readings is only one letter: θ or κ.

The arguments from transcriptional and intrinsic probabilities are also not easy to weigh. On one hand, the phrase ἡ ἐκκλησία τοῦ κυρίου occurs nowhere else in the NT, which suggests that the reading κυρίου may be original, since a scribe might amend κυρίου to θεοῦ, the more usual NT usage.[3] On the other hand, the reading θεοῦ is theologically difficult, since in combination with τοῦ αἵματος τοῦ ἰδίου, θεοῦ might be thought to imply that God gave his own blood, and therefore a scribe would alter θεοῦ to κυρίου, in

---

[1] Metzger, *Text of the NT*, p. 234 is clearly right to see the variants κυρίου καὶ θεοῦ and θεοῦ καὶ κυρίου as later conflations preserved in Byzantine texts.

[2] DeVine, 'Blood of God', pp. 382–91; Metzger, *Text of the NT*, p. 234 set the evidence out in full.

[3] e.g. 1 Cor. 1.2; 10.32; 11.16, 22; 15.9; 2 Cor. 1.1; Gal. 1.13; 1 Thess. 2.14; 2 Thess. 1.4; 1 Tim. 3.5, 15; 1 Pet. 5.2.

order to make it clear that the blood shed was that of the Lord, that is, Jesus. Further, the expression ἡ ἐκκλησία τοῦ κυρίου occurs in the LXX,[4] so a Septuagintally literate scribe might think of this phrase rather than the NT phrase using θεοῦ.

Perhaps decisive is the possible allusion to Ps. 73.1–2a LXX (MT 74.1–2a).[5] The Psalm also contains the combination of shepherding and flock imagery with the language of obtaining, although not using precisely the vocabulary in Acts 20.28: ἵνα τί ἀπώσω ὁ θεός εἰς τέλος ὠργίσθη ὁ θυμός σου ἐπὶ **πρόβατα** νομῆς σου; μνήσθητι τῆς συναγωγῆς σου ἧς **ἐκτήσω** ἀπ᾽ ἀρχῆς ('Why do you cast us off, O God, to the end? Why are you angry with the sheep of your pasture? Remember your congregation which you obtained from the beginning'). In Ps. 73 it is God who is being addressed, and it is his συναγωγή[6] which he has obtained (κτάομαι). Such an allusion reinforces the argument for θεοῦ as original in Acts 20.28, and that is the reading we shall adopt.[7]

The second variant is more straightforward, in that the attestation of the reading favoured in NA[27]/UBS[4] is clearly superior to its competitors.[8] Τοῦ αἵματος τοῦ ἰδίου has wide support, being found in Alexandrian manuscripts, both early (𝔓[74] ℵ B) and later (A C Ψ 33 326 945), as well as in Western witnesses (D E 1739). The reading τοῦ αἵματος τοῦ ἰδίου is found in the same Byzantine witnesses which support the conflation κυρίου καὶ θεοῦ earlier in this verse.[9] The external evidence here overwhelmingly supports τοῦ αἵματος τοῦ ἰδίου, and the change can be understood as a scribe seeking to overcome the confusion over the meaning of ἰδίου which we noted above.

---

[4] Deut. 23.2, 3, 4 (twice), 9; 1 Chron. 28.8; Micah 2.5.

[5] Harris, *Jesus as God*, p. 135.

[6] Schrage (*TDNT*, vol. VII, p. 829 n. 199) argues that Acts 20.28 emends συναγωγή in Ps. 73.2 LXX to ἐκκλησία because the reference is to a distinctively *Christian* community, in spite of the fact that the underlying Hebrew is never translated ἐκκλησία in the LXX.

[7] In agreement with DeVine, 'Blood of God', pp. 391–7; Metzger, *Text of the NT*, pp. 234f; Metzger, *Textual Commentary* (1st edn), pp. 480f; Dupont, *Discours de Milet*, pp. 150f; Conzelmann, *Acts*, p. 175; Bruce, *Acts* (3rd edn), p. 434; Hanson, *Acts*, p. 205; Johnson, *Acts*, p. 363; Harris, *Jesus as God*, pp. 134–6; Schmeichel, 'Does Luke', pp. 503f; Barrett, *Acts,* vol. II, p. 976; *contra* Foakes Jackson and Lake, *Beginnings*, vol. III, pp. 197f; Clark, *Acts*, p. 134.

[8] Harris, *Jesus as God*, pp. 136f; Metzger, *Textual Commentary* (1st edn), p. 482.

[9] Metzger, *Textual Commentary* (1st edn), p. 482.

Translation and meaning

The meaning of the text as established is then a matter for further discussion. Harris notes four possible translations,[10] to which we may add two others: 'to shepherd the church of God (= Jesus) which he acquired with his own blood'; 'to shepherd the church of God (the Father) which he acquired with his own blood'; 'to shepherd the church of God (the Father) which he (Christ) obtained through his own blood'; 'to shepherd the church of God (the Father) which he obtained with the blood of his own Son/one'; 'to feed the church of God which he obtained with the blood of his own one [Paul]';[11] and 'to shepherd the congregation of God, the existence of which he preserved by means of the one nearest to him(self)'.[12]

The first is the view of DeVine,[13] but it seems unlikely, in that phraseology such as 'the blood of God' does not occur in Christian usage until the second century.[14]

The second proposal is based on the view that the blood of the Son was the 'heart blood' of the Father, because Father and Son are one in thought and action. This has three difficulties: that ἰδίου implies that the blood belongs to the subject of περιεποιήσατο, which is God; that αἷμα refers to real blood, signifying death;[15] and that such a perspective is Johannine, rather than Lukan.[16]

The third view stems from one of two perspectives: either Dupont's view that there is a 'glissement' (slippage) in the thinking of the verse: the actions of Father and Son are so intertwined that Luke can pass from one to the other without an explicit transitional phrase;[17] or the view that Luke here combines a traditional formula, τοῦ αἷματος τοῦ ἰδίου (which was understood to refer to the blood of Christ), with τὴν ἐκκλησίαν τοῦ θεοῦ without indicating any change of subject.[18] While neither idea is impossible, both have the difficulty that there is no explicit change of subject –

[10] Harris, *Jesus as God*, pp. 137–41; cf. Schmeichel, 'Does Luke', 505f.

[11] Schmeichel, 'Does Luke', esp. 507–14; Walaskay, *Acts*, pp. 189f.

[12] Dolfe, 'Greek Word of Blood', p. 70.

[13] DeVine, 'Blood of God', esp. 398–408.

[14] Harris, *Jesus as God*, p. 138, referring to Ignatius *Eph.* 1.1; *Rom.* 6.3.

[15] Harris, *Jesus as God*, p. 138.

[16] e.g. John 14.7–11; 17.21–3.

[17] Dupont, *Discours de Milet*, p. 152. He points to Rom. 8.31–9 as a possible parallel, in which he sees Paul moving from the love of Christ (v. 35) to the love of God shown in Christ (v. 39).

[18] Aejmelaeus, *Rezeption*, p. 133; Conzelmann, *Acts*, p. 175.

and the latter view is unverifiable in the absence of Luke's sources for Acts.

The fourth translation hinges on seeing τοῦ ἰδίου as substantival, as it is in Acts 4.23; 24.23 (in the plural in both cases; cf. John 1.11; 13.1).[19] Such use is not unknown in the papyri[20] and is paralleled by other NT expressions functioning as Christological titles, such as ὁ ἀγαπητός,[21] ὁ ἠγαπημένος[22] and ὁ δίκαιος.[23] This would allow the possibility of translating in such a way.[24] The difficulty with this is that such a use of τοῦ ἰδίου as both substantival and a Christological title would be unique in the NT.[25] Nevertheless, there are other unique features in this speech, so that consideration alone should not rule out this translation.

Schmeichel argues that the fourth view of the meaning of τοῦ ἰδίου is accurate, but the ἴδιος referred to is Paul himself: 'it is Paul and his martyr blood which was shed in the service of establishing and obtaining the church of God'.[26] He sees αἷμα in verse 26 as introducing a conception of 'blood' in a non-soteriological sense, analogous to the uses found elsewhere in oath formulae in Luke-Acts.[27] Thus the reference to blood being shed in verse 28 is to the same event mentioned in verses 22–7, 38, that is, to Paul's forthcoming martyrdom. The use of ἴδιος to mean Paul is deliberately veiled language: throughout the speech, when there is explicit reference to the sufferer, the form and depth of the suffering is vague (verses 22–5); likewise, when the language about suffering to come is explicit, the identity of the sufferer is vague (verse 28b).

It is hard, however, to understand why Luke provides Paul with an aorist form (περιεποιήσατο) at this point if the reference is to Paul's *future* death, given that the tenses are so carefully used in the rest of the speech.[28] It must also be doubted whether the author of Luke 23, with its elements pointing to the death of Jesus as

[19] Bruce, *Acts* (3rd edn), p. 434. For other NT examples, see Harris, *Jesus as God*, p. 140. LXX usage is no help, since τοῦ ἰδίου is never found without a noun, e.g. Prov. 9.13; 16.13; 27.15; Dan. 13.60.

[20] Moulton, *Grammar*, vol. I, p. 90; Harris, *Jesus as God*, p. 140.

[21] e.g. Mark 1.11; 9.7; 2 Pet. 1.17.

[22] Eph. 1.6.

[23] e.g. Acts 3.14; 7.52; 22.14.

[24] Bruce, *Acts* (3rd edn), p. 434; Marshall, *Acts* (TNTC), p. 334; Harris, *Jesus as God*, pp. 139–41; Jervell, *Apostelgeschichte*, p. 512; Barrett, *Acts*, vol. II, pp. 976f.

[25] Schmeichel, 'Does Luke', p. 506.

[26] Schmeichel, 'Does Luke', p. 507.

[27] Schmeichel, 'Does Luke', p. 504 cites Luke 11.50f; Acts 5.28; 18.6; 20.26.

[28] Gempf, 'Historical and Literary Appropriateness', p. 300 n. 86.

redemptive,[29] would have intended his language in verse 28b to be so unclear that it has taken two thousand years for it to be unravelled. While Schmeichel has made a significant point in showing that the use of ἴδιος proposed in the fourth option would be very unusual in the NT, his overall position must be adjudged doubtful.

Finally, Dolfe proposes that we should understand αἷμα through non-biblical use, in which it can mean 'blood-relative'.[30] He argues that we should read 20.28 as implying that God preserved his congregation (which is thus the continuation of Israel) by the life of the one close to him – presumably Jesus (although Dolfe fails to say this). Dolfe further argues that this interpretation fits better with Luke's focus on the resurrection, rather than the death, of Jesus.[31]

This interpretation is open to some of the same objections as Schmeidel's view, discussed above, particularly in the light of Luke's interpretation of the death of Jesus in Luke 23. Further, given that Luke is an author steeped in the LXX,[32] where αἷμα is used almost 400 times, to interpret the word without any reference to that context is unlikely to yield a view close to Luke's own.

We therefore conclude that the fourth translation, 'to shepherd the church of God (the Father) which he obtained with the blood of his own one', has fewest difficulties attached to it, and it is our working translation.

[29] Marshall, *Luke: Historian and Theologian*, pp. 169–75; Tannehill, *Narrative Unity*, vol. I, pp. 125–7, 197–9; Johnson, *Luke*, pp. 373–5, 380f, 384f; Moberly, 'Proclaiming Christ Crucified', pp. 36–9.

[30] Dolfe, 'Greek Word of Blood', pp. 64f.

[31] Dolfe, 'Greek Word of Blood', p. 67.

[32] Barrett, 'Luke-Acts', p. 231 rightly observes: 'It is safe to say that there is no major concept in the two books [*sc.* Luke and Acts] that does not to some extent reflect the beliefs and theological vocabulary of the OT.'

4

THE MILETUS SPEECH AND LUKE'S GOSPEL

4.1 Introduction

What is Luke seeking to accomplish by the use of the Miletus speech? A key clue is provided by parallel material in his first volume. Because Acts is to be read as the follow-on to the Gospel,[1] a reading strategy which looks for links commends itself over against a strategy which atomises material and isolates individual speeches or incidents, as classical form and redaction criticism sometimes do.[2]

4.1.1 The context in Acts

We have noted that there are significant individual verbal links with Paul's Ephesian ministry (Acts 19),[3] but otherwise our speech seems to form something of an island in the sea of Acts. There are no clusters of parallels with 20.17–38 elsewhere in Acts, which is not greatly surprising, for this is the only recorded address given by Paul to Christians in the book.[4] Conceptual parallels come only as the action develops in the remainder of the journey to Jerusalem in Acts, although even these are sketchy.[5]

4.1.2 Parallels in Luke's Gospel

Three longer passages in the Gospel invite consideration: 22.14–38; 12.1–53; 21.5–31. In particular, 22.14–38 and 21.5–31 represent

---

[1] See § 2.3.   [2] See § 2.4 for the approach here taken.   [3] § 3.2.2.
[4] There are mentions of Paul speaking with Christians, sometimes at length (Acts 20.7–11!), but there are no other actual speeches.
[5] e.g. the idea of suffering to come predicted by the Spirit (20.22f; cf. 21.4, 10–14; 22.5, 29; 24.24; see Johnson, *Acts*, p. 361; Squires, *Plan of God in Luke-Acts*, pp. 151f), determination to do God's will (20.27 has τὴν βουλὴν τοῦ θεοῦ, cf. 21.14), and the sense of divine necessity (20.22; cf. 21.11, 13). The speeches in chs. 22, 24 and 26 could also be seen as embodying the principle of 20.24.

possible candidates for an *Abschiedsrede* in Luke. In addition there are four brief passages (7.38, 44; 9.2; 10.3; 13.32f) where interesting verbal parallels occur, often with words found in Luke-Acts only in the relevant passage in Luke and the Miletus speech.

4.2   Luke 22.14–38

This is the clearest candidate for a 'farewell discourse' in Luke's Gospel, and the parallels with the Miletus speech are rich and suggestive. In this case not only are the four themes we identified in the Miletus address present, but the sequence of the themes in the speeches is also similar:

	Luke 22	*Acts 20*
suffering to come	verses 15 (28, 31f, 37)	verses 22–4
efficacy of the death of Jesus	verses 19f	verse 28
leadership	verses 24–30	verse 28
money	verses 35f	verses 33–5

4.2.1   The Last Supper discourse as a farewell speech

As with our discussion of the Miletus speech, we shall examine the occasion and contents of the Lukan Last Supper discourse for signs that it might fit a 'farewell' genre.[6]

Occasion

It is noteworthy that it is Jesus who creates this situation by sending Peter and John to prepare the Passover in the upstairs room (Luke 22.7–13). Not only that, but the question of verse 11 implies preparation on the part of Jesus by prior arrangement with the owner of the house – Luke's Jesus summons the hearers for the discourse. Farewell speeches commonly have the departing one calling the hearers together, and this feature of Luke 22 fits the genre.

A second prominent feature is the nearness of the death of the speaker, and in Luke 22 the death of Jesus is clearly on the

---

[6] For the features of a farewell speech discussed below, see § 3.2.1; in relation to this discourse, see Kurz, 'Luke 22:14–38'; Nelson, 'Leadership and Discipleship', pp. 117–26; Neyrey, *Passion according to Luke*, pp. 5–48.

horizon.[7] This is a feature of the speech, rather than the framework, and its prominence is evident: verse 15b explicitly refers to Jesus' forthcoming suffering (unparalleled in Mark/Matthew); verse 16 reinforces the prediction of Jesus' death by indicating that he will not take food again until the kingdom's arrival (unparalleled in Mark/Matthew); verse 18a repeats the same point in relation to the cup (cf. Mark 14.25; Matt. 26.29); verses 19f picture the death of Jesus in the bread broken and the wine poured out (cf. Mark 14.22–4; Matt. 26.26–8 – although the command to repeat (verse 19), which implies Jesus' future absence, is peculiar to Luke); verses 21f warn that Jesus will be betrayed and die (Luke alone using πορεύεται, 'go', which connotes death, 22.33[8]); and verse 27c hints that Jesus' service will include his death (without exact parallel in Mark/Matthew).[9]

Contents

In common with farewell speeches, Luke's Last Supper discourse contains extensive recollections of the past, all unparalleled in Mark/Matthew.[10] Jesus recalls his service to the disciples, for verse 27c has a *double entendre*, pointing both to his forthcoming death and to his past service to the disciples during his life.[11] Verse 28 then speaks of the past trials (the substantival participle διαμεμενη-κότες is perfect) which he and his disciples have experienced, and verse 35 recalls the disciples' experience of the mission of the seventy(-two) (Luke 10.4, and possibly the mission of the twelve, Luke 9.3[12]). These past events provide a key context for Jesus' words about forthcoming suffering (e.g. verses 15, 19f, 21f).

Another mark of farewell addresses is their hortatory nature: the departing one calls the hearers to a particular future lifestyle and conduct. Luke's discourse offers at least four examples of this.[13] First, the command to repeat the action with the bread (verse 19b)

---

[7] Nelson, 'Leadership and Discipleship', p. 117; Tannehill, *Narrative Unity,* vol. I, p. 263; Neyrey, *Passion according to Luke*, pp. 5–48, esp. 7, 48.

[8] Nelson, 'Leadership and Discipleship', p. 117.

[9] Nelson, 'Leadership and Discipleship', pp. 180–3.

[10] Nelson, 'Leadership and Discipleship', p. 118.

[11] Nelson, 'Leadership and Discipleship', p. 183 points to the context of the following clause (v. 28) which looks to Jesus' past.

[12] See pp. 115f.

[13] Neyrey, *Passion according to Luke*, pp. 22f; Nelson, 'Leadership and Discipleship', p. 118; Senior, *Passion in Luke*, p. 55.

implies that Jesus bequeaths the eucharist to his disciples as a parting gift[14] – a gift seen later in Acts (2.42, in a programmatic passage; 20.11, just before the Miletus scene). Second, the exhortation of verses 25–7 (probably Lukan rather than based on Mark/Matthew[15]) calls on the disciples to give up worldly ideas of greatness and follow Jesus on the path of humble servanthood. Third, verse 32 (unique to Luke) sees Jesus instructing Peter on his conduct after he has 'turned again'. And fourth, verse 36 (again, found in Luke alone) instructs the disciples for the forthcoming time of pressure.

Farewell addresses generally include predictions about the future, and here Luke presents predictions of the following events:[16] the coming of the kingly rule of God (twice, linked to Jesus' death, verses 16, 18); Jesus' forthcoming betrayal by one of the apostolic band (κατὰ τὸ ὡρισμένον,[17] verses 21f: different from Matthew and Mark's καθὼς γέγραπται); the bestowal of kingly rule on the disciples, including their sitting on seats at Jesus' banquet and on thrones judging Israel (verses 29f: no parallel in Mark; partial parallel in Matt. 19.28), which implies a future renewal of Israel; Peter's denial of Jesus (verse 34: paralleled in a different context, on Olivet, Mark 14.30; Matt. 26.34); and future adversity and conflict (verse 36: no parallels).[18]

A further mark of farewell speeches is that the departing person makes provision for life after his demise.[19] We have already noted

[14] Neyrey, *Passion according to Luke*, pp. 15f.

[15] See § 4.2.4.

[16] Nelson, 'Leadership and Discipleship', p. 119; Neyrey, *Passion according to Luke*, pp. 17–19.

[17] Of only eight NT uses of ὁρίζω (whose perfect passive participle is used here), six are Lukan (Luke 22.22; Acts 2.23; 10.42; 11.29; 17.26, 31); the passive suggests that God has determined the way things will happen (*EDNT*, vol. 2, p. 532; BAGD, p. 581; *TDNT*, vol. V, pp. 452f; Squires, *Plan of God in Luke-Acts*, p. 171).

[18] We may note that Luke offers his readers an immediate ground for confidence in Jesus' predictive powers in 22.7–13, where Jesus' prediction of meeting the man with the water pot is fulfilled (Talbert, *Reading Luke*, pp. 207f; Nelson, 'Leadership and Discipleship', p. 121); cf. also the fetching of the colt (19.29–34).

[19] Some phrase this aspect of the Last Supper discourse as 'provision for succession', in line with farewell speeches in general, but in Luke's view Jesus does not become a dead (and therefore absent) leader, but is living and active by the Spirit in the church (note ἤρξατο in Acts 1.1 in conjunction with 1.4–6, 8: Bruce, *Acts* (3rd edn), p. 98; *contra* Haenchen, *Acts*, p. 137 n. 4, who regards ἤρξατο as merely stylistic); cf. Denney, *Studies in Theology*, p. 154. So Jesus does not have a single successor, as a king might have, and the leadership of the Christian community does not focus on one person alone. There is a 'succession', but it is centred on a *group* of leaders, seen, e.g., in the process of decision-making in Acts 15.6ff.

several elements of this discourse which fit such a need (e.g. provision for the meal of remembrance, exhortations and predictions), but we may add the leadership commission of the disciples in general (verses 28–30, in the immediate context of Jesus' model of leadership in verses 24–7) and Peter in particular (verses 31f) – commissions which they will exercise in Acts.[20]

Some object that Luke's Last Supper discourse is a dialogue, not a monologue, and this disqualifies it from being seen as a farewell speech.[21] However, dialogical examples exist,[22] and this feature alone cannot rule the speech out.

Again, Jesus' death does not take place until 23.46 – whereas the death of the speaker is often the conclusion of an *Abschiedsszene*. But there are sufficient pointers that this discourse has the major themes of a farewell address, along with the flexibility which is characteristic of the genre, to conclude that the Lukan Last Supper discourse is from the 'farewell speech' family.[23]

Turning to consider the major themes, this scene falls into five or six panels:[24] the Passover enacted and reinterpreted (verses 14–20); prediction of betrayal (verses 21–3); Jesus' example and statement of true leadership (verses 24–7); the promise of kingly rule (verses 28–30); the testing of the disciples and Simon's commission (verses 31–4); and the warning of the coming crisis (verses 35–8). While past scholarship has focused on the diverse materials brought together by Luke,[25] we shall seek a more holistic, final-form reading of the text,[26] informed by what knowledge of sources is available. This will allow us both to discern Luke's purpose and to evaluate the possible parallels with the Miletus speech.

[20] e.g. 1.15–22; 2.14, 37, 42, 43; 3.1–7, 12; 4.8–12, 13, 19f, 33, 35, 37; 5.1–11, 15, 29–32; 6.2–4, 6 (Johnson, *Luke*, p. 349; Tannehill, *Narrative Unity,* vol. I, p. 263).
[21] Kurz, 'Luke 22:14–38', p. 252; Nelson, 'Leadership and Discipleship', p. 122.
[22] See § 3.2.1.
[23] In agreement with Kurz, 'Luke 22:14–38'; Green, *Death of Jesus*, p. 52; Nolland, *Luke 18:35–24:53*, p. 1049; Karris, *Luke: Artist and Theologian*, pp. 65f; Senior, *Passion in Luke*, p. 55; Neyrey, *Passion according to Luke*, pp. 7, 48; Johnson, *Luke*, p. 348; Talbert, *Reading Luke*, pp. 207f; Ernst, *Lukas*, p. 589; Schürmann, *Ursprung und Gehalt*, p. 148.
[24] Depending on whether vv. 24–30 are seen as a unity or not. For the case that Luke conceived vv. 24–30 as a unity, see Nelson, 'Leadership and Discipleship', pp. 5–7, 254–7.
[25] Notably Schürmann, *Paschamahlbericht*; *Einsetzungsbericht*; and *Jesu Abschiedsrede*.
[26] Comparable with Johnson, *Luke*; Tannehill, *Narrative Unity*; Neyrey, *Passion according to Luke*; Nelson, 'Leadership and Discipleship'.

4.2.2   Suffering to come

The theme of Paul's foreboding of suffering to come (Acts 20.22–4) is extensively paralleled in the Lukan Last Supper discourse. In both cases it comes in a context of meeting with those to whom the torch is being passed before the suffering occurs: for Jesus at the Last Supper with his disciples, and for Paul at Miletus with the elders of a key church which he has founded.

The (re-)reader of Luke-Acts knows that both are to suffer in Jerusalem:[27] in Paul's case this is made explicit (Acts 9.16, using the same verb as Luke 22.15, πάσχω;[28] Acts 20.22), and in the case of Jesus it has already been stated explicitly (Luke 9.22; 17.25, again using πάσχω in both cases[29]; 9.31; 18.31) and hinted at (Luke 13.33f). In Luke-Acts the suffering of Jesus is seen as necessary[30] – indeed, it fulfils Scripture (Luke 24.46), which implies that the necessity is divine.[31]

There is some debate whether Luke 22.15 should be seen as peculiar to Luke, or whether verses 15f (or 15–18) are Luke's version of Mark 14.25. In favour of the latter view it is argued that Luke wishes to stress the paschal nature of the Last Supper, and that he wishes to follow the meal with discussion of the death of Jesus, his betrayal and the disciples' denial of him (Luke 22.21–38). Thus he re-orders Mark's narrative to bring out these emphases.[32] However, it is 22.18 which parallels Mark 14.25, if any verse in Luke does, and it is hard to see why Luke would provide two parallels to the one Markan verse in such close proximity.[33] Further, Jeremias and Schürmann have argued persuasively that there are many words distinctive of a Lukan special source in

[27] On silences in narrative and the possible use of 'assumed knowledge', see Magness, *Sense and Absence*, esp. pp. 15–24, 65–85; Kurz, *Reading Luke-Acts*, pp. 31–6 (esp. 35).

[28] This verb is used frequently in Luke-Acts (eleven times from 42 total NT uses, although note twelve uses in 1 Peter). There is an interesting parallelism (mostly unnoticed, although see Fitzmyer, *Luke X–XXIV*, p. 1396) in 22.15 between τὸ πάσχα which Jesus greatly desires to eat and his forthcoming παθεῖν.

[29] Nolland, *Luke 18:35–24:53*, p. 1050.

[30] Expressed by the use of δεῖ (Luke 9.22; 13.33; 17.25; 22.37; 24.7, 26, 44, 46; cf. Acts 3.18; 17.3) and μέλλω (Luke 9.31, 44; Acts 26.23). Cf. Squires, *Plan of God in Luke-Acts*, p. 2 nn. 6–7; Peterson, 'Motif of Fulfilment', p. 86.

[31] Cosgrove, 'Divine ΔΕΙ', 173f; Peterson, 'Motif of Fulfilment', p. 93.

[32] Pesch, *Das Abendmahl*, pp. 26–31.

[33] Soards, *Passion according to Luke*, p. 27.

22.15f, and that when Luke does not share Mark's sequence, this is usually a sign that he is following another source, rather than transposing Markan order.[34]

Whatever the resolution of this debate, it is widely agreed that the phrase πρὸ τοῦ με παθεῖν is derived from either Luke's special source or Luke's own hand.[35] It can therefore be taken with some confidence as showing Luke's own interests. Thus we may conclude that 22.15 points to an expectation on Luke's part of forthcoming suffering for Jesus, an expectation that parallels Acts 20.22–4 at a conceptual level.

The likelihood of this conceptual parallel being significant is increased by the further parallels between the Lukan Last Supper discourse and the Miletus speech on the matter of suffering. First, a verbal parallel links Jesus' trials and Paul's trials, namely the use of the plural[36] of πειρασμός in Luke 22.28 and Acts 20.19.[37] The phrase ἐν τοῖς πειρασμοῖς μου (Luke 22.28) is absent in the possible Matthean parallel (Matt. 19.28),[38] and Acts 20.19 represents the only use in Acts. This combination suggests that Luke is drawing attention to the parallel by the choice of vocabulary. It is also notable, in the light of our discussion of leadership below,[39] that the comment of Jesus in Luke 22.28 is immediately followed by words of promise about leadership for the disciples – the readiness to undergo trials is a necessity for leadership in the community of Jesus. And Paul is

[34] Jeremias, *Eucharistic Words*, pp. 160–4, cites καὶ εἶπεν, ἐπιθυμεῖν + infinitive, λέγω γὰρ ὑμῖν, οὐ μή, ἕως ὅτου, ἀπὸ τοῦ νῦν as words from the special Lukan source; cf. Schürmann, *Paschamahlbericht*, pp. 1–74; Taylor, *Passion Narrative of Luke*, pp. 47–50; Smith, *Jesus' Last Passover Meal*, pp. 67–73; Goulder, *Luke: New Paradigm*, p. 722.

[35] Johnson, *Luke*, p. 337. Goulder, *Luke: New Paradigm*, p. 728 appears to argue that πρὸ τοῦ + infinitive is Lukan, in agreement with Schürmann, *Paschamahlbericht*, pp. 12f; Marshall, *Luke*, p. 795; Evans, *Saint Luke*, p. 784. Of the nine NT uses, three are found in Luke-Acts (Luke 2.21; 22.15; Acts 23.15; elsewhere Matt. 6.8; John 1.48; 13.19; 17.5; Gal. 2.12; 3.23).

[36] Nelson, 'Leadership and Discipleship', pp. 206f suggests that the plural implies 'repeated or continuing experiences'.

[37] Nelson, 'Leadership and Discipleship', p. 206; Schürmann, *Jesu Abschiedsrede*, p. 39; Evans, *Saint Luke*, p. 798; Marshall, *Luke*, p. 816; Neyrey, *Passion according to Luke*, p. 45; Jervell, *Apostelgeschichte*, p. 509.

[38] Nelson, 'Leadership and Discipleship', pp. 187f, 206–12. Mark uses πειρασμός only once (14.38) and Matthew just twice (6.13; 26.41), compared to seven uses in Luke-Acts (Luke 4.13; 8.13; 11.4; 22.28, 40, 46; Acts 20.19); Soards, *Passion according to Luke*, pp. 46, 139 n. 76.

[39] § 4.2.4

the exemplar of this, having faced trials through 'the plots of the Jews' (Acts 20.19).⁴⁰

Second, in a passage unique to Luke (22.37),⁴¹ it is said of Jesus' subsequent suffering, 'it is necessary for this Scripture to be fulfilled (τελεσθῆναι: aorist passive infinitive of τελέω) in me', and this forthcoming suffering is described as τέλος. The final phrase of the verse, τό περὶ ἐμοῦ τέλος ἔχει, is best translated 'my life's work is at an end', for if it means 'the references in the Scriptures to me are being fulfilled' (as often in modern translations) it merely repeats what was said in the first part of the verse, and there is evidence that τέλος ἔχω can have the sense 'to come to an end' – the singular form τὸ περὶ ἐμοῦ more naturally points to the task of Jesus as that which is coming to an end.⁴² This offers a striking parallel to the use of τελειόω in Acts 20.24, there of Paul completing his course in suffering.⁴³ Luke alone of the Synoptics uses τελειόω,⁴⁴ and the Miletus speech is the only use of the verb in Acts.

Third, in a passage without parallel in the other Synoptics, forthcoming pressure on Peter is predicted by Jesus (Luke 22.31f; cf. verses 35–8), and this is echoed by Paul's warning of pressure to come on the elders (Acts 20.29f).⁴⁵ The command to 'strengthen (στήρισον) your brothers' after turning (ἐπιστρέφω, verse 32) is fulfilled by Paul in Acts (e.g. Acts 14.22; 15.41; 18.23 – each using ἐπιστηρίζω, a compound of στηρίζω).⁴⁶ Further, Acts 20.31 carries

⁴⁰ Tannehill, *Narrative Unity,* vol. I, p. 211 suggests that 'persecution must be a major part of the meaning [of πειρασμός]'. Cf. Marshall, *Luke,* p. 816.

⁴¹ Soards, *Passion according to Luke,* pp. 31, 53f, argues that Luke composed vv. 35–8 on the basis of some traditional material with the help of Luke 10.4 and Isa. 53.12. Taylor, *Passion Narrative of Luke,* pp. 66–9 sees the material as derived from a pre-Lukan source which has been lightly edited by Luke.

⁴² Marshall, *Luke,* p. 826, cites Josephus *Life* 154: καὶ τὰ μὲν περὶ ἐκείνους τοῦτ' ἔσχε τὸ τέλος ('And this was the conclusion of what concerned these men', Whiston's translation) as evidence for the proposed sense of τέλος ἔχω. See also Nolland, *Luke 18:35–24:53,* p. 1077 (citing Mark 3.26); Fitzmyer, *Luke X–XXIV,* p. 1433; *contra* Evans, *Saint Luke,* p. 806; Johnson, *Luke,* p. 347, who see the phrase as describing a particular fulfilment, rather than the general principle enunciated earlier in the verse, and argue that the use of τέλος echoes the verb earlier in the verse. Cf. *TDNT,* vol. VIII, pp. 49f for extra-biblical use.

⁴³ Neyrey, *Passion according to Luke,* p. 45.

⁴⁴ Luke 2.43; 13.32; Acts 20.24. Luke also uses τελέω (Luke 2.39; 12.50; 18.31; 22.37; Acts 13.29), as does Matthew (seven times, particularly in connection with the fulfilment of Scripture and at the end of his five major discourses). Mark uses neither verb. See further Peterson, 'Motif of Fulfilment', p. 86; *NIDNTT,* vol. II, pp. 59–65.

⁴⁵ Neyrey, *Passion according to Luke,* p. 44.

⁴⁶ Marshall, *Luke,* p. 822; Nolland, *Luke 18:35–24:53,* p. 1072; Johnson, *Luke,* p. 346. Neyrey, *Passion according to Luke,* p. 45 suggests that the combination of

the implicit message that the elders are to be alert as Paul has been alert, that is, by warning the flock with tears – a 'strengthening' activity.

Finally, the theme of glory through suffering is important to both speeches. Jesus' forthcoming suffering (Luke 22.15, 28) leads to his glory (Luke 22.16f, 29) – both in its fulfilment in the kingdom[47] and in Jesus himself receiving a kingdom.[48] Likewise, the pressure the disciples have faced and will face (Luke 22.28, 31f) will lead to a kingdom for them, dining at Jesus' table and judging from thrones (Luke 22.29f).[49]

Paul's ministry in Acts reflects a pattern of falling and rising.[50] Each account of his commissioning shows him being humbled as he is blinded and falls to the ground, but each also leads to his rise to prominent leadership in spearheading the mission (Acts 9.1–8, 15; 22.6–16, 15, 21; 26.12–15, 16–18). Similarly, he goes through an experience of apparent death and rising in Lystra (Acts 14.19f; notice ἀναστάς, verse 20). In the Miletus speech the very fact that Paul can speak of having endured trials and plots (Acts 20.19) implies this same reversal motif, that God exalts those humbled for him (and note that Paul's humility is important, Acts 20.19, contrasting with the disciples' attitude in Luke 22.24).

Taken together, these various aspects of the suffering theme in the Lukan Last Supper discourse link closely with the same theme in the Miletus speech.

4.2.3 The efficacy of the death of Jesus

The death of Jesus does not occur in the other possible Lukan parallel passages we shall consider, and it is therefore of particular interest in Luke 22. The context is the Last Supper, and Jesus invests the Passover ceremonies (verses 8, 13, 15) with new meaning by his actions and interpretative words (verses 17–20).[51]

Jesus' concern for Peter's faith and Peter's turning (Luke 22.32) should be compared with Paul's preaching of repentance and faith (Acts 20.21).

[47] Senior, *Passion in Luke*, p. 56.

[48] Dawsey, *Lukan Voice*, p. 141.

[49] Nelson, 'Leadership and Discipleship', p. 242 notes that the subjunctives ἔσθητε and πίνητε suggest a *future* meal.

[50] Nelson, 'Leadership and Discipleship', p. 101. The exhortation in Acts 14.22 shows a similar reversal motif.

[51] The literature on the eucharistic words is considerable. For a valuable recent survey, see O'Toole, 'Last Supper' (with bibliography). There is a difficult textual

Thus verse 20 speaks of the cup as the new covenant ἐν τῷ αἵματί μου, a phrase closely paralleled by διὰ τοῦ αἵματος τοῦ ἰδίου (Acts 20.28). The phraseology in Luke is different from Matthew and Mark, and closer to Paul: Matt. 26.28; Mark 14.24 both have τοῦτο ἐστιν τὸ αἷμά μου τῆς διαθήκης; 1 Cor. 11.25 has τοῦτο τὸ ποτήριον ἡ καινὴ διαθήκη ἐστὶν ἐν τῷ ἐμῷ αἵματι. Luke differs from the other accounts of the eucharistic words in its use of the participle διδόμενον (verse 19) in connection with the bread.

Both Luke 22.20 and Acts 20.28 speak of the efficacy of the death of Jesus using the image of blood.[52] Zehnle[53] objects that verses 19–20 do not contain 'satisfaction theology', since they do not speak of the death of Jesus being 'for sins', but simply ὑπὲρ ὑμῶν. He further suggests that such language may not be Lukan, but simply show his fidelity to church traditions – as he believes is the case in Acts 20.28. However, several factors suggest that we ought to see a redemptive theology in Luke 22.19–20.

First, there is the phrase ὑπὲρ ὑμῶν (verses 19, 20). The preposition ὑπὲρ in LXX and NT usage frequently means 'in place of' and 'on behalf of'.[54] Thus it can connote both representation and substitution.[55] Hence Fitzmyer asserts that the use of ὑπὲρ ὑμῶν in the bread saying (verse 19) 'adds a vicarious dimension of meaning to his "body", and probably a sacrificial nuance'.[56] The context of verse 15 implies that there will be a redemptive significance for 'you' – the disciples and (by implication) others who will follow Jesus in the future – in the forthcoming suffering of Jesus.[57] Further, the phrasing of the Markan parallel to the cup saying is

question regarding Luke 22.17–20. What follows is based on the view that vv. 19b–20 are part of the autograph (see Excursus 2).

[52] These are the only uses of αἷμα in relation to the redemptive significance of the death of Jesus in Luke-Acts.

[53] Zehnle, 'Salvific Character', p. 440.

[54] *EDNT*, vol. III, pp. 396f estimates that 130 out of 150 NT uses are of this sort; cf. BAGD, pp. 838f; *NIDNTT*, vol. III, pp. 1196f; Johnson, *Luke*, p. 339. For Lukan use see Acts 5.41; 8.24; 9.16; 15.26; 21.13, 26.

[55] The latter is seen in John 11.50, where it is clear from Caiaphas' following remark, καὶ μὴ ὅλον τὸ ἔθνος ἀπόληται, that Jesus' death ὑπὲρ τοῦ λαοῦ denotes his death *in place of* the people (*NIDNTT*, vol. III, p. 1197).

[56] Fitzmyer, *Luke X–XXIV*, pp. 1391, 1401, citing Josephus, *Antiquities* 13.1.1 (= 13:6), ὁ δ᾽ Ἰωνάθης φήσας ἑτοίμως ἔχειν ἀποθνήσκειν ὑπὲρ αὐτῶν ('And Jonathan said that he was ready to die for them'), and *Jewish War* 2.10.5 (= 2:201), ὑπὲρ τοσούτων ἑτοίμως ἐπιδώσω τὴν ἐμαθτοῦ ψυχήν ('on behalf of the lives of so many to give over my own'), as examples of ὑπὲρ in a vicarious sense. See further Stein, *Luke*, p. 543 n. 23; Kurz, 'Luke 22:14–38', pp. 266f.

[57] Fitzmyer, *Luke X–XXIV*, p. 1391.

ὑπὲρ πολλῶν (14.24), an allusion to the Suffering Servant's vicarious suffering (Isa. 53.11–12).[58] Luke appears to have used ὑμῶν in order to parallel the bread saying (verses 19, 20), without necessarily intending the allusion to Isaiah 53 to be lost, since he has the participle ἐκχυννόμενον (= 'being poured out') which also alludes to Isaiah 53.12.[59]

Second, the presence of διδόμενον (verse 19) uniquely in Luke's version of the bread saying points to the forthcoming giving of Jesus' body in sacrifice, especially since it parallels ἐκχυννόμενον in the cup saying (verse 20). Δίδωμι is used in such a way in Luke 2.24.[60]

Third, the mention of ἡ **καινὴ** διαθήκη (verse 20) is unique to Luke amongst the Synoptics, although it is present in 1 Corinthians 11.25. This is a clear allusion to Jeremiah 31.31, adding to the allusion to Exodus 24.8 already present in διαθήκη.[61] The covenant is ἐν τῷ αἵματί μου, alluding to the place of blood in the OT's understanding of sacrifice, particularly Leviticus 17.11, 14. Fitzmyer rightly observes that, 'the cultic overtones of Jesus' words are unmistakable'.[62]

Zehnle draws the conclusion that Luke's incorporation of early tradition into his narrative means that this material does not reflect Luke's own perspective. But the opposite should be argued, that Luke's incorporation of the material implies that he believed and accepted it. Had he disagreed, it was open to him to omit the material from his Gospel.[63]

The redemptive nature of the statement in Luke 22.19–20 seems secure, and the parallel with Acts 20.28 evident. That these should be the two places where Luke's understanding of the death of Jesus is 'told' rather than simply 'shown' is significant. Luke's Paul

[58] France, *Jesus and OT*, pp. 120f, 122; *TDNT*, vol. VIII, pp. 510f. Marshall, *Luke*, p. 807 sees Luke's ὑμῶν as secondary to Mark's πολλῶν, which alludes to Isa. 53.10 [?a slip for 11], 12.

[59] France, *Jesus and OT*, p. 122. Contrast 1 Cor. 11.25, which lacks the whole phrase τὸ ὑπὲρ ὑμῶν ἐκχυννόμενον.

[60] Fitzmyer, *Luke X–XXIV*, p. 1400 cites as similar Mark 10.45; Gal. 1.4; 2 Cor. 8.5; John 6.51; 1 Tim. 2.6; Tit. 2.14; 1 Macc. 2.50; 6.4. Nolland, *Luke 18:35–24:53*, p. 1054 offers Thucydides, *History* 2.43.2; Libanius, *Oration* 24.3 as examples of 'to give one's body' for dying in battle for the sake of the people. The former uses δίδωμι and the latter δέχομαι.

[61] France, *Jesus and OT*, pp. 66f, 94; Fitzmyer, *Luke X–XXIV*, p. 1402; Evans, *Saint Luke*, p. 791; Nolland, *Luke 18:35–24:53*, p. 1054; Marshall, *Luke*, p. 806.

[62] Fitzmyer, *Luke X–XXIV*, p. 1402. Similarly Stein, *Luke*, pp. 543f; Green, *Death of Jesus*, pp. 194–7.

[63] Stein, *Luke*, p. 545.

understands his Master's death in terms similar to those enunciated by the Master himself.

4.2.4   Leadership

Luke 22.24–30 is the section of the discourse most clearly focused on leadership, for it begins with a dispute about greatness (verse 24), involves Jesus contrasting his style of leadership with others (verses 25–7), and closes with the apostles being given a position of leadership as judges of the twelve tribes of Israel (verses 29f). In discussing possible parallels with the Miletus speech, we shall first consider the source(s) of this Lukan passage. We shall then examine Luke 22.24–30 for the treatment of Jesus as servant and leader and the leadership the apostles are to exercise, and for the parallels with Paul's speech.

It is a matter of debate how far Luke 22.24–30 should be seen as expressing Lukan thought, since verses 24–7 have a possible parallel in Mark 10.41–5; Matthew 20.24–8, and verses 28–30 in Matthew 19.28.

However, Nelson argues cogently that verses 24–7 should be seen as independent of the Markan parallel.[64] Although Mark 10.41–5 is superficially parallel, the verbal agreement is poor: of the 67 words in verses 24–7, only sixteen appear in the same form, including four definite articles, four conjunctions, three third-person plural pronouns, and the phrases οὐχ οὕτως and ἐν ὑμῖν. Moreover, no verbal forms are common to the two passages, and the only noun they share is ἐθνῶν.[65] The two verbal forms κυριεύουσιν and ἐξουσιάζοντες (verse 25) are 'paralleled' in Mark (verse 42) by compound forms which are more commonly found in Luke[66] – whereas we might expect that Luke would have the compound forms if he were editing Mark.[67] Again, Luke uses a comparative adjective, μείζων (verse 26), whereas Mark uses a

---

[64] Nelson, 'Leadership and Discipleship', pp. 132–40; similarly Soards, *Passion according to Luke*, pp. 30f; Page, 'Authenticity of Ransom Logion', pp. 148–54; Green, *Death of Jesus*, pp. 44–6; Taylor, *Passion Narrative of Luke*, pp. 61–4; Nolland, *Luke 18:35–24:53*, pp. 1062f.

[65] Page, 'Authenticity of Ransom Logion', p. 149.

[66] Nelson, 'Leadership and Discipleship', pp. 196f (asserting that 275 out of 593 NT uses of διά- compounds are found in Luke-Acts); Moulton and Howard, *Grammar,* vol. II, p. 300 (claiming 200 out of 343 for the same phenomenon) and p. 11 (arguing cogently that compound verbs should not be used as a test of more 'literary' Greek).

[67] Nelson, 'Leadership and Discipleship', p. 136; Green, *Death of Jesus*, p. 46;

positive, μέγας (verse 43). There is no material shared by Luke 22.24 and Mark 10.41, and only one word in common between Luke 22.27 and Mark 10.45 (διακονέω, although Luke has an articular substantival present active participle and Mark an aorist passive infinitive).[68] Finally, Luke rarely relocates material from its Markan sequence, but rather uses the material in the same order. Jeremias points to only two small deviations before the passion narrative (Luke 6.17–19; 8.19–21) and concludes that deviations imply that Luke is not using Mark.[69]

By contrast, it seems likely that a common source is used by Matthew (19.28) and Luke (22.28–30) for the second half of the passage.[70] There is a high level of verbal agreement between Luke 22.30b and Matthew 19.28c (καθήσεσθε, ἐπί, θρόνους/θρόνων, κρίνοντες, τὰς δώδεκα φυλὰς, τοῦ Ἰσραήλ), and there is clear conceptual and structural parallelism earlier in the passages. Further, the dissimilarities between the two can largely be explained on the basis of the redactional tendencies of the two authors.[71] That said, there is clearly Lukan redaction, for the Lukan version is very much longer than the Matthean: verse 29 is unparalleled in Matthew, for example. Thus in seeking parallels with the Miletus speech we shall look for signs of Lukan emphasis or redaction in verses 28–30.

So we turn to examine the key themes of the Lukan passage in relation to the Miletus speech.

In Luke 22 Jesus is the leader: he takes the role of the father/host at the Passover (verses 19f); he is the departing one delivering his farewell; he exhorts his disciples (verses 19b, 25–7, 36); he has authority to confer kingship (verse 29); and he prophesies about their future (verses 15f, 18, 21f, 30, 31–4).[72] But Jesus' leadership is not conventional, for he is ὁ διακονῶν (verse 27). The use of ὁ

Cadbury, *Making*, pp. 163, 174, 305. Luke 22.25 is the only NT use of κυριεύω outside the Pauline corpus (where it is used six times).

[68] Taylor, *Passion Narrative of Luke*, pp. 62f; Nelson, 'Leadership and Discipleship', p. 136.

[69] Jeremias, *Eucharistic Words*, p. 98.

[70] Green, *Death of Jesus*, pp. 46–8; Nelson, 'Leadership and Discipleship', pp. 187–93; Neyrey, *Passion according to Luke*, pp. 23f; Marshall, *Luke*, p. 815; *contra* Taylor, *Passion Narrative of Luke*, p. 64.

[71] Nelson, 'Leadership and Discipleship', p. 188; Green, *Death of Jesus*, p. 47. For example, ἀκολουθήσαντές is used more frequently by Matthew than Luke of the disciples following Jesus (and may in any case be an assimilation to Matt. 19.27), although the word may be close in sense to the Lukan διαμεμενηκότες.

[72] Nelson, 'Leadership and Discipleship', p. 158.

διακονῶν three times in verses 26f implies that this idea is central to the passage, especially because it contrasts with three uses of μείζων (verses 24, 26, 27).[73] And by the use of the emphatic personal pronoun ἐγώ (verse 27), Jesus identifies strongly with ὁ διακονῶν.

Jesus critiques the kings of the Gentiles (verse 25), who provide a foil to his idea of servanthood. In Graeco-Roman society, those called 'benefactors' had this honorific title conferred, generally publicly.[74] The conferral could include a formal statement of the goodness of the benefactor, the gift of a gold crown to wear, a seat of honour in the theatre, the right to wear purple for life, citizenship, and other honours.[75] Jesus contrasts the attention to social status in such procedures with his demand of his followers: ὑμεῖς δὲ οὐχ οὕτως.[76]

This demand is developed by the sequence of contrasts in verses 26f:[77]

Position A	*Position B*
the greatest	the youngest (verse 26b)
the leader	the servant (verse 26c)
the diner	the table servant (verse 27a)
the diner	Jesus the table servant (verse 27b–c)

In each case 'position B' is lower in status than 'position A'. Jesus' identification with the lower-status role implies that he calls his disciples to the same identification. However, for Jesus such identification does not involve a disavowal of leadership, for we have already seen that he exercises considerable leadership in this

---

[73] Nelson, 'Leadership and Discipleship', p. 184.

[74] Danker, *Benefactor*, pp. 436–41; Winter, 'Public Honouring', pp. 90f.

[75] Danker, *Benefactor*, pp. 467f; Winter, 'Public Honouring', pp. 91f.

[76] Lull, 'Servant-Benefactor', p. 295 proposes that καλεῖσθε ('you are called') ought to be understood as the verb in this clause, thus making the sense more neutral about Gentile kings: it is simply that the apostles are not *called* benefactors. The introduction of ἀλλ' (v. 26b) leads to the contrast, whereas v. 26a is simply a statement of fact. However, Nelson, 'Leadership and Discipleship', pp. 143–6 argues persuasively that the flow of thought in vv. 24–7, and particularly the contrasts in vv. 26–7, cannot bear such an interpretation. The last phrase of v. 27 clinches the argument: since Jesus identifies with the low-status member of each pair, he wants his disciples to do the same – they should not identify with 'the greatest' (ὁ μείζων) or 'the leader' (ὁ ἡγούμενος, v. 26). Thus, 'Since the kings and rulers function as negative examples whom Luke contrasts with the positive example of Jesus, v. 26a would have the sense of a prohibition' (p. 145). See further Danker, *Benefactor*, p. 324; Winter, *Seek the Welfare*, p. 40 n. 50.

[77] Nelson, 'Leadership and Discipleship', p. 143.

discourse. Rather, it is that the greatest is to be ὡς the youngest, the leader ὡς the servant, for Jesus is among his disciples ὡς the servant. The service Jesus offers is compared to that of the household table servant, particularly in the second and third uses of ὁ διακονῶν (verse 27).[78]

It is to such a combination of leadership and servanthood that Jesus calls his disciples. They will exercise leadership too, for they are being given kingly rule by Jesus (verse 29).[79] They will sit on thrones judging the twelve tribes of Israel (verse 30). Indeed, the statement 'let the greatest among you become as the youngest' (verse 26) paradoxically implies that there *is* a 'greatest among you'.[80]

But the apostles' leadership is to be 'as the youngest . . . as the one who serves' (verse 26). As they have continued with Jesus in his trials (verse 28), so they are to exercise leadership in a Jesus-like servant manner (verses 26f). As Jesus serves his people by laying down his life for them (verses 15, 19–22), so their leadership is to seek the good of those they lead rather than their own (verses 25f).[81]

This material links in three ways with the Miletus speech. First, Paul's leader/servant ministry is described in similar terms to those of Jesus and the disciples. Paul exercises leadership, for he can 'summon'[82] the elders to come to meet with him (Acts 20.17). He

---

[78] See Nelson's translation in the table above. Tannehill, *Narrative Unity*, vol. I, p. 256 and Johnson, *Luke*, p. 345 observe that διακονέω is usually used by Luke of serving meals (Luke 4.39; 10.40; 12.37; 17.8; cf. Acts 6.2), and therefore refers to a task usually undertaken by slaves or women. If so, this reinforces the point Luke presents about servant leadership; cf. Morris, *Luke*, p. 308. Marshall, *Luke*, p. 813 argues that the Lukan redaction of Mark has produced an emphasis on the 'force of Jesus' saying for church leaders', although without noting the parallels in Acts 20.24, 28 (discussed below).

[79] Note that διατίθεμαι (v. 29) is a present verb, which implies that it is during the Last Supper that Jesus is conferring kingship upon the disciples (Nelson, 'Leadership and Discipleship', pp. 214, 241; Neyrey, *Passion according to Luke*, p. 27). Johnson, *Luke*, pp. 345f; Johnson, *Literary Function of Possessions*, p. 120 sees this role exercised in the apostle's 'judging' (v. 30) function in the post-Easter community (e.g. Acts 5.1–11), observing that Luke lacks the phrase ἐν τῇ παλιγγενεσίᾳ found in the parallel (Matt. 19.28), whereas Nelson, 'Leadership and Discipleship', pp. 241–8 argues (among other points) that, because the subjunctives ἔσθητε and πίνητε (v. 30) imply a future, eschatological eating and drinking, the 'judging' will also be eschatological.

[80] Nelson, 'Leadership and Discipleship', p. 167.

[81] Johnson, *Literary Function of Possessions*, p. 167 argues, 'The authority of the Twelve over Israel is to be *expressed* in their διακονεῖν τραπέζαις (Acts 6.2), in the distribution of goods to the community' (italics his). But Acts 6.1–7 shows the Twelve declining this function on the grounds that their ministry should be prayer and ἡ διακονία τοῦ λόγου (v. 4)!

[82] Μετακαλέω, only found in Acts in the NT (7.14; 10.32; 20.17; 24.25), and only

also leads through his teaching ministry (Acts 20.20), in which he speaks of the βασιλεία which Jesus received from his Father (Acts 20.25; Luke 22.29).

Paul also shows traits of the servant ministry described in Luke 22.24–30.[83] The noun διακονία (Acts 20.24, cf. the articular participle ὁ διακονῶν, Luke 22.26f) puts Paul's ministry into servant categories. Luke's Paul speaks of himself 'serving the Lord' (Acts 20.19, using δουλεύω), and he has served in ταπεινοφροσύνη (Acts 20.19) – a quality central to the style of leadership commended by Jesus (Luke 22.26f). Paul's servant ministry includes care for the weak (Acts 20.34f, using ὑπηρετέω, verse 34[84]), which accords with our previous observation that Jesus-style servant ministry is intended to benefit those served, rather than the servant. And the costliness of Jesus' servant ministry, extending to death, is borne by Paul in tears and trials (Acts 20.19, 31), as well as in readiness to die (Acts 20.23f) – a cost from which he does not shrink (Acts 20.20, 24). Further, the tone of the Miletus speech is one of a concerned pastor pleading, rather than a domineering leader giving orders to subordinates. Tannehill summarises well:

> The humble service that Jesus commended by including himself among the waiters and waitresses is now being carried out through Paul's dedicated service to the Lord and others in his mission.[85]

Not only that, but Paul charges the elders to exercise this kind of leadership in the Christian community at Ephesus (Acts 20.28): a feeding leadership which 'oversees'[86] and 'shepherds',[87] not a

---

in the middle voice, which seems to have a reflexive sense 'to call to oneself' (BAGD, p. 511). *NIDNTT*, vol. I, p. 273 notes that Luke uses the compounds of καλέω more frequently than other NT writers: ἐπικαλέω (30 times NT, 20 times Acts); προσκαλέομαι (29 times NT, 13 times Luke-Acts); εἰσκαλέω (Acts 10.23 only).

[83] Cf. Spencer, *Acts*, p. 194, linking Luke 22.26f with Acts 20.35.

[84] Found only in Acts in the NT (13.26; 20.34; 24.23). The noun ὑπηρέτης (often meaning 'guard') is a favourite of John (nine occurrences), but is also found twice in Luke (1.2; 4.20) and four times in Acts (5.22, 26; 13.5; 26.16). It is only found at 1 Cor. 4.1 in the Pauline corpus. Cf. Dupont, *Discours de Milet*, p. 302 n. 3.

[85] Tannehill, *Narrative Unity*, vol. II, p. 260.

[86] The cognate verb of ἐπίσκοπος is ἐπισκέπτομαι, which is used in the LXX for the work of shepherds (e.g. Zech. 10.3; 11.16; Jer. 23.2), and in the NT for caring provision (e.g. Jas. 1.27). Ἐπισκέπτομαι is a Lukanism, being used twice only in Matthew, three times in Luke (1.68, 78; 7.16), four times in Acts (6.3; 7.23; 15.14, 36), and only twice elsewhere in the NT.

[87] Ποιμαίνω is used twice only in Luke-Acts (Acts 20.28; Luke 17.7 – of literal

domineering leadership. That this is the intention is evident from the nature of Paul's example of servant leadership in the whole speech. This general intention finds specific expression when Paul offers the elders his example of supporting the weak (Acts 20.35). The servant leadership model which Paul exemplifies and which Jesus originated is being commended to other Christian leaders.

As with other themes, there is an accumulation of parallels, both verbal and conceptual, on the question of leadership, particularly focused on servant-style leadership. We suggest that Luke meant his readers to hear the echoes.

4.2.5   Money and work

Evans describes Luke 22.35–8 as 'perhaps the most puzzling passage in the Gospel [of Luke], indeed in all the gospels'[88] – a judgement with which it is easy to agree. Nevertheless, the passage evidently considers money and possessions, and is therefore worth investigating in connection with Acts 20.33–5. Because it is so difficult, we shall indicate briefly how the passage as a whole should be read before turning to the potential parallel with the Miletus speech.

First, verses 33–5 are unparalleled in Matthew and Mark, and the majority judgement of scholars is that these verses have been woven out of pre-Lukan tradition,[89] even where it is thought that some of the material is Lukan creation.[90] Either way, we may reasonably look to this passage for a Lukan perspective, for Luke's incorporation of the material into his Gospel implies that he can at least countenance it.

There is a clear allusion in verse 35 to the sending of the seventy(-two) (Luke 10.3f), particularly in the three items βαλλάντιον, πήρα and ὑποδήματα, which come in the same sequence.[91] Some also see an allusion to the sending of the twelve (Luke 9.3f),

---

shepherding of a herd, cf. 1 Cor. 9.7). Cf. 1 Pet. 5.2, which uses it of church leadership.

[88] Evans, *Saint Luke*, pp. 803f.

[89] Taylor, *Passion Narrative of Luke*, p. 67; Soards, *Passion according to Luke*, p. 31; Stein, *Luke*, p. 554; Marshall, *Luke*, p. 824; Nolland, *Luke 18:35–24:53*, p. 1075; Fitzmyer, *Luke X–XXIV*, p. 1429; Schürmann, *Jesu Abschiedsrede*, pp. 116–39; Bock, *Luke*, vol. II, pp. 1745f.

[90] Lampe, 'Two Swords', pp. 336, 342.

[91] Fitzmyer, *Luke X–XXIV*, p. 847; Nolland, *Luke 18:35–24:53*, p. 1075.

suggesting that the requirement to take 'nothing for the way' could include the unmentioned purse and sandals.[92]

But although there is a clear allusion to 10.3f, there is also a clear contrast: ἀλλὰ νῦν (verse 36) is a very strong adversative, used here alone in Luke's writings.[93] A new phase is beginning, in which conditions will be different.[94]

The mark of the new situation is that Satan will test the apostolic band,[95] and thus they cannot expect the same welcome and provision that they experienced when sent out by Jesus previously (verse 35): that is why they need to take purse, bag and sword (verse 36).[96] The urgency of this is stressed by the need for the one without a sword to sell his ἱμάτιον, the outer garment which kept its owner warm at night.[97] Thus Jesus effectively annuls the earlier instruction (Luke 10.4), which was relevant to the former conditions alone.[98] The period beginning with ἀλλὰ νῦν (verse 36) will be a time of testing in which the apostles will need to be self-sufficient and must have the wherewithal to defend themselves, as any other traveller might.[99] That the 'sword' is intended by Luke's Jesus to be metaphorical – but misunderstood literally by the apostles (verse 38) – is suggested by Jesus' reaction to the use of an actual sword (22.50f): 'Since their [the apostles'] self-defence had reflected faulty hearing, his [Jesus'] undiminished power was manifested in his healing of the ear.'[100] Further, there is no sign of sword-bearing

---

[92] Tannehill, *Narrative Unity,* vol. I, p. 266 n. 110; similarly Stein, *Luke*, p. 555; Senior, *Passion in Luke*, pp. 79f; Minear, 'Note on Luke xxii 36', p. 129.

[93] Marshall, *Luke*, p. 824; Evans, *Saint Luke*, p. 805. Ἀλλὰ νῦν is used quite rarely in the NT (clearly only in Luke 22.36; 2 Cor. 5.16; Phil. 2.12; 1 Pet. 2.25; possibly 1 Cor. 3.2; John 11.22, *v.l.*).

[94] There is some debate whether this new phase is the whole church period (Conzelmann, *Theology of St Luke*, pp. 16, 80f, 103 n. 1; Stein, *Luke*, p. 556; Fitzmyer, *Luke X–XXIV*, p. 1431) or only the period of Satanic pressure during the passion (Marshall, *Luke*, p. 824; Nolland, *Luke 18:35–24:53*, pp. 1976, 1078; Minear, 'Note on Luke xxii 36', pp. 130f, 133), but for our present purposes we need only note the shift of conditions.

[95] Note ὑμᾶς (v. 31), contrasted with σοῦ (v. 32).

[96] Johnson, *Literary Function of Possessions*, p. 164.

[97] Marshall, *Luke*, p. 825. Cf. Luke 6.29; Exod. 22.25f LXX.

[98] Schweizer, *Luke*, p. 341; Conzelmann, *Theology of St Luke*, pp. 186 n. 1 (found on p. 187); 232f.

[99] Lampe, 'Two Swords', pp. 337f; Johnson, *Luke*, p. 347.

[100] Minear, 'Note on Luke xxii 36', p. 132. Others who hold the metaphorical reading include: Talbert, *Reading Luke*, p. 211; Neyrey, *Passion according to Luke*, pp. 40f; Senior, *Passion in Luke*, p. 82; Johnson, *Luke*, p. 347; Fitzmyer, *Luke X–XXIV*, p. 1432; Marshall, *Luke*, p. 823.

apostles in Acts,[101] and a sword could be understood metaphorically as indicating division (note Matt. 10.34//Luke 12.51).[102]

There are two links to the Miletus speech in such an understanding of this difficult passage. First, the warning of distress (verses 35–7) parallels a similar warning to the elders (Acts 20.29–31)[103] – a warning natural in a situation of 'leave-taking'.

But second, and more significant, is the link to the discussion of finance in the Miletus address (Acts 20.33–5). The 'fend for yourself' attitude of Luke 22.36 conceptually parallels Paul's determination not to be dependent on anyone (Acts 20.34). Schweizer observes astutely: 'But he [Paul] lived the fine carelessness of Jesus' messengers in other ways (Acts 20.33–5; Phil. 4.12–16).'[104]

4.2.6 Summary

We noted above that the Last Supper discourse fits the 'farewell speech' genre rather well, and we have now observed extensive and significant parallels with the Miletus speech. While some can be seen as 'standard' farewell speech items, the correspondences of language and concepts seem too close for the similarity to be limited to the level of genre. It is the clustering of themes which is particularly notable, and this series of connections is reinforced by the sequence of the themes in the two passages. It is not too much to say that Luke gives us two similarly structured farewell discourses which mirror each other: the departing Jesus passes on to his disciples/apostles a model of life and leadership in his community which the departing Paul later passes on to the elders of one of his key churches.[105]

---

[101] The only mentions of μάχαιρα in Luke-Acts (apart from Luke 22.36, 38, 49) are in the hands of the enemies of Jesus and his people (Luke 21.24; 22.52; Acts 12.2; 16.27).

[102] Neyrey, *Passion according to Luke*, p. 40; Senior, *Passion in Luke*, p. 82.

[103] Lampe, 'Two Swords', p. 337.

[104] Schweizer, *Luke*, p. 341. Kurz, *Farewell Addresses*, pp. 68f suggests that the contrasting approaches of missionaries to financial support in the apostolic church (some seeking support from the churches in line with Luke 10.4, others being self-supporting in line with Luke 22.36) might lead to a need to defend Paul from criticism that he was not following the Master's instructions.

[105] A further link between the scenes is that both are followed by kneeling for prayer (Acts 20.36; Luke 22.41, different from Matt. 26.39; Mark 14.35, who have Jesus prostrate), which is not the usual posture for prayer in Judaism (e.g. 1 Sam. 1.26; Mark 11.25), according to Bock, *Luke,* vol. II, p. 1758; Marshall, *Luke*, p. 830. That the posture is likely to be Lukan redaction is suggested by the fact that Luke

4.3   Luke 12.1–53

Jesus here teaches about discipleship: in verse 1 he turns from the (large) crowd to speak to his disciples. Following an interruption by a member of the crowd (verse 13) Jesus turns again to his disciples (verse 22). Then, when Peter asks whom Jesus intends as the target of this teaching (verse 41), he answers by telling the parable of the steward (verses 42–8). Finally, Jesus stresses the pressures and divisions which discipleship brings, both for himself and for his followers (verses 49–53). The amount of material addressed specifically to the disciples suggests that their future leadership responsibility may be in view, and at certain points this becomes explicit (verses 32, 42, 44, 45f, 47: see discussion below).

It is evident from an examination of parallels in the other Synoptics that Luke has brought this material together:[106]

Luke 12	Mark	Matthew	Thomas[107]
1	8.15	16.5f	
2–9		10.26–33	
10	3.28f	12.31f	44
11f	13.11	10.19f	
13–15			72 (verses 13f)
16–21			63
22–32		6.25–33	36 (verse 22)
33f		6.19–21	76 (verse 33)
35–8	?13.33–7	?25.1–13	
39–46		24.43–51	21 (verse 39)
47f			
49f	?10.38f		10 (verse 49)
51, 53		10.34–6	
52			16 (verses 52f)

The chapter begins with a warning to the disciples about the Pharisees (verses 1–3, possibly located here in juxtaposition to the

alone among the Evangelists records kneeling as a prayer posture (although cf. Eph. 3.14; Mark 1.40; 10.17; Matt. 17.14); see Evans, *Saint Luke*, pp. 809, 811; Mattill, 'Jesus-Paul Parallels', p. 39. I owe the suggestion of the link to my student, Mr Simon Hawthorne.

[106] Klostermann, *Lukasevangelium*, p. 132 calls Luke 12 'eine komponierte Rede, ja ein Musterbeispiel lukanischer Redaktion' (a speech which has been composed, truly a model of Lukan redaction).

[107] Material from the Gospel of Thomas is added for illustrative purposes without a presupposed hypothesis about the origin of the material. See Kloppenborg, *Q Parallels*, pp. 116–43 for the parallels set out synoptically.

altercation in 11.33–54), which broadens into a warning to fear God above people (verses 4–7). This leads on to more specific words about acknowledging Jesus before people, especially in a public tribunal (verses 8–12). The focus is then shifted by the interrupting question of a bystander, in response to which Jesus declines to take the role of a religious 'ruler' and warns against covetousness (verses 13–15). This warning is underlined by a parable (verses 16–21). Turning again to his disciples, Jesus teaches about the futility of worry (verses 22–32),[108] before drawing the conclusion that wealth is not to be hoarded, but given to the needy (verses 33f). The focus then moves to teaching about readiness, including a group of parables (verses 36–48), and the section ends with Jesus' sayings about division (verses 49–53).

The section is thus full of material about discipleship, some for outsiders and some for those who already follow Jesus. Three major themes of this passage parallel the Miletus speech: leadership, suffering (and the priority of discipleship), and money.[109]

4.3.1 Leadership

Given the context of Jesus teaching the disciples – who will themselves be the leaders of the church – we should not be surprised that Luke 12.1–53 contains material on leadership. While Jesus declines to be 'set over' people as a judge of material things (verses 13f), he speaks of the household manager who is 'set over' the master's house in his absence (verses 42, 44, using καθίστημι, as in verse 14), implying the apostles' future leadership role in his own absence.[110] Moreover, in this parable Luke alone uses οἰκονόμος (verse 42; δοῦλος in Matt. 24.45), which denotes a slave put over other slaves of the same master.[111] Indeed, Peter's question (verse 41, Luke alone) puts the parable in a context which implies that it is

---

[108] Nolland, *Luke 9:21–18:34*, p. 690 suggests that vv. 22–32 parallel vv. 13–21, but are aimed at disciples rather than outsiders.

[109] Cf. Tannehill, *Narrative Unity,* vol. I, p. 250.

[110] Johnson, *Luke*, p. 204. Καθίστημι appears just these three times in Luke plus five times in Acts (6.3; 7.10, 27, 35; 17.15), in all but one of which (17.15) the appointment to leadership is in view. It occurs in Matthew four times, and never in Mark and John. Stein, *Luke*, p. 361; Bock, *Luke,* vol. II, p. 1179 and Johnson, *Literary Function of Possessions*, p. 166, noticing the future tenses (vv. 42, 44: in v. 42 Luke uses a future by contrast with Matthew's aorist, whereas in v. 44 both use a future), believe that this implies a reference to the Twelve's future leadership over the church.

[111] Marshall, *Luke*, p. 540. Luke shows that this is his understanding by using

for the disciples as future leaders.[112] Further, the disciples are to be given τὴν βασιλείαν (verse 32), which may carry the same sense of 'kingly rule' as in 22.29.

Jesus contrasts the attitudes he seeks with those of the Pharisees[113] (verses 1–3), whom he criticises for their hypocrisy (only mentioned by Luke). This follows criticism of their lack of inner cleanliness (11.37–41) and not practising what they preach (11.42–4). Further, the lawyers, who are associated with the Pharisees (11.45), are criticised by Jesus for hiding the truth from the people (11.52).

In contrast to their hidden hypocrisy which will one day be revealed for all to see (verses 2f) and their hiding the truth (11.52), the teaching of Paul is open to inspection: he has not hidden anything profitable to the Ephesian Christians (Acts 20.20, 27). This is a conceptual contrast, and parallel to the lifestyle to which Jesus calls his teaching followers. Paul is a model of his own teaching, for which he has suffered (Acts 20.19) and is willing to suffer (Acts 20.23f) – again, by contrast with the comfortable lifestyle of those whom Jesus criticises (Luke 11.43).

This line of thought is taken further in verses 8–12, where readiness to acknowledge Jesus publicly marks true disciples. The substance (and mostly the vocabulary) of the sayings in verses 8–9 is identical in Luke and Matthew. What marks Luke's account as distinctive is the bringing together of the material in verses 8–12, which is found in disparate locations in Mark and Matthew. Luke provides a grouping of sayings which highlight the responsibility of the disciples in their missionary/leadership role: verses 11f particularly are more specific than their Matthean and Markan equivalents in stating before whom the apostles will be tried – synagogues, rulers and authorities.

Luke links the requirement of faithfulness to the responsibilities of an οἰκονόμος (verse 42; Matthew has δοῦλος), a word that suggests leaders.[114] Πιστός, which embodies the task of leadership,

δοῦλος for the same person later in the parable (v. 43). It is noteworthy that Luke alone among the Evangelists uses οἰκονόμος (Luke 12.42; 16.1, 3, 8).

[112] Johnson, *Literary Function of Possessions*, p. 166 argues that the redactional placing of the parable in vv. 42–8 establishes 'a separation between the rest of the disciples to whom these sayings have been addressed and those whom Peter calls "us" which in context can only mean the Twelve'.

[113] Luke focuses the criticism on the Pharisees alone, by contrast with Matthew (who also has Sadducees, 16.6) and Mark (who also has Herod, 8.15).

[114] Marshall, *Luke*, p. 540; Ellis, *Luke*, p. 181 argue that this difference highlights

is a favourite word of Luke.[115] Christian leaders have a responsibility of stewardship over the household of God (verses 35–48, esp.
41–8). Verses 35–48 picture a situation where the disciples' master
is absent but due to return, and the disciples are leaders with
pastoral responsibility. Their leadership is not to abuse those they
lead: verses 45f show a contrasting example of bad leadership in the
striking of fellow servants (not unlike the manner of the Gentile
kings of 22.24–7[116] and the wolves of Acts 20.29).

Most surprising in the teaching of this section is the idea that the
returning master will wait upon his faithful servants (verse 37,
found in Luke alone). The returning master would be understood
in the early church to be the Lord Jesus, and this verse provides a
strong parallel to the saying in Luke 22.27,[117] particularly because
it mentions the servants reclining at table (cf. Luke 22.14) and the
master serving them (using διακονέω, as 22.37): 'To picture the
returning Lord as still serving gives this aspect of his work
unexpected prominence. It suggests that service is a permanent
characteristic of the Lord, even when he is exalted'[118] – more, it
suggests that service is to characterise the leaders of the Lord's
community.

The idea of the οἰκονόμος as serving, particularly clear in verses
35–8, is taken up in the Miletus speech, where Paul uses the word
δουλεύω (Acts 20.19) of his ministry. The verbal parallel is strong
here, for the noun δοῦλος is used in Luke 12.37, 43, 45, 46. Thus we
may see here both a verbal and a conceptual parallel.

Luke presents Paul as faithful (cf. Luke 12.42) in passing on the
tradition (Acts 20.20f, 24, 27), which forms a conceptual parallel to

a clearer focus on church leaders in Luke's account. Cf. Talbert, 'Redaction Critical
Search', pp. 188f, who sees v. 42 as 'very much like Luke's description of the ideal
elder of his own time in Acts 20.28.'

[115] Luke-Acts uses it ten times (Luke 12.42; 16.10 (twice), 11, 12; Acts 10.45;
13.34; 16.1, 15); Matthew five times, in the parallel to this passage (24.45) and in the
parable of the talents (25.21 (twice), 23 (twice)) – all paralleled in Luke; John uses it
once (20.27); Mark not at all. Cf. 1 Cor. 4.2, where Paul declares that the
characteristic of a steward should be faithfulness.

[116] Tannehill, *Narrative Unity*, vol. I, p. 250. Ellis, *Luke*, p. 181 proposes that
'Luke apparently is addressing a situation in which some Christian leaders have
become corrupt and despotic ... he distinguishes and emphasizes the additional
responsibility resting upon Christian leaders.' Likewise, Schmithals, *Lukas*, p. 148
sees Luke teaching the church leaders of his day, when false teachers were a danger
(he cites Acts 20.28ff; 1 Tim. 1.3ff; 3.1ff).

[117] Johnson, *Literary Function of Possessions*, p. 167; see discussion, § 4.2.4.

[118] Tannehill, *Narrative Unity*, vol. I, p. 249 (italics his). Similarly Johnson, *Luke*,
p. 206; Marshall, *Luke*, p. 536.

the idea of stewardship in Luke 12. Paul exemplifies the carrying out of this calling: he makes strenuous efforts in his service (Acts 20.19, 20, 27, and the use of πᾶς throughout the speech;[119] cf. the vocabulary of effort in Luke 12.35f); he faces trials as a result of his faithful proclamation (Acts 20.19–21, 27); and he is ready to face future suffering (Acts 20.22f) in order to complete the road which the Lord Jesus has set before him (Acts 20.24).

Further, Paul calls the Ephesian elders to the same readiness to proclaim the message despite the coming of others who will either deny or distort it (Acts 20.28–31). They too are to make strenuous efforts to carry out their service (Acts 20.28, 31). 20.28–31, in parallel with Luke 12.41–8, indicate that church leaders should not 'browbeat their fellow Christians or ... run riot':[120] the parallel with the Miletus speech operates in both positive and negative forms. Both Paul's own activities and his charge to the elders are instantiations of Luke's record of the teaching of Jesus in this respect.

4.3.2   Suffering

The readiness to suffer for Jesus' sake is another theme from Luke 12 with strong echoes in the Miletus speech. It connects with another significant theme of the section – fear:[121] φοβέω[122] is used frequently (verses 4, 5 (three times), 7, 32), as is μεριμνάω (verses 11, 22, 25, 26). As we shall see from the contrasts which are made, this fear is not common human fear, but anxiety arising out of discipleship.[123]

The conjunction of these themes is seen first when Jesus says that physical suffering imposed by other people is not the greatest thing to fear; rather, God,[124] who can cast the whole person into Gehenna, is the one to fear (verses 4–7). This comes in the context of the threat to Jesus from the scribes and Pharisees (Luke 11.53f) following his criticisms of them (11.37–52).[125] Paul speaks of the

---

[119] See p. 84f.

[120] Evans, *Saint Luke*, p. 536.

[121] Tannehill, *Narrative Unity*, vol. I, pp. 244f; Johnson, *Literary Function of Possessions*, p. 152.

[122] Around a third of the NT uses are found in Luke-Acts (37 of 95). Goulder, *Luke: New Paradigm*, pp. 800, 809 cites the verb (of fearing God) and the noun as distinctive Lukan vocabulary.

[123] Seccombe, *Possessions*, pp. 150–2.

[124] Fitzmyer, *Luke X–XXIV*, p. 959.

[125] Johnson, *Literary Function of Possessions*, p. 152.

value of his own life in very similar terms. He models what it is to fear God rather than people, for he will face imprisonment (Acts 20.23) rather than fail to follow the path the Lord Jesus has prepared for him (Acts 20.24).[126]

Likewise, the readiness to testify (ὁμολογέω, Luke 12.8[127]) before[128] the Jewish ('synagogue') and Gentile ('rulers and authorities'[129]) authorities (verses 11f), of which Jesus speaks in verses 8–12,[130] is the other side of the coin to not denying Jesus (verses 8f[131]).

Paul speaks in similar terms of threats to him, particularly naming his Jewish opponents in the Miletus address (Acts 20.19), but also stating that he testifies (διαμαρτύρεω, Acts 20.21, 22, 24) to Jews and Greeks (Acts 20.21). A link with Luke 12.8–12 is that the disciples are to bear testimony before synagogues and rulers (Luke 12.11), with particular mention of the Jews. A conceptual parallel may thus, we suggest, be seen here.[132]

Discipleship takes higher priority than one's own family (verses 49–53). Jesus brings division[133] because he demands absolute priority above all other people and loyalties – and this has been a major theme, stretching back to the division between the followers of Jesus and the Pharisees (11.37–12.3).[134] The sense of the priority demanded by discipleship is also clear in Paul's speech (esp. Acts 20.24), and Paul has faithfully carried out his leadership task with the same priority (Acts 20.19, 20, 26f, 31). He is prepared to go to

[126] Paul is twice told by God not to be afraid (Acts 18.9; 27.24).

[127] Reiling and Swellengrebel, *Luke*, p. 466 suggest (following BAGD, p. 568) the sense 'acknowledge'; cf. 2 Macc. 6.6.

[128] Ἔμπροσθεν shows that public testimony is involved (cf. Luke 5.19; 19.2, 27; Acts 18.17). See Marshall, *Luke*, p. 515.

[129] Note the parallel with Luke 20.20 (Lukan redaction), where Pilate has ἀρχή καὶ ἐξουσία. See Goulder, *Luke: New Paradigm*, p. 531.

[130] Evans, *Saint Luke*, p. 519; Stein, *Luke*, p. 349 both note the reference to the two kinds of tribunal.

[131] Using ἀρνέομαι and ἀπαρνέομαι, next found at Luke 22.34, 57, 61, all significantly of Peter's denial of Jesus (Tannehill, *Narrative Unity*, vol. I, p. 245).

[132] Evans, *Saint Luke*, p. 519 sees Paul's testimony before the elders as an example of such activity (Acts 20.22ff). But Evans' other proposed examples (Acts 22–6) are more likely, since they are in a judicial setting; there is no suggestion in Acts 20 that Paul is before a tribunal, either formally or informally.

[133] Using a Lukan word, διαμερισμός (v. 51), where Matthew uses μάχαιρα (10.34); cf. the uses of participles of the cognate verb διαμερίζω (vv. 52, 53). The noun and verb are found nine times in Luke-Acts (Luke 11.17, 18; 12.51, 52, 53; 22.17; 23.34; Acts 2.17, 34), compared to once each in Matthew, Mark and John. No other NT uses exist. Cf. Goulder, *Luke: New Paradigm*, p. 802.

[134] Johnson, *Literary Function of Possessions*, pp. 151f.

prison rather than fail to carry out his task (Acts 20.22–4) – he is, we might say, 'bound' (cf. δεδεμένος, verse 22) by God to carry it through, captive to God's desires. Not only that, but Paul summons the Ephesian elders to share his wholeheartedness in keeping watch and being alert day and night (Acts 20.28, 31).

4.3.3   Money

The attitude to wealth is very similar in both passages. Luke's Jesus teaches both negatively and positively. Negatively, he criticises excessive acquisitiveness and points to the relativisation of wealth in the light of the need to be 'rich toward God' (verses 13–21, unique to Luke). The sequence of first-person references in verses 17–19, both the fourfold μου[135] and the series of eight first-person singular verbs (ποιήσω, ἔχω, συνάξω, ποιήσω, καθελῶ, οἰκο-δομήσω, συνάξω, ἐρῶ),[136] contrasts sharply with the verdict of verse 21, with its emphatic placing of οὕτως ὁ θησαυρίζων ἑαυτῷ.

Positively (verses 22–31//Matt. 6.25–33), God is able to provide for his own and therefore worry is folly (verses 22–6). Those who seek God's kingdom (verses 31f; verse 32 in Luke alone) will discover that God's care is expressed in the same way as his care for the birds and the lilies (verses 24, 27f; cf. verse 7). Luke goes on to record teaching about the disciples now being free to give to those in need (verses 33f; verse 33a unique to Luke) because they possess heavenly treasure.[137]

In the main section of the Miletus speech relating to wealth (Acts 20.33–5), a striking verbal parallel to the use of δίδωμι (Acts 20.35) in the quotation of a saying of Jesus is the same verb (in the imperative mood) in Luke 12.33a (unparalleled in Matthew), where Jesus encourages giving. Luke's lexical choice draws attention to the invitation of Jesus to give, which Paul models – and which he in turn delivers to the elders by word and example (Acts 20.35).

Paul also records his lack of covetousness (verse 33), thus embodying the teaching of Luke 12.13–21 (especially verse 15, which makes the point explicit). Paul contrasts with the rich fool, for Paul works with his hands to provide for his companions as well as

---

[135] Plummer, *Luke*, p. 324; Ellis, *Luke*, p. 177 ('Thinking he was an owner, he found that he himself was owned').

[136] Rienecker, *Lukas*, p. 311.

[137] Cf. Talbert, *Reading Luke*, pp. 141, 143.

himself (Acts 20.34), whereas the rich fool wishes not to have to work with his hands (Luke 12.19).[138]

Further, Paul includes in his list of non-coveted items clothes (Acts 20.33, ἱμάτιον), which resonates with language about the body being more than clothes (Luke 12.23, ἔνδυμα) and God clothing the grass and those of little faith (Luke 12.28, ἀμφιέζω[139]).

A further lexical link is the contrast in the use of κληρονομία in Luke 12.13f, where Jesus refuses to be a divider of an inheritance, and in Acts 20.32, where Paul tells the elders that God will *give* them an inheritance.[140] God's generosity, exemplified by his treatment of the birds and lilies, is great to those who respond to him.

4.3.4 Other verbal parallels

Again, it is not so much the paralleling of individual themes that is remarkable, but the clustering of several themes from the Miletus speech in Luke 12.1–53. In the speech Luke seems to be presenting Paul, in his own following of Jesus, as modelling the discipleship described in Luke 12.1–53. We may note five further verbal parallels between Luke 12.1–53 and the Miletus address which are not linked directly to the major themes of the Pauline speech.

First, the blessing on those found awake (γρηγοροῦντας, verse 37[141]) at the master's return is paralleled in the Miletus speech by the use of the same verb in the imperative mood in Acts 20.31.[142] This becomes the more significant when we notice that γρηγορέω occurs nowhere else in Luke-Acts:[143] Luke only uses the word in Jesus' blessing, which acts as an instruction to his disciples to stay awake, and Paul's similar injunction to the elders. Luke thus draws

---

[138] Seccombe, *Possessions*, p. 158.

[139] A Hellenistic spelling of ἀμφιάζω (BAGD, p. 47).

[140] Κληρονομία is not used greatly in the NT (fourteen times, six in the Gospels and Acts); Luke-Acts provides four uses. Apart from the two discussed, the other uses are in the parable of the wicked tenants (Luke 20.14, also found in the Matthean and Markan parallels) and in Stephen's speech (of the promised land, Acts 7.5).

[141] Γρηγορέω is also present in a variant reading in Luke 12.39, but the evidence is against its being present in the autograph in spite of the range of manuscripts containing it, because of the probability of assimilation to the parallel in Matt. 24.43 (Metzger, *Textual Commentary* (1st edn), pp. 161f; Marshall, *Luke*, p. 538; Fitzmyer, *Luke X–XXIV*, p. 989; Nolland, *Luke 9:21–18:34*, p. 698).

[142] Marshall, *Luke*, p. 536.

[143] It occurs six times each in Matthew and Mark, but there is no parallel to Luke 12.37 in the other Synoptics.

126   Leadership and Lifestyle

attention to the parallel between Jesus and Paul in their exhortation
to those who follow them in leadership.

Second, Jesus describes himself as constrained ἕως ὅτου τελεσθῇ
(Luke 12.50; found in Luke alone[144]), and Paul speaks of his own
desire to complete the task God has given to him using the closely
related verb τελειόω (Acts 20.24[145]). Luke presents Paul as sharing
his Master's focus on carrying out his God-given task – and the
two verbs both give a sense of purpose to their respective work,[146]
both of which will result in suffering in Jerusalem (Luke 12.50; Acts
20.23f).

Third, Jesus describes his disciples as τὸ μικρὸν ποίμνιον[147]
(Luke 12.32, peculiar to Luke), and Paul describes the church in
Ephesus using ποίμνιον (Acts 20.28, 29).[148] These are the only uses
of ποίμνιον in Luke-Acts,[149] and the word is only used once
elsewhere in the NT.[150] Luke's Paul also uses the cognate verb
ποιμαίνω (Acts 20.28). Paul is again portrayed in the tradition of
his Master, conceiving those whom he cares for as a 'flock' who are
to be 'shepherded', as he expounds Christian leadership to the
elders.

Fourth, the language of alerting is common to the two passages.
The unusual ὑποδείκνυμι is used by Jesus to set a pattern for the
disciples of fearing God (Luke 12.5, unparalleled in Matthew) and

[144] Luke also uses συνέχω here, a favourite word of his: nine of the twelve NT
uses are found in Luke-Acts (Luke 4.38; 8.37, 45; 12.50; 19.43; 22.63; Acts 7.57; 18.5;
28.8). Goulder, *Luke: New Paradigm*, p. 808 lists it in his 'Lukan vocabulary'.
[145] Tannehill, *Narrative Unity*, vol. I, pp. 250f.
[146] Concerning τελέω, see Marshall, *Luke*, p. 547: 'τελέω ... conveys the idea
that the death envisaged by Jesus ... is no mere fate or accident but a destiny to be
fulfilled'. Similarly Nolland, *Luke 9:21–18:34*, p. 709. Concerning τελειόω, see
Bruce, *Acts* (3rd edn), p. 532; Conzelmann, *Acts*, p. 174; Schneider, *Apostelgeschichte*, vol. II, p. 295.
[147] Fitzmyer, *Luke X–XXIV*, p. 980 sees this as an allusion to Isa. 41.14 LXX;
Jervell, *Apostelgeschichte*, p. 512 adds Jer. 2.8; 23.1ff; Ezek. 34.2; Ps. 23.1, regarding
the allusion to the church as 'the renewed Israel'. Morris, *Luke*, p. 215 notes that this
phrase is found only here in the NT. Talbert, 'Redaction Critical Search', p. 189
observes that the image of a flock for the disciples occurs in Luke 12 and the Miletus
speech.
[148] Marshall, *Luke*, p. 530; Evans, *Saint Luke*, p. 530; Kee, *To Every Nation*,
p. 241; Jervell, *Apostelgeschichte*, p. 512. Stein, *Luke*, p. 356 suggests that there may
also be a link with the idea of being sent out as lambs in the midst of wolves (Luke
10.3), which might provide a further link with Acts 20.29. See § 4.5.3.
[149] Seccombe, *Possessions*, p. 149.
[150] 1 Pet. 5.2f, also in the context of leadership. Achtemeier, *1 Peter*, pp. 325f
notes the collocation of ποίμνιον, ποιμαίνω and words from the ἐπίσκοπος word-
group in 1 Pet. 5.2; Acts 20.28.

by Paul who sets a pattern for the elders' conduct (Acts 20.35).[151] Προσέχω also occurs in both places with a reflexive second person pronoun,[152] each using the imperative (Luke 12.1, paralleled in Matthew but not Mark; Acts 20.28).[153]

Finally, the use of verbs of knowing is of interest. Luke 12 contains a number of uses of γινώσκω and οἶδα (verses 2, 30, 39, 46, 47, 48). Jesus speaks of God's knowledge, which means that he will provide (verse 30); he will reveal secret things (verse 2). There is also a contrast between the slave who knows and the one who does not (verses 47f), for knowledge should lead to action (verse 39b). Hidden knowledge appears at three points (verses 2, 39b, 46). The Miletus speech also abounds in use of these two verbs[154] and highlights the need to act on knowledge (Acts 20.29–31: the use of διό at the beginning of verse 31 indicates a conclusion being drawn from verses 29f), as well as an understanding of Paul's imperfect knowledge (Acts 20.22), implicitly contrasted with God's full knowledge.

4.3.5 Summary

Throughout Luke 12.1–53 parallels with the Miletus speech occur, both verbal and conceptual. As with our study of Luke's Last Supper discourse, some parallels appear closer than others, but they should be seen as having a cumulative effect: one or two alone could be coincidence, but several clear-cut verbal parallels clustered together lead us to take seriously the likelihood of conceptual parallels.

A key significance of these parallels is that Luke presents Paul as modelling the teaching of Jesus in his lifestyle and as he passes on the tradition to the Ephesian leaders. Tannehill summarises well:

> The portrait of Paul in his farewell address in Acts 20.18–35, which corresponds to major themes in Jesus' teaching to the disciples in Luke 12.4–53, suggests a highly favourable view of Paul, which in turn indicates that Paul's life story is a faithful interpretation of God's purposes in Jesus.[155]

---

[151] See p. 83 on ὑποδείκνυμι.

[152] Goulder, *Luke: New Paradigm*, p. 808 notes that προσέχω ἑαυτοῖς (Luke 12.1) is characteristically Lukan (never found in Matthew or Mark, five times in Luke-Acts: Luke 12.1; 17.3; 21.34 (see § 4.4); Acts 5.35; 20.28), in agreement with Marshall, *Luke*, p. 782; Plummer, *Luke*, p. 317; Fitzmyer, *Luke X–XXIV*, p. 954.

[153] Cf. Stein, *Luke*, p. 346.   [154] See p. 70.

[155] Tannehill, *Narrative Unity,* vol. I, p. 253.

4.4   Luke 21.5–36

This passage could be considered as a 'farewell speech' of Jesus, in which he prepares his disciples for what is to come.[156] He speaks of future suffering and persecution (verses 12–19, 36), the need to be ready for what will follow (verses 29–36), the dangers of false teachers or prophets who will come after him (verses 8–9), and the need to be watchful (verses 34–6).

The focus of the discourse is entirely in the future, however: there is no retrospect of the past as is common in farewell speeches. Further, Jesus' future absence is assumed rather than explicitly predicted, which further limits the sense in which this may be seen as a 'farewell speech'. Nevertheless, some of the themes of this discourse are present in the Miletus speech. Four particular points call for comment.

First, Jesus warns of future suffering and persecution (verses 12–19, 36). We have already noticed the prominence of suffering in the Miletus speech (Acts 20.19, 22–4);[157] it is prominent here too. In particular, the persecution will come both from official sources (verses 12–15) and from family and kin (verses 16–19). The mention of 'kin' (i.e. συγγενής, verse 16, a Lukanism[158]) among those who will deliver up the disciples is found in Luke alone (cf. Matt. 10.21; Mark 13.12). In addition, the fourfold opposition (parents, brothers, kin, friends) reflects a Lukan liking for groups of four.[159] This mention of 'kin' forms a conceptual parallel to the Miletus speech's statement that the Jews – Paul's own kin – oppose and persecute Paul (Acts 20.19, 22f). Luke's Paul lives out the teaching of Jesus – and this fits him to warn the elders of opposition and suffering to come in the Miletus speech.

Second, the use of μαρτύριον (verse 13) provides a link with the use of the cognate compound verb διαμαρτύρομαι (Acts 20.21, 24) describing Paul's own ministry. The meaning of μαρτύριον here is debated, for the more usual sense in the NT seems to be 'evidence, testimony' (e.g. Luke 5.14; 22.71), and μαρτυρία is more regularly

---

[156] Evans, *Saint Luke*, p. 730.   [157] § 3.5.2.

[158] Goulder, *Luke: New Paradigm*, pp. 709f, 808. The word-group (συγγενής, συγγενίς, συγγένεια) occurs once in Mark, never in Matthew, and nine times in Luke-Acts (Luke 1.38, 58, 61; 2.44; 14.12; 21.16; Acts 7.3, 14; 10.24). In the NT it is otherwise found only once in John and four times in Romans.

[159] Goulder, *Luke: New Paradigm*, pp. 709, 113f cites four Beatitudes, four Woes and the fourfold groups in Luke 6.27f, 37f; 14.12f, 21; 12.19; 17.27, all unparalleled in Matthew and Mark.

used for the act of giving testimony (e.g. John 1.7).[160] Such a distinction leads some to argue that Luke's phrase ἀποβήσεται ὑμῖν εἰς μαρτύριον should be understood as referring to a testimony for the disciples at the eschatological judgement.[161] Evans rightly observes that this proposal would be more convincing if a Greek equivalent of 'for you'[162] followed εἰς μαρτύριον. The translation 'this will give you an opportunity to testify' is most likely because of the context of verbal testimony by the disciples (verses 12, 14f) and the use of μαρτύριον in Acts 4.33.[163] With such an understanding of μαρτύριον, we observe that, just as Luke's Jesus calls his disciples to bear witness and to testify of him, so Luke's Paul in the Miletus speech is presented as having lived this out.[164]

Third, the need to be watchful and ready is emphasised in both the Miletus speech and the Lukan apocalypse.[165] The elders must be watchful of themselves (Acts 20.28: προσέχετε ἑαυτοῖς[166]), a Lukan phrase[167] used by Jesus to warn the disciples (verse 34, within a section unparalleled in Matthew and Mark[168]). Luke again presents Paul as being in the tradition of his Master.

Fourth, the future includes false teachers or prophets in both passages. Luke's version of Jesus' warning is closer to Mark than Matthew (Luke 21.8f; Mark 13.5f; Matt. 24.4f), but differs in some respects from both. Many who come 'in my name' will say ἐγώ εἰμι. This combination of the two phrases seems to point to the latter phrase being understood in the light of the former, that is that these people will come claiming Jesus' office as Messiah, and

---

[160] BAGD, pp. 493f.

[161] *EDNT*, vol. II, p. 393; Marshall, *Luke*, p. 768 sees LXX use pointing this way, citing Deut. 31.26; Hos. 2.12; Micah 1.2; 7.18; Zeph. 3.8.

[162] Presumably a dative, as Col. 4.13, although Evans, *Saint Luke*, p. 742 is not specific.

[163] *TDNT*, vol. IV, pp. 503f; *NIDNTT*, vol. III, p. 1043; Trites, *NT Concept of Witness*, pp. 128, 131; Nolland, *Luke 18:35–24:53*, p. 996; Goulder, *Luke: New Paradigm*, p. 708; Fitzmyer, *Luke X–XXIV*, p. 1340; Stein, *Luke*, p. 517; Schneider, *Lukas*, p. 420; Bock, *Luke,* vol. II, pp. 1669f.

[164] Johnson, *Luke*, p. 322 sees Acts 20.26 (among other passages in Acts) as a fulfilment of the opportunity to bear witness predicted by Jesus here.

[165] Barrett, *Acts,* vol. II, p. 964, following Rackham, *Acts*, p. 383.

[166] The parallel with Acts 20.28 is noted by Johnson, *Luke*, p. 328; Tannehill, *Narrative Unity,* vol. II, p. 261; Stein, *Luke*, p. 346; Jervell, *Apostelgeschichte*, p. 512.

[167] See n. 152 (above) for evidence that the phrase is Lukan, plus Nolland, *Luke 18:35–24:53*, p. 1012; Evans, *Saint Luke*, p. 762.

[168] Schweizer, *Luke*, p. 322. Nolland, *Luke 18:35–24:53*, p. 1012 suggests that vv. 34–6 should be seen as a Lukan replacement for Mark 13.33–7.

therefore Matthew has correctly understood ἐγώ εἰμι to mean, 'I am the Messiah.'[169] Paul, similarly, wants the elders of Ephesus to be alert to the 'wolves' who will come after him, whose characteristic will be distortion of the truth, that is, false teaching (Acts 20.29f; cf. Luke 10.3f[170]). Again, Paul gives a similar warning to that of his Lord – and Luke thereby hints that we may conclude that Paul is in the authentic tradition of Jesus.

As in Luke 12 and 22, it is not simply that one or two parallels with the Miletus speech occur, but the clustering of several parallels implies that it is no accident. Luke is drawing his readers' attention to the requirement that the servant is as the Master, in consistency of both lifestyle and leadership, expressed particularly in the parallels between Luke 21 and Paul's teaching role in the Miletus speech.

4.5   Briefer passages

Finally, four briefer passages in Luke's Gospel merit comment.

4.5.1   Luke 7.38, 44

The story of the woman (Luke 7.36–50) offers a fascinating series of parallels to the Miletus meeting in connection with weeping and kissing. Three words used in the Lukan story form the links with Paul's meeting with the elders: δάκρυον, κλαίω and καταφιλέω.

It is debated whether the Lukan story should be considered part of the Lukan *Sondergut*[171] or a Lukan adaptation of material he has derived from elsewhere.[172] There are both similarities and differences between the stories found in Mark 14.3–9; Matt. 26.6–13; Luke 7.36–50 and John 12.1–8.[173] In the event, this issue is not decisive for our study, since all of the words we shall discuss

[169] Nolland, *Luke 18:35–24:53*, p. 991; Evans, *Saint Luke*, p. 308; Ernst, *Lukas*, p. 555; Stein, *Luke*, p. 513; Marshall, *Luke*, p. 763; *contra* Ellis, *Luke*, p. 243; Fitzmyer, *Luke X–XXIV*, pp. 817, 1336 – the latter two see the warning as vaguer, against people who claim to be Jesus' representative.

[170] Discussed in § 4.5.3.

[171] Schneider, *Lukas*, p. 176; Fitzmyer, *Luke X–XXIV*, p. 684; Stein, *Luke*, p. 235; Bock, *Luke*, vol. I, p. 690; Johnson, *Luke*, p. 128; Evans, *Saint Luke*, p. 360; Nolland, *Luke 1–9:20*, p. 352.

[172] Elliott, 'Anointing of Jesus'; Goulder, *Luke: New Paradigm*, pp. 398–401.

[173] Ably documented in Fitzmyer, *Luke X–XXIV*, p. 684; Elliott, 'Anointing of Jesus', p. 15; Bock, *Luke*, vol. I, pp. 689–91.

are peculiar to the Lukan account, so that they at least provide evidence of Lukan redaction.

Δάκρυον is very rare in Luke-Acts: it only occurs here (Luke 7.38, 44) and in the Miletus speech (Acts 20.19, 31).[174] The tears of the woman here are not 'light whimpering' (Bock) but enough for the feet of Jesus to need drying.[175] Indeed, the verbs of verse 38 have continuous aspects, implying that she goes on doing the various things.[176] She is overcome by the occasion and can no longer hold back her tears.[177]

Κλαίω is a Lukanism[178] and is echoed by the related noun κλαυθμός (Acts 20.37) recording the reaction of the elders to Paul's address. Καταφιλέω is another Lukanism,[179] even though not a very common word in Luke-Acts, and the only place in Acts where it is used is in recording the elders kissing Paul (Acts 20.37).[180]

But what is the meaning of the weeping and kissing in Luke 7? The tears of the woman may indicate her penitence or her joy at her (antecedent) forgiveness.[181] The latter seems more likely for two reasons. First, the perfect tenses of ἀφίημι (verses 47, 48) imply that the woman is already in a state of forgiven-ness.[182] Second, the statement of verse 47a should be understood as 'her sins ... are forgiven, as evidenced by the fact that she loved much', since the parable of the debtors (verses 41–3) and the following summary

---

[174] It is found only six times elsewhere in the NT.

[175] Bock, *Luke*, vol. I, p. 696 observes that βρέχω (v. 38) is used of rain showers elsewhere (e.g. Matt. 5.45; Jas. 5.17; confirmed in BAGD, p. 147). Evans, *Saint Luke*, p. 360 points to Ps. 6.6 LXX as an example of βρέχω used for tears.

[176] Κλαίουσα is a present participle; βρέχειν is a present infinitive; ἐξέμασσεν is imperfect indicative; κατεφίλει is imperfect indicative; ἤλειφεν is imperfect indicative (Bock, *Luke*, vol. I, p. 697 notices the imperfects; Evans, *Saint Luke*, p. 362 appears to identify the last as an aorist; the aorist would be ἤλειψεν, the form found in v. 46, after the anointing is completed).

[177] Ernst, *Lukas*, p. 256.

[178] Goulder, *Luke: New Paradigm*, p. 805. Found twice in Matthew, four times in Mark (one of which is 16.10!), eleven times in Luke and twice in Acts, thirty-nine times in the NT in total (excluding Mark 16.10).

[179] Found three times in Luke (7.38, 45; 15.20) and once in Acts (20.37), but elsewhere in the NT only at Matt. 26.49//Mark 14.45.

[180] Bock, *Luke*, vol. I, p. 697.

[181] Bailey, *Through Peasant Eyes*, p. 17f sees a further element, of anger at the inhospitality of Simon to Jesus, for he has failed to provide the normal courtesies due to a guest. Some argue that it is not clear that the washing of feet was a *normal* courtesy in this period (Marshall, *Luke*, pp. 311f; Nolland, *Luke 1–9:20*, p. 357). However, Thomas, *Footwashing*, pp. 26–56 concludes his thorough discussion of Jewish contexts, 'references to footwashing for the purpose of hospitality are very frequent' (p. 42).

[182] Bailey, *Through Peasant Eyes*, p. 17; Fitzmyer, *Luke I–IX*, p. 692.

comment (verse 47b) have the same sequence of forgiveness then love. This suggests that verse 47a ought to be understood to have a similar sequence, rather than meaning (in contradiction of the surrounding phrases) that her forgiveness was the reward for her love.[183] There are examples elsewhere of ὅτι used in this sense.[184] Significantly, a reliable character in the narrative (Jesus) gives a positive evaluation of the woman's tears (verse 44), suggesting that tears on other occasions may have a positive value too.

Paul's tears (Acts 20.19, 31) show his love for the Ephesian church (demonstrated in that he has not spared any effort to help them), as well as his sincerity and earnestness. Luke may thus be presenting Paul as a model of discipleship, a model copied from the woman commended by Jesus. Not only that, but the weeping of the elders and their kissing Paul (Acts 20.37) show the same devotion to the one who has helped them experience the forgiving love of God as the woman expresses toward Jesus. Once again, this is a suggestive link.

4.5.2   Luke 9.2

Κηρύσσω + τὴν βασιλείαν only occurs twice elsewhere in the NT (Acts 20.25; 28.31). In Luke 9.2 the disciples are sent out κηρύσσειν τὴν βασιλείαν τοῦ θεοῦ, again a rare phrase. Neither of the Markan or Matthean parallels have this phrase (Mark 6.6ff; Matt. 10.1, 7ff), which suggests that at the least the phrase represents Lukan redaction.[185]

For Luke, Jesus is the original and supreme preacher of the kingdom: Luke omits mention of the Baptist preaching about the kingdom (Luke 3.2; cf. Matt. 3.2),[186] and introduces the kingdom of God on the lips of Jesus (Luke 4.43; contrast Mark 1.38, which lacks the reference to the kingdom of God).[187] Jesus will shortly be seen preaching the kingdom of God himself (Luke 9.11).[188] Thus in

[183] Bailey, *Through Peasant Eyes*, p. 18. See also Johnson, *Luke*, pp. 127f; Marshall, *Luke*, pp. 306, 309; Tannehill, *Narrative Unity,* vol. I, pp. 95, 117f; Bock, *Luke*, vol. I, p. 703; Ellis, *Luke*, p. 122; Evans, *Saint Luke*, p. 364; Stein, *Luke*, p. 237; Nolland, *Luke 1–9:20*, p. 354.

[184] Marshall, *Luke*, p. 313 cites Luke 1.22; 6.21; 13.2; Gal. 4.6. Cf. Turner, *Grammatical Insights*, pp. 37–40.

[185] Fitzmyer, *Luke I–IX*, p. 753; Evans, *Saint Luke*, p. 395; Marshall, *Luke*, p. 352 (although the latter regards the change as not having theological significance).

[186] Conzelmann, *Theology of St Luke*, p. 23.

[187] Fitzmyer, *Luke I–IX*, pp. 154, 157, 753.

[188] Schweizer, *Luke*, p. 152.

9.2 Jesus is extending his kingdom-preaching ministry through the apostolic band, and so associating them with a central thrust of his own ministry.[189]

Luke's use of κηρύσσω + τὴν βασιλείαν to describe Paul's ministry in the Miletus speech (Acts 20.25)[190] therefore implies that Paul is also to be seen as extending the ministry of (the by now risen and exalted) Jesus, and he too is close to the heartbeat of the preaching of Jesus.

4.5.3   Luke 10.3

Both Luke 10.1ff and the Miletus address include the charging of a group with a task: in Luke the seventy(-two) and in Acts the elders of Ephesus. The link is the use of λύκος, which is only used in Luke-Acts in these two passages (Luke 10.3; Acts 20.29).[191] In both cases wolves are contrasted with the flock (Luke 10.3; Acts 20.28, 29). Luke's version of the saying differs slightly from Matthew's, using 'lamb' (ἀρήν) rather than 'sheep' (πρόβατον, Matt. 10.16),[192] which increases the sense of vulnerability of the disciples being sent out – and this seems to be the major point of the metaphor: lambs are defenceless before wolves.[193] There is thus an implicit warning in the metaphor: those being charged with the task need to beware people who are like wolves.

Luke presents Jesus and Paul using a similar metaphor to warn those who will be leaders in the mission of God – the disciples as

---

[189] Fitzmyer, *Luke I–IX*, p. 753; Tannehill, *Narrative Unity,* vol. I, pp. 81, 217.

[190] Tannehill, *Narrative Unity,* vol. I, p. 78 n. 4; Goulder, *Luke: New Paradigm*, p. 432; Evans, *Saint Luke*, p. 395; O'Toole, *Unity of Luke's Theology*, p. 76. Fitzmyer, *Luke I–IX*, p. 157 observes this parallel as well as the parallel with others in Acts who preach the kingdom of God (although not using precisely the same verb as Luke 9.2; Acts 20.25): Philip (Acts 8.12), Barnabas and Saul (Acts 14.22), and Paul himself (Acts 19.8; 28.23, 31). This reinforces the sense that Luke is presenting these people (including Paul at Miletus) as faithful instantiations of the ministry of Jesus.

[191] Marshall, *Luke*, p. 417; Evans, *Saint Luke*, p. 447; Johnson, *Acts*, p. 363. It is used only four other times in the NT (Matt. 7.15; 10.16 (parallel with Luke 10.3); John 10.12 (twice)), and only nine times in the LXX (Gen. 49.27; Prov. 28.15; Sir. 13.17; Hab. 1.8; Zeph. 3.3; Isa. 11.6; 65.25; Jer. 5.6; Ezek. 22.27).

[192] Goulder, *Luke: New Paradigm*, p. 466 suggests that Luke, editing Matthew, saw the apostles (Matt. 10.16) as sheep and the lesser disciples, the seventy, as lambs.

[193] Marshall, *Luke*, p. 417; Geldenhuys, *Luke*, p. 299. Cf. especially Isa. 11.6; 65.25; Sir. 13.17, 1 Enoch 89.14, 18–20, 55 where similar contrasts are drawn to this effect. Possibly the source of the metaphor is Jewish apocalyptic writing (Ernst, *Lukas*, p. 332; Evans, *Luke*, p. 173) or simply the Isaiah passages (Nolland, *Luke 9:21–18:34*, p. 551).

the harbingers of Jesus himself and the elders as guardians of the flock in Ephesus.

4.5.4   Luke 13.32

We note here the parallel use of τελειόω[194] in verse 32 and Acts 20.24.[195] The Lukan passage is unparalleled in the other Synoptics[196] – and it is probable that the use of the same word is no mere verbal coincidence, since both passages use the word in the context of a completion in Jerusalem (Luke 13.33; Acts 20.22[197]). This underlines the growing sense that Luke presents Paul in the Miletus speech as an exemplar of his Master, one who follows his Master all along the way of discipleship, even to suffering in Jerusalem.

4.6   Conclusion: leadership

Our examination of passages in Luke's Gospel has provided a rich seam of parallels to the Miletus speech, suggesting that Luke intends to draw attention to the parallel between Jesus and Paul at this point. Luke presents Paul as both the model of the discipleship lived and taught by Jesus, and the model of leadership in the tradition of Jesus – and this precisely in the context of expounding that leadership to the church leaders of Ephesus. Tannehill correctly asserts:[198]

> Although it is largely independent in wording, Paul's fare-well to the Ephesian elders is remarkably close to Jesus' admonitions to church leaders in basic themes, an indication that Paul is being presented as the ideal church leader who fulfils Jesus' commands and therefore is an example to others.

Therefore, the idea that in the Miletus speech Paul is being presented as embodying and passing on the model of Christian

---

[194] Cf. p. 106, noting particularly that Luke alone amongst the Synoptics uses this verb.

[195] Marshall, *Luke*, p. 572; Johnson, *Luke*, p. 218.

[196] Schneider, *Lukas*, p. 308.

[197] Thus Fitzmyer, *Luke X–XXIV*, p. 1031, who understands the 'completion' as being Jesus' arrival in the city of destiny, Jerusalem, and thus to his death, in common with Nolland, *Luke 9:21–18:34*, p. 741; Marshall, *Luke*, p. 572; Evans, *Saint Luke*, p. 562; Schneider, *Lukas*, 310; *contra* Plummer, *Luke*, p. 350; Ellis, *Luke*, p. 190, who claim the sense 'to perfect' as in Heb. 2.10; 5.9; 7.28.

[198] Tannehill, *Narrative Unity*, vol. I, p. 250.

discipleship and leadership taught and lived by Jesus has a sound exegetical basis in the text of Luke-Acts. Luke presents Paul as the personification of the teaching of Jesus. Paul passes on the teaching of Jesus to those he teaches. He follows Jesus along the path of suffering leading to Jerusalem.

The Lukan parallels to Acts 20.17–35 show a 'clustering' of themes and verbal parallels remarkably close to those found in the Miletus speech – particularly the substantial parallels in Luke 12, 21 and especially 22. This comparison has two implications for our study. First, it demonstrates the strong probability that the final form of Paul's speech owes a good deal to Luke's shaping and editing. The depth and breadth of allusions and parallels in the Gospel leave this conclusion beyond cavil.

This consideration of parallels has a second implication, namely that there is a clear concept of Christian leadership being promulgated in Luke's work, focused on the manner and 'conditions of service' (to use a modern phrase) of leadership, rather than being taken up with considerations of 'office'.[199] The shape of this understanding of leadership, which emerges from our exegetical study, can be sketched as follows.

For Luke the heart of Christian leadership is to be like Jesus, and the extent to which both the disciples and Paul do and teach what Jesus did and taught – frequently using similar vocabulary – makes this clear. Such following in the way of Jesus includes servanthood (e.g. Luke 22.24–7; Acts 20.19), for Jesus, his disciples and Paul serve others at cost to themselves, including past and future personal suffering (e.g. Luke 12.4, 11; 22.15, 28, 31f, 37; Acts 20.19–21, 22f, 27). This is why Paul calls the elders to such costly, watchful service (Acts 20.28–31). Jesus, his disciples and Paul served in humility (e.g. Luke 22.26f; Acts 20.19), valuing others' needs above their own (Luke 22.26f; Acts 20.19, 21, 22, 24, 28, 34f). They taught and testified faithfully (e.g. Luke 9.2; 12.1–53; 21.13; 22.14–38; Acts 20.20f, 24, 25, 26f, 31). This costly commitment drew out the affection of those they led (Luke 7.38, 44; Acts 20.37), as they saw the faithful ministry (Luke 12.42; Acts 20.20f, 24, 27)

---

[199] Contrast, e.g., Prast, *Presbyter und Evangelium*, whose study of the Miletus speech focuses on the question of church structures and 'office'. If the conclusions of Campbell, *The Elders* are well-founded, as we suggest they are (see p. 86 above), this suggests that πρεσβύτερος (Acts 20.17) should not be seen as an 'office', and therefore there is very much less material which might be relevant at all to a consideration of 'office' – such an idea may be anachronistic for Luke's day.

they received. Their ministry was comparable to that of a household steward, whose leadership was real, but who was also answerable to his master (e.g. Luke 12.35–48, esp. 42; Acts 20.19, 24).

The suffering which Jesus and Paul experienced are an inevitable part of Christian leadership as Luke understands it (e.g. Luke 21.12–19, 36; 22.28; Acts 20.19, 23f, 31), but should not be feared above God himself (e.g. Luke 12.4–7; Acts 20.24). Certainly, such suffering and threats from false teachers (e.g. Luke 10.3; 21.8f; Acts 20.29f) call for watchfulness (e.g. Luke 12.1, 5, 37; 21.34; Acts 20.28, 31), but in the end suffering and struggle lead purposefully to glory (e.g. Luke 13.32; Acts 20.22; Luke 22.16f, 29f; Acts 20.19).

The faithfulness of Paul and his Master is particularly seen in their approach to money and work, where Luke portrays both men living and teaching openness, generosity to others and straightforwardness (e.g. Luke 12.13–34; Acts 20.33–5). God provides for such faithful servants as he does for the birds and the flowers (Luke 12.24, 27f), but Paul also carries out the admonition of Jesus to provide for himself and others by working (Acts 20.33–5).

This represents far more than a collection of vague platitudes; it offers a dynamic, sharply focused model of Christian leadership rooted in Luke's understanding of Jesus, in contrast with other approaches to leadership available in the ancient world (Luke 22.25). A comparison with Paul's understanding in 1 Thessalonians will be instructive.

EXCURSUS 2: THE TEXT OF LUKE 22.17–20

The textual witnesses divide into three groups over the knotty problem of the text of Luke 22.17–20.[1] First, the Greek manuscripts (except D), the lage majority of the versions, and references in the early Fathers include verses 19b–20. The oldest manuscript, $\mathfrak{P}^{75}$, which Jeremias dates to AD 175–225,[2] has this reading.

Second, a shorter text which omits verses 19b–20 is found in D and some Old Latin manuscripts, dating from fourth to eighth century (a, d, ff², i, l).

Third, variations of sequence are found, some with the longer text and some the shorter. Two fifth-century Old Latin manuscripts (b, e) have verse 19a before verse 17. The Curetonian Syriac (sy^c) has 1 Corinthians 11.24 added to verse 19a. The Sinaitic Syriac (sy^s) has the sequence: verse 19, part of verse 20a (καὶ μετὰ τὸ δειπνῆσαι), verse 17, a rearranged part of verse 20b (τοῦτό ἐστιν τὸ αἷμά μου ἡ διαθήκη ἡ καινή[3]), verse 18. The Peshitta omits verses 17–18 in company with the eleventh-century l^{32}, a Boharic manuscript and two Sahidic manuscripts.

The real options for the original text are one of the first two readings, for other variants can be explained in terms of either of these. Scholarly opinion has lately come to a consensus (with some exceptions) that the longer text is original, after for some time being persuaded by Westcott and Hort's arguments that verses

---

[1] The evidence is set out fully in International Greek New Testament Project, *Luke, Part 2*, pp. 177f. Metzger, *Textual Commentary* (2nd edn), p. 149 helpfully displays the variants synoptically (based on Kenyon and Legg, 'Textual Data', pp. 284f).

[2] Jeremias, *Eucharistic Words*, p. 139.

[3] According to Metzger, *Textual Commentary* (2nd edn), p. 149; NA^27 translates the Syriac: τοῦτό μού τὸ αἷμά ἡ καινὴ διαθήκη.

19b–20 represent a so-called 'Western non-interpolation'.[4] The arguments for each reading follow.[5]

In favour of the shorter reading it is argued: (1) in general the shorter reading should be preferred;[6] (2) the shorter reading is harder because it inverts the traditional bread–cup order found in 1 Corinthians 11.24f; Matthew 26.26f; Mark 14.22–4; (3) verses 19b–20 are similar to 1 Corinthians 11.24b–25; Mark 14.24 and are an interpolation using words from those passages; (4) verses 19b–20 are a 'Western non-interpolation', i.e. one of the (nine) passages where all but the Western manuscripts have suffered interpolation;[7] (5) Luke 22.19b–20 show non-Lukan features – in particular, the lack of ἐστίν (verse 20b) and the clumsiness of placing τὸ ὑπὲρ ὑμῶν ἐκχυννόμενον (verse 20b) in the nominative if it is meant to agree with αἵματί;[8] (6) Luke's general lack of atonement theology implies that verses 19b–20 are not from his hand – for example Luke 22.27 differs from its ostensible Markan parallel (10.45) in this respect;[9] (7) Luke did not realise that the reference to τὸ πάσχα (verse 15) included the bread without using the word ἄρτος, and therefore inserted it at verse 19a: this explains the oddness of the shorter text.[10]

In favour of the longer reading it is argued: (1) the external evidence is heavily weighted towards this reading, including most Western manuscripts; (2) it is more likely that the scribe/editor of Codex Bezae eliminated a second cup than that a scribe/editor added a second cup; (3) the longer reading is more difficult because of the presence of two cups; (4) verses 15–18, 19–20 display a structural unity which suggests verses 19b–20 are original – particularly because the parallelism in verses 15–18 is incompatible with

---

[4] Westcott and Hort, *NT in the Original Greek*, 'Notes on Selected Readings', pp. 63f; for a discussion of 'Western non-interpolations' see Metzger, *Textual Commentary* (1st edn), pp. 191–3.

[5] See the excellent summary in Metzger, *Textual Commentary* (1st edn), pp. 173–7. For good bibliographies of major treatments, see Marshall, *Luke*, p. 801; Fitzmyer, *Luke X–XXIV*, pp. 1405f; Nolland, *Luke 18:35–24:53*, p. 1040; Marshall, *Last Supper*, pp. 36–8.

[6] Metzger, *Text of the NT*, pp. 120, 209f; *contra* Elliott and Moir, *Manuscripts*, p. 33.

[7] Fitzmyer, *Luke X–XXIV*, p. 1388. The passages are: Matt. 27.49; Luke 22.19b–20; 24.3, 6, 12, 36, 40, 51, 52 (Westcott and Hort, *NT in the Original Greek*, pp. 175–7; Metzger, *Textual Commentary* (1st edn), p. 192 n. 2).

[8] Chadwick, 'Shorter Text', p. 252.

[9] Marshall, *Luke*, p. 800; Nolland, *Luke 18:35–24:53*, p. 1041.

[10] Chadwick, 'Shorter Text', pp. 257f.

the presence of verse 19a (if the shorter reading is original);[11]
(5) the similarity between verses 19b–20 and 1 Corinthians 11.24b–
25; Mark 14.24 is more apparent than real, for the verbal correspondence is not exact;[12] (6) Acts 20.28 shows that Luke has a
'ransom' theology, even if not frequently expressed explicitly;[13]
(7) the actual eucharistic words were removed from editions of
Luke for non-Christians to protect the eucharist from profanation,
and this resulted in the longer text being abbreviated;[14] (8) features
in the rest of Luke 22 presuppose the presence of verses 19b–20:[15]
(i) πλὴν ἰδού ('but behold', verse 21) is a strong adversative
referring back to ὑπὲρ ὑμῶν (verse 20), and it would be incon-
gruous following verse 19a; (ii) the verb διατίθημι (verse 29, twice)
develops the reference to καινή διαθήκη (verse 20); (iii) τοῦτο τὸ
ποτήριον (verse 42) refers back to the same phrase in verse 20.

It is clear that both the longer and shorter readings have
difficulties, but the overwhelming weight of the manuscript evidence is a strong factor, along with the possibility of scribal
misunderstanding or deliberate change because of a different
liturgical practice in the scribe's church or because of unfamiliarity
with the passover practice of more than one cup.[16] The editors of
UBS[4] were therefore right, in my judgement, to include the longer
reading in their text and to increase the 'rating' of the longer
reading from C (UBS[3]) to B.

[11] Nolland, *Luke 18:35–24:53*, p. 1041; Ellis, *Luke*, p. 255.
[12] Chadwick, 'Shorter Text', p. 252.
[13] Nolland, *Luke 18:35–24:53*, p. 1041. See § 3.5.4.
[14] Jeremias, *Eucharistic Words*, p. 158. However, Chadwick, 'Shorter Text', p. 255 observes, 'it is a severe difficulty that the hypothetical abbreviator left untouched xxii.19a containing the very *mysterium fidei*, "This is my body"'.
[15] Ellis, *Luke*, p. 255.
[16] Ellis, *Luke*, p. 256.

5

THE MILETUS SPEECH AND 1 THESSALONIANS

5.1 Introduction

How Pauline is the Miletus speech? We shall now consider this question by evaluating possible parallels to the speech in one Pauline letter.[1] Several scholars have drawn attention to the numerous parallels in the Pauline letters to individual points in the speech,[2] but a systematic comparison of the speech with an individual letter has not previously been made.

5.1.1 Why 1 Thessalonians?

At first glance the Miletus speech and 1 Thessalonians look different; in particular, the eschatological material in the letter (1 Thess. 4.13–5.11) has no obvious parallel in the speech, and the letter is about five times the length of the speech.[3] In addition, the occasions of the two appear different: the Miletus speech has a strong 'farewell' colouring, which 1 Thessalonians lacks, as a pastoral letter from the founders of a church to their converts. So why consider this letter for possible parallels to the Miletus speech?

First, since our concern is to see how *Pauline* the speech is, it is vital to work with a document which is acknowledged to be from the hand of the apostle. As we shall see, this is not in dispute for 1 Thessalonians. This concern eliminates two obvious candidates for parallels, namely Ephesians and 2 Timothy, since the authorship of both is disputed.[4] In both cases one natural link is with

---

[1] See the justification for limiting our discussion to one letter, § 2.5.1.

[2] See § 1.3.1.

[3] The UBS[4]/NA[27] text has 1580 words in 1 Thessalonians and 342 in the Miletus speech (vv. 18b–35); there are 410 words in the whole scene, vv. 17–38.

[4] As is the case (to varying degrees) also for Philippians, Colossians, 2 Thessalonians, 1 Timothy and Titus, although the links with Ephesus are not as clear in these cases.

Ephesus,[5] and 2 Timothy has a 'farewell' sense similar to the Miletus speech.[6] This is not to say that it would not be helpful and valuable to study these letters in parallel with the Miletus speech:[7] simply that it would not be recognised as providing the Pauline comparison we seek.

Second, 1 Thessalonians is pastorally oriented and full of the personal concern and practical instruction of the apostle and his companions (e.g. 2.7f, 11f, 17–20; 3.1–13; 4.1–5.11); in this respect it is not dissimilar in atmosphere to the Miletus speech, where Paul speaks as a pastor to pastors (especially verses 28–35). This link provides a *prima facie* reason for seeking possible parallels. This consideration means that a clearly polemical letter, such as Galatians, is inappropriate for our study.

Third, there are some reasonably clear parallels between the speech and 1 Thessalonians which suggest that further study of the links might be profitable. In particular, there are numerous references to Paul's past conduct in both (1 Thess. 1.5; 2.1–12; 2.17–3.3; Acts 20.18–21, 27, 31, 33f), and several references to suffering (1 Thess. 2.2, 14–16; 3.3f, 7; Acts 20.19, 23f, 29f).

Fourth, 1 Thessalonians has material on leadership (5.12ff), which is evidently a, if not the, central concern of the Miletus speech.

Taken together, these points suggest that 1 Thessalonians is a good place to search for parallels to the Miletus speech, as we listen to Paul speaking to a young church and its leaders.

5.1.2   Our approach to parallels

We shall consider potential parallels between the Miletus speech and 1 Thessalonians from two directions. First, we shall look in 1 Thessalonians for material which parallels the key themes from Acts 20.18–35 identified above.[8] Then we shall consider whether there are other themes or ideas in the letter echoed in the speech. If such parallels exist, they may be significant as evidence for Luke's understanding of Paul.

[5] If ἐν Ἐφέσῳ is original in Eph. 1.1 (which is doubtful), or if the Ephesian church is part of the group of churches to whom the letter is addressed (which is possible, perhaps probable). For discussion, see Caird, *Letters from Prison*, pp. 9–11; Martin, *Ephesians, Colossians and Philemon*, pp. 3–6; Barth, *Ephesians*, vol. I, pp. 10–12, 67; Lincoln, *Ephesians*, pp. lxxxi–lxxxiii, 1–4; Schnackenburg, *Ephesians*, pp. 29, 40f.
[6] e.g. 4.6–8.   [7] Cf. chapter 6.   [8] §§ 3.5.1–4.

If the picture that emerges contains uses of similar vocabulary or synonyms in connection with similar themes, this at least suggests that Luke and Paul inhabited related thought-worlds. If not, it places a question mark over Luke's understanding of Paul; for if the Miletus speech, where Paul is presented as addressing Christians, were to bear little similarity in themes and vocabulary to a Pauline letter such as 1 Thessalonians, it would be harder to see Luke's portrait of Paul throughout Acts as consonant with the portrait emerging from the Pauline letters.

5.2   Orientation to 1 Thessalonians

In considering parallels between the Miletus speech and 1 Thessalonians we need first to review briefly the background to the letter, in order to give a context to our detailed study. This involves the authorship, date, provenance and exigency(-ies) of the letter.

5.2.1   Authorship

1 Thessalonians remains a letter generally recognised as Pauline, to the extent that Wanamaker writes in 1990, 'no contemporary scholars of repute seem to doubt the authentic Pauline character of the letter'.[9] The letter's evident early eschatology would be unthinkable for a later pseudepigraphic document.[10] As we shall see,[11] it can be placed – both historically and in provenance – with considerable confidence within the ministry of Paul.

A question, however, does arise which is of interest for our considerations of parallels below, namely the use of the plural in virtually the entire letter, in combination with the opening address (1.1).

The use of the plural

The letter is sent from Παῦλος καὶ Σιλουανὸς καὶ Τιμόθεος (1.1). It is noticeable that plural verbs are used throughout, with the sole

---

[9] Wanamaker, *Thessalonians*, p. 17. This is also true of those who see 1 Thessalonians as composite, e.g. Richard, *Thessalonians*, pp. 11–19; Schmithals, *Paul and Gnostics*, pp. 123–218. For summaries and cogent critiques of Schmithals, see Best, *Thessalonians*, pp. 31–5; Marshall, *Thessalonians*, pp. 15f.

[10] Best, *Thessalonians*, p. 23 observes, 'Would a later writer allow the implication in 4.13–18 that Paul would be alive at the parousia?'

[11] § 5.2.2.

exceptions of 2.18; 3.5; 5.27. Further, the personal pronoun ἐγώ is used only once, in contrast to ἡμεῖς (49 times). Granted that in other letters generally accepted as authentic Paul opens with a salutation from himself and others (e.g. 1 Cor. 1.1; 2 Cor. 1.1) and then continues in the singular, how should the plurals of 1 Thessalonians be understood?

Askwith's discussion of this question remains comprehensive, and it is noticeable that Best (writing more than sixty years later) adds little to Askwith's arguments, save responding to computer-based analyses which were not, of course, available in Askwith's time.[12]

Askwith examines the uses of the singular and shows in each case that there is a good explanation for such usage. At 2.18 the emphatic ἐγώ is particularly marked by the presence of μέν without an answering δέ,[13] and should not be seen as Paul setting himself over against Silvanus and Timothy (i.e. he wanted to see them but his associates did not), but rather Paul is stressing that what was true of them was particularly true of him – he wanted to visit the city again in person.[14] In other words, Askwith understands μέν as being used absolutely, in the sense 'indeed'.[15]

Regarding 3.5, Paul is here impressing upon the Thessalonian Christians his personal care for them,[16] not least since he was the one left alone while Timothy and Silvanus were away.[17] It also suggests that Paul was the senior of the writers. This implies that the letter has Paul's *imprimatur*, as the senior missionary.

Askwith understands the 'sign-off' phrase in 5.27 in precisely this sense, as Paul concluding the letter with something from his own hand (cf. Gal. 6.11; 1 Cor. 16.21). It would be natural to do this in the first person singular.[18] Askwith therefore concludes that Paul's letters really are his own, even when written in partnership.

The importance of this conclusion is that we are correct in understanding 1 Thessalonians as a Pauline letter, for Paul surely

---

[12] Askwith, 'I and We'; Best, *Thessalonians*, pp. 25–9.

[13] Richard, *Thessalonians*, p. 130.

[14] Askwith, 'I and We', p. 155.

[15] Similarly Best, *Thessalonians*, p. 126; Bruce, *Thessalonians*, p. 55; Robertson, *Grammar*, p. 1151; BDF, § 447. Contrast Wanamaker, *Thessalonians*, p. 121.

[16] Askwith, 'I and We', p. 157f.

[17] Marshall, *Thessalonians*, p. 93.

[18] Askwith, 'I and We', p. 159; similarly Best, *Thessalonians*, p. 246; Bruce, *Thessalonians*, p. 135; Marshall, *Thessalonians*, p. 165; Wanamaker, *Thessalonians*, p. 208.

would not have put his name to a letter with which he disagreed. Further, as the senior partner, it is likely that Paul took the lead in composing the letter. The involvement of Silvanus and Timothy would have been real (and may be a partial explanation of the relative lack of distinctively Pauline vocabulary at points in the letter[19]) – and we must allow that they also would not have put their names to the letter had they disagreed with its substance – but nevertheless Paul's mind is the driving force of the letter.[20] Accordingly, we are justified in the use of 1 Thessalonians as a source for *Pauline* parallels to the Miletus speech.

5.2.2   Date

In discussing issues of date and occasion, we need to be aware of the potential dangers of 'mirror-reading' a text to deduce information which it does not directly give. 'Mirror-reading' examines a text in order to understand the nature of the situation to which it responds, including the identity and views of any opponents of the writer(s). The dangers of 'mirror-reading' have been highlighted by Barclay, who observes a number of pitfalls:[21] the need to make choices as to which parts of the text under consideration reveal the views of the opponents, while still seeking a view that explains the whole text; the danger of understanding every statement in the text as being directed against an opposing view of the opponents; the distorting effect of polemics on the nature, accuracy and objectivity of the language used by the author; and the danger of latching onto particular words as 'catchwords' of the opponents and then hanging a thesis on flimsy evidence. These dangers are undoubtedly real, and Barclay illustrates them well from the study of Galatians.

A letter such as 1 Thessalonians, which is not obviously polemical, has the further danger that opponents of Paul may be assumed to be present, and the text may then be interpreted in the light of that assumption. This is a difficult point on which to find the right balance, but it is vital both that the undoubted presence of opponents of Paul in some churches (of which Galatians is a clear example) should not become an assumption in every church, and

---

[19] Best, *Thessalonians*, p. 23; cf. Bruce, *Thessalonians*, pp. xxxiif; Marshall, *Thessalonians*, p. 21; more fully, Marshall, 'Pauline Theology'.

[20] Wanamaker, *Thessalonians*, p. 121; *contra* Prior, *Paul the Letter-Writer*, pp. 37–45, 57–9.

[21] Barclay, 'Mirror-reading', pp. 79–83.

that we should look at the text carefully for evidence of conflict, without assuming that all was sweetness and light in the earliest churches.

The date of the letter

The traditional solution to the date and occasion of 1 Thessalonians is that it was written shortly after the initial visit to the city by Paul, Silas and Timothy. Its competitors are an early date (41–44)[22] or a much later (third 'missionary journey') date.[23] Neither fits the evidence as well as the traditional dating.

The shortness of the interval between the initial visit and the letter is suggested by: (1) 2.17, which indicates a short gap; (2) the lack of description of events between Paul's visit and the writing of the letter (excluding Satan's hindrance, 2.18, and Timothy's visit, 3.2); (3) the vivid language used of the initial visit and Paul's oral teaching (e.g. 3.4; 4.2); (4) the indication that Paul sent Timothy soon after the initial visit and that the letter is now being sent very shortly after Timothy's return (3.1–6); (5) if the interval had been long, Paul would surely have had fuller information about the Thessalonian situation, rather than writing as he does in 3.1.[24]

The 'fit' between the information of 1 Thessalonians and Acts 17f at this point is good,[25] including agreement that Paul first came to Thessalonica from Philippi (Acts 16.40; 1 Thess. 2.1f), where he had been humiliated (Acts 16.22–4; 1 Thess. 2.2); that Paul was opposed in Thessalonica by Jews who also persecuted the church there (Acts 17.5ff; 1 Thess. 2.2); that Paul visited Athens after Thessalonica (Acts 17.16; 1 Thess. 3.1); and that Paul sent Timothy to Thessalonica (Acts 17.14f; 18.5; 1 Thess. 3.2). This combination

[22] Lüdemann, *Paul*, pp. 157–78; Donfried, '1 Thessalonians, Acts and Early Paul', pp. 4–8, both arguing on the basis of the equation of the edict of Claudius (Acts 18.2) with that mentioned by Suetonius (*Caesar Claudius* 25), and the belief that Acts 18.1ff represents a conflation of two distinct visits by Paul to Corinth. For response, see Bruce, 'Chronological Questions', 280–2.

[23] Thus Schmithals, *Paul and Gnostics*, pp. 123–218, whose argument involves postulating numerous (Pauline) fragments which were reassembled into our 1 and 2 Thessalonians. His study is of a piece with his theory that Gnostics were everywhere opponents of Paul. For critique, see Best, *Thessalonians,* pp. 10f; Marshall, *Thessalonians*, pp. 22f; Wanamaker, *Thessalonians*, pp. 34f; Jewett, *Thessalonian Correspondence*, pp. 33–6; Johanson, *To All the Brethren*, pp. 169–72.

[24] Best, *Thessalonians*, pp. 8f; Bruce, *Thessalonians*, pp. xxxiv–xxxvi; Marshall, *Thessalonians*, pp. 20f; Kümmel, *Introduction*, pp. 257–60.

[25] Johnson, *Acts*, pp. 308f; cf. Riesner, *Frühzeit*, pp. 325f.

leads many to suppose that 1 Thessalonians was written from Corinth, which was where Timothy returned after his visit to Thessalonica.[26] The result is a relative dating of the letter within months, if not weeks, of the initial visit to Thessalonica.[27]

Some point to tensions between the Acts account and the letters,[28] and therefore suggest that the accounts are incompatible. The length of the initial stay appears different, since a cursory reading of Acts suggests a visit of three to four weeks (Acts 17.2), whereas the letter implies a longer visit, because the missionaries needed to work (1 Thess. 2.9), and there was time for the news of the Thessalonians' Christian standing to spread far and wide (1 Thess. 1.7f; 4.10).[29] In addition, the letter implies that Timothy had been with Paul in Athens (1 Thess. 3.1f), whereas Acts 17.14; 18.5 do not mention a visit by Timothy to Athens. Finally, the account in Acts implies that there were Jewish and Gentile converts (Acts 17.4), whereas the reference to 'turning to God from idols' (1 Thess. 1.9) suggests only Gentile converts.[30]

None of these objections is decisive. A careful reading shows that neither Acts nor the letter defines the length of the initial visit closely: the reference to 'three sabbaths' is most probably simply a record of the initial evangelism Paul conducted in the synagogue.[31] Timothy and Silas may have visited Paul in Athens after Paul's first arrival (Acts 17.14f), which would give added poignancy to Paul choosing *again* to lose his companion Timothy (1 Thess. 3.1f), having also sent Silas off elsewhere.[32] The converts of Thessalonica are implied by Acts to be largely Gentile (note the contrast between τινες and πλῆθος πολύ ... οὐκ ὀλίγαι, Acts 17.4), even though Luke's concentration is on ministry in the synagogue.[33]

To go further with dating, the initial visit to Corinth (Acts 18.1–18) can be dated with considerable confidence by the use of an inscription addressed to the citizens of Delphi.[34] This dates

---

[26] Best, *Thessalonians*, p. 11; Marshall, *Thessalonians*, p. 21; Bruce, *Thessalonians*, p. xxxv; Morris, *Thessalonians* (revised edn.), p. 12; Jewett, *Thessalonian Correspondence*, pp. 52f; *pace* Lüdemann, *Paul*, pp. 204f, 238.

[27] Riesner, *Frühzeit*, p. 325 estimates no more than six months.

[28] Best, *Thessalonians*, pp. 5–7; Kümmel, *Introduction*, pp. 257f.

[29] Further, money came from Philippi 'more than once' (Phil. 4.15f), perhaps suggesting a longer stay.

[30] Haenchen, *Acts*, p. 507.

[31] Malherbe, *Paul and the Thessalonians*, pp. 13f; Marshall, *Thessalonians*, p. 5.

[32] Marshall, *Thessalonians*, p. 6; Best, *Thessalonians*, pp. 131f.

[33] Johnson, *Acts*, pp. 309f.

[34] *SIG*³, 801D; text and translation in Conzelmann, *Acts*, pp. 152f; translation

Paul's visit to Corinth to the period 50–52, on the basis of Gallio's proconsulship being dated 51–52. Accordingly, the initial visit to Thessalonica would be between one and two years earlier, dated at 49–50, and the letter would be written in 50–51, shortly after the visit.[35]

5.2.3 Occasion

The immediate 'occasion' of the letter was Timothy's return to Paul following his visit to Thessalonica (3.6ff), but we shall seek an understanding of the situation which gave rise to the letter, as an aid to better understanding of key themes and ideas in 1 Thessalonians.

The nature of the letter

The function of the letter was to serve *in lieu* of a visit by Paul.[36] Paul expresses his desire to visit (2.17f); the frustration of this desire was dealt with by sending Timothy (3.1–3, 6) and then by writing. Paul continues to express the desire to visit (3.10f), and we may therefore take it that 1 Thessalonians is, in Paul's mind, a temporary substitute for his personal presence and 'a means of pastoral care given at a distance'.[37]

The news from Timothy has encouraged Paul that the Thessalonian Christians are staying the course in spite of persecution (3.6–9) – the sense of relief in Paul's words here is tangible. But what form did the information to which Paul responds take? It could have been a letter from the Thessalonians to Paul; the arguments in favour of this are as follows.

and discussion in Barrett (ed.), *NT Background*, pp. 51f; see also Lüdemann, *Paul*, pp. 163f; Jewett, *Dating Paul's Life*, pp. 38–40; Hemer, 'Observations', pp. 6–9; Hemer and Gempf, *Book of Acts*, pp. 251–3.

[35] Frame, *Thessalonians*, p. 9; Milligan, *Thessalonians*, pp. xxxvf; Plummer, *Thessalonians*, p. xiii; Moore, *Thessalonians*, pp. 6f; Schürmann and Egenolf, *Thessalonians*, p. xi; Jewett, *Thessalonian Correspondence*, pp. 59f; Morris, *Thessalonians* (revised edn.), pp. 12–14; Best, *Thessalonians*, pp. 7–11; Bruce, *Thessalonians*, p. xxxv; Hemer and Gempf, *Book of Acts*, p. 270; Carson, Moo and Morris, *Introduction*, pp. 347f.

[36] Bruce, *Thessalonians*, p. xxi; Best, *Thessalonians*, p. 14; Malherbe, 'Did the Thessalonians?', pp. 252f; Koester, '1 Thessalonians', p. 35.

[37] Richard, *Thessalonians*, p. 31. The letter could be seen as a Pauline *speech*, for it would be read aloud to the church assembled (Walton, 'What Has Aristotle', p. 249; Walton, 'Rhetorical Criticism', p. 6; more fully Botha, 'Verbal Art').

First, the use of περὶ δέ (4.9, 13; 5.1) is compared with the use of that phrase in 1 Corinthians (e.g. 1 Cor. 7.1, 25; 8.1; 12.1), where until recently there has been a consensus that it refers to a letter sent by the Corinthians to Paul, particularly because he writes Περὶ δὲ ὧν ἐγράψατε.[38] Accordingly, the phrase should be understood to have a similar meaning here.[39]

Second, the transitions at 4.9, 13; 5.1 would seem abrupt were they not responses to specific points put to Paul. Faw believes that Paul seems reluctant to discuss the topics of brotherly love and the times and seasons (4.9; 5.1), and therefore understands these verses to indicate that Paul is writing in response to a specific question.[40]

Third, the use of καί at 2.13 may indicate that Paul is adding his own thanksgivings to those of the Thessalonians in their letter; and the frequent use of 'you know' (in the phrases οἴδατε γάρ (2.1; 3.3; 4.2; 5.2), καθὼς οἴδατε (1.5; 2.2, 5; 3.4) and καθάπερ οἴδατε (2.11)) can be seen to relate to the points mentioned by the Thessalonians in their letter.[41]

Fourth, ancient epistolographic conventions may point to a prior letter from the Thessalonians.[42] Malherbe cites the expression of longing for absent friends; the convention that a letter of friendship would stress the constant remembrance in which the friends were held; the use of περὶ δέ (although with caution[43]); the reference to the correspondent's needs; the expression of joy on receipt of a letter; thanks to the gods for the letter received; and the use of a letter 'as a surrogate for one's own physical presence'.[44]

Malherbe suggests that Paul may have sent a (now lost) letter with Timothy to the Thessalonians, to which their letter was in part a reply.[45] He conjectures this on the basis of an analysis of 2.17–3.10 in parallel with ancient epistolographic conventions, arguing that: in 1 Thessalonians 1–3 Paul has used features of the style of

[38] 1 Cor. 7.1. See recently Fee, *1 Corinthians*, pp. 266f; however, Mitchell, 'Concerning περὶ δέ' asserts that περὶ δέ merely introduces the next topic in a letter, a topic which is readily known to author and reader, without any clarity as to the source of the topic. This clearly limits the cogency of this argument in 1 Thessalonians.

[39] Cf. Faw, 'Writing of First Thessalonians', 220f; similarly Frame, *Thessalonians*, p. 140; Bicknell, *Thessalonians*, p. 40; Jewett, *Thessalonian Correspondence*, p. 92.

[40] Faw, 'Writing of First Thessalonians', pp. 221f.

[41] Best, *Thessalonians*, p. 14.

[42] Malherbe, 'Did the Thessalonians?', pp. 250–5.

[43] Malherbe, 'Did the Thessalonians?', p. 251.

[44] Malherbe, 'Did the Thessalonians?', p. 252.

[45] Malherbe, 'Did the Thessalonians?', p. 248f.

the 'friendly letter' to express his feelings towards them; the expressions of loneliness come from the same standard form; and the mention of himself by name (2.18), unusual in the body of a letter, finds its counterpart in such 'friendly letters'.

Malherbe does not overstate his case, pointing out that the statements noted also fit naturally with what is known of Paul's circumstances at the time of writing 1 Thessalonians; and that the conventions described have not been seen in a letter where the writer is seeking to re-establish contact after separation, as Paul is doing in 1 Thessalonians (albeit a brief separation).[46]

Four points may be made in response. First, the use of περὶ δέ need not carry the sense which Faw proposes. Malherbe and Mitchell's caution seems appropriate – accepting the use in 1 Corinthians as referring to a letter from Corinth need not imply that other uses of περὶ δέ have the same sense in other places without other evidence for a letter.[47]

Second, the alleged abruptness of the transitions at 4.9, 13; 5.1 may have the implication that Paul is responding to questions, but it does not show whether the questions were written or oral, possibly relayed by Timothy.[48]

Third, the arguments from the use of καί in 2.13[49] and the references to 'you know' are weak.[50] In each case the texts can more naturally be taken in other ways,[51] particularly referring back to their knowledge of Paul and his teaching from his earlier visit (as seems natural in every case cited). In any case this argument, if valid, would not demonstrate whether the communication with Paul was written or oral.

Fourth, Malherbe's criticism of the case for a letter from Paul to the Thessalonians taken by Timothy also applies to his own

[46] Malherbe, 'Did the Thessalonians?', p. 249.

[47] Best, *Thessalonians*, p. 15; Mitchell, 'Concerning περὶ δέ', 253f. Johanson, *To All the Brethren*, p. 51 n. 266, citing Aristotle, *Poetics* 6.1 (περὶ μὲν οὖν τῆς ἐν ἑξαμέτροις μιμητικῆς καὶ περὶ κωμῳδίας ὕστερον ἐροῦμεν, 'with the representation of life in hexameter verse and with comedy we will deal later'); Isocrates, *Panegyric* 15 (περὶ δὲ τῶν κοινῶν, 'but as to our public interests'); Josephus, *Contra Apionem* 2.291 (περὶ τῶν νόμων οὐκ ἐδέσε λόγου πλείονος, 'upon the laws it was unnecessary to expatiate'); Diogenes Laertius 8.67 (περὶ δὲ τοῦ θανάτου διάφορός ἐστιν αὐτοῦ λόγος, 'as to his death different accounts are given').

[48] Best, *Thessalonians*, p. 15.

[49] Holtz, *Erste Brief*, p. 97 n. 435 argues that the second καί in 2.13 should be seen as resumptive, indicating that Paul is adding further reasons for thanksgiving to those expressed in 1.2. So also Wanamaker, *Thessalonians*, p. 110.

[50] Best, *Thessalonians*, pp. 14, 110.

[51] See Best, *Thessalonians*, ad loc.

arguments from ancient epistolographic conventions for a letter from the Thessalonians to Paul. By demonstrating a parallel (if his case is accepted) he has not necessarily demonstrated that Paul has *in this case* followed the conventions. The use of phraseology found elsewhere as epistolographic clichés may be patient of another explanation if, as in 1 Thessalonians, it also seems apposite to the circumstances of the author of the letter.

We may conclude that there are two certain sources for Paul's knowledge of the Thessalonian situation: his own memory of the situation when he left Thessalonica, some weeks or months previously, and the information brought by Timothy on his return. If Timothy was the bearer of a letter or spoken message from Thessalonica, we may add that as a source, but one that would inevitably be mediated through Timothy's explanatory glosses; for it is inconceivable that Paul would not enquire of Timothy for expansion and explanation of particular points (and broader issues) within any letter or oral message from Thessalonica.

To these sources we may add that Paul, by this time, was a church-planting missionary of not inconsiderable experience. Accordingly, he would have knowledge of likely issues that would arise in a fairly new congregation, such as that in Thessalonica. This knowledge would contribute to the concerns expressed in his writing 1 Thessalonians.

Exigencies of the letter

By the exigency(-ies) of 1 Thessalonians we understand the particular thing (or things) which prompted its writing.[52] It is a situation which calls forth a response aimed at changing it.

Any rhetorical situation will have at least one controlling exigency, which becomes the organising principle of the response of the speaker or writer. This exigency leads to the audience being addressed and the change desired as a result of the rhetorical response.[53] It is clearly possible for there to be more than one controlling exigency in a rhetorical situation, and this is certainly possible in the case of 1 Thessalonians, which ranges over a lot of territory. Nevertheless, it is possible that one main exigency may be

---

[52] Bitzer, 'Rhetorical Situation', p. 252; cf. Kennedy, *NT Interpretation*, p. 35.
[53] Bitzer, 'Rhetorical Situation', p. 253.

behind the whole letter, and we shall consider such 'global' explanations.

Four main exigencies have been proposed, sometimes with underlying overall explanations of the situation of the Thessalonian Christians. These centre around the eschatological material, persecution, Pauline self-defence, and ecstatic manifestations in Thessalonica.

Eschatology

That there was confusion over eschatology in Thessalonica is widely agreed. However, the precise nature of the confusion or misunderstanding is not agreed. There are elements in the text which suggest issues that were around in the young Thessalonian church.

The most prominent is the death of believers before the parousia.[54] It is likely that Paul believed there to be confusion, or at least concern, about the situation of believers who had died (4.13ff), most probably as a result of information or questions given to him via Timothy.

Johanson believes that the death of believers before the parousia is *the* controlling exigency of the letter and that other features of 1 Thessalonians follow from this. He understands this concern on the part of the Thessalonian Christians to raise potential questions about the reliability of Paul and his co-workers, as well as casting a shadow over the Thessalonians' hope and faith. These concerns give rise to an emphasis on establishing the ethos of Paul and his co-workers, particularly in the earlier part of 1 Thessalonians.[55]

Wanamaker likewise believes there to have been eschatological confusion, particularly concerning Christians who had died. He sees the use of δὲ ... περί (4.13) as indicating an issue that the Thessalonians had raised with Paul via Timothy. Paul's response indicates either that he had been misunderstood by the Thessalonians or that he had not explained fully the implications of his eschatological teaching.[56]

Jewett sees the church in Thessalonica as millenarian, by which

---

[54] Frame, *Thessalonians*, pp. 10f; Morris, *Thessalonians* (revised edn.), p. 9; Richard, *Thessalonians*, pp. 231f; Jewett, *Thessalonian Correspondence*, pp. 94–100.

[55] Johanson, *To All the Brethren*, p. 54. He understands the 'defence' of 2.1ff as a prophylactic response to potential criticisms of Paul and his colleagues.

[56] Wanamaker, *Thessalonians*, p. 62; cf. Bruce, *Thessalonians*, p. xxxvii.

he means 'religious movements which expect the total transforma-
tion of this world to occur in connection with a cataclism [*sic*] in the
near future'.[57] Thus he views 4.13ff as responding to the difficulty
caused by the Thessalonian Christians' (mistaken) belief that there
would be no death for Christians, and their lack of any assurance
of resurrection after death.[58] He further reads 5.1ff as aiming to
restore a proper sense of urgency in the face of the Thessalonians
relaxing too much. Paul underlines the unpredictability of the time
of the parousia in response to this error.[59]

Clearly the eschatological material provides an important dimension to the letter. However, Jewett and Johanson's attempts to
demonstrate that eschatological difficulties were *the* exigency of the
letter seem to go beyond the evidence. In particular, the presence of
persecution, evidenced by the references to this topic discussed
below, was significant for Paul, seen in his concern 'that somehow
the tempter had tempted you and our labour had been in vain'
(3.5).

Persecution in Thessalonica

The young church faced persecution in its new faith.[60] Barclay
draws attention to key texts which explicitly refer to the pressure
they experienced (e.g. 1.6; 2.14), along with the implication that
Timothy was sent because of Paul's concern that they should not
give way under the pressure (3.3). Paul reminds the Christians that
he had already warned them that suffering would come to them
(3.4). Barclay suggests that the principal cause of the pressure on
the Christians was the offensive nature of the claims made for their
faith, not least in the refusal to take part in, or even to allow as
valid, the worship of other gods.[61] Donfried focuses this in the
social and political pressures resulting from the civic cult which he
identifies in Thessalonica and the obligations to the emperor (cf.
Acts 17.7),[62] pressures which could lead to the young Christians
giving up their new-found faith.

This persecution would give rise to questions in the minds of the

---

[57] Jewett, *Thessalonian Correspondence*, p. 161.
[58] Jewett, *Thessalonian Correspondence*, p. 94.
[59] Jewett, *Thessalonian Correspondence*, pp. 96f.
[60] Barclay, 'Thessalonica and Corinth', pp. 52f.
[61] Barclay, 'Thessalonica and Corinth', p. 53; Barclay, 'Conflict', pp. 2–7.
[62] Donfried, 'Cults of Thessalonica', 342–7; cf. Bruce, *Acts* (3rd edn), pp. 371f.

Thessalonian Christians, which seems a likely explanation of much of the emphasis on suffering in the letter. It may also be a partial explanation of the strong emphasis on kinship language in the letter:[63] Paul regularly refers to the Christians as ἀδελφοί,[64] and describes his relationship with them using parental imagery (2.11). Such an emphasis on mutual love would be important where they were a small minority in a society which rejected their beliefs and consequently ostracised them. Bruce speculates that the persecution might raise questions concerning Christians who had died, if their deaths were the result of persecution.[65]

Persecution cannot be regarded as *the* exigency of the letter, for it would leave the presence of much other material unexplained; but it seems to have been a significant factor in Paul's response in 1 Thessalonians.

Ecstatic manifestations

Jewett believes that 1.5 implies that the initial evangelisation of Thessalonica was accompanied by miraculous events[66] and that the joy mentioned (1.6) has a supernatural source and is ecstatically experienced.

He interprets references to sobriety (5.6–8) as counterpoints to the association of drunkenness with ecstatic behaviour involving loss of self-control; and 5.19–22 as confirming the presence of conflict over ecstatic manifestations, balancing advice to the leaders not to quench the Spirit – that is, to allow legitimate ecstatic manifestations – with the insistence that everything should be tested according to moral standards, as a response to those who believed that such manifestations were beyond such assessment.[67]

That 1.5f is likely to be referring to 'signs and wonders' that accompanied the initial evangelisation of Thessalonica we may grant, on the basis of the knowledge that Paul's apostolic ministry

---

[63] Malherbe, *Paul and the Thessalonians*, p. 48; Riesner, *Frühzeit*, p. 330.

[64] Eighteen times, proportionately more than any other Pauline letter.

[65] Bruce, *Acts* (3rd edn), p. 372, but with caution; cf. Bruce, *Thessalonians*, p. 98.

[66] Jewett, *Thessalonian Correspondence*, p. 100. He cites Marshall, *Thessalonians*, pp. 53f in support, but Marshall only allows that this is a *possible* understanding of the text. Wanamaker, *Thessalonians*, p. 79 holds a similar view to Jewett, referring to the gifts of the Spirit in 1 Cor. 12.8–10. But those gifts are for edification of the church (e.g. 1 Cor. 14.17f), rather than for evangelism, which seems to be Wanamaker's understanding here.

[67] Jewett, *Thessalonian Correspondence*, pp. 101f.

was at times followed by such things (e.g. Gal. 3.5; Rom. 15.18f; 2 Cor. 12.12f).[68] It seems, however, to be stretching a point to argue that this is the referent in 5.6–8, where a more general ethical exhortation takes place in the light of the potential for ethical laxity resulting from the young church's eschatology.[69]

Further, 5.19–22 could simply be Paul trying to head off an over-reaction to what he says about the dangers of their eschatological perspective. It would be wrong to press the use of the present imperatives μὴ σβέννυτε (5.19) and μὴ ἐξουθενεῖτε (5.20) to imply that the recipients are being instructed to stop an activity that they are already performing, since Paul generally commends the behaviour of the Thessalonians. In the same manner as the positive imperatives in 5.16–18, 21f, these negative imperatives should be read as statements of what Paul wants them (not) to do habitually.[70]

We may therefore agree with Jewett that it is likely that there were specific manifestations of the Spirit's activity during initial evangelism in Thessalonica, and that at least some of the Thessalonian Christians particularly valued such manifestations. Jewett fails, however, to demonstrate the presence of conflict over such manifestations: Paul does not instruct the Christians about the need for mutual edification in the use of such manifestations as he does in 1 Corinthians 12–14, for example. There is silence concerning explicit references to conflict within the Christian community at Thessalonica, to the extent that Paul can write that the Thessalonians need no lessons in love of their fellow Christians (4.9f). We therefore doubt that conflict over such manifestations was a significant exigency of the letter.

Paul defending himself

It is sometimes suggested that a key reason for writing 1 Thessalonians was Paul being attacked by opponents within the Christian community in the city. I have discussed elsewhere the question

---

[68] Marshall, *Thessalonians*, pp. 53f; Wanamaker, *Thessalonians*, p. 79. Schmithals, *Paul*, p. 172 sees 5.19–22 as directed against the effects of agitation by pneumatics within the community.

[69] Best, *Thessalonians*, pp. 211ff; Frame, *Thessalonians*, pp. 185ff; Morris, *Thessalonians* (revised edn.), pp. 156f; Marshall, *Thessalonians*, p. 137.

[70] Bruce, *Thessalonians*, p. 125; *contra* Wanamaker, *Thessalonians*, p. 202.

whether there were opponents of Paul within the Thessalonian church,[71] and here summarise key points.

The major planks in favour of this view of opponents within the church are the 'self-defence' (2.1–12) and Paul's explanation of his failure to return (3.1ff). Schmithals, in particular, sees gnostic opponents attacking Paul's integrity, both in general and in the specific of his non-return.[72] Jewett (as we have seen) believes there were 'enthusiastic' opponents of Paul in the church, who criticised Paul because he was not more explicitly ecstatic in his leadership.[73]

However, Schmithals' view stands or falls with his general thesis, that there were gnostic opponents of Paul nearly everywhere in the early churches, a thesis which fails to command agreement because it is 'a contention for which not a shred of credible evidence within the correspondence itself is available'.[74]

As we have seen, Jewett similarly fails to offer evidence for conflict within the community. Indeed, there is strong evidence of cohesion within the church and in the church's relationship with Paul – he is pleased with their progress (2.14), their love (1.3; 4.9–12), and their positive memory of him (3.6). This is the only group of Christians of whom it is said that they *already* imitate Paul (1.6)[75] – and they have become a τύπος for other churches (1.7).[76]

It is better to see the autobiographical material, especially 2.1–12, as being implicitly paraenetic: Paul is presenting his conduct as a model to be followed.[77] Lyons identifies a number of topics from Paul's conduct which reappear as exhortations to the Thessalonians elsewhere in the letter: encouragement (2.3, 11f; 4.1, 18, 5.11); holy and blameless conduct (2.3, 9–12; 4.1–7; 5.22f); a sense of the responsibility to please God (2.4, 15; 4.1); brotherly love and constant friendship (2.5–8, 17f; 3.6, 10, 12; 4.9–12; 5.15); manual work and self-support (2.8f; 4.9–12; 5.12–14); prayers of

---

[71] Walton, 'What Has Aristotle', 240–9.

[72] Schmithals, *Paul and Gnostics*, pp. 142ff.

[73] Jewett, *Thessalonian Correspondence*, pp. 100–2.

[74] Jewett, *Thessalonian Correspondence*, p. 148.

[75] Contrast the use of the imperative in 1 Cor. 4.16; 11.1; Gal. 4.12; Phil. 3.17; 2 Thess. 3.7, 9. Discussion in Lyons, *Pauline Autobiography*, pp. 190f; Malherbe, 'Exhortation in 1 Thessalonians', 246f; Malherbe, 'Hellenistic Moralists', 267–333, 290; Castelli, *Imitating Paul*, pp. 89–117 (esp. 90–5 on 1 Thess. 1.6; 2.14).

[76] Castelli, *Imitating Paul*, p. 92.

[77] Lyons, *Pauline Autobiography*, pp. 189–221; Wanamaker, *Thessalonians*, pp. 90f.

thanksgiving (1.2; 2.13; 3.10; 5.17f); joy amidst affliction (1.6; 3.9f; 5.16–18); and eschatological hope (1.10; 2.19f; 3.13; 4.13–5.11).[78]

The antitheses of 2.1–12 should be seen within a wider context, for opponents holding the opposite pole of Paul's antithetical statements are an unnecessary hypothesis. The antithetical style is used throughout the letter (e.g. 1.5, 8; 2.13, 17; 4.7, 8; 5.6, 9, 15) and in at least some cases there surely cannot have been people holding the opposite view (5.9, 15).[79] Such an antithetical style was part of the armoury of wandering philosophers in teaching their views,[80] and could therefore have been adopted by Paul. In the antitheses Paul may be contrasting himself with such professional orators, rather than opponents within the church, since the professional rhetors sought the very things which Paul denied were important – glory, praise and financial gain (cf. 2.4–6) – and used methods which Paul deprecated – deception and flattery (cf. 2.3–5).[81]

We may allow that Paul's observations are designed to have a prophylactic effect, in case such accusations are made within the community – or, more likely, in assisting the Christians to respond to potential accusations made by their non-Christian compatriots.[82] But the hypothesis of opponents within the church at the time of 1 Thessalonians is misguided and unnecessary.

Conclusions on exigencies

Overall, we may see three major exigencies of the letter. First, the letter serves as a substitute for a visit, and by way of explanation for Paul and his colleagues' inability to visit. Second, Paul responds to the news of persecution with encouragement and support (including a reminder of his own care for them), as well as reminding the church of his teaching about persecution. Third, Paul replies to questions relayed to him, received by letter or through Timothy (or both, where Timothy might give an oral

---

[78] Lyons, *Pauline Autobiography*, pp. 218f.
[79] Lyons, *Pauline Autobiography*, p. 184.
[80] Malherbe, 'Hellenistic Moralists', pp. 283 n. 67, 290, 297f, citing Dio Chrysostom, *Orations* 32.11f. See also Isocrates, *Oration I: To Demonicus* 9–15 for a good example of antithesis in paraenesis; cf. Lyons, *Pauline Autobiography*, pp. 105–12; Collins, *Studies on 1 Thessalonians*, pp. 183–5.
[81] Winter, 'Entries and Ethics', pp. 67f; Smith, *Comfort One Another*, p. 78.
[82] Johanson, *To All the Brethren*, p. 164.

commentary on a letter), specifically about eschatology (including the situation of believers who died before the End).[83]

5.2.4 Summary

We have seen that the letter is regarded as indubitably Pauline and therefore provides as good as possible a check on Paul's own expression of his thought in our comparision with Pauline speech reported by Luke. The letter pre-dates the ostensible date of the speech – by some time. In both cases there appears to have been a good relationship between apostle and audience, and pressure from outside was probably a significant exigency.[84] We are now in a good position to consider detailed parallels with the Miletus speech.

5.3 From the Miletus speech to 1 Thessalonians

The four key themes of the Miletus speech are leadership, suffering, wealth, and the death of Jesus. Do parallels exist in 1 Thessalonians?

5.3.1 Leadership

The Miletus speech and its Lukan parallels make much of leadership, but it stands out less clearly in 1 Thessalonians. Nevertheless, a careful reading of the letter finds a considerable amount on leadership, particularly concerning the leadership of Paul and his companions, and leadership within the congregation.

Verbs of knowing

In the Miletus speech the hearers know (Acts 20.18b–21, 31, 34, using οἶδα and γινώσκω) that Paul has fulfilled his responsibilities towards the Ephesian Christians (cf. Acts 20.2). 1 Thessalonians has a rich seam of references to both the conduct of Paul and his colleagues, and the recipients' knowledge of that conduct.[85] Οἶδα is used considerably to this end, notably in οἴδατε γάρ (2.1; 3.3; 4.2;

---

[83] Cf. Martin, *NT Foundations,* vol. II, pp. 161–3.
[84] In 1 Thessalonians this is past and present; in the Miletus speech it is future (Acts 20.29f).
[85] Dupont, *Discours de Milet,* p. 32; Dunn, *Acts,* p. 271; Aejmelaeus, *Rezeption,*

5.2), καθὼς οἴδατε (1.5; 2.2, 5; 3.4) and καθάπερ οἴδατε (2.11).[86]
Paul appeals to the Thessalonians' knowledge of his conduct and,
as in Acts 20,[87] verbs of knowing coincide at times with emphatic
personal pronouns (αὐτοί, 2.1; 3.3; 5.2), underlining that it is *these*
people's knowledge to which Paul appeals.

The use of οἶδα in 1 Thessalonians is particularly notable when
compared with other Pauline letters. It is used thirteen times in this
letter, whereas Pauline letters of comparable length have nothing
like this frequency of οἶδα.[88] Further, the use of οἶδα with emphatic
personal pronouns is also a particular feature of this letter: it is
found elsewhere in the Pauline letters in just five places, only one of
which has αὐτοί.[89] This suggests that the appeal to the addressees'
knowledge of the exemplary conduct of Paul and his companions is
a particular concern in 1 Thessalonians.

The appeal to the readers' knowledge of Paul goes wider than
this verb. The readers are told, 'For you remember (μνημο-
νεύετε[90]), brothers, our labour and toil' (2.9), appealing to their
knowledge of the apostle's conduct, and this is followed by, 'You
are witnesses (μάρτυρες), and God also, how pure, upright and
blameless our conduct was' (2.10). Paul appeals to the lessons on
Christian living that the Thessalonians had learned from him and
his colleagues, 'just as you learned (παρελάβετε) from us how it is
necessary to walk and to please God' (4.1), and uses the language
of imitation (καὶ ὑμεῖς μιμηταὶ ἡμῶν ἐγενήθητε, 1.6),[91] which
presupposes a knowledge of the one(s) to be imitated.

The kinds of knowledge appealed to in the letter and the speech
are closely parallel. In the letter Paul draws attention to the readers'
knowledge of his lifestyle and that of his companions (1.5f; 2.2, 5,

p. 101; Witherington, *Acts*, p. 616 n. 231 draw attention to some parallels between
the Miletus speech and 1 Thessalonians in this regard.
[86] Γινώσκω is used only once in the letter (3.5), of Paul's lack of knowledge about
the situation in Thessalonica.
[87] See p. 70 above.
[88] Galatians 3; Ephesians 5; Philippians 6; Colossians 4; Philemon 1; 2 Thessalonians 3. The number of occurrences in Romans (16), 1 Corinthians (25) and
2 Corinthians (16) is greater, but οἶδα occurs more than twice as frequently in
1 Thessalonians as in those three letters.
[89] 2 Cor. 5.16; Eph. 6.21; Col. 4.1; Phil. 4.15; 2 Thess. 3.7 (αὐτοί).
[90] This verb could be imperative, but is taken by the large majority as indicative
on the basis that the uses of οἶδα (vv. 1, 5, 11) are indicative (Frame, *Thessalonians*,
p. 102; Bruce, *Thessalonians*, p. 34). Blight, *Thessalonians*, p. 52 notes that NEB,
NAB and *TNT* take it as imperative.
[91] See the helpful discussion of 'imitation' in Paul in Clarke, 'Be Imitators', esp.
pp. 333–40 (on 1 Thessalonians).

9, 10, 11) – they shared their own selves with the Thessalonians
(2.8) and sought their good (2.2, 5f, 7, 9–12; 3.5, 10) – their lifestyle
took the shape it did δι' ὑμᾶς (1.5).[92] Likewise, Luke's Paul speaks
of the elders' knowledge of his exemplary conduct amongst them
(Acts 20.20, a clause dependent on the main verb ἐπίστασθε, verse
18), and this conduct the elders know to have been at cost to
himself (Acts 20.19, 22f, 31), to the extent that Paul provided for
the weak, as they should (Acts 20.34f).[93]

A similar parallel concerns Paul's teaching, for the Thessalonians
know this (4.1, 2; 5.2) – as do the Ephesian elders (Acts 20.20).
Again, both in letter and speech Paul appeals to the hearers'
knowledge that future suffering as Christians is inevitable – both
for him and for them (1 Thess. 3.3f; Acts 20.25, 29f).

Finally, in the letter Paul draws attention to the recipients'
knowledge that the visit had not been in vain, for the gospel had
borne fruit among them (2.1f; cf. 1.5);[94] and in the speech Luke's
Paul stresses how much he has done (20.26f).

This appeal to the Thessalonians' knowledge has a paraenetic
function, serving to offer a model for imitation to the readers:
descriptions of the missionaries' conduct often become exhortations
elsewhere in the letter.[95] This links strongly with the Miletus
speech, where Paul's reminder of his conduct is the springboard for
his call to the elders to serve.[96]

The theme of knowing provides a range of parallels between the
letter and the speech which begin with a verbal coincidence, but
extend to the use of other verbs of knowing and, strikingly, to the
kinds of knowledge mentioned.

Paul's 'defence'

1 Thessalonians 2.1–12 proffers a reminder of Paul's conduct while
in Thessalonica.[97] One mark of Paul's conduct mentioned is not

[92] De Boer, *Imitation of Paul*, pp. 112f.
[93] Cf. the Lukan Jesus' understanding of leadership as humble service for the sake
of those led (Luke 22.24–30, discussed pp. 111–13).
[94] Collins, '1 Thessalonians', p. 775.
[95] Lyons, *Pauline Autobiography*, pp. 189–221; Marshall, *Thessalonians*, p. 61;
Wanamaker, *Thessalonians*, p. 80.
[96] Esp. v. 35, but also vv. 18–21, 26–31 – note the use of διό in verse 31, showing
that an implication is being drawn from what precedes; cf. Dunn, *Acts*, p. 275.
[97] Wanamaker, *Thessalonians*, pp. 91, 98 argues that 2.1–12 serves the purpose of
implicit paraenesis, providing role-models of Christian moral behaviour, an interesting parallel point to the paraenetic function of farewell speeches (see § 3.2.1).

seeking glory[98] from people (2.6), using vocabulary which is not used in the Miletus speech (ζητέω, δόξα), although it is used elsewhere in Acts.[99] By contrast, the δόξα to be sought is that of God (2.12), before whom the Thessalonians are the δόξα of the missionaries (2.20).[100] Ζητέω is used only on this occasion in 1 Thessalonians.

1 Thessalonians 2.6 interestingly parallels Acts 20.19 conceptually, where Paul describes himself as δουλεύων τῷ κυρίῳ μετὰ πάσης ταπεινοφροσύνης.[101] The vocabulary is different (although it is in some cases fairly rare vocabulary), but the thought of the two phrases is not dissimilar, for they present two sides of the same coin, one phrased positively ('with all humility') and the other negatively ('not seeking glory from people').[102]

The call to the Thessalonian leaders

The other material on leadership in 1 Thessalonians is the call to the leaders of the Thessalonian church to fulfil their leadership responsibilities. 5.12f have these leaders in view, since they are described as προϊσταμένους ὑμῶν ἐν κυρίῳ.[103] These verses should be seen as echoing the description of the missionaries' work (2.1–12) and turning the description, which was implicitly paraenetic, into explicit exhortation.[104]

---

[98] Wanamaker, *Thessalonians*, p. 98 rightly claims that δόξα here does not carry its usual religious sense but rather should be read as having the common non-biblical sense of 'honour' or 'fame'. He cites Dio Chrysostom (*Oration*, 32.7–12, esp. 32.10) as saying that a genuine philosopher will not speak for the sake of δόξα. Thus Paul is contrasting his motives with those of popular philosophers who sought honour from their audiences. Similarly, Best, *Thessalonians*, p. 99; Morris, *Thessalonians* (revised edn.), p. 66; Rigaux, *Thessaloniciens*, p. 415; Bruce, *Thessalonians*, p. 30; Milligan, *Thessalonians*, p. 21.

[99] Ζητέω: 9.11; 10.19, 21; 13.8, 11; 16.10; 17.5, 27; 21.31; 27.30; δόξα: 7.2, 55; 12.23; 22.11.

[100] These are the only uses of δόξα in the letter.

[101] Ταπεινοφροσύνη is rare in the NT, used only seven times in total; this is its only use in Acts. Cf. § 3.4.1.

[102] Bruce, *Acts* (3rd edn), p. 430; Marshall, *Acts* (TNTC), p. 330.

[103] Morris, *Thessalonians* (revised edn.), p. 165 notes that the sentence has one article governing three participles, implying that it is one group of people with a threefold function, namely the elders. Similarly Lightfoot, *Notes on the Epistles*, pp. 78f; Best, *Thessalonians*, p. 224; Milligan, *Thessalonians*, p. 71; Blight, *Thessalonians*, p. 174; Moore, *Thessalonians*, p. 80; Neil, *Thessalonians*, p. 121; Wanamaker, *Thessalonians*, p. 192; Rigaux, *Thessaloniciens*, pp. 576f; Marshall, *Thessalonians*, p. 147; Bruce, *Thessalonians*, p. 118; *contra* Richard, *Thessalonians*, pp. 281f; Malherbe, *Paul and the Thessalonians*, pp. 88f who see 5.12f as being about the exercise of *charismata* by the whole congregation.

[104] Richard, *Thessalonians*, pp. 275f.

Προΐστημι is used eight times in the NT, always intransitively, dividing between the two senses[105] 'be at the head (of), rule, direct', taking a genitive of the person/people led,[106] and 'be concerned about, care for, give aid'.[107] It is used once clearly of church leaders (1 Tim. 5.17), although it is there not a title. In Romans 12.8 it could refer to a type of minister, or to the service provided by that minister. The noun προστάτης is not found in the NT, but the feminine form προστάτις describes the work of Phoebe in relation to the Romans and Paul (Rom. 16.2). Again it is not titular, since Phoebe's role is as a διάκονος (if that is a title at this date), and προστάτις is likely here to mean 'benefactor', since she can hardly be a 'leader' in relation to Paul.[108] It is not necessary to suppose that there was a formal structure to the church or formal 'orders of ministry' in Thessalonica to accept that certain people exercised leadership, and were recognised by the congregation to do so.

Paul describes the leaders' responsibilities using the terms κο-πιῶντας and νουθετοῦντας. In 5.14 he again uses νουθετέω, speaking to the church at large.[109] In both cases he is describing the leaders' task and encouraging its fulfilment, not least by presupposing that it is happening.

Νουθετέω is not widely used in the NT, only seven times in total; apart from Acts 20.31, it is found only in Pauline letters. Νουθετέω is used by Paul for his own relationships with the churches (1 Cor. 4.14f), for the way that those responsible within churches should act (1 Thess. 5.12; Col. 1.28), and for the way that all Christians should act towards one another (1 Thess. 5.14; Col. 3.16; Rom. 5.14).[110] The occurrence of as clearly Pauline a word as νουθετέω

---

[105] BAGD, p. 707; cf. *EDNT*, vol. III, pp. 156f.

[106] e.g. 1 Tim. 3.4f, 12 of 'directing' a household.

[107] e.g. Titus 3.8, 14 of 'caring for', i.e. promoting, good works.

[108] Wanamaker, *Thessalonians*, p. 193; this last point leads Wanamaker to propose that we should see the leaders of the church as those of highest social status and wealth (so also Jewett, *Thessalonian Correspondence*, p. 103). See the excellent discussion of προστάτις in Whelan, 'Amica Pauli', concluding that Phoebe is a 'patron' of Paul.

[109] Milligan, *Thessalonians*, p. 73; Morris, *Thessalonians* (revised edn.), p. 168; Wanamaker, *Thessalonians*, p. 196; Best, *Thessalonians*, p. 299; Frame, *Thessalonians*, p. 196, on the grounds that the address ἀδελφοί in 5.14 resumes the discussion begun in 5.12, where the address is also ἀδελφοί, and that the vocative indicates the beginning of a new topic.

[110] Morris, *Thessalonians* (revised edn.), p. 226. Wanamaker, *Thessalonians*, pp. 193 offers a similar summary of usage. That usage is Pauline (including the Acts context) is also noted by Barrett, 'Paul's Address', p. 115; Roloff, *Apostelgeschichte*, p. 301; Schneider, *Apostelgeschichte*, vol. II, p. 298 n. 64; Pesch, *Apostelgeschichte*,

in a Pauline speech[111] points to some understanding by Luke of the vocabulary that Paul used.[112]

The κόπος word-group has a strongly 'Pauline' feel to it, too. Of twenty-three uses of κοπιάω in the NT, eleven occur within Pauline letters[113] (and three more in the Pastorals[114]). Of nineteen uses of the noun κόπος in the NT, eleven occur within the Pauline letters.[115] The word-group is used of physical toil (e.g. 1 Thess. 2.9; 3.5; 1 Cor. 4.12; 2 Thess. 3.8) and also of 'evangelical activity' (e.g. 1 Cor. 15.10; 16.16; Gal. 4.11; Phil. 2.16; Rom. 16.6, 12).[116] The only use in relation to Paul's work in this letter is 2.9.

In this context it is interesting that the uses of κοπιῶντας in Acts 20.35 and 1 Thessalonians 5.12 are the only uses of the verb in those two books.[117] In both cases it is the leaders of the community whose activity is being described by the verb:[118] in Acts 20.35 the elders are to toil like Paul; in 1 Thessalonians 5.12 the leaders of the community are described as 'those who toil amongst you'. Here is a Pauline idea used in a Pauline way with Pauline vocabulary in the Miletus speech.

Finally, the fact that their leadership is to be exercised ἐν κυρίῳ suggests that it is to be exercised in the same spirit of service as that of the Lord himself.[119] This characteristically Pauline phrase[120] is used often of Christian actions, such as welcome (Rom. 16.2; Phil.

vol. II, p. 205; Marshall, *Thessalonians*, p. 148; Morris, *Thessalonians* (revised edn.), p. 166; Frame, *Thessalonians*, p. 194; Moore, *Thessalonians*, p. 80.

[111] Best, *Thessalonians*, p. 226; Plummer, *Thessalonians*, p. 93.

[112] Aejmelaeus, *Rezeption*, p. 153, who comes to a similar conclusion, also notices the use of παραμυθέομαι, found in the NT only in 1 Thess. 5.14; 2.12; John 11.19, 31, which binds 1 Thess. 2.9–12; 5.14 further together.

[113] Rom. 16.6, 12; 1 Cor. 4.12; 15.10; 16.16; Gal. 4.11; Eph. 4.28; Phil. 2.16; Col. 1.29; 1 Thess. 5.12.

[114] 1 Tim. 4.10; 5.17; 2 Tim. 2.6.

[115] 1 Cor. 3.8; 15.58; 2 Cor. 6.5; 10.15; 11.23, 27; Gal. 6.17; 1 Thess. 1.3; 2.9; 3.5; 2 Thess. 3.8. Κόπος is not used in the Pastorals.

[116] Best, *Thessalonians*, p. 224.

[117] Plummer, *Thessalonians*, p. 91; Aejmelaeus, *Rezeption*, p. 170, the latter also observing that the noun occurs at 1 Thess. 1.3; 2.9; 3.5 (as do Best, *Thessalonians*, p. 224; Marshall, *Thessalonians*, p. 147).

[118] *TDNT*, vol. III, p. 829 notes the parallel.

[119] Dunn, *Jesus and the Spirit*, p. 324. Donfried and Marshall, *Theology of Shorter Paulines*, p. 61; Marshall, *Thessalonians*, p. 148 note 1 Thess. 1.6, where imitation of the Lord consists in suffering, as Paul's had; 2.7–12, where Paul stresses the gentleness he showed as their leader; and 3.12, where it is ὁ κύριος whom Paul invokes to increase the mutual love of the Thessalonians.

[120] Used 47 times in the Pauline corpus (never in the Pastorals), and only once elsewhere in the NT (Rev. 14.13).

2.29) or greeting (Rom. 16.8, 11, 22).[121] In 1 Thessalonians it is used three times, the other uses being of standing firm (3.8) and Paul urging them 'in the Lord Jesus' (4.1), which bears a similar sense as 5.12. Thus in 5.12, as the Lord gave himself for the church, so the leaders are to give themselves for the church.

This is a link to the Miletus speech, where references to Jesus' gift of Paul's ministry and Jesus' teaching (Acts 20.24, 35) show Luke's Paul focused on acting as Jesus did (especially verse 35, which is in a position of emphasis at the end of the speech). Indeed, Luke's presentation of Paul's ministry is modelled on that of Jesus' life and teaching, particularly the Lukan Last Supper discourse.[122]

5.3.2 Suffering

The theme of suffering in the Miletus speech focuses particularly on Paul's own (past and future) suffering, although he also warns the elders of future suffering to come.[123] The suffering theme is also prominent in 1 Thessalonians, in three ways: Paul writes of his own suffering, the Thessalonian Christians' suffering, and he teaches about a right Christian attitude to suffering

Paul's own suffering

Paul reminds the Thessalonian Christians that they already know about his suffering (καθὼς οἴδατε, 2.2). He describes his ministry in Thessalonica in terms of sharing his life (2.8). He mentions his suffering at the hands of the Jews (2.15f[124]) and refers to present

---

[121] Cf. Best, *Thessalonians*, p. 225.
[122] See § 4.2.4.   [123] See § 3.5.2.
[124] It has been argued that 1 Thess. 2.13–16 (or 14–16) are a non-Pauline interpolation (Pearson, 'Deutero-Pauline Interpolation'; Boers, 'Form-Critical Study', esp. pp. 150–2; Schmidt, 'Linguistic Evidence'; Koester, '1 Thessalonians', p. 38; Richard, *Thessalonians*, pp. 17–19). The main grounds for this view are: (1) the passage is theologically incompatible with Paul's positive view of the Jews in Rom. 11, esp. vv. 25–32; (2) there is no evidence of persecution of Christian Jews by non-Christian Jews in Judaea before AD 50; (3) ἔφθασεν (v. 16), because aorist, implies a specific act of God's wrath on the Jews, and only the destruction of Jerusalem in AD 70 fits this; (4) v. 13 looks like the start of another thanksgiving period (cf. 1.2f), whereas if vv. 13–16 are deleted there is a smooth transition from v. 12 to v. 17; (5) the language of imitation (v. 14) differs from Paul's usual use of such language, which is of imitating himself or Christ (1 Cor. 4.16; 11.1; Phil. 3.17; 1 Thess. 1.6); (6) the linguistic usage of vv. 13–16 is un-Pauline in its use of καί rather than γάρ or no conjunction (v. 13), in the number of levels of 'embedding' of dependent clauses in v. 15, and the separation of κυρίος and Ἰησοῦς by a participle;

(or recent) affliction and distress (3.7), partly arising from not seeing the Thessalonian Christians (3.1, 5[125]). In various ways, these are parallels to material in the Miletus speech that we have already discussed.

The sharing of Paul's very self with the Thessalonians (2.8) uses vocabulary reminiscent of the Miletus speech in the use of ψυχή in both places (Acts 20.24).[126] In both cases it is Paul's ψυχή being discussed: in 1 Thessalonians he shares it with the Thessalonian Christians; in Acts 20 he values his ψυχή less than completing the work given to him by God. In both cases Paul is taking risks in his ministry (note 1 Thess. 2.2 as part of the context of 2.8).[127]

The opposition to Paul is Jewish, caused by his mission to Gentiles (2.15f). Paul describes his experience as that of having been 'driven out' or 'persecuted'.[128] It is most likely the experience

and the combination τῶν ἐκκλησιῶν τοῦ θεοῦ τῶν οὐσῶν ἐν τῇ Ἰουδαίᾳ ἐν Χριστῷ Ἰησοῦ (v. 14) is not found elsewhere in Paul, even though the individual elements are.

But each of these points can be answered (Donfried, 'Paul and Judaism'; Okeke, 'Fate of Unbelieving Jews'; Weatherly, 'Authenticity'; Hurd, 'Paul Ahead of His Time'; Schlueter, *Filling up*, pp. 29–38; Wanamaker, *Thessalonians*, pp. 29–34; Jewett, *Thessalonian Correspondence*, pp. 36–41; Marshall, *Thessalonians*, pp. 11f; Smith, *Comfort One Another*, pp. 77f): (1) the geographical focus of τῶν Ἰουδαίων (v. 14) is on the Jews *of Judaea*, since it is they who persecute the Christian Jews of Judaea, and who killed the Lord Jesus; (2) there is evidence for persecution of Christian Jews in Judaea pre-50 in Acts and the Pauline letters, not least by Paul/Saul himself (e.g. Acts 4.1ff; 5.17ff; 6.9–7.60; 8.1; 11.19; 12.1ff; Gal. 1.13, 23; Phil. 3.6; 1 Cor. 15.9); (3) there are events, such as the expulsion of the Jews from Rome under Claudius in AD 49 which would fit the aorist use, or the aorist is of an imminent event; (4) there is a parallelism between 1.2–10 and 2.13–16 which shows 1.2–2.16 to have a 'ring' composition with 2.1–12 as its centre; (5) it is typical of Paul to move from the general to the specific, and his thanksgiving moves from the general (1.6–9a, their imitation of the missionaries) to the more specific (2.13–16, their endurance of persecution) to the consequence (5.9, they will receive not wrath, but salvation, contrasting with the Judaean Jews of 2.16), so that there is a logic to the references to imitation in the letter; (6) each of the linguistic uses is arguably Pauline: the use of καί (e.g. Rom. 1.28; 2.27; 3.8; 5.16; 1 Thess. 1.6), the number of levels of 'embedding' (Rom 4.16f contains nine levels), the separation of noun from attributing adjective by a verb form, which parallels the separation of 'Lord' and 'Jesus' (e.g. 1 Cor. 7.7, 12; Phil. 2.20; 3.20), and the combination of Pauline phrases, which can be explained in the context.

[125] Cf. Jervell, *Apostelgeschichte*, p. 509.

[126] Aejmelaeus, *Rezeption*, pp. 126f; Munck, *Acts*, p. 204; Bruce, *Thessalonians*, p. 32 note the parallel of 1 Thess. 2.8 and 2 Thess. 3.9. There is a further link in τὸ εὐαγγέλιον τοῦ θεοῦ, see pp. 261f.

[127] It is also interesting to note that ψυχή, which is widely used in the NT, is only used on two occasions in 1 Thessalonians (2.8; 5.23). The verse we are considering assumes greater importance because of this.

[128] The Greek is ἐκδιωξάντων (an NT *hapax legomenon*), which Wanamaker, *Thessalonians*, p. 115 understands as literal driving out, noting Luke's description of

of Paul and his companions that is being described here[129] and this
may be explained by Luke's description of the initial mission to
Thessalonica (Acts 17.1ff).

The parallel with Acts 20.19 is notable here.[130] There also Paul
persists in his work in spite of pressure from Jewish persecutors.[131]
Strelan sees the Miletus speech as Jewish in 'flavour', and suggests
that this shows the Ephesian elders to include Jews at this
period:[132] he cites the use of 'elder', which was a synagogue term
(verse 17), the continued commitment to teaching Jews as well as
Gentiles (verse 21), the emphasis on 'the kingdom' (verse 25),
language of 'the whole will of God' (verse 27), the imagery of
shepherd and flock (verse 28), God obtaining (περιποιέομαι) the
church (verse 28), the λύκοι βαρεῖς (verse 29, recalling Deut. 31.29;
Ezek. 22.27; Zeph. 3.3), and δοῦναι τὴν κληρονομίαν ἐν τοῖς
ἡγιασμένοις πᾶσιν (verse 32) recalling the promises of God to
Israel of an inheritance. Likewise, the body language of falling on
Paul's neck and kissing him (verse 37) echoes the actions of Esau
and Jacob (Gen. 33.4), Joseph and Benjamin (Gen. 45.14), Joseph
and his father (Gen. 46.29) and Raguel and his relatives (Tobit
7.6f). The Jewishness of the speech prompts the observation that
debate and disagreement are often sharpest and most acrimonious
(from an outsider's perspective) when the opposing people are
closest in background – and this is the case with Paul and his
persecutors in the Miletus speech (Acts 20.19) and 1 Thessalonians
(2.14–16).

Paul's ministry in Thessalonica (Acts 17.5–10). Schlueter, *Filling up*, pp. 68f argues
that ἐκδιώκω means 'persecute' here because of its association with 'killing the Lord
Jesus'.

[129] Best, *Thessalonians*, p. 116 cites the argument from consistency of usage in 1
Thessalonians for 'us' meaning Paul and his companions here. Similarly, Malherbe,
Paul and the Thessalonians, p. 62; Marshall, *Thessalonians*, p. 79; Lightfoot, *Notes on
the Epistles*, p. 33; Bruce, *Thessalonians*, p. 47. Cf. Schlueter, *Filling up*, pp. 70–3,
who compares Gal. 5.11; 2 Cor. 11.24, and suggests that 'us' should be understood
as 'us apostles', since it is not easy to understand why Jews should persecute the
Gentile Timothy.

[130] Aejmelaeus, *Rezeption*, p. 102 argues that the picture in Acts 20.18b–19 and
1 Thess. 2.2 is in essentials the same; so also Jervell, *Apostelgeschichte*, p. 509;
Barrett, *Acts,* vol. II, p. 967.

[131] Marshall, *Acts* (TNTC), p. 330. Barrett, 'Paul's Address', p. 111 also observes
the allusion in 1 Thess. 2.15 to the Jews being the enemies of the apostolic church.
Cf. Davies, 'Paul and the People', 6–9.

[132] Strelan, *Paul, Artemis*, pp. 266–9.

The Thessalonian Christians' suffering

Paul compares the suffering of the Thessalonian Christians with
that of the churches of Judaea (2.14, resulting from persecution by
Jews[133]), having already compared it to his own and the Lord's
(1.6). He also refers to the Thessalonian Christians' suffering prior
to teaching about the attitude they should have (3.3).

In the Miletus speech Paul does not discuss the past suffering of
the elders, but does hint (Acts 20.29f) that they will in future
experience suffering not dissimilar to his own. This forms an
interesting parallel of thought to 1 Thessalonians 3.3f, where Paul
states that he warned the Thessalonian Christians of suffering to
come, using an emphatic personal pronoun to underline the point
that he had taught them this during his visit – and the present tense
of κείμεθα (verse 3) underlines that this is still his expectation.[134]
The inevitability is further stressed by the use of μέλλω (verse 4),
and the whole provides encouragement to persevere amidst afflic-
tions – not dissimilar to the call to the Ephesian elders to stay alert
when pressures from outside ('savage wolves', Acts 20.29) and
inside (verse 30) come on the horizon.

A Christian attitude to suffering

This is the concern of 3.3f, where Paul is concerned to help the
Thessalonian Christians understand that their suffering should be
no surprise, for they were warned beforehand that this would be
the case.

Paul uses the noun θλῖψις (verse 3) and the verb θλίβω (verse 4)
in teaching about suffering here. The verb is relatively unusual in
the NT,[135] although the noun is more common.[136] The parallel
with Acts 14.22 at first appears stronger than that with Acts 20.23,
as Lightfoot notes,[137] but the parallel with Acts 20.23 is clear,

[133] Marshall, *Thessalonians*, p. 78.
[134] Johanson, *To All the Brethren*, p. 105.
[135] Ten uses, six in Paul (2 Cor. 1.6; 4.8; 7.5; 1 Thess. 3.4; 2 Thess. 1.6, 7), one in
the Pastorals (1 Tim. 5.10), never in Acts.
[136] Forty-five times in the NT, of which twenty-four are in the Pauline letters
(including 1 Thess. 1.6; 3.3, 7) and five in Acts (7.10, 11; 11.19; 14.22; 20.23; only
11.19 is in narrative; the others are in speeches).
[137] Lightfoot, *Notes on the Epistles*, p. 43. The parallel with Acts 14.22 is also
noted in Aejmelaeus, *Rezeption*, p. 92; Morris, *Thessalonians* (revised edn.), pp. 97f;
Bruce, *Thessalonians*, p. 63.

particularly in the unexpectedness of θλῖψις.[138] Paul prophesies suffering for himself in both places:[139] the normality of persecution is a theme common to Acts 20.23 and 1 Thessalonians 3.3f, using the same vocabulary in both places. Again we see the use of a 'Pauline' term by Luke.

5.3.3   Money and work

Attitudes to money and work are important themes of the Miletus address. Paul's own conduct (Acts 20.33–5) is one focus of the theme there, the other being (by implication) the attitude to wealth expected of the elders (especially Acts 20.28, 33–5). In 1 Thessalonians this theme is prominent, focused on three passages, 2.5ff, 9; 4.11f; and 5.14.

1 Thessalonians 2.5ff, 9

A number of parallels with the Miletus speech coincide in these verses. Paul's assertion that he did not 'lay burdens' (ἐπιβαπῆσαι) on the Thessalonians (2.9) means financial burdens, since in the first half of the verse Paul writes of his 'labour and toil', referring to his self-support by tentmaking.[140] This is a significant parallel to Acts 20.33f, where Luke's Paul describes his Ephesian ministry in similar terms.[141] Paul's policy of not demanding financial support from churches which he was in the process of planting is a common thread to both passages,[142] and this is a Pauline theme in other places.[143]

As an apostle, Paul claims, he could have made such demands (ἐν βάρει, 2.7, a phrase that most probably refers to financial support[144]), but this was a right he waived – a strong parallel with

---

[138] *NIDNTT*, vol. II, p. 809.

[139] Aejmelaeus, *Rezeption*, p. 117.

[140] Hock, *Social Context*, p. 30 cites Lucian, *De Mercede conductis* 20, 37 as examples of the client as a burden to the patron (although the latter reference should probably be 38), seeing Lucian and Paul's usage as 'technical' (p. 80 n. 44).

[141] Schürmann and Egenolf, *Thessalonians*, pp. 28f; cf. Jervell, *Apostelgeschichte*, p. 514.

[142] Aejmelaeus, *Rezeption*, pp. 168f.

[143] Bruce, *Thessalonians*, p. 34 cites 1 Cor. 4.12; Acts 19.12; 2 Thess. 3.8.

[144] Milligan, *Thessalonians*, p. 20; Bruce, *Thessalonians*, p. 31; Marshall, *Acts* (TNTC), p. 336; *pace* Frame, *Thessalonians*, pp. 99f, who argues that the use of βάρος (2.7) is more to do with the requirement of honour than a stipend, finding no reference to a stipend in the immediate context; and Best, *Thessalonians*, p. 100, who

the assertions of Acts 20.34f. The theme of not making demands on the particular church being served at a given time recurs throughout the Pauline corpus.[145]

The parallel between 1 Thessalonians 2.5ff and Acts 20 is the more striking because of the use of common vocabulary in the expression of the idea. Paul uses both the noun βάρος (2.7) and the related (rare) verb ἐπιβαρέω (2.9) – wording echoed by Luke's record of the Miletus speech when Luke's Paul speaks of the coming wolves, using the adjective βαρύς (Acts 20.29):[146] the wolves will be the kind of people Paul and his companions have declined to be, for they will be burdensome to the Ephesian church.

The common vocabulary runs further than this. Νυκτός καὶ ἡμέρας (2.9)[147] also bespeaks Paul's tentmaking labours,[148] which were long and during which Paul most probably carried out evangelism.[149] This phrase is echoed in Acts 20.31, νύκτα καὶ ἡμέραν,[150] where it again speaks of Paul's long and arduous ministry, most probably alongside his work.[151] We have found here

---

concurs with Frame on the ground that the clause in v. 7 is more closely linked to v. 6, which discusses dignity, than v. 5, which discusses exploitation. Wanamaker, *Thessalonians*, p. 99 thinks that there is a *double entendre* in the use of the word in v. 7. We may therefore take there to be at least *some* reference to financial support in the use of βάρος (v. 7).

[145] e.g. 1 Cor. 9.3–18; 2 Cor. 11.7–12; 2 Thess. 3.7–9. It is clear from these references that Paul achieved this at times by relying on financial support from other churches, esp. 2 Cor. 11.8f.

[146] Aejmelaeus, *Rezeption*, p. 147 believes the use in Acts 20.29 is derived from 1 Thess. 2.7, 9.

[147] Lightfoot, *Notes on the Epistles*, p. 27 notes that the order of the words need not imply that the phrase is based on the Jewish understanding of the beginning of the day being sunset, for Jewish writers use the reverse order also, e.g. Jer. 16.13; 33.25. Equally Roman writers, who reckoned the day as beginning at sunrise, sometimes speak of 'night and day', e.g. Cicero, *De Finibus Bonorum et Malorum* 1.16.51; *De Oratore* 1.61.260 (misprinted as 1.16.260 in Lightfoot); Caesar, *De Bello Gallico* 5.38.1. (These authors write, of course, in Latin, not Greek.)

[148] Hock, *Social Context*, p. 31 sees the use of the genitive as meaning 'during night and day', rather than 'throughout the whole night and day', and relates this to Paul's tentmaking.

[149] Hock, *Social Context*, pp. 37–42.

[150] Bruce, *Thessalonians*, p. 35; Williams, *Thessalonians*, p. 42; Haenchen, *Acts*, p. 593 n. 7; Marshall, *Acts* (TNTC), p. 335; Aejmelaeus, *Rezeption*, p. 152; Dunn, *Acts*, p. 274.

[151] Bruce, *Acts* (3rd edn), p. 410 notes that Acts 19.12 mentions σουδάρια ἢ σιμικίνθια, which have Latin origin in *sudaria*, sweat-rags worn on the head, and *semicinctia*, aprons, both of which were worn while working – presumably by Paul as he worked on tents; so also Haenchen, *Acts*, p. 562 n. 1; *contra* Johnson, *Acts*, p. 340, who envisages small pieces of cloth being pressed against Paul and then carried to the sick.

a considerable clustering of themes and vocabulary found in both the Miletus speech and 1 Thessalonians.

1 Thessalonians 4.11f; 5.14

We note first the mention of hands in 1 Thessalonians 4.11f and Acts 20.34.[152] In both cases it is work with the hands that is mentioned: in the letter Paul is urging the duty of work with the hands on the Christians; in the speech Paul reminds the elders of his own work with his hands.

1 Thessalonians 4.11 is the only use of χείρ in the letter, whereas it is quite common in Acts (forty-five uses). 4.11 links back to 2.9, where Paul speaks of his own work; Paul is offering his practice and attitude (2.9) as a model for imitation (4.11).[153] Paul's urging that the Thessalonians should work with their hands may suggest that the church was composed principally of manual workers,[154] or that Paul was seeking to remove Christian clients from the kind of client-patron relationships which meant that they had no need to work (because of the benefactions of their patrons), and no opportunity to work, since they had to focus attention on their patron's affairs, being present for the morning *salutatio* and then going with the patron and supporting his causes.[155] In general Judaism valued manual work, whereas the Greeks regarded it with disdain,[156] although there is evidence of philosophers who chose to work manually and regarded this as honourable, since it meant

---

[152] Hanson, *Acts*, p. 205; Neil, *Acts*, p. 215; Taylor, *Les Actes VI*, p. 97. Conzelmann, *Acts*, p. 176; Lüdemann, *Acts*, p. 228 suggest that Luke may have used 1 Thess. 2.9; 4.11 in constructing Acts 20.34f, although Lüdemann thinks it more likely that Luke derived the material from oral tradition.

[153] Collins, *Studies on 1 Thessalonians*, p. 187; Hock, *Social Context*, pp. 42–9.

[154] Best, *Thessalonians*, p. 176; Morris, *Thessalonians* (revised edn.), p. 132; Malherbe, *Paul and the Thessalonians*, pp. 15f.

[155] Juvenal, *Satires* I, lines 127f; Saller, *Personal Patronage*, pp. 128f; Winter, *Seek the Welfare*, pp. 42–60; Winter, '*Christentum und Antike*', p. 124. In the latter, Winter considers that 2 Thess. 3.6, 10 point to such a reading of 1 Thess. 4.11f, for it was a person who 'did not *want* to work' (τις οὐ θέλει ἐργάζεσθαι, 2 Thess. 3.10) who was censured, implying that they did not *need* to work. This view, if correct, makes it unlikely that the cause of Paul's instructions was over-enthusiastic eschatological fervour leading the Thessalonians to give up working (thus Hock, *Social Context*, p. 43; *contra* Agrell, *Work*, pp. 101–3; Jewett, *Thessalonian Correspondence*, pp. 173f, 176f).

[156] Best, *Thessalonians*, p. 176; Bicknell, *Thessalonians*, p. 41; Marshall, *Thessalonians*, p. 116.

they were not dependent on a wealthy patron.[157] It was normal for a Jew – even a rabbi – to learn a trade.[158]

Three purposes are involved in manual work of this kind. First, it will command the respect of outsiders (4.12a), for clients were not generally admired[159] and working will provide a testimony to outsiders.[160] Second, working will produce financial independence, rather than the dependence which was inherent in certain patron-client relationships (4.12b),[161] or the possibility of leaning upon fellow Christians for support.[162] Third, working will provide the ability to support the weaker members of the church (4.11), for it is in response to that question (4.9ff) that Paul introduces the specific point of working with one's hands. 4.9–12 should be seen as focused on one subject, namely the love of fellow Christians: in 4.9–10a the general principle is enunciated, and in 4.10b–12 its specific meaning is explained.[163] Verse 11 is then not necessarily advocating 'political quietism' in the sense of withdrawal from public affairs,[164] but is contrasting the client, who had to be busy about the patron's affairs, with the financially independent person, who could 'mind your own affairs'.

This provides a real parallel with the Miletus speech, for χείρ is used there in relation to Paul's manual work (Acts 20.34), his provision for his fellow workers (Acts 20.34) and his urging on the elders the duty of care for the weak (Acts 20.35; cf. 1 Thess. 5.14, discussed below). Although the owner of the χείρ is different in the two texts, the idea focused by the use of χείρ is very similar in the two cases. It is also of interest that the parallel extends to a reminder that the hearers know this already (καθὼς ὑμῖν παρηγγεί-λαμεν, 1 Thess. 4.11; αὐτοὶ γινώσκετε, Acts 20.34) and to the same word for 'needs' (χρεία, Acts 20.34; 1 Thess. 4.12).[165]

The theme of support of the weak appears in the exhortation ἀντέχεσθε τῶν ἀσθενῶν (1 Thess. 5.14), forming an interesting

---

[157] Hock, *Social Context*, pp. 52–9, 220.

[158] *TDNT*, vol. II, p. 649 (mis-cited in Richard, *Thessalonians*, p. 211 as p. 249) cites later rabbinic sources to this effect, but also notes, 'there are also critical voices arguing that the two [*sc.* a manual trade and being a rabbi] are incompatible'.

[159] Cf. Juvenal, *Satires* V, esp. lines 1–5; Winter, *Seek the Welfare*, p. 51.

[160] Agrell, *Work*, pp. 99f.

[161] i.e. the kind which precluded work discussed above. See also Winter, *Seek the Welfare*, pp. 51–3.

[162] Agrell, *Work*, p. 100.

[163] Best, *Thessalonians*, pp. 171, 175.

[164] Winter, *Seek the Welfare*, pp. 48–50; *contra* Hock, *Social Context*, pp. 46f.

[165] Aejmelaeus, *Rezeption*, pp. 168f.

parallel to δεῖ ἀντιλαμβάνεσθαι τῶν ἀσθενούντων (Acts 20.35).[166]
The participle ἀσθενούντων is derived from the verb ἀσθενέω,
which is used in Acts (9.37; 19.12; 20.35), but never in 1 Thessalonians.[167] The noun ἀσθενής is used in Acts (4.9; 5.15, 16), but
1 Thessalonians 5.14 represents its only use in that letter.[168] In
general use it often connotes physical sickness, as well as being used
metaphorically for ethical weakness or poverty.[169]

The meaning of this word-group in 1 Thessalonians is debated.
Lightfoot understands it as the spiritually weak (comparing Rom.
4.19; 14.1, 2; 1 Cor. 8.7–12; 9.22).[170] Frame proposes that the
morally weak are in view.[171] Agrell sees this group as the economic-
ally weak.[172] Best agrees that it is unlikely that 'weak' should have
a physical sense here, and notes that in other letters Paul uses the
participle of those who are hesitant about matters on which others
have clear minds (e.g. Rom. 14.1–15.6; 1 Cor. 8.10). He therefore
argues that, even though we have no knowledge of such difficulties
in Thessalonica, it is likely that such questions came up wherever
issues of Christian freedom arose. Thus Best understands the thrust
of the exhortation to be an encouragement to help those who are
struggling in matters of faith and Christian freedom.[173] However,
Wanamaker suggests that προϊσταμένους (5.12) may include an
allusion to caring for the materially needy. Accordingly, he suggests
that this possibility should be included while observing that Paul
may have left these exhortations vague because the Thessalonians
would have known what he meant, and there was therefore no need
to be more specific.[174]

[166] Aejmelaeus, *Rezeption*, pp. 170f.
[167] Elsewhere in Paul it is used literally (Rom 4.19; 2 Cor. 12.10; 13.3) and
metaphorically (Rom. 8.3; 14.1f; 1 Cor. 8.11f).
[168] Found twenty-six times in the NT, including twelve uses in Paul (Rom. 5.6;
1 Cor. 1.25, 27; 4.10; 8.7, 9; 9.22; 11.30; 12.22; 2 Cor. 10.10; Gal. 4.9; 1 Thess. 5.14).
[169] BAGD, pp. 115f; *EDNT*, vol. I, pp. 170f. Cf. Stark, 'Antioch', pp. 193–5,
describing the health hazards of ancient urban life, especially in the lack of pure
water supplies, which would result in poor general health.
[170] Lightfoot, *Notes on the Epistles*, p. 80. Morris, *Thessalonians* (revised edn.),
p. 169 sees the reference to the spiritually weak, but argues that we cannot know the
specific weakness referred to here.
[171] Frame, *Thessalonians*, p. 198. He goes to argue that, since 'the idlers' and 'the
faint-hearted' refer to groups already addressed (in 4.11f and 4.13–5.1 respectively),
it is likely that 'the weak' here were subject to particular temptation to impurity
(already mentioned in 4.3–8).
[172] Agrell, *Work*, p. 137; similarly Witherington, *Acts*, p. 625.
[173] Best, *Thessalonians*, p. 230; similarly Marshall, *Thessalonians*, p. 151.
[174] Wanamaker, *Thessalonians*, pp. 197f.

There must be a measure of agnosticism over the sense of 'weak' here – and whatever the sense in 1 Thessalonians, the same ambiguity exists in the use of ἀσθενούντων in Acts 20.35. It seems probable that some reference to financial help because of physical weakness (leading to the inability to support oneself through manual work) is included in both cases, and it is accordingly proper to include this parallel under our consideration of attitudes to wealth.

Conclusions

We have seen significant parallels between the letter and the speech of the themes of money and work, reinforced in many cases by similar vocabulary. Particularly, in 1 Thessalonians 2.5ff, 9; 4.11f and 5.14 groupings of ideas and vocabulary occur which form close parallels with the closing section of the Miletus speech (Acts 20.33–5).

5.3.4   The death of Jesus

It is quite rare for a theological interpretation of the death of Jesus to be mentioned explicitly in Acts, 20.28 being a place where it comes particularly clearly into focus. The language used there has a notable parallel in 1 Thessalonians 5.9f.[175] The parallel includes both the use of περιποιέομαι and the presence of an explanatory διά-clause.[176]

The περιποιέομαι word-group is used little in the NT.[177] Bruce observes that Paul more often uses ἀγοράζω, ἐξαγοράζω or ἀπολύτρωσις when he refers to God's acquisition of his people,[178] the thought in view in Acts 20.28. The language has a parallel in biblical Greek in Isa. 43.21 LXX,[179] λαόν μου ὃν περιεποιησάμην. This suggests that Luke's Paul is using language which sees God's

---

[175] Rigaux, *Thessaloniciens*, p. 571.

[176] Aejmelaeus, *Rezeption*, p. 135.

[177] The verb περιποιέομαι is used only three times (Luke 17.33; Acts 20.28; 1 Tim. 3.13) and the noun περιποίησις five times (Eph 1.11; 1 Thess. 5.9; 2 Thess. 2.14; Heb. 10.39; 1 Pet. 2.9).

[178] Bruce, *Acts* (3rd edn), p. 434, citing 1 Cor. 6.20; 7.23 (ἀγοράζω); Gal. 3.13; 4.5 (ἐξαγοράζω); Rom. 3.24 (ἀπολύτρωσις).

[179] Aejmelaeus, *Rezeption*, p. 138 proposes that Isa. 43.20f LXX is one of Luke's sources here.

relationship with the Ephesian church as modelled on the relationship of God to Israel.[180]

Best[181] notes that περιποίησις can be used actively or passively, and (rightly) favours taking the word actively here, on the ground that a passive reading would make no sense of the dependent genitive σωτηρίας. The active sense is the sense of the cognate verb in its three NT uses.

The verb and the noun are used in slightly different senses: in Acts 20 the verb speaks of God obtaining the church, whereas in 1 Thessalonians the noun describes Christians obtaining salvation. Nevertheless, in both contexts there are clear references to this taking place through the death of Jesus in the διά-clauses which follow: διὰ τοῦ αἵματος τοῦ ἰδίου (Acts 20.28); διὰ τοῦ κυρίου ἡμῶν Ἰησοῦ Χριστοῦ τοῦ ἀποθανόντος ὑπὲρ[182] ἡμῶν (1 Thess. 5.9f). In 1 Thessalonians 5.9f the hope of salvation from wrath is grounded in Christology, particularly in the death of Jesus.[183] There is an important contrast in 1 Thessalonians between wrath and salvation, since this is the third time they have appeared as polar opposites in the letter (cf. 1.10; 2.16).

This parallel, while not word for word, is nevertheless significant, for it offers a similar use of a rare NT word-group in a common sense followed by a similar grammatical construction which states the same ground for the obtaining of the church/salvation. While the spread of the word-group in the NT argues against the words being seen as especially 'Pauline', Luke's Paul and the Paul of 1 Thessalonians use the word-group in the same way on the only occasions that they both use it.

5.3.5 Conclusions

The themes of the Miletus speech that we have identified have significant parallels in 1 Thessalonians. In particular, the use of verbs of knowing, especially with reference to the addressees' knowledge of Paul, is important in both cases. Paul's example as a

[180] Tannehill, *Narrative Unity,* vol. II, pp. 258f.

[181] Best, *Thessalonians,* pp. 216f; in agreement with Morris, *Thessalonians* (revised edn.), p. 160; Wanamaker, *Thessalonians,* p. 187; Marshall, *Thessalonians,* pp. 139f.

[182] There is a variant reading, περί, here, and the manuscript evidence is not strongly weighted on one side. Nevertheless, περί and ὑπέρ could be synonyms in Hellenistic Greek, both having the sense of 'on behalf of' (Moule, *Idiom-Book,* p. 63; LSJ, vol. II, pp. 1366 (§ A.II), 1857 (§ A.II)).

[183] Wanamaker, *Thessalonians,* pp. 187f.

leader is frequently referred to in both cases, both to demonstrate that he has faithfully fulfilled his own leadership responsibilities, and to be used as a model to be followed and imitated.

Paul's view of suffering in 1 Thessalonians seems very close to that in the Miletus speech, in his understanding of his own and the Thessalonian Christians' suffering, and also in his more general teaching on the topic. As with the theme of leadership, there are significant parallels of vocabulary.

1 Thessalonians also offers material on attitudes to money and work showing remarkable parallels to the Miletus speech, again using common vocabulary.

While the death of Jesus may not be so extensive a theme as the others discussed, we have again seen that the significant references in the two cases run parallel, using a rare NT word-group in a similar grammatical construction with the same force in both places.

In sum, the four major themes of the Miletus speech are paralleled within 1 Thessalonians, often using similar vocabulary. This suggests that Luke and Paul inhabited closely related thought-worlds, to the extent that when Luke presents Paul speaking to Christians in the Miletus speech, the Paul he presents sounds remarkably like the Paul of 1 Thessalonians.

5.4   From 1 Thessalonians to the Miletus speech

An ensuing question is whether further parallels between the Miletus speech and 1 Thessalonians exist, by seeking ideas and vocabulary in the letter which are not covered by the major themes in the speech, but which are paralleled in Acts 20.18–35.

5.4.1   Δουλεύω

Paul uses this verb in describing the Thessalonian Christians' conversion (1 Thess. 1.9f), and the participle is also used in Acts 20.19 in the description of Paul's own ministry. The sense is not precisely the same in the two places, but the similarity of language merits further investigation, since the verb is unusual in Acts (only at 20.19; 7.7) and only occurs here in 1 Thessalonians.[184]

---

[184] The noun δοῦλος does not occur in 1 Thessalonians, and is found only three times in Acts: 2.18 (quoting Joel 2.28ff); 4.29 (the church as the servants of God); 16.17 (Paul and Barnabas described as servants of the Most High God).

The verb is used frequently in the LXX of Israel's relationship with Yahweh – or with other gods.[185] To apostatise is to 'serve other gods' (Exod. 23.32f), whereas Israel should 'serve the Lord alone' (1 Sam. 7.3f).[186] Key leaders of Israel (Joshua, David, Abraham, Moses) are described as 'servants' of God, using δοῦλος (Josh. 24.30 (MT 29); Pss. 88.4, 21 (MT 89.4, 21); 104.26, 42 (MT 105.26, 42)).

With this background it is not surprising that a Jewish Christian like Paul would use such language to describe the Christian profession of the Thessalonians and, by implication (for it is a present infinitive) their continuing walk with the true and living God.[187] Paul certainly uses the language of slavery in his letters. He can introduce himself in later letters as Παῦλος δοῦλος Χριστοῦ Ἰησοῦ (Rom. 1.1; cf. Gal. 1.10; Phil. 1.1). He also writes of serving the Lord in contrast to serving sin (Rom. 6.16–20; 7.25) or the law (Rom. 7.6). Best suggests that the use in 1 Thessalonians 1.9 of serving God is not characteristic of Paul,[188] but Wanamaker, observing the breadth of terms with which δουλεύω can be combined, argues that there is no 'standard' Pauline use of the verb.[189] Conzelmann[190] sees the parallel as being the result of 'flowery phrases from ecclesiastical language [being] woven into the speech', whereas Barrett is more positive about the possibility that the phraseology could be Pauline.[191]

It is of interest, then, that Luke's Paul speaks with the same accent as 1 Thessalonians 1.9f in describing his own ministry in the Miletus speech. The parallel we note, then, is the use of the language of slavery of Christian belonging and Christian life and ministry, used of Paul and his converts.

---

[185] *TDNT*, vol. II, pp. 265–8; Rigaux, *Thessaloniciens*, p. 390; Richard, *Thessalonians*, p. 55.

[186] Peterson, *Engaging with God*, p. 150 sees the use of the verb in Acts 20.19 as evidence that Christian living was regarded as the sphere of worship, rather than simply the 'cultic' meeting of Christians together; cf. Walton, 'Sacrifice and Priesthood', esp. pp. 138–41.

[187] Schürmann and Egenolf, *Thessalonians*, p. 21. It could be argued that the Lukan and Pauline use are both derived from the LXX use, which would imply that Luke and Paul are using the LXX similarly at this point.

[188] Best, *Thessalonians*, pp. 83, 85.

[189] Wanamaker, *Thessalonians*, p. 86, citing 'sin' (Rom. 6.6) 'spirit' (Rom. 7.6), 'law' (Rom. 9.25), 'those which by nature are not God' (Gal. 4.8), as well as 'Christ' (Rom. 14.18; 16.18; Col. 3.24).

[190] Conzelmann, *Acts*, p. 173.

[191] Barrett, 'Paul's Address', p. 111; cf. Hanson, *Acts*, p. 203.

5.4.2   Ἐπιστρέφω

Paul speaks of the Thessalonians' conversion using this term in 1.9, a *hapax legomenon* in 1 Thessalonians.[192] It occurs more frequently in Acts,[193] and the only other NT uses are in the Pauline letters.[194] All the NT uses refer to turning, either to God (in the sense of conversion) or away from God.[195] The use in Acts closely parallels that in the letter.[196]

Paul uses ἐπιστρέφω (1 Thess. 1.9) with similar significance to μετάνοια (Acts 20.21).[197] Μετάνοια and its cognate verb μετανοέω are relatively rare in the Pauline letters, whereas they are more common in Acts.[198] The equivalence of μετάνοια and ἐπιστρέφω in the two places may be taken as highly likely, given the relative rarity of the terms in the Pauline corpus. Further, both verses speak of the converts having turned to God.[199]

Schneider suggests that in Acts 20.21 Luke is using a formula which describes the conversion of Gentiles, just as Paul is using a similar formula in 1 Thessalonians 1.9f.[200] In agreement, Best reasons that vocabulary is used which is unusual for Paul – turned, real, to serve (in relation to God rather than Jesus), out of heavens, ἀναμένω for 'wait', the use of the article in 'raised from the dead', deliver – and that Paul characteristically makes the cross central (alongside the resurrection), whereas it receives no mention here.[201]

However, Wanamaker[202] argues that to speak of a 'pre-Pauline

---

[192] Best, *Thessalonians*, p. 82 suggests that the use in 1 Thess. 1.9 may be dependent on Isa. 6.9f LXX.

[193] Eleven times (3.19; 9.35, 40; 11.21; 14.15; 15.19, 36; 16.18; 26.18, 20; 28.27). Bruce, *Thessalonians*, p. 17 notes that it is commonly used of conversion.

[194] 2 Cor. 3.16 (alluding to Exod. 34.34, but not quoting directly: Belleville, *Reflections of Glory*, pp. 250–2; Thrall, *2 Corinthians*, pp. 268f; Hafemann, *Paul, Moses, and the History of Israel*, pp. 387f); Gal. 4.9 (speaking of the possibility of the Galatians turning back to 'weak and beggarly elemental spirits').

[195] Wanamaker, *Thessalonians*, p. 85; Bruce, *Thessalonians*, p. 17.

[196] Marshall, *Thessalonians*, p. 57.

[197] Moore, *Thessalonians*, p. 30; cf. Aejmelaeus, *Rezeption*, pp. 110f; Dunn, *Acts*, p. 271; Pesch, *Apostelgeschichte*, vol. II, p. 202.

[198] Paul: Rom. 2.4; 2 Cor. 7.9, 10 (noun); 2 Cor. 12.21 (verb). Acts: 2.38; 3.19; 8.22; 17.30; 26.20 (verb); 5.31; 11.18; 13.24; 19.4; 20.21; 26.20 (noun).

[199] Witherington, *Acts*, p. 617.

[200] Schneider, *Apostelgeschichte*, vol. II, p. 295; similarly Best, *Thessalonians*, p. 81; Conzelmann, *Acts*, pp. 173f. Marshall, *Acts* (TNTC), p. 331 notes the parallel without commenting on the presence of a formula.

[201] Best, *Thessalonians*, pp. 85f; in agreement with Bruce, *Thessalonians*, p. 18; Havener, 'Pre-Pauline Christological Credal Formulae', p. 105.

[202] Wanamaker, *Thessalonians*, p. 85. Munck, 'I Thess. I.9–10', esp. pp. 100–2,

formula' is a misnomer, since Paul's ministry went back to the first days of the Christian mission – prior to him there was no known organised mission to Gentiles. Further, the linguistic usage here can be construed as Pauline, and the 'formula' does not seem to have the smoothness which might be expected – for example, there is a shift from second person plural to first person plural at the end of verse 10. The possibility of a pre-Pauline formula is unproven, we may conclude, and it is probable that we have a parallel of synonyms between the letter and the speech.

5.4.3 The Christian message

Two interesting phrases used in 1 Thessalonians to describe Paul's message find potential parallels in the Miletus speech.

Τὸ εὐαγγέλιον τοῦ θεοῦ

In 1 Thessalonians 2.2, 8, 9, Paul writes of τὸ εὐαγγέλιον τοῦ θεοῦ,[203] a phrase found elsewhere in his letters (Rom 1.1; 15.16; 2 Cor. 11.7).[204] Richard[205] notes that all three references in the letter come in close proximity, and suggests that this implies there is a particular issue in Thessalonica over the divine accreditation of the missionaries and their message. Certainly a theme of 2.1–12 is the validity of Paul's ministry, but we have shown[206] that there need not be actual accusations in the background of this section.

The unusual phrase τὸ εὐαγγέλιον τῆς χάριτος τοῦ θεοῦ (Acts 20.24) is an interesting parallel with the 1 Thessalonians passages. Barrett is correct that the precise phrase τὸ εὐαγγέλιον τῆς χάριτος τοῦ θεοῦ does not occur in the Pauline letters, for the phrase is unique in the NT, but the collocation of acknowledged Pauline terms in Acts 20.24 suggests that Luke could use Pauline language in consonance with Paul's own use.[207] Barrett does not suggest that

104–8 argues that 1.9f should be understood by reference to the rest of the letter, considering that it is unpacked by 4.13–5.11, which it anticipates.

[203] The genitive is most probably subjective, that is, God is the origin or author of the message, rather than objective, which would mean that God was the content of the message (Lightfoot, *Notes on the Epistles*, p. 20; Best, *Thessalonians*, p. 91).

[204] Τὸ εὐαγγέλιον τοῦ θεοῦ is found only twice more in the NT (Mark 1.14; 1 Pet. 4.17).

[205] Richard, *Thessalonians*, pp. 78f.

[206] § 5.2.3, *Paul defending himself*; more fully, Walton, 'What Has Aristotle', pp. 240–9.

[207] Barrett, 'Paul's Address', p. 112; see § 3.4.2.

Luke misrepresents Paul, or that what Luke presents has a quite different emphasis to Paul. This verbal parallel may therefore be noted as implying a common thought-world inhabited by Paul and Luke at this point.

The probability of this parallel is increased by observing that Acts 20.24 contains a combination of factors also found in the letter's references to τὸ εὐαγγέλιον τοῦ θεοῦ,[208] namely Paul's voluntary giving of himself (1 Thess. 2.2, 8, 9) and the use of ψυχή (1 Thess. 2.8).[209] This cluster shows Luke's Paul speaking in similar manner and phraseology to the Paul of 1 Thessalonians.

(Ὁ) λόγος τοῦ θεοῦ

1 Thessalonians 2.13 contains two interesting uses of this term: the Thessalonian Christians' welcome of the message (λόγος ... τοῦ θεοῦ) which Paul brought is rejoiced in by Paul because they received it not as a merely human word, but as λόγος θεοῦ.[210] The phrase ὁ λόγος τοῦ κυρίου also occurs (1.8), as does ἐν λόγῳ κυρίου (4.15).[211] The phrase ὁ λόγος τοῦ κυρίου is found in the Pauline corpus[212] (although Paul uses ὁ λόγος τοῦ θεοῦ more often[213]), while also being used in Acts.[214]

In Acts 20.32 Luke's Paul speaks of τῷ λόγῳ τῆς χάριτος αὐτοῦ. Marshall observes that Paul's and Luke's thought coincide in using χάρις and in linking the blessings received to the λόγος.[215] Aejmelaeus[216] also sees a parallel between the speech and the letter in the idea of the word as a 'power' which effects things – almost being

---

[208] Aejmelaeus, *Rezeption*, p. 126.

[209] See § 5.3.2, *Paul's own suffering*.

[210] Subjective genitive, a message *from* God (Lightfoot, *Notes on the Epistles*, p. 31; Rigaux, *Thessaloniciens*, p. 440).

[211] Although this is a special use to refer to a saying of Jesus: see § 5.4.4.

[212] Here and Col. 3.16; 2 Thess. 3.1 (Marshall, *Thessalonians*, pp. 55f; Morris, *Thessalonians* (revised edn.), p. 51 n. 45).

[213] Ὁ λόγος τοῦ θεοῦ is found seven times in Paul (Rom. 9.6; 1 Cor. 14.36; 2 Cor. 2.17; 4.2; Col. 1.25; 1 Thess. 2.13 (twice)), and ὁ λόγος τοῦ κυρίου four times (Col. 3.16; 1 Thess. 1.8; 4.15; 2 Thess. 3.1). This seems rather closer than suggested by the statement that he 'usually' uses the one in preference to the other (Marshall, *Thessalonians*, pp. 55f), and a somewhat small sample for such a statement.

[214] 8.25; 13.44, 48, 49; 15.36; 19.10, 20. It is also a variant reading in 12.24. Wanamaker, *Thessalonians*, p. 83 sees the phrase as having OT origins, offering Gen. 15.1, 4; Isa. 1.10; Jer. 2.4 as examples, although his examples are not always ὁ λόγος τοῦ κυρίου in the LXX: Gen. 15.1 uses ῥῆμα κυρίου and Gen. 15.4 has φωνή κυρίου.

[215] Marshall, *Acts* (TNTC), p. 335.

[216] Aejmelaeus, *Rezeption*, p. 158.

hypostatised by Luke. Further, in both contexts the power of the word is reinforced by additional phrases in which the presence of other 'power' words is noticeable, τῷ δυναμένῳ οἰκοδομῆσαι καὶ δοῦναι τὴν κληρονομίαν ἐν τοῖς ἡγιασμένοις πᾶσιν (Acts 20.32) and ὃς καὶ ἐνεργεῖται ἐν ὑμῖν τοῖς πιστεύουσιν (1 Thess. 2.13).[217]

As with τὸ εὐαγγέλιον τῆς χάριτος τοῦ θεοῦ (Acts 20.24, discussed above), the combination of words found in Acts shows Luke using Pauline language in ways consonant with Paul's thought.

5.4.4 The teaching of Jesus as the basis for ethical exhortation

This point occurs in both 1 Thessalonians and the Miletus speech and is interesting because explicit references to the teaching of Jesus are so rare in the NT outside the Gospels, and particularly in Paul.[218] Paul states that he writes ἐν λόγῳ κυρίου (1 Thess. 4.15f); Luke's Paul cites an (otherwise unknown) saying of Jesus, using a similar formula, τῶν λόγων τοῦ κυρίου Ἰησοῦ (Acts 20.35).

The presence of what are likely to be traditional materials in 1 Thessalonians 4.16f (the Lord's descent, the angels and trumpets, the 'rapture' and probably the κέλευσμα) is evidence for the 'word of the Lord' here being a (traditional) word of Jesus.[219] When Paul cites the teaching of Jesus explicitly, he uses a similar formula.[220] Jeremias observes that 4.16f has ideas in common with Matthew 24.30f, but adds new thoughts (the living and dead meeting the Lord in the air at his coming), and concludes that 4.16f should be seen as an *agraphon.*[221] On either view, Paul's intention in 1 Thess. 4.16f is to claim the authority of Jesus for his teaching at this point.[222]

[217] Pesch, *Apostelgeschichte*, p. 205 observes that 'Paul "commits" the elders to "God and the word of his grace" ... which "is powerful"' (my translation), at which point he parallels 'mächtig' (presumably δυναμένῳ) in Acts 20.32 with 1 Thess. 2.13 (presumably ἐνεργεῖται).
[218] Best, *Paul and His Converts*, pp. 78f; cf. Thompson, *Clothed with Christ*, pp. 15–17, 70–6; Wenham, *Paul*, esp. ch. 1.
[219] Wenham, 'Paul and Synoptic Apocalypse', pp. 367f n. 17; Wenham, *Paul*, pp. 309f. Wenham acknowledges that Paul is here expounding the teaching of Jesus 'freely', and cites Rom. 14.14 as a similar example. Thompson, *Clothed with Christ*, pp. 185–99 concludes his careful discussion, 'a dominical echo is virtually certain'. An alternative view is that this is the word of a Christian prophet, as proposed by Aune, *Prophecy*, pp. 253–6 (a particularly well-documented discussion); Best, *Thessalonians*, pp. 189–94.
[220] Marshall, *Thessalonians*, p. 125, citing Rom. 14.14; 1 Cor. 7.10; 9.14; cf. Longenecker, 'Acts', p. 514.
[221] Jeremias, *Unknown Sayings*, p. 5.
[222] Wanamaker, *Thessalonians*, p. 171.

This is the likeliest understanding of Acts 20.35 also, particularly because of the introductory formula.[223] A saying of Jesus provides a clinching argument in earliest Christianity.

What we see here is not so much a parallel of vocabulary, although the introductory wording is similar in both places, but a parallel of an unusual event, a citation of a saying of Jesus used to back up an ethical exhortation.[224] The question of the authenticity of the saying in either case is neither here nor there for our present purpose: what is significant is that in both cases Paul is portrayed as regarding the citation of a saying of Jesus as conclusive. On this point Luke's Paul and the Paul of 1 Thessalonians inhabit the same thought-world.

5.4.5   Οἰκοδομέω

The Miletus speech contains in Acts 20.32 what Longenecker describes as 'a catena of Pauline terms'; he lists οἰκοδομέω as an example, and offers 1 Thessalonians 5.11 as one case of Pauline use.[225]

Οἰκοδομέω[226] is used in the Pauline corpus, although its use is focused in just four letters.[227] The cognate noun, οἰκοδομή, occurs more frequently in the Pauline letters, but is again found only in four letters, and never in 1 Thessalonians.[228] In Acts the verb is used four times and the noun never.[229] Acts 20.32 is the only use of the verb in Acts within a Pauline speech.[230]

---

[223] Jeremias, *Unknown Sayings*, p. 4; Pesch, *Apostelgeschichte*, vol. II, p. 206; Barrett, 'Sayings of Jesus', pp. 686f.

[224] Best, *Paul and His Converts*, pp. 79, 94 n. 6; cf. Dunn, *Acts*, p. 275.

[225] Longenecker, 'Acts', pp. 513f, citing other uses of οἰκοδομέω in 1 Cor. 8.1; 10.23; 14.4, 17. Aejmelaeus, *Rezeption*, p. 163 lists extensive parallels in Ephesians, as well as 1 Thess. 5.11. Pesch, *Apostelgeschichte*, vol. II, p. 205; Weiser, *Apostelgeschichte*, p. 572 cite the 1 Corinthians references and 1 Thess. 5.11 (misprinted in Peach as 5.1). Cf. Bruce, *Thessalonians*, p. 115; Best, *Thessalonians*, p. 220; Lightfoot, *Notes on the Epistles*, p. 78; Wanamaker, *Thessalonians*, p. 190; Dunn, *Acts*, p. 274; Barrett, *Acts*, vol. II, p. 981, who note the Pauline use of the term.

[226] Wanamaker, *Thessalonians*, p. 189 traces the metaphorical use back to the LXX, especially Jeremiah (e.g. 38.4 (MT 31.4); 40.7 (MT 33.7); 49.10 (MT 42.10)); see also Richard, *Thessalonians*, p. 257; Best, *Thessalonians*, pp. 219f.

[227] Rom. 15.20; 1 Cor. 8.1, 10; 10.23; 14.4, 17; Gal. 2.18; 1 Thess. 5.11.

[228] Rom. 14.19; 15.2; 1 Cor. 3.9; 14.3, 5, 12, 26; 2 Cor. 5.1; 12.19; 13.10; Eph. 2.21; 4.12, 16, 29.

[229] Acts contains the one NT use of οἰκοδόμος (4.11, quoting Ps. 118.22, but not 117.22 LXX; cf. Matt. 21.42; Mark 12.10; Luke 20.17; 1 Pet. 2.7).

[230] The others are in the speech of Stephen (7.47, 49) and a Lukan summary (9.31).

The verb has different subjects in the two contexts: in Acts 20.32 it is the word of God which is able to build up the church,[231] whereas in 1 Thessalonians 5.11 Paul is urging the Thessalonian Christians to build up one another.[232] Nevertheless, in both cases it is the building up of the church that is in view, and this is both a Pauline and a Lukan idea, using common vocabulary.

5.4.6 Ἡ ἐκκλησία τοῦ θεοῦ

Giles has discussed the use of this term in Acts 20.28 and suggests that the ecclesiology present is non-Lukan.[233] He offers three arguments for this assertion: first, this is the only case where the extended designation ἐκκλησία τοῦ θεοῦ is found in Acts – the other eight NT references come within the Pauline letters or the Pastorals;[234] second, the church has been called into existence by God, rather than becoming a community through meeting together; third, 'the redemptive work of Christ here is said to be for the church'[235] – this Giles understands to introduce ideas of communal salvation and substitutionary atonement, both of which are more characteristic of Paul than Luke.

This leads Giles to consider why this use of ἐκκλησία τοῦ θεοῦ might be here. He excludes the possibility that the ideas about ἐκκλησία are Lukan, since his argument has shown that they are not. He proposes that Luke is either using Pauline ideas or using traditional ideas that sound Pauline to our ears. For his purposes, he does not need to choose between these proposals, since on either view the ecclesiology and soteriology are close to Paul's.[236]

When we turn to the use of ἐκκλησία in 1 Thessalonians 1.1; 2.14 (the only uses of the term in the letter), we find the kind of use

---

[231] *Contra* Barrett, *Acts,* vol. II, p. 981, who observes, 'God in his word ... is able to build up the elders.'

[232] Best, *Thessalonians,* p. 220 acutely observes that in Paul's conception 'the Christian does not build up himself, he builds up his fellow-Christians'.

[233] Giles, 'Luke's Use of ἐκκλησία', pp. 136f.

[234] Giles, 'Luke's Use of ἐκκλησία', pp. 141 n. 9 and Schneider, *Apostelgeschichte,* vol. II, p. 297 list 1 Cor. 1.2; 10.32; 11.22; 15.9; 2 Cor. 1.1; Gal. 1.13; 1 Tim. 3.5, 15. There are, as Giles observes ('Luke's Use of ἐκκλησία', pp. 141 n. 10), three further uses where ἐκκλησία is plural, namely 1 Cor. 11.16; 1 Thess. 2.14; 2 Thess. 1.4.

[235] Giles, 'Luke's Use of ἐκκλησία', p. 136.

[236] Giles, 'Luke's Use of ἐκκλησία', p. 137; cf. Schneider, *Apostelgeschichte,* vol. II, p. 297; Weiser, *Apostelgeschichte,* p. 572; Pesch, *Apostelgeschichte,* vol. II, p. 204.

which Giles describes as Pauline.[237] For a Greek speaker, the term ἐκκλησία would certainly need delimiting, because it was a secular term for a citizen-assembly[238] – hence in both places ἐκκλησία is followed by a further designation (ἐν θεῷ πατρί καὶ κυρίῳ Ἰησοῦ Χριστῷ, 1.1; τῶν οὐσῶν ἐν τῇ Ἰουδαίᾳ ἐν Χριστῷ Ἰησοῦ, 2.14). This extended designation in each case marks the church as God's people, called into being by him.[239] Further, the mention in each case of Jesus Christ alludes to the church having become his by his death (cf. 5.10).[240] So in the use of the term ἐκκλησία with a delimiting phrase, Luke presents Paul speaking with a similar accent to the one we hear in 1 Thessalonians.

5.4.7   Μαρτύρομαι, διαμαρτύρομαι

Μαρτύρομαι[241] is used only five times in the NT[242] – the use in 1 Thessalonians 2.12 is a *hapax legomenon* in the letter, and the use in Acts 20.26 is one of only two uses in that book.[243] In these verses we have the use of a rare word used by the same person: in Acts he

---

[237] Witherington, *Acts*, p. 623 cites the parallel with 1 Thess. 2.14 and notes that the use in Acts 20.28 is Pauline in flavour.

[238] Wanamaker, *Thessalonians*, p. 112; Lightfoot, *Notes on the Epistles*, p. 32; Moore, *Thessalonians*, p. 44 suggest that all of the delimitation τοῦ θεοῦ τῶν οὐσῶν ἐν τῇ Ἰουδαίᾳ ἐν Χριστῷ Ἰησοῦ (1 Thess. 2.14) was necessary, since τοῦ θεοῦ τῶν οὐσῶν ἐν τῇ Ἰουδαίᾳ could have referred to the Jewish synagogues. Aejmelaeus, *Rezeption*, p. 137 believes that Luke is using Isa. 43.20f LXX here, but substitutes ἐκκλησία for λαός because the latter meant the *Jewish* people of God. In fact, ἐκκλησία θεοῦ is found only once in the LXX (Neh. 13.1); ἐκκλησία is used without qualification for 'assembly', and can be qualified by κυρίου (Deut. 23.2, 9; 1 Chron. 28.8; Micah 2.5) or Ἰσραήλ (Deut. 31.30; 1 Kings 8.14, 22, 55; 1 Chron. 13.2; 2 Chron. 6.3, 12f; 10.3; 1 Macc. 4.59; Sir. 50.13). Thus Dunn, *Acts*, p. 273 overstates his point in claiming that ἐκκλησία τοῦ θεοῦ is simply regular OT usage taken over by the Christians.

[239] Best, *Thessalonians*, p. 62; Richard, *Thessalonians*, pp. 38, 41f.

[240] Best, *Thessalonians*, p. 62; Bruce, *Thessalonians*, p. 7.

[241] Lightfoot, *Notes on the Epistles*, p. 29 states that it invariably means 'to invoke witnesses' and so 'to appeal to as in the sight of witnesses, to charge, protest', by contrast with μαρτύρουμαι, the passive form of μαρτυρέω, which means 'to be borne witness to'. BAGD, p. 494 offers 'testify, bear witness' and 'affirm, insist, implore'.

[242] Acts 20.26; 26.22; Gal. 5.3; Eph. 4.17; 1 Thess. 2.12. The nouns are used more frequently: μάρτυς is a favourite of Luke (Luke 11.48; 24.48; Acts 1.8, 22; 2.32; 3.15; 5.32; 6.13; 7.58; 10.39, 41; 13.31; 22.15, 20; 26.16) but is also used by Paul (Rom. 1.9; 2 Cor. 1.23; 13.1; Phil. 1.8; 1 Thess. 2.5, 10); μαρτύριον is used much less by both authors (Luke 5.14; 21.13; Acts 4.33; 7.44; 1 Cor. 1.6; 2 Cor. 1.12); and μαρτυρία is a favourite word of John (fourteen uses), but used a little by Luke (Luke 22.71; Acts 22.18), though not in the undisputed Paulines (it is used twice in the Pastorals).

[243] Schneider, *Apostelgeschichte*, vol. II, p. 296 n. 37 observes that the other use in Acts (26.22) is also found on the lips of Paul.

is bearing witness to his own innocence and in 1 Thessalonians he is bearing witness to, or delivering, a solemn demand to the Christians.[244] Morris, commenting on 1 Thessalonians 2.12, cites Acts 20.26 as another place where μαρτύρομαι has the same sense of 'solemn affirmation'.[245] Again, this appears to be a case of the same vocabulary being used by both authors in the same sense.

Διαμαρτύρομαι is also unusual, used fifteen times in the NT in total.[246] Ten are in Luke-Acts,[247] including nine in Acts and three in the Miletus speech (Acts 20.21, 23, 24). 1 Thessalonians 4.6 represents the only use in that letter – indeed, in the Pauline letters outside the Pastorals.[248] Διαμαρτύρομαι may be stronger than μαρτύρομαι, suggesting that it means either 'call to witness' or 'solemnly affirm or protest'.[249] The subject of the verb in two of the three uses in the Miletus speech is Paul himself (verses 21, 24; the other subject is the Spirit, verse 23). In 1 Thessalonians 4.6 the subject is Paul and his colleagues. The two pictures are very close, both presenting Paul in both situations as bearing solemn testimony.[250]

5.5   Leadership in 1 Thessalonians

A striking discovery from our study of Lukan parallels to the Miletus speech was a clear and powerful understanding of Christian leadership.[251] In drawing the threads of our study of 1 Thessalonians together, it is noticeable both how sharply defined a view of leadership emerges, and how similar it is to that found in the Lukan writings. The summary which follows traces similar categories to those in our summary of the Lukan conception of leadership.

---

244 Marshall, *Thessalonians*, p. 74.

245 Morris, *Thessalonians* (revised edn.), p. 77, comparing Gal. 5.3.

246 Luke 16.28; Acts 2.40; 8.25; 10.42; 18.5; 20.21, 23, 24; 23.11; 28.23; 1 Thess. 4.6; 1 Tim. 5.21; 2 Tim. 2.14; 4.1; Heb. 2.6.

247 Nelson, 'Leadership and Discipleship', pp. 196–200 argues that Luke prefers διά-compound verbs, and that the presence of διά adds a nuance of 'thoroughly'; similarly Moulton and Howard, *Grammar*, vol. II, pp. 300–3, esp. 302 concerning διαμαρτύρομαι.

248 Plummer, *Thessalonians*, pp. 62f notes the parallel between 1 Thess. 2.6 and the Miletus speech uses.

249 Frame, *Thessalonians*, p. 154; Plummer, *Thessalonians*, p. 62; Moulton and Howard, *Grammar*, vol. II, p. 302; Blight, *Thessalonians*, p. 126; Trites, *NT Concept of Witness*, p. 74.

250 Trites, *NT Concept of Witness*, p. 75 sees the verb in 1 Thess. 4.6 as having the same meaning as the Acts examples.

251 § 4.6.

Leadership, and Christian discipleship, are fundamentally about Christlikeness, about doing and teaching what Jesus taught and did (ἐν κυρίῳ (᾽Ιησοῦ) 4.1; 5.12; the teaching of Jesus 4.16f), a model that is to be passed on to the next generation of believers (1.6; 4.1). Servanthood, which humbly places the needs of others higher than one's own (δι᾽ ὑμᾶς, 1.5; cf. 2.2, 5f, 7, 9–12; 3.5, 10) is central to this conception – particularly support of the weak (5.14).

This leadership is a costly form of service (2.9; 5.6, 12), and will inevitably involve suffering, both in the past (2.2; 3.3f) and the future (3.3f; 4.1f; 5.2). But Paul, who has experienced such pain, can call others to walk the same path of costly, watchful service of God and his people (5.6, 12). A further focus of this ministry is faithful teaching and testimony concerning the Lord Jesus, a faithfulness of which the readers are well aware ('you know' is said frequently, especially 1.5; 2.10, 11f) – and a faithfulness which is not afraid to 'admonish' at times (5.12, 14), knowing that it is not the fear of people that is to dominate (2.2), but the fear of God (2.4; 3.13; cf. language of God's wrath in 2.16; 5.9). Suffering in the service of God there may be, but there is also future glory to come for the faithful who stay awake (4.15–18; 5.9–11[252]).

This faithful ministry produced a bond of affection between leaders, based, in the case of the missionaries and the nascent church, on lives shared with one another (e.g. 1.9; 2.8; 2.17–3.6; 3.9f, 12). And that sharing was no mere abstract idea, but expressed in the hard currency of work in self-support (2.7, 9; 4.11f) and generosity (2.5f, 8f; 4.11; 5.14) – faithful finances matched the faithful teaching and testimony.

As with the Lukan understanding of leadership, it is clear that this is no vacuous ideal, but an understanding of this ministry worked out by Paul and his colleagues, and expected to be worked out in the congregation's life. The similarities between the two views of leadership are evident: Donfried's suggestion[253] that the view of Paul in Acts may be similar to the earlier epistles has something to be said for it.

---

[252] Note the common ending to these two pieces of teaching: both are intended as the basis of mutual encouragement in the face of pressures of various kinds; cf. Smith, *Comfort One Another*, p. 73.

[253] Donfried and Marshall, *Theology of Shorter Paulines*, pp. 67–70.

5.6 Conclusions

We have considered a number of possible verbal parallels between the Miletus speech and 1 Thessalonians, and in case after case have found that the thought of the two texts, and often its verbal expression, runs remarkably parallel. The conclusion seems inescapable that Luke and Paul *did* inhabit similar thought-worlds. Luke is clearly capable of presenting Paul speaking in ways that sound very like the *ipsissima vox* of the apostle himself. The possible conclusions for an understanding of the relationship between Acts and the Pauline corpus will be considered below.[254]

[254] § 7.2.2.

6

THE MILETUS SPEECH, EPHESIANS AND 2 TIMOTHY

In defining our task we specifically excluded Ephesians and 2 Timothy from consideration because their authorship is disputed. This was not because a comparison with those letters is not worthwhile or productive, but simply because we were seeking *Pauline* parallels to the Miletus speech, and the authorship of 1 Thessalonians is undisputed. However, some scholars have compared the speech with these letters, and have concluded that the letters are close to the speech. The question of the authorship of these disputed Paulines does not fall within the purview of this study[1] – on grounds of space alone. However, we shall outline and evaluate the links proposed with the Miletus speech.

6.1 Ephesians and the Miletus speech

Mitton sets out a series of parallels between the Miletus speech and Ephesians as part of a wider effort to demonstrate parallels between Ephesians and Acts which leads him to conclude that Ephesians was written after Acts.[2] His proposed parallels are:

Miletus speech	*Ephesians*	*Colossians*[3]
verse 19 δουλεύων τῷ κυρίῳ	6.7 μετ᾽ εὐνοίας δουλεύοντες ὡς τῷ κυρίῳ καὶ οὐκ ἀνθρώποις	3.23f ὃ ἐὰν ποιῆτε, ἐκ ψυχῆς ἐργάζεσθε ὡς τῷ κυρίῳ καὶ οὐκ ἀνθρώποις

---

[1] See the valuable discussion of whether pseudonymity was deceptive in Wilder, 'NT Pseudonymity' (with excellent bibliography), concluding that it was, and the contrary view of Bauckham, 'Pseudo-Apostolic Letters'.

[2] Mitton, *Epistle to the Ephesians*, pp. 210–13.

[3] Mitton provides Colossians parallels where he sees them as relevant, usually because he believes that the author of Ephesians has derived the phrase from Colossians.

Miletus speech	Ephesians	Colossians
verse 19 **μετὰ πάσης ταπεινοφροσύνης**	4.1f Παρακαλῶ οὖν ὑμᾶς ἐγὼ ὁ δέσμιος ἐν κυρίῳ ἀξίως περιπατῆσαι τῆς κλήσεως ἧς ἐκλήθητε, **μετὰ πάσης ταπεινοφροσύνης** καὶ πραΰτητος	3.12 Ἐνδύσασθε … ταπεινοφροσύνην πραΰτητα μακρουθμίαν, ἀνεχόμενοι ἀλλήλων
verse 21 διαμαρτυρόμενος Ἰουδαίοις τε καὶ Ἕλλησιν τὴν εἰς θεὸν μετάνοιαν καὶ **πίστιν εἰς τὸν κύριον ἡμῶν Ἰησοῦν**	1.15 ἀκούσας τὴν καθ᾽ ὑμᾶς **πίστιν ἐν τῷ κυρίῳ Ἰησοῦ**	1.4 ἀκούσαντες τὴν πίστιν ὑμῶν ἐν Χριστῷ Ἰησοῦ
verse 24 ὡς τελειῶσαι τὸν δρόμον μου καὶ τὴν **διακονίαν** ἣν ἔλαβον παρὰ τοῦ κυρίου Ἰησοῦ, διαμαρτύρασθαι **τὸ εὐαγγέλιον τῆς χάριτος τοῦ θεοῦ**	3.2, 6f εἴ γε ἠκούσατε τὴν οἰκονομίαν **τῆς χάριτος τοῦ θεοῦ** τῆς δοθείσης μοι εἰς ὑμᾶς … διὰ **τοῦ εὐαγγελίου**, οὗ ἐγενήθην **διάκονος** κατὰ τὴν δωρεὰν **τῆς χάριτος τοῦ θεοῦ**	1.23, 24f τοῦ εὐαγγελίου … οὗ ἐγενόμην ἐγὼ Παῦλος … διάκονος … ἡ ἐκκλησία, ἧς ἐγενόμην ἐγὼ διάκονος κατὰ τὴν οἰκονομίαν τοῦ θεοῦ τὴν δοθεῖσάν μοι εἰς ὑμᾶς
verse 27 οὐ γὰρ ὑπεστειλάμην τοῦ μὴ ἀναγγεῖλαι πᾶσαν **τὴν βουλὴν τοῦ θεοῦ** ὑμῖν	1.11 ἐκληρώθημεν προορισθέντες κατὰ πρόθεσιν τοῦ τὰ πάντα ἐνεργοῦντος κατὰ **τὴν βουλὴν** τοῦ θελήματος **αὐτοῦ**	

Miletus speech	Ephesians
verse 28 προσέχετε	4.11f αὐτὸς ἔδωκεν
ἑαυτοῖς καὶ παντὶ τῷ	... τοὺς δὲ **ποιμένας**
ποιμνίῳ, ἐν ᾧ ὑμᾶς	... εἰς οἰκοδομὴν τοῦ
τὸ πνεῦμα τὸ ἅγιον	σώματος τοῦ
ἔθετο ἐπισκόπους	Χριστοῦ 1.13f
ποιμαίνειν τὴν	ἐσφραγίσθητε τῷ
ἐκκλησίαν τοῦ θεοῦ,	πνεύματι τῆς
ἣν **περιεποιήσατο**	ἐπαγγελίας τῷ ἁγίῳ,
διὰ τοῦ αἵματος τοῦ	ὅ ἐστιν ἀρραβὼν
ἰδίου	τῆς κληρονομίας
	ἡμῶν, εἰς
	ἀπολύτρωσιν τῆς
	περιποιήσεως
	1.7 ἀπολύτρωσιν **διὰ**
	τοῦ αἵματος αὐτοῦ
verse 32 Καὶ τὰ νῦν	1.18 εἰς τὸ εἰδέναι
παρατίθεμαι ὑμᾶς τῷ	ὑμᾶς τίς ἐστιν ἡ
θεῷ καὶ τῷ λόγῳ τῆς	ἐλπὶς τῆς κλήσεως
χάριτος αὐτοῦ, τῷ	αὐτοῦ, τίς ὁ πλοῦτος
δυναμένῳ	τῆς δόξης **τῆς**
οἰκοδομῆσαι καὶ	**κληρονομίας** αὐτοῦ
δοῦναι **τὴν**	**ἐν τοῖς ἁγίοις**
κληρονομίαν ἐν τοῖς	4.12, 16 εἰς
ἡγιασμένοις πᾶσιν	**οἰκοδομήν**

Martin has a similar list, largely agreeing with Mitton.[4] In addition, Martin parallels Ephesians 4.11f with Acts 20.24, and Ephesians 1.11, 14 with Acts 20.32, although he does not specify parallel wording in those cases. In the former case a clear verbal link is the common use of διακονία (Eph. 4.12), and perhaps the use of the cognate nouns εὐαγγελιστής (Eph. 4.11) and εὐαγγέλιον (Acts 20.24); in the latter case the only clear verbal link is the use of κληρονομία.

6.1.1   Evaluation of proposed parallels

How should we evaluate these proposed parallels? It is of interest that only Martin appears to have taken up Mitton's suggestion,

---

[4] Martin, *NT Foundations*, vol. II, p. 231. Martin makes the observations as part of his case that Luke was the author of Ephesians (see further Martin, 'An Epistle in Search').

made in the early 1950s, that Acts and Ephesians are close.[5] Neither of the recent major English scholarly commentaries on Ephesians discusses Mitton's proposals at any length.[6] A closer examination of his proposed parallels with the Miletus speech is in order.

Mitton regards the use of δουλεύων τῷ κυρίῳ (Acts 20.19), which he sets in parallel to Ephesians 6.7 (derived, in his view, from Colossians 3.23f), as suggesting that the author of Acts knows Pauline tradition well, for it is found elsewhere in the undisputed Paulines (Rom. 12.11; 1 Thess. 1.9[7]). Mitton does not argue, however, that Luke is actually using Pauline tradition in Acts 20, but rather that Luke utilises either eye-witness memory of the speech or general knowledge of Paul's ways of speaking derived from personal acquaintance with the apostle. On either explanation, this parallel carries no weight for our purposes.[8]

The use of μετὰ πάσης ταπεινοφροσύνης (Eph. 4.2) is in a context of explicit parenesis, and its parallel in Acts 20.19 is implicit paraenesis, for Paul is there being presented as an example for imitation. Both Lincoln and Best note the use of ταπεινοφροσύνη in Philippians 2.3, 8,[9] although neither mention Acts 20.19. Mitton regards the Ephesians' use as derived from Colossians 3.12, but observes that the use of this phrase in the only occurrence of ταπεινοφροσύνη in Acts and Ephesians is notable.

Mitton's use of Acts 20.21 is more debatable. He claims that 'the faith in our Lord Jesus Christ' appears in all three passages which he cites (Acts 20.21; Eph. 1.5; Col. 1.4), but notes again that this phrase is often used by Paul. However, the phrase is not the same in the three passages: Colossians lacks 'Lord' and adds 'Christ' (which is absent in the other passages). Moreover, the use of εἰς in Acts 20.21 should not be seen as inferring the same kind of 'faith' as in Ephesians and Colossians (where ἐν is used), for the Acts passage is discussing Paul's evangelistic message (note the context of 'repentance toward God'), whereas the Ephesians and Colossians

---

[5] Käsemann, 'Ephesians and Acts', p. 291 n. 1 acknowledges Mitton's work, but says that he is attempting a quite different task in comparing Acts and Ephesians; Käsemann considers major themes rather than showing specific verbal coincidences as evidence, and hardly mentions the Miletus speech, our focus of attention.

[6] I can find no mention of them in Lincoln, *Ephesians*. Best, *Ephesians*, pp. 17f presents them briefly to dismiss them.

[7] See § 5.4.1.

[8] Mitton, *Epistle to the Ephesians*, p. 210.

[9] Lincoln, *Ephesians*, p. 236; Best, *Ephesians*, pp. 362f.

references seem to be about the continuing faith of the recipients.[10] The language may be similar (although not identical), but the reference appears to be different.

On Acts 20.24, Mitton sees four common elements with Ephesians 3.2, 6f: (1) Paul's ministry is διακονία (Acts 20.24), reflected in Ephesians' description of Paul as a διάκονος (3.7); (2) God/ Christ has given Paul this minstry, rather than Paul taking the initiative; (3) the διακονία is linked to the gospel; (4) the διακονία is linked to the grace of God. Again, Mitton sees Ephesians as dependent on Colossians for the first three ideas, which are found in Colossians 1.23, 25.

However, διάκονος/διακονία is such a common Pauline description of his task or the task of Christian leadership that we may doubt the significance of the parallel.[11] Further, it is not simply that Paul's διακονία is associated with the gospel, but in Ephesians 3.7 and Colossians 1.23, 25 (uniquely in the Pauline corpus) that Paul is a servant of the gospel – this is a different thought to Acts 20.24, where Paul's ministry is characterised as διακονία, and the context implies that it is service of the Lord Jesus. As before, this looks like a case of similar wording, but with the word(s) used in different senses.

Again, the thought that Paul's ministry stems from God's initiative is hardly unique to the Miletus speech and Ephesians, being prominent throughout the Pauline corpus,[12] so it is hard to see why Mitton sees this as so significant, particularly given that the vocabulary used in the passages differs so much. The verb of giving is different (λαμβάνω, Acts 20.24; δίδωμι, Eph. 3.2; Col. 1.25) and the one giving differs ('the Lord Jesus', Acts 20.24; God, Eph. 3.2;

[10] Lincoln, *Ephesians*, p. 55 notes that, although popular Greek did not always distinguish rigorously between εἰς and ἐν (see Moule, *Idiom-Book*, pp. 67, 75f), use of ἐν with πίστις in the Pauline corpus generally refers to the realm in which faith operates (Gal. 3.26; 5.6; Col. 1.4; 1 Tim. 1.15; 3.13; 2 Tim. 1.13; 3.15). Gal. 2.16 shows the cognate verb used with εἰς in a context speaking of the initial response of faith to the gospel message.

[11] Διάκονος is used of Paul and other early Christian leaders (e.g. Rom. 16.1; 1 Cor. 3.5; 2 Cor. 3.6; 6.4; 11.23; Phil. 1.1; cf. similar use in Col. 1.7; 4.7; 1 Tim. 4.6). Διακονία is used similarly (Rom. 11.13; 15.31; 2 Cor. 4.1; 5.18; 6.3; 11.8; cf. Col. 4.17; 1 Tim. 1.12; 2 Tim. 4.5, 11), as well as with a wider meaning of 'service' (such as the collection, 2 Cor. 8.4; 9.1, 12, 13). The verb διακονέω has both the narrower sense (2 Cor. 3.3; Phm 13; cf. 1 Tim. 3.10, 13; 2 Tim. 1.18) and a similar wider sense (the collection, Rom. 15.25; 2 Cor. 8.19, 20).

[12] e.g. Gal. 1.1, 10–12, 15f; 2.7; 1 Cor. 1.17; 15.8ff with 9.1; Rom. 1.1; 1 Thess. 2.4. For discussion see Kim, *Origin of Paul's Gospel*, pp. 56–66; Dunn, *Theology of Paul*, pp. 571–80; Donaldson, 'Israelite, Convert'.

Col. 1.25). Overall, Mitton's conclusion that there is a 'large measure of similarity'[13] between Acts 20.24 and Ephesians 3.2, 7 seems considerably overstated.

Concerning Acts 20.27, we have already observed that Luke and Paul both use βοθλή or the cognate verb, although it is clear that Luke uses this language more frequently than Paul.[14] Nevertheless, when Mitton fails to mention the use of the cognate verb by Paul he is only giving selective evidence – and Ephesians does not use the same phrase as Acts, for it is 'the plan of his will', which is a similar idea, but not the same language.

Acts 20.28 contains a relatively unusual use of 'flock' and 'shepherd' as metaphorical language for the church and its pastors, and Mitton is right in observing that Ephesians 4.11f uses similar language.[15] However, contrary to Mitton's assertion, this language is used by Paul; 1 Corinthians 9.7 in context is describing Paul and Barnabas' ministry using this language – three times in that verse.

Mitton also observes that the rare περιποιέομαι/περιποίησις are found in these verses (Acts 20.28;[16] Eph. 1.14), and notes that this verse, containing the only use in Ephesians, links περιποίσις with ἀπολύτρωσις. He then connects this with the use of ἀπολύτρωσις in 1.7, which is διὰ τοῦ αἵματος αὐτοῦ,[17] as in Acts 20.28. An explanatory διὰ-clause is found in the parallel in 1 Thessalonians 5.9f too, which suggests that Mitton goes beyond the evidence in suggesting that the parallel is particularly significant – for again it reflects Pauline language found elsewhere. Mitton's further observation, that in both cases there is an association with the Holy Spirit, is stretching the point to breaking, for in Acts 20.28 the Spirit appointed the elders as overseers, but in Ephesians 1.13f the Spirit is the 'earnest' of redemption – two different actions, and the former not associated with περιποιέομαι. Overall, there is a link

[13] Mitton, *Epistle to the Ephesians*, p. 211.
[14] See p. 80 n. 111.
[15] Ephesians uses ποιμήν and Acts uses the cognate noun ποίμνη and the cognate verb ποιμαίνω; cf. Barrett, *Acts,* vol. II, p. 974.
[16] Cf. § 5.3.4.
[17] It is hard to see how Mitton can claim that Eph. 1.7 is taken 'word for word' from Col. 1.14 (Mitton, *Ephesians* (NCB), p. 52), since blood is not mentioned in Col. 1.14 and a different word for 'sin' is used (as also argued in Lincoln, *Ephesians*, p. 27). Mitton earlier suggested Col. 1.20 as the source for διὰ τοῦ αἵματος αὐτοῦ in Eph. 1.7 (Mitton, *Epistle to the Ephesians*, p. 65), but the link of blood with redemption was made early in Christian tradition, including by Paul (e.g. Rom. 3.24f), so it seems more likely that Acts (to say nothing of Ephesians) uses Pauline tradition (Best, *Ephesians*, p. 129).

between Acts 20.28 and Ephesians 1.14 in the use of περιποιέομαι/ περιποίησις, but Mitton considerably overstates it.

Mitton observes that Acts 20.32 and Ephesians 1.18 both use κληρονομία in combination with a phrase meaning 'among (ἐν) the saints'[18] for believers' 'share in the blessings of Christ's kingdom'.[19] He claims that this word is characteristic of Ephesians,[20] and that it is the only use of the word in this sense in the Pauline writings (except Colossians 3.24); however, he fails to notice that the participle of the cognate verb κληρονομέω is used by Paul in this sense in a number of places,[21] which considerably reduces the significance of his observation.

Mitton also draws attention to the uses of οἰκοδομέω (Acts 20.32) and the cognate noun οἰκοδομή (Eph. 4.12, 16), but without seeing that the contexts are very different. In Acts the building up is done by 'the Lord and the word of his grace', whereas in Ephesians it is the work of the apostles, prophets, evangelists, pastors and teachers (4.12) or the whole body (4.16). Again, the language coincides, but the use does not.

Mitton concludes by claiming that these phrases all come within the Miletus speech, and that six such coincidences are suggestive, particularly since the speech is Paul's farewell to the elders of Ephesus.[22] However, in case after case we have seen Mitton offering selective evidence or overstating what the evidence will bear. That there are parallels between the Miletus speech and Ephesians we may grant; that they are extensive enough to merit Mitton's conclusion we must doubt. The distance between the Miletus speech and Ephesians appears considerably greater than that between the speech and 1 Thessalonians.

6.2.   2 Timothy and the Miletus speech

In the case of 2 Timothy there is a *prima facie* case for expecting parallels with the Miletus speech, since the atmosphere of both documents is one of farewell.[23] Several scholars believe that there

---

[18] Acts uses an aorist substantival participle in combination with πᾶς; Ephesians uses the adjective ἅγιος substantivally.
[19] Mitton, *Epistle to the Ephesians*, p. 213.
[20] Of fourteen NT uses, three are found in Ephesians (1.14, 18; 5.5).
[21] Rom. 8.17; 1 Cor. 6.9, 10; 15.50 (twice); Gal. 3.29; 4.7; 5.21.
[22] Mitton, *Epistle to the Ephesians*, p. 213.
[23] This represents the consensus view of 2 Timothy, particularly because of 4.6–8 (including those favouring pseudepigraphical and those favouring Pauline author-

are similarities between the speech and the Pastoral Epistles, particularly 2 Timothy;[24] we shall summarise and respond to Schmithals' presentation, which we consider since he offers evidence (rather than merely asserting that there are similarities).

We note first, however, that it can be unhelpful to group the Pastorals together in an undifferentiated way – although this has been common for the last two hundred years. There are several dangers inherent in this approach.[25] In particular, and relevant to our discussion, a composite description of the situation(s) assumed is frequently drawn from all three letters and then applied equally to each of them.[26] A notable example is the common assertion that the Pastorals present a model of church order closer to later Ignatian models than the undisputed Paulines. In fact, 2 Timothy says virtually nothing about church order and Titus only a little; the bulk of the material on this topic is in 1 Timothy (e.g. 3.1–13; 5.17–22). The situations presupposed in the three letters may be different, and there is evidence that the opponents in the background of each letter do not have the same profile.[27] So we shall consider parallels between the Miletus speech and 2 Timothy without importing evidence from the other Pastorals.

6.2.1   Schmithals' evidence

Schmithals believes that a Pauline travel source containing elements of the speech (Acts 20.18–19a, 25a, 26–32) lies behind Luke's version.[28] Nevertheless, he seeks parallels through the speech.

He begins with the clear parallel of Acts 20.24 and 2 Timothy

ship); see, e.g., Dibelius and Conzelmann, *Pastoral Epistles*, p. 121; Hanson, *Pastoral Epistles*, p. 155; Barrett, *Pastoral Epistles*, pp. 118f; Lock, *Pastoral Epistles*, pp. 114f; Kelly, *Pastoral Epistles*, pp. 7, 207f; Fee, *Timothy, Titus*, pp. 288f; Houlden, *Pastoral Epistles*, pp. 132f; Knight, *Pastoral Epistles*, pp. 458f; Johnson, *Letters to Paul's Delegates*, p. 93; *contra* Prior, *Paul the Letter-Writer*, pp. 91–112 (arguing that the language used indicates that Paul expected release).

[24] e.g. Schmithals, 'Apg 20,17–38'; Lock, *Pastoral Epistles*, p. xxv; Houlden, *Pastoral Epistles*, p. 133; Knight, *Pastoral Epistles*, p. 23; Rackham, *Acts*, p. 384; Wilson, *Luke and Pastoral Epistles*, pp. 117f; Roloff, *Apostelgeschichte*, p. 302; Pesch, *Apostelgeschichte*, vol. II, pp. 206f; Barrett, *Acts*, vol. II, pp. 964f.

[25] Johnson, *Letters to Paul's Delegates*, pp. 7f; Prior, *Paul the Letter-Writer*, p. 61.

[26] e.g. Barrett, *Acts*, vol. II, p. 965; Wilson, *Luke and Pastoral Epistles*, pp. 117f.

[27] Johnson, *Letters to Paul's Delegates*, p. 13.

[28] Schmithals, 'Apg 20,17–38', p. 313, based on Schmithals, *Apostelgeschichte*, pp. 188f. Schmithals also believes that the speech targets Gnostics (whom he sees as Paul's opponents everywhere; see § 1.3.2, p. 35); for critique, see Lüdemann, *Acts*, p. 229.

4.7.[29] Both passages combine τελειόω and the rare δρόμος.[30] This is a clear parallel of vocabulary, which Schmithals ascribes to the use of a Pauline itinerary source by both authors.

Schmithals goes on to observe that there are generally very few clear agreements; rather, there are obvious divergences between the speech and the Pastorals. Acts 20.33–5 differs from 1 Timothy 5.17f; 2 Timothy 2.6 in its view of the payment of church leaders, and the lack of knowledge of Paul's future in the speech (Acts 20.22) differs from 2 Timothy 4.6. His case for the resemblance of the speech and the Pastorals is built, therefore, on similar themes, and does not have the rigour of working with similar vocabulary. His argument has two parts: first, he claims that there are similar general situations underlying both speech and letter; and second, he proposes details of the speech and the letter as parallel.

Schmithals identifies six common factors in the situations of the letter and the speech (by contrast with other speeches in Acts):[31] (1) both are aimed at a Christian audience; (2) both are speaking to congregational leaders and set out the meaning of taking or holding office; (3) the theme in both cases is Paul as an example; (4) both speak directly to a church situation; (5) the label *'Abschiedsrede'* or 'testament' fits them both; (6) both were written in the expectation of the death of Paul (Acts 20.25a; 2 Tim. 4.6–8), who has completed his work in the eastern Mediterranean (2 Tim. 1.17), and neither text shows knowledge of a further period of freedom for Paul, whether in Rome or further west.

In response, it must be said that (1), (3) and (4) apply equally well to 1 Thessalonians (to say nothing of other undisputed Paulines), and that (2) applies to significant parts of 1 Thessalonians, particularly 2.1–12; 5.12ff.[32] The only potentially significant points of contact with the Miletus speech are (5), which we accepted

---

[29] Schmithals, 'Apg 20,17–38', p. 313; cf. Moule, 'Problem of the Pastorals', pp. 125f; Strobel, 'Schreiben des Lukas?'; Wilson, *Luke and Pastoral Epistles*, p. 117; Schneider, *Apostelgeschichte*, vol. II, p. 295 n. 30; Haenchen, *Acts*, p. 592; Schille, *Apostelgeschichte*, p. 402; Roloff, *Apostelgeschichte*, p. 304; Rackham, *Acts*, p. 391; Williams, *Acts* (NIBC), pp. 353f; Williams, *Commentary on Acts*, p. 233; Marshall, *Acts* (TNTC), p. 332; Pesch, *Apostelgeschichte*, vol. II, p. 203; Bruce, *Acts* (3rd edn), p. 432; Dunn, *Acts*, p. 272; Barrett, *Acts,* vol. II, p. 965; Johnson, *Letters to Paul's Delegates*, p. 361; Lock, *Pastoral Epistles*, p. 114; Hanson, *Pastoral Epistles*, p. 155; Fee, *Timothy, Titus*, p. 289; Houlden, *Pastoral Epistles*, p. 133; Knight, *Pastoral Epistles*, pp. 459f.

[30] Found in the NT only in these two passsages and Acts 13.25.

[31] Schmithals, 'Apg 20,17–38', p. 313.

[32] See § 5.3.1.

in a qualified form for the Miletus speech,[33] and (6), which is highly debatable.[34]

Schmithals discusses five more detailed proposed points of contact between the Pastorals and the speech. We shall focus on suggested links with 2 Timothy.

First, there are warnings about false teachers in both cases.[35] Acts 20.29f alerts the elders to the coming 'wolves' from within and without the congregation, as do 2 Timothy 3.1ff; 4.3f. Schmithals states that in both cases the false teachers are presented as a future threat, a feature which he regards as fictional, although in line with Luke's presentation of the apostolic age as a 'heresy free zone'. He regards Acts 20.30 as presenting a picture of outsiders who teach falsely and infiltrate the church, in similar manner to 2 Timothy 2.17; 3.6–9; 4.3f, and oberves that the false teachers are Ephesian in provenance (2 Tim. 1.15; 2.17).

However, Schmithals' reconstruction does not stand up to examination. The false teachers in 2 Timothy are already known to the congregation – some are named (1.15; 2.17f; 4.14f), unusually in the Pauline corpus. Further, at least some are insiders rather than outsiders (a picture more consistent with Acts 20.29f[36]). It is hard to see how the mention of these specific, named people in 2 Timothy implies that the threat of false teachers is located entirely in the future – the present tenses of 3.6–8 suggest otherwise.

Second, Schmithals claims that the views of the false teachers are not described in the Miletus speech or the Pastorals.[37] He sees Acts 20.27 as suggesting that the false teachers see some deficit in orthodox teaching which they will try to fill, and 2 Timothy not as defending orthodoxy against other views, but merely stating its validity and sufficiency (2.24; 3.13ff; 4.2), and its basis in Scripture (3.15–17). Further, Acts 20.28 appeals to the readers' memory of 'sound teaching' in similar manner to 2 Timothy 1.9f; 2.8, and the denial of other teaching is only brief in both speech and letter.

Certainly we know little of the specific beliefs of the false teachers in either case (2 Tim. 2.18 is perhaps the best hint), but the same

[33] § 3.2.2.

[34] See § 3.4.3 on the Miletus speech. Johnson, *Letters to Paul's Delegates*, pp. 32, 38–41 challenges the view that 2 Timothy is a 'testament', arguing that it should be seen as a personal paraenetic letter.

[35] Schmithals, 'Apg 20,17–38', p. 314; similar are Wilson, *Luke and Pastoral Epistles*, p. 117; Dunn, *Acts*, p. 273; Barrett, *Acts*, vol. II, pp. lxiii, 965.

[36] As Wilson, *Luke and Pastoral Epistles*, p. 117 notes.

[37] Schmithals, 'Apg 20,17–38', pp. 314f.

could be said of other NT contexts, such as Colossians (where there is considerable debate over the context into which the letter is written[38]). There are other places where Paul calls Christians to recall his teaching, in which he alludes briefly to what were clearly major themes (e.g. 1 Thess. 1.9f; 1 Cor. 15.1ff). The call to remember past teaching looks like a common Pauline theme found in the Miletus speech and closely resembling what is found in 2 Timothy. The parallel proposed is therefore not significant for our discussion.

Third, Schmithals believes that orthodox teaching is to be safe-guarded by a succession of orthodox teachers in both cases.[39] He regards the use of παρατίθημι (Acts 20.32) as a 'succession formula' parallel to 2 Timothy 2.2. Schmithals notes the insistence on Paul's innocence (2 Tim. 4.7; 1.3; Acts 20.20, 26f), showing that Paul is presented as passing on this 'sound teaching' himself (2 Tim. 1.13; 2.10; 3.10) – a task to which his successors are called (2 Tim. 2.14, 25f; 4.1ff). Käsemann similarly asserts that in the Miletus speech Paul is contrasting the dangers of his time with the ideal of the one true church whose teaching office safeguards its faithfulness to the faith.[40]

However, there is no suggestion anywhere in the speech that the elders are Paul's successors or that Paul is handing office on to them. They are already leaders in the congregation(s) of Ephesus, and in Acts 20.32 they are being commended to God, rather than having an office handed on to them. Barrett rightly observes that the idea of apostolic succession is absent from the speech.[41] We know nothing about how they became elders, except that it was the Holy Spirit's work (verse 28).[42] If Luke were providing a *frühkatho-lisch* model, we would expect some reference to the process of

---

[38] See, e.g., Wright, *Colossians*, pp. 23–34 (Judaism); Dunn, *Colossians*, pp. 23–35 (Jewish apologetics); Barth and Blanke, *Colossians*, pp. 21–41 (inconclusive); DeMaris, *Colossian Controversy* (an ascetic philosophy based on Middle Platonism); Hooker, 'False Teachers' (no false teachers at all).

[39] Schmithals, 'Apg 20,17–38', pp. 315f; cf. Barrett, *Acts,* vol. II, p. 965.

[40] Käsemann, *Disciples of John*, p. 145.

[41] Barrett, 'Apollos', pp. 35f; Barrett, *Acts,* vol. II, pp. xcvif, 976; cf. Witherington, *Acts*, pp. 615, 623; Jervell, *Apostelgeschichte*, p. 513; Haenchen, *Apostelgeschichte* (16th edn), p. 62: 'Von "Frühkatholizismus" sollte man besser hier [*sc.* in Acts] noch nicht sprechen, ebensowenig von einem Fortleben der paulinischen Verkündigung.' ('It would be better to speak neither of "early catholicism" [in Acts], nor of the continuing life of the Pauline proclamation.') – a comment absent from the 15th edition and therefore not in the English translation, Haenchen, *Acts*.

[42] Barrett, *Acts,* vol. II, p. xc.

handing over office. Similarly, in 2 Timothy 2.2 there is no suggestion that an office is to be handed on from Timothy; rather, it is the apostolic teaching which he is to pass on to these 'faithful people'.[43] If the Miletus speech and 2 Timothy are close at this point, they are not close in the way Schmithals suggests.

Fourth, Schmithals asserts that only in the Pastorals and the Miletus speech do 'elders' and 'bishops' meet.[44] However, he concedes that there is no mention of either designation in 2 Timothy, which means that there is no parallel here between this letter and the speech.

Fifth, Schmithals points to a look back to the past relationship Paul had with the congregation or individual (Acts 20.18–19a; 2 Tim. 1.3ff), and to their memory of Paul's ministry (Acts 20.31; 2 Tim. 4.7). This seems accurately observed, but it is hardly of great significance in relating the speech and the letter closely, for Paul's letters contain other retrospective views of earlier relationships, notably 1 Thessalonians 1.4–2.12, recalling the initial visit of Paul and his colleagues to Thessalonica. What is lacking in 2 Timothy, but present in 1 Thessalonians and the Miletus speech, are details concerning the relationship or Paul's conduct – again, the distance between 2 Timothy and the Miletus speech is considerably greater than that between 1 Thessalonians and the speech.

Wilson further observes that the theme of suffering is found in the speech and 2 Timothy.[45] Acts 20.19–24 and 2 Timothy 1.11f speak similarly of Paul suffering for the ministry he is engaged in, but without any coincidence of vocabulary: πάσχω (2 Tim. 1.12) is not found in the Miletus speech.[46]

Schmithals concludes by asserting that each thought of the Miletus speech can be found in the Pastorals, particularly 2 Timothy. He believes that they share a common author.[47] However, our investigation suggests that the speech does not appear particularly close to 2 Timothy. Certainly there are some

[43] Cf. Barrett, *Acts,* vol. II, p. 980.

[44] Schmithals, 'Apg 20,17–38', pp. 316–18; also Wilson, *Luke and Pastoral Epistles,* p. 118; Barrett, *Acts,* vol. II, p. 965. For discussion of the relationship of the two terms in the Pastorals, see Towner, *Goal of Our Instruction,* pp. 223–9; Campbell, *The Elders,* pp. 176–205.

[45] Wilson, *Luke and Pastoral Epistles,* p. 118; Barrett, *Acts,* vol. II, p. 965.

[46] It is reserved by Luke almost invariably for the suffering of Jesus (Luke 9.22; 17.25; 24.26, 46; Acts 1.3; 3.18; 17.3). Luke uses the verb in relation to Paul only twice (Acts 9.16; 28.5) – although in the latter he is said *not* to suffer!

[47] Schmithals, 'Apg 20,17–38', p. 320.

parallels of thought; however, such parallels lack the coincidence of vocabulary which we found in 1 Thessalonians.[48] We may also agree that there is one clear parallel of vocabulary. But these examples do not support Schmithals' extravagant conclusion. Indeed, if the relationship of thought were as close as Schmithals proposes, we should expect eschatological motives to be cited in the Miletus speech as they are in 2 Timothy 4.1f – but eschatology is notably absent from the speech. Similarly, as Barrett concedes, it is surprising that there is nothing in any of the Pastorals to parallel Acts 20.28, 'the most explicit theological verse in the speech'.[49]

6.3   Conclusion

Our examination of proposed parallels in Ephesians and 2 Timothy leads to a clear conclusion. Ephesians and 2 Timothy, where they are close to the Miletus speech, are close at the level of ideas sometimes, and in the vocabulary expressing those ideas only rarely. By contrast, 1 Thessalonians appears close to the speech in both words and ideas. Thus the Miletus speech does not belong with the 'deutero-Paulines', for the similarities proposed with these particular 'deutero-Paulines' are not close, by contrast with the close parallels found in 1 Thessalonians.

[48] A fact which is of interest since the proportion of words in the speech shared by 1 Thessalonians and 2 Timothy is not very different: 49.4% of the words found in the speech are found in 1 Thessalonians (being 22.7% of the vocabulary of the letter), and 50.0% in 2 Timothy (being 18.3% of the vocabulary of the letter). (These statistics are derived from a combination of the total vocabulary found in Morgenthaler, *Statistik*, p. 164 and use of *Accordance*.) 51.2% of the words of the speech are found in Ephesians (16.3% of the vocabulary of the letter). Large numbers of these shared words are unlikely to be relevant (e.g. prepositions, copulas, pronouns).

[49] Barrett, *Acts,* vol. II, p. 965.

7

CONCLUDING REFLECTIONS

Our detailed study is ended, and the time has come to summarise and discuss the implications of our results – as well as to consider what avenues future research on questions raised in this study might follow.

7.1 Review and summary of results

We began by observing the importance of the Miletus speech for two interlocking debates (chapter 1): concerning the relationship between the portrait of Paul found in Acts and that derived from the epistles; and concerning whether Luke knew the Pauline epistles. We also reviewed the history of scholarship on this speech – a 'set piece' for most modern critical approaches to Acts. We set out to examine the speech in its Lukan contexts (within Acts and in relation to the whole of Luke-Acts), and to consider potential parallels in 1 Thessalonians. Our aim was to see how Lukan and how Pauline the speech is.

We then outlined our method (chapter 2), and discussed how parallels are to be recognised. We acknowledged the inevitable subjective element in seeking parallels, but sought a measure of objectivity by using a hierarchical approach, beginning with lexical parallels (including cognate words and compounds) before considering synonyms, conceptual parallels, and parallel styles of argumentation. We saw 'clustering' of such parallels in particular passages as likely to be significant. We explained our decision to focus on one Pauline letter, by contrast with traditional approaches which compare the Miletus speech with a wider Pauline letter-group.

After we outlined the immediate context in Acts (§ 3.1), consideration of the Miletus speech in the context of ancient 'farewell speeches' (§ 3.2) suggested that it has much in common with this genre, although care needs to be taken not automatically to attribute to our speech all the features of the genre, bearing in mind that a genre is a construct from the extant examples.

Concerning structure (§ 3.3), the speech appears at first sight to be well organised. A number of features reinforce this view: the repetitions of key words and phrases, the time references, and the change of subject. However, the lack of any scholarly consensus on the sub-divisions of the speech suggests that this appearance may be deceptive, and we concluded that it is better to see the speech as a tapestry, where the major themes are like threads interwoven with each other, often in subtle ways.

Consideration of the contents of the speech therefore took two forms: a consecutive reading, section by section through the speech, seeing its main threads (§ 3.4); and a thematic reading, tracing the four major themes through the whole speech (leadership, suffering, wealth and work, and the death of Jesus, § 3.5).

In the light of these readings, we sought parallels in Luke's Gospel (chapter 4), finding three extensive and suggestive passages (22.14–38; 12.1–53; 21.5–36). The Last Supper discourse (22.14–38, § 4.2) in particular is part of a similar 'farewell' scene, but parallels with the Miletus speech go well beyond the generic, echoing the four major Miletus themes in both structure and sequence, including reference to the redemptive significance of the death of Jesus – a rare explicit mention of this theme in Luke-Acts. The discourse on discipleship (12.1–53, § 4.3) offers considerable parallels to the Miletus speech on the themes of leadership, suffering and wealth, as well as paralleling some unusual words in Luke-Acts. The Lukan Apocalypse (21.5–36, § 4.4) contains a 'cluster' of parallels to Paul's speech. Four briefer passages (7.38, 44; 9.2; 10.3; 13.32, § 4.5) offer suggestive individual points of comparison with the speech. A sharply focused portrait of Christian leadership as Luke understands it emerges (§ 4.6) – a portrait seen first in the life and teaching of Jesus, and then reflected in the ministry and teaching of Paul. Moreover, the Miletus meeting presents Paul calling the Ephesian leaders to imitate this model. One fresh contribution of this study is to show that a key aim of Paul's address is the presentation of a model of leadership for imitation, contrasting with the focus on questions about ministerial office in previous studies.[1]

---

[1] e.g. Prast, *Presbyter und Evangelium*; Knoch, *Die Testamente*.

The portrait of Christian leadership emerging from the study to this point gave particular interest to consideration of the Miletus speech in relation to 1 Thessalonians (chapter 5). The value of studying this letter stems from its authenticity as a Pauline letter (thus providing a sound database for comparison), from its pastoral nature, and from *prima facie* evidence of similar themes (including Paul's past conduct, suffering and leadership) (§ 5.1.1). An initial orientation (§ 5.2) confirmed its indubitably Pauline nature and outlined its likely date and occasion. The letter serves as a substitute for a visit which the missionary team of Paul, Silas and Timothy was unable to make, responds to the news of persecution with encouragement and support, and responds to questions raised by the Thessalonian Christians.

Our examination of the letter began by observing the presence of the four major Miletus themes in 1 Thessalonians, often with the same or similar vocabulary (§ 5.3). This is particularly clear in considering leadership, but also evident in relation to suffering, money and work, and the death of Jesus. We then considered whether other emphases in the letter are paralleled in the address (§ 5.4), and found several examples which reinforce the parallel. Turning to leadership, where such a striking portrait emerged from examination of Luke-Acts, we found a similar picture in the letter (§ 5.5). Our study suggests that the Paul of 1 Thessalonians and the Paul of the Miletus speech sound very similar – and the similarities extend to vocabulary and to manner and style of teaching.

An examination of the speech in parallel with Ephesians (§ 6.1) and 2 Timothy (§ 6.2) showed how meagre the parallels with those two letters seem to be – surprisingly, in view of the claims made by Mitton and Martin (Ephesians) and Schmithals and others (2 Timothy) that there are significant parallels. The speech is far closer to 1 Thessalonians, on this showing, than to these so-called 'deutero-Paulines'. This suggests that the oft-claimed closeness of the later Paulines and the Miletus speech is mistaken – the speech is far closer to an indubitably Pauline (and early Pauline, at that) letter.

7.2   Implications for study of the Miletus speech

Two areas invite discussion in the light of our study so far: the place of the speech in the wider scheme of Luke-Acts; and Luke's sources. We shall suggest implications of our research for each.

7.2.1   The Miletus speech in Luke-Acts

Three issues are intertwined: to what extent the speech should be understood as a 'farewell' by Paul; why the speech is located at this point in the narrative; and the overall portrait of Paul in Acts.

To the question whether the address is Paul's 'farewell' in Acts we must answer both 'yes' and 'no'. It shows significant parallels to other ancient farewell speeches, especially from Jewish contexts, and Paul is presented as taking leave of a group he never expects to see again (Acts 20.25, 38). To that extent it is a farewell to this set of people.

However, the argument that Luke assumes Paul to be dead at the time of writing Acts is inconclusive (§ 3.4.3). Acts 20.25, 38 together do not necessarily say any more than that Luke's Paul is uncertain about his future, although his firm expectation is that he will not re-visit Ephesus.[2] Further, the evidence is lacking that Luke intends this as his narrative farewell for Paul, since Paul goes on being active for some time and makes further speeches.

The Paul for whom this speech may be a farewell is the missionary Paul, for from Acts 21.27 onwards we see the prisoner Paul. At this transition point, the church-planting Paul teaches the key themes of Christian leadership to the Ephesian church leaders, who will later pass the torch on to their successors. Luke's use of the speech here adds the final lines to his portrait of Paul the missionary, for without this address we would know little of Paul the pastor – up to Acts 21.26 the focus has been on Paul the church-planting missionary.[3] Paul here models for Luke's readers how to lead and pastor a church at a time when he has planted many churches, and when he has recently (Acts 20.7–12) taught a church, raised a church member from the dead[4] and broken bread.[5]

---

[2] Cf. Rom. 15.23f, which imply (about two to three years prior to Luke's ostensible dating of the Miletus speech) that the historical Paul intended to travel westward to Spain, with Rome as a staging post along the way.

[3] Hengel, *Acts and the History*, p. 110; Marshall, *Acts* (TNTC), p. 43 n. 4. Cf. Maddox, *Purpose of Luke-Acts*, pp. 67, 76–80; Pervo, *Luke's Story of Paul*, p. 73; Rapske, *Paul in Roman Custody*, pp. 429–36.

[4] Ἤρθη νεκρός (20.9) 'should not be weakened to "as if" dead' (Conzelmann, *Acts*, p. 169); similarly Haenchen, *Acts*, p. 585; Bruce, *Acts* (3rd edn), p. 426 (noting the different phraseology in 14.19, νομίζοντες αὐτὸν τεθνηκέναι); Marshall, *Acts* (TNTC), p. 326; *contra* Tannehill, *Narrative Unity*, vol. II, pp. 248f.

[5] Pervo, *Luke's Story of Paul*, p. 74, noting the proximity of 20.7–12 and the Miletus speech, suggests that they are Luke's portrait of Paul the pastor.

7.2.2   Luke's source(s)

The natural question, given the amount of parallelism between the Miletus speech and 1 Thessalonians that we have found (§§ 5.3–5.5), is whether one account might be dependent on the other. It has not been proposed that the letter is dependent on Luke's record of the speech, because 1 Thessalonians is generally thought to be early, but it has been suggested that Luke has used the letter in composing the Miletus speech.[6]

Before turning to detailed reasons for this thesis, we should first review the logical possibilities for the relationship of the speech and the letter. There are at least five possible explanations of the parallels we have observed. First, Luke had 1 Thessalonians before him as he wrote Acts, and used it extensively in composing the Miletus speech. Second, Luke had knowledge of 1 Thessalonians, but in writing Acts – at least while writing the Miletus speech – he relied upon his memory of the letter, rather than having the text before him. Third, Luke had access to other written (non-letter) Pauline sources (such as a diary of the companion of Paul who was present in the 'we' sections) as he wrote the Miletus speech, perhaps including a source for the Miletus speech itself, and the parallels between the speech and 1 Thessalonians are due to both being based on Pauline tradition (for the letter in the shape of the apostle himself, and for the speech in the form of written materials). Fourth, Luke had access to oral Pauline tradition, which he utilised in writing the Miletus speech. Fifth, Luke knew Paul personally, and used his memory of Paul, perhaps including the Miletus speech, in writing the account in Acts 20. Choosing between these options is not easy, but we shall focus upon two attempts to argue for the first or the second explanation.

Schulze

Schulze[7] argues that the parallels between the speech and the letter are so extensive (he cites twenty-four verses of the letter paralleled in the speech) that there must be a literary explanation. Schulze also believes that Luke used other Pauline letters, especially Ephesians, Romans, Philippians and 2 Corinthians, but sees the pre-

[6] Schulze, 'Unterlagen'; Aejmelaeus, *Rezeption*.
[7] Schulze, 'Unterlagen', p. 123.

ponderance of parallels pointing to 1 Thessalonians as the major source of the speech. His parallels are as follows:

Miletus speech	*1 Thessalonians*
verse 18 ὑμεῖς ἐπίστασθε	2.1 Αὐτοὶ γὰρ οἴδατε 1.5 οἴδατε
verse 19 ἐν ταῖς ἐπιβουλαῖς τῶν Ἰουδαίων	2.14 καὶ αὐτοὶ ὑπὸ τῶν Ἰουδαίων
verse 23 διαμαρτύρεταί μοι λέγον ὅτι δεσμὰ καί θλίψεις με μένουσιν	3.4 προελέγομεν ὑμῖν ὅτι μέλλομεν θλίβεσθαι, καθὼς καὶ ἐγένετο καὶ οἴδατε
verse 24 ψυχὴν... τὸ εὐαγγέλιον τῆς χάριτος τοῦ θεοῦ	2.8 τὸ εὐαγγέλιον τοῦ θεοῦ ... ψυχάς
verse 25 οὐκέτι ὄψεσθε το πρόσωπόν μου ὑμεῖς πάντες	3.10 εἰς τὸ ἰδεῖν ὑμῶν τὸ πρόσωπον
verse 26 the theme of Paul's innocence	2.10 the theme of Paul's conduct with the Thessalonians
verse 26 μαρτύρομαι	2.10 μάρτυρες
verse 27 the theme of Paul telling everything	4.13 the theme of Paul not wanting the Thessalonians to be ignorant
verse 27 ἀναγγεῖλαι	4.2 παραγγελίας
verse 28 the Spirit's appointment of ἐπισκόπους	5.12 those who are προϊσταμένους ὑμῶν ἐν κυρίῳ (contrast 2.7)
verse 31 γρηγορεῖτε	5.6 γρηγορῶμεν
verse 31 νύκτα καὶ ἡμέραν	2.9 νυκτὸς καὶ ἡμέρας
verse 31 ἐπαυσάμην	2.11f παρακαλοῦντες[8]
verse 32 prayer to God for the Ephesians	5.23 prayer to God for the Thessalonians
verse 33 the theme of not taking advantage	The theme of not imposing authority
verse 34 the theme of providing with Paul's own hands	2.9 the theme of working night and day
verse 35a Paul has shown that everyone should work	4.11 the theme that everyone should work with the hands
verse 35b δεῖ ἀντιλαμβάνεσθαι τῶν ἀσθενούντων	5.14 ἀντέχεσθε τῶν ἀσθενῶν

---

[8] This proposed parallel is listed by Schulze, 'Unterlagen', p. 122, although there is no verbal parallel in the Greek.

Schulze does not really *argue* for his conclusion: he regards the listing of the parallels as so conclusive that he can simply conclude 'QED'. We shall therefore consider Aejmelaeus' arguments in more detail.

Aejemelaus

Aejmelaeus' work is much more careful and thorough. The heart of his work lies in a long and detailed study of the speech against the backcloth of the Pauline letters, seeking parallels. Aejmelaeus seeks to distinguish in every case (Pauline and other) tradition from Lukan redaction by minute word study and analysis. Prior to his verse-by-verse study he offers a listing of Pauline and Lukan vocabulary in the Miletus speech, evaluated by comparative use.[9] The parallels he finds are:

Miletus speech	word/phrase	parallel(s)	Aejmelaeus' comment
verse 18		1 Sam. 12.2 LXX	self-defence theme from farewell speech form
		1 Thess. 1.5c; 2.1	Luke has blended the two in his head
	knowing	1 Thess 2.5, 9, 10, 11; 3.3, 4; 4.2; 5.2	typical feature of farewell speech
verse 19	ταπεινοφροσύνη	1 Thess. 2.6f; Eph. 4.2	Pauline word (statistics)
	δουλεύω		Pauline word (statistics)
	distress from Jews	1 Thess. 2.15f; 3.4f	
verses 20, 27		1 Thess. 2.2, 16; Gal. 2.12f	ὑποστέλλω as 'negative synonym' of παρρησιάζομαι
verse 21		1 Thess. 1.9f	cf. parallels in Acts 14.15 (more literal); 17.30 (free citation)
	διαμαρτύρομαι	1 Thess. 4.6	only Pauline use

[9] Aejmelaeus, *Rezeption*, pp. 90f.

Miletus speech	*word/phrase*	*parallel(s)*	*Aejmelaeus' comment*
verses 22f	θλῖψις	1 Thess. 3.4 (verb)	similar case of Paul prophesying suffering for himself
		Acts 21.11	authentic because not literally fulfilled
	καὶ νῦν ἰδού	LXX	farewell speech colouring
	πορεύομαι εἰς Ἰερουσαλήμ	Rom. 15.25	
	hardship theme	1 Thess. 3.4, 7; Phil. 1.17f	
verse 24		Phil. 2.16f (paraphrased)	picture agrees, although words different
	διακονία	Rom. 15.25 (both about journey to Jerusalem)	
	ψυχή	1 Thess. 2.8	
	εὐαγγέλιον	1 Thess. 2.8; Eph. 3.6f	
verses 25f	ὁρᾶν/θεωρεῖν τὸ πρόσωπόν τινος	1 Thess. 2.17; 3.10f	not derived from LXX farewell speeches, because Paul doesn't die at the end of the scene
	βασιλεία	1 Thess. 2.12	
verse 28	περιποιέομαι	1 Thess. 5.9 (noun); Isa. 43.20f LXX	more significant of parallels with this verse
	προσέχετε ἑαυτοῖς	1 Thess. 5.11, 12, 14	
	παντὶ τῷ ποιμνίῳ ... ποιμαίνειν	1 Thess. 5.11	
	ὑμᾶς τὸ πνεῦμα τὸ ἅγιον ἔθετο	1 Thess. 5.9	
	ἐπισκόπους	1 Thess. 5.12	Pauline office title
	διὰ τοῦ αἵματος τοῦ ἰδίου	1 Thess. 5.9f; Eph. 1.7	more significant of parallels with this verse

Miletus speech	*word/phrase*	*parallel(s)*	*Aejmelaeus' comment*
verse 28		1 Thess. 5.9–12	used by Luke because it is about leaders
	τίθημι + ἐν τινί + accusative	1 Cor. 12.28; Eph. 4.11	
verses 29f		Mark 13.21–3	
	βαρύς	1 Thess. 2.7, 9	
verse 31	γρηγορέω	1 Thess. 5.6, 10 (imperative in both cases)	eschatological technical term in early Christianity
	μνημονεύω	1 Thess. 2.9	Paul reminding of his lifestyle in both cases
	νύκτα καὶ ἡμέραν	1 Thess. 2.9	
	νουυετέω	1 Thess. 2.9–12; 5.12, 14	Acts 20.31 only use outside Paulines
	εἷς ἕκαστος	1 Thess. 2.11	
	οὐκ ἐπαυσάμην	1 Thess. 2.9	Paul's persistence (thematic link)
	μετὰ δακρύων	1 Thess. 2.7–12; 3.7–10	expressions of Paul's love
verse 32	λόγος	1 Thess. 2.13	
	τῷ δυναμένῳ	Rom 16.25; Eph. 3.20; Jude 24	liturgical formula, non-Pauline
	οἰκοδομέω	1 Thess. 5.11; Eph. 4.12, 16, 29	
	κληρονομία	Eph. 1.18, 14; 5.5	
	τῆς χάριτος αὐτοῦ	Eph. 1.6, 7; 2.7	
	τῆς χάριτος (τοῦ θεοῦ)	Eph. 3.2, 7	
	δοῦναι τὴν κληρονομίαν ἐν τοῖς ἡγιασμένοις πᾶσιν	τοῦ θεοῦ τοῦ καλοῦντος ὑμᾶς εἰς τὴν ἑαυτοῦ βασιλείαν καὶ δόξαν 1 Thess. 2.12b	identical in content

Miletus speech	word/phrase	parallel(s)	Aejmelaeus' comment
verses 33–35a	lack of guilt	1 Sam. 12.3–5	standard theme of farewell speech
	lack of covetousness	1 Thess. 2.5, 3, 10	
verse 34	χρεία χείρ	1 Thess. 2.9; 4.11f	idea from 2.9, content from 4.11f
verse 35a	Paul's love for the churches	1 Thess. 2.7–12	his love as a father means he serves them without fee
	κοπιάω	1 Thess. 1.3; 2.9; 3.5; 5.12 (only of Paul's work in 2.9)	
	ἀσθενούντων	1 Thess. 5.14; Eph. 4.28	
verse 35b	idea of word of Jesus	1 Thess. 4.15	
	actual words	1 Clem. 13.1f; 46.7f	

In our earlier discussion (chapter 5), we considered many of the parallels identified by Aejmelaeus, although he has extended the search more widely. Aejmelaeus' case for a parallel looks at its strongest when he finds clusters of parallels, such as in Acts 20.18–20 (cf. 1 Thess. 2.1f), 24 (cf. Phil. 4.16f), 28 (cf. 1 Thess. 5.9–12) and 31 (cf. 1 Thess. 2.9–12). In other cases he claims a cumulative case, although it is sometimes hard to tell whether the dependence of the speech on the letters is his conclusion or presupposition; for example, he argues on the use of βασιλεία (Acts 20.25) that, since it is likely that Luke used 1 Thessalonians 2, it is probable that 2.12 is the source for this word.[10]

A number of points can be made in response to Aejmelaeus' arguments. First, and most seriously, his proposed process of composition of the speech is difficult to believe. Aejmelaeus confidently distinguishes tradition and redaction in the speech, but his use of word-statistics is at least debatable, since the Miletus speech contains a number of words used never or rarely elsewhere in Acts (and in some cases in Luke-Acts) because the subject-matter of the speech is unusual in Acts – this is the only recorded speech to

[10] Aejmelaeus, *Rezeption*, p. 131.

Christians made by Paul, and speeches by others to Christians in Acts are also in special circumstances, as well as being relatively brief.[11] It is probable that unusual words go with unusual subject-matter.

Further, Aejmelaeus takes words in isolation from their contexts in some of his parallels.[12] His parallel between Acts 20.28 and 1 Thessalonians 5.9 involves quite different uses of τίθημι (itself common[13]), in the one case of the Holy Spirit appointing overseers and in the other of God not appointing the Thessalonians to wrath, but salvation; but Aejmelaeus regards the use of τίθημι as significant.[14]

He also runs into difficulties when Paul and Luke use the same word in different senses, as with the use of γρηγορέω (Acts 20.31; 1 Thess. 5.6, 10), for in spite of his claim that this was a technical term in early Christianity for eschatological watchfulness,[15] it does not appear to be used in this sense in Acts 20.31, especially when the link with the previous verses, signalled by διό, and the previous call προσέχετε ἑαυτοῖς καὶ παντὶ τῷ ποιμνίῳ (verse 28) are taken into account.[16] Thus if Paul is using the term for eschatological watching in 1 Thessalonians 5.6, as he appears to be, he is using the term differently from Luke. The language may be the same, but the thought is not.

A difficulty of separating tradition and redaction as tidily as Aejmelaeus seeks to do is that the processes he proposes for the composition of the Miletus speech by Luke appear psychologically implausible for a first-century writer. Even granted the greater power of memory at that period in Hellenistic and Jewish cultures,[17] the combinations of passages from different Pauline letters and the LXX proposed by Aejmelaeus require CD-ROM and computer search facilities unavailable to Luke. For example, Aejmelaeus sees Acts 20.24 as a conflation of seven Pauline texts

---

[11] 1.15–17, 20–2 (Peter asking for the choice of a successor to Judas); 15.7–11 (Peter at the 'Jerusalem Council'); 15.13–21 (James on the same occasion).

[12] Brawley, review of Aejmelaeus, *Die Rezeption*, p. 533.

[13] 100 times in NT, including twenty-three in Acts, sixteen in Luke. This is the only use of τίθημι in 1 Thessalonians. The grammatical form is the same, the aorist middle (used in 1 Thess. 5.9) being a favourite of Luke (twice in Luke, nine times Acts, four times Paul, once in the Pastorals) – other forms are more common in the other Evangelists.

[14] Aejmelaeus, *Rezeption*, p. 135.

[15] Aejmelaeus, *Rezeption*, p. 149.

[16] Cf. § 4.3.4.

[17] Riesner, 'Jesus as Preacher', esp. pp. 203–8; Aune, 'Prolegomena'.

(1 Thess. 2.8; Phil. 2.16f; Eph. 3.6f; Phil. 3.12f; 1 Cor. 9.24–7; Rom. 11.13; 15.25);[18] Acts 20.28 as a conflation of seven texts (1 Thess. 5.9–12; Isa. 43.21 LXX; Eph. 1.7, 14; 4.11; 1 Cor. 12.28 and the use of the title ἐπίσκοπος from the Paulines);[19] and Acts 20.22f as the result of a complex process of redaction involving the Agabus story (Acts 21.11), the LXX (for καὶ νῦν ἰδού), Romans 15.25 (for πορεύομαι εἰς Ἰερουσαλήμ), 1 Thessalonians 3.4, 7 (for the 'hardship' theme) and Philippians 1.17f (similarly).[20] He comments on the latter that Luke probably had Philippians memorised,[21] but his case elsewhere seems to require that Luke not only had virtually the whole Pauline corpus memorised, but also that he could instantly recall material across the various letters using a mental 'concordance'.

In other cases, Aejmelaeus provides evidence that a phrase is Septuagintal[22] but then argues that because the phrase is only found in 1 Thessalonians among the Paulines, the derivation must be from that letter, even though Septuagintal use shows that the phrase was common currency.[23] In such cases it is hard to argue that Luke has derived the material from 1 Thessalonians.

Aejmelaeus believes that 'church officials' such as ἐπίσκοποι did not exist in Ephesus at the ostensible time of the Miletus speech,[24] but Philippians 1.1 provides evidence from roughly this period of such people in a Pauline church, and there is no reason to think that Ephesus was different. Part of the stumbling-block for Aejmelaeus here is the equation of πρεσβύτεροι and ἐπίσκοποι in the Miletus speech, but the former need not be seen, at least at this period, as an office title.[25] That allows the two designations to be used for the same group of people, and to read the evidence differently from Aejmelaeus.

Aejmelaeus struggles to explain why Luke makes no use of the

---

[18] Aejmelaeus, *Rezeption*, pp. 119–27.

[19] Aejmelaeus, *Rezeption*, pp. 132–42.

[20] Aejmelaeus, *Rezeption*, pp. 112–19.

[21] Aejmelaeus, *Rezeption*, p. 119.

[22] e.g. Aejmelaeus, *Rezeption*, p. 128 offers examples of the use of ὁρᾶν/θεωρεῖν τὸ πρόσωπόν τινος in the LXX (Gen. 32.21; 43.3, 5; 44.23, 26; 46.30; Exod. 10.28; 2 Kings 3.13; 14.24, 32; Jdt 6.5; 1 Macc. 7.28, 30).

[23] In this particular case, Aejmelaeus, *Rezeption*, p. 128 acknowledges that the phrase is also used elsewhere in the NT (Matt. 18.10; Acts 6.15; Rev. 22.4), but argues that the meaning and context in those cases is different. This looks rather like an attempt to have his cake and eat it!

[24] Aejmelaeus, *Rezeption*, pp. 225–35.

[25] § 3.5.1, based on Campbell, *The Elders*.

eschatological section of 1 Thessalonians (4.13–5.11) in composing the Miletus speech.[26] He believes Luke has a different eschatology from Paul, but even so the evidence of 2 Timothy is that eschatological motives were significant in a call to leaders left behind at a 'farewell' (e.g. 2 Tim. 4.1ff). Given that Luke may be in some ways close to the author of 2 Timothy,[27] it seems curious to find such distance here – especially since, on Aejmelaeus' hypothesis, the material was so easily available.

Again, if Luke used 1 Thessalonians in writing the Miletus speech, then he surely would use the letter in writing Acts 17.1–15, the account of the initial evangelisation of Thessalonica. Why, then, should there be evident tensions between the letter and this account? We have argued that these tensions are not without resolution,[28] but their presence tells against Aejmelaeus' proposal, even on his suggestion that Luke used a travel document as an alternative source and either altered or ignored information in 1 Thessalonians for stylistic or theological reasons.[29] Further, a non-extant document as a solution to this difficulty involves the multiplication of hypotheticals.

Equally, if Luke had access to the letters in the manner Aejmelaeus envisages, why does he never even hint that Paul wrote letters, and why do other speeches of Paul not contain such parallels to the letters? It is an acknowledged difficulty that the evangelistic speeches of Paul in Acts cannot be paralleled straightforwardly in the letters, and Aejmelaeus' theory offers no help in dealing with this. He suggests that Luke never mentions Paul's letter-writing because he does not see the letters as of particular interest or value for his task.[30] But if this is so, why does Luke make such extensive use of them in this one speech?

Overall, Aejmelaeus' ingenious and well-presented case fails to convince because it does not take account of enough factors or consider alternative hypotheses. Similar problems exist with Schulze's case – merely exhibiting parallels does not demonstrate dependence. The portraits of Paul in the Miletus speech and

[26] Aejmelaeus, *Rezeption*, p. 184.
[27] Moule, 'Problem of the Pastorals', esp. pp. 123–7; Wilson, *Luke and Pastoral Epistles*; Kaestli, 'Luke-Acts and the Pastorals'.
[28] § 5.2.2.
[29] Aejmelaeus, *Rezeption*, pp. 196–210.
[30] Aejmelaeus, *Rezeption*, p. 47.

1 Thessalonians are consonant in key areas, but Aejmelaeus and Schulze fail to provide persuasive evidence of literary dependence.

Luke and Paul

What overall impression emerges from our comparison with the Lukan corpus and 1 Thessalonians? We may state three theses which draw together what can reasonably be concluded.

First, in the light of our critique of Aejmelaeus, Luke knows Pauline tradition independently of the epistles. This is suggested by the presence of material in the Miletus speech that sounds like Paul without quite matching what we know from 1 Thessalonians, in combination with the probability that Luke did not know the letters.

Second, Luke knows Pauline tradition rather better than is sometimes suggested. The use of Pauline language, turns of phrase, and methods of argument or teaching in the Miletus address all point to this conclusion. This conclusion is compatible with both the view that Luke knew Paul personally and the view that Luke was using independent Pauline tradition. The data we have considered is insufficient to decide between these positions.

Third, Luke seeks to pass on and commend Paul's tradition, especially concerning Christian leadership, to his readers. This is a major result of our study of the speech in the context of Luke-Acts, underlining the oft-made claim that Paul is Luke's 'hero'.[31] It is seen particularly in the way that in the speech Paul mirrors the life and teaching of his Master as seen in the Third Gospel. This conclusion, based on observation from the texts, is independent of any reconstruction of the circumstances, aims and date of the author of Acts.

7.3   Implications for the Paul of Acts / Paul of the epistles debate

Luke's portrait of Paul is often compared unfavourably with a portrait reconstructed from the letters, but to compare the epistles as a whole with Paul's speeches in Acts as a whole is mistaken – hence, we compared the one Pauline speech given to Christians

---

[31] e.g. Lentz, *Luke's Portrait*; Rapske, *Paul in Roman Custody*, esp. pp. 429–36.

with 1 Thessalonians. We found extensive and suggestive parallels between the two portraits of Paul, significantly in a speech from an 'epistle-like' situation. More, we found such parallels clustered in one letter, rather than isolated parallels of individual words or ideas. This suggests that Luke not only knows individual threads from the Pauline sewing basket, but also understands how Paul combines these into tapestries.

Thus our contribution to the Paul of Acts / Paul of the epistles debate is to move the discussion on a stage. Luke's Paul, when he speaks to Christians as a pastor, sounds like Paul writing as a pastor. Further, when Paul himself writes about pastoral ministry in 1 Thessalonians he sounds similar to Luke's portrayal of him teaching pastors about pastoral ministry. Therefore the Vielhauer/ Haenchen view, that the 'two Pauls' are at variance, is over-stated, for our research suggests that at this point Luke's Paul sounds like the Paul of the epistles. It would require further work to demonstrate this for other Pauline letters, but our conclusion implies that such a quest would be worthwhile.

7.4 Future work suggested by this study

How could this discussion be further developed? It is beyond the scope of this work to consider wider questions of the Pauline corpus and other Pauline speeches in Acts, but two particular issues suggest themselves as potentially fruitful.

First, it would be valuable to study leadership elsewhere in the NT, to assess whether the common elements to the Lukan and Pauline views can be found elsewhere. *Prima facie* we might expect a variety of perspectives among the different NT authors – and the evidence appears to support such a view.[32] If there are unifying factors within the understanding and practice of leadership and

---

[32] e.g. Caird and Hurst, *NT Theology*, pp. 232–4 characterises the earliest churches as lacking organisation; Dunn, *Unity and Diversity*, pp. 103–23 catalogues a range of concepts of ministry, concluding that there is as much diversity in forms of ministry as in understandings of community within the NT; see also Guthrie, *NT Theology*, pp. 738–42, 760–74 and (esp.) 789: 'it is clear that on the matter of leadership there was no universal policy'. This diversity over leadership contrasts with Johnson's view that there is a consistent picture of Christian *discipleship* across the range of NT writings, including the four Gospels, Paul, Hebrews and 1 Peter (Johnson, *Real Jesus*, pp. 151–65).

ministry among the churches, that might be suggestive for our understanding of leadership in the earliest communities.

Second, our study has focused on the only Pauline speech to Christians in Acts. Another approach to the relationship of the 'two Pauls' would be from the epistles, by seeking passages suggestive of Paul's evangelistic preaching and speaking (e.g. 1 Thess. 1.9f; 1 Cor. 15.1ff) and comparing them in detail with Pauline evangelistic speeches in Acts to comparable audiences – for the two examples cited, to predominantly Gentile groups. This comparison would provide further evidence of the degree of 'fit' between the two portraits of Paul.

Both of these are fascinating prospects, but space forbids pursuing them here. That privilege must await further work to give a greater insight into the growth and development of earliest Christianity – a growth and development in which both Paul and Luke played important roles.

BIBLIOGRAPHY

Texts and translations

Apart from texts and translations listed below, works by ancient authors are cited from the Loeb Classical Library edition.

Aland, Barbara, Aland, Kurt, Karavidopoulos, Johannes, Martini, Carlo M. and Metzger, Bruce M. (eds.), *Novum Testamentum Graece*, 27th edn, Stuttgart: Deutsche Bibelgesellschaft, 1993.

Aland, Barbara, Aland, Kurt, Karavidopoulos, Johannes, Martini, Carlo M. and Metzger, Bruce M. (eds.), *The Greek New Testament*, 4th revised edn, Stuttgart: Deutsche Bibelgesellschaft/United Bible Societies, 1994.

Aland, Kurt, Black, Matthew, Martini, Carlo M., Metzger, Bruce M. and Wikgren, Allen (eds.), *The Greek New Testament*, 3rd (corrected) edn, Stuttgart: United Bible Societies, 1983.

Barrett, C. K. (ed.), *The New Testament Background: Selected Documents*, revised edn, London: SPCK, 1987.

Clark, A. C., *The Acts of the Apostles: A Critical Edition*, Oxford: Clarendon Press, 1933.

Dittenberger, W. (ed.), *Sylloge Inscriptionum Graecarum*, 4 vols., 3rd edn, Leipzig: S. Hirzelium, 1915–24.

International Greek New Testament Project, American and British Committees, *The Gospel according to St Luke, Part 2, Chapters 13–24*, The NT in Greek 3, Oxford: Clarendon Press, 1987.

Kramer, Fr., Dittenberger, W. and Meusel, Heinrich (eds.), *Caesar, 'De Bello Gallico'*, 18th edn, Berlin: Weidmannsche Verlagsbuchhandlung, 1960.

Kühn, Carl G. (ed.), *Galeni Opera Omnia*, 20 vols., Leipzig: Officia Libraria Car. Cnoblochii, 1821–33.

Malherbe, Abraham J., *The Cynic Epistles: A Study Edition*, SBLSBS 12, Missoula: Scholars Press, 1977.

Marsden, E. W. (ed.), *Greek and Roman Artillery: Technical Treatises*, Oxford: Clarendon Press, 1971.

Milne, H. J. M. (ed.), *Greek Shorthand Manuals: Syllabary and Commentary*, London: Egypt Exploration Society, 1934.

Rahlfs, Alfred (ed.), *Septuaginta*, 2 vols., Stuttgart: Deutsche Bibelgesellschaft, 1935, repr. 1982.

Russell, D. A. and Wilson, N. G. (eds.), *Menander Rhetor: Edited with Translation and Commentary*, Oxford: Clarendon Press, 1981.

Whiston, William (ed.), *The Works of Flavius Josephus*, London: Nimmo, no date.

Reference tools

Accordance 3.5 for Macintosh, Altamonte Springs, Fla: Oak Tree Software Specialists, 1998.

Aland, Kurt (ed.), *Synopsis of the Four Gospels*, Stuttgart: United Bible Societies, 1976.

Balz, Horst and Schneider, Gerhard (eds.), *Exegetical Dictionary of the New Testament*, 3 vols., ET of *Exegetisches Wörterbuch zum Neuen Testament*, Grand Rapids: Eerdmans, 1990–3.

Bauer, Walter, Arndt, W. F., Gingrich, F. W. and Danker, F. W. (eds.), *A Greek-English Lexicon of the New Testament and Other Early Christian Literature*, 2nd edn, University of Chicago Press, 1979.

Blass, F., Debrunner, A. and Funk, Robert W., *A Greek Grammar of the New Testament and Other Early Christian Literature*, Cambridge University Press, 1961.

Brown, Colin (ed.), *The New International Dictionary of New Testament Theology*, 3 vols., Exeter: Paternoster Press, 1975–8.

Brown, Francis, Driver, S. R. and Briggs, Charles A., *A Hebrew and English Lexicon of the Old Testament*, corrected edn, Oxford: Clarendon Press, 1953, repr. 1977.

Freedman, David N. (ed.), *Anchor Bible Dictionary*, 6 vols., New York: Doubleday, 1992.

Green, Joel B., McKnight, Scot and Marshall, I. Howard (eds.), *Dictionary of Jesus and the Gospels*, Leicester: IVP, 1992.

Hammond, N. G. L. and Scullard, H. H. (eds.), *The Oxford Classical Dictionary*, 2nd edn, Oxford: Clarendon Press, 1970.

Hawkins, Sir John C., *Horae Synopticae: Contributions to the Study of the Synoptic Problem*, Oxford: Clarendon Press, 1899.

Hawthorne, Gerald F., Martin, Ralph P. and Reid, Daniel G. (eds.), *Dictionary of Paul and the Letters*, Leicester/Downers Grove: IVP, 1993.

Hornblower, Simon and Spawforth, Antony (eds.), *Oxford Classical Dictionary*, 3rd edn, Oxford/New York: Oxford University Press, 1996.

Kittel, G. and Friedrich, G. (eds.), *Theological Dictionary of the New Testament*, 10 vols., ET of *Theologisches Wörterbuch zum Neuen Testament* (tr. Bromiley, G. W.), Grand Rapids: Eerdmans, 1964–76.

Kloppenborg, John S., *Q Parallels: Synopsis, Critical Notes and Concordance*, Foundations and Facets, Sonoma, Calif.: Polebridge Press, 1988.

Liddell, Henry G., Scott, Robert, Jones, Henry S., Sir and McKenzie, Roderick (eds.), *A Greek-English Lexicon*, 2 vols., 9th edn, Oxford: Clarendon Press, 1940, repr. 1951.

Metzger, Bruce M., *A Textual Commentary on the Greek New Testament*, London: United Bible Societies, 1975.

A Textual Commentary on the Greek New Testament, 2nd edn, Stuttgart: Deutsche Bibelgesellschaft/United Bible Societies, 1994.

Morgenthaler, R., *Statistik des neutestamentlichen Wortschatzes*, Zürich/ Frankfurt-am-Main: Gotthelf-Verlag, 1958.

Morton, A. Q. and Michaelson, S. (eds.), *A Critical Concordance to the Acts of the Apostles*, The Computer Bible VIII, Wooster, Ohio: Biblical Research Associates, 1976.

Morton, A. Q., Michaelson, S. and Thompson, J. David (eds.), *A Critical Concordance to I, II Thessalonians*, The Computer Bible XXVI, Wooster, Ohio: Biblical Research Associates, 1983.

Moule, C. F. D., *An Idiom-Book of New Testament Greek*, 2nd edn, Cambridge University Press, 1959.

Moulton, James H., *A Grammar of New Testament Greek, vol. I Prolegomena*, 3rd edn, Edinburgh: T. & T. Clark, 1908.

Moulton, James H. and Howard, Wilbert F., *A Grammar of New Testament Greek, vol. II: Accidence and Word Formation*, Edinburgh: T. & T. Clark, 1929.

Moulton, W. F, Geden, A. S. and Moulton, H. K. (eds.), *A Concordance to the Greek Testament*, 5th edn, Edinburgh: T. & T. Clark, 1978.

Norbury, James and Agutter, Margaret, *Odhams Encyclopaedia of Knitting*, London: Odhams, 1957.

Porter, Stanley E., *Idioms of the Greek New Testament*, Biblical Languages: Greek 2, 2nd edn, Sheffield: JSOT Press, 1994.

Rengstorf, K. H. (ed.), *A Complete Concordance to Flavius Josephus*, 4 vols., Leiden: Brill, 1973–83.

Robertson, A. T., *A Grammar of the Greek New Testament in the Light of Historical Research*, London: Hodder & Stoughton, 1914.

Turner, Nigel, *A Grammar of New Testament Greek, vol. III: Syntax*, Edinburgh: T. & T. Clark, 1963.
   Grammatical Insights into the New Testament, Edinburgh: T. & T. Clark, 1965.

Turner, Nigel and Moulton, James H. (ed.), *A Grammar of New Testament Greek, vol. IV: Style*, Edinburgh: T. & T. Clark, 1976.

Zerwick, Max, *Biblical Greek Illustrated by Examples*, Rome: Pontifical Biblical Institute, 1963.

Articles, books, dissertations, etc.

Achtemeier, Paul J., *1 Peter*, Hermeneia, Minneapolis: Fortress Press, 1996.

Aejmelaeus, Lars, *Die Rezeption der Paulusbriefe in der Miletrede (Apg. 20:18–35)*, Helsinki: Suomalainen Tiedeakatemia, 1987.

Agrell, Göran, *Work, Toil and Sustenance: An Examination of the View of Work in the New Testament, Taking into Consideration Views Found in Old Testament, Intertestamental, and Early Rabbinic Writings*, Lund: Verbum/Håkan Ohlssons Förlag, 1976.

Aland, Kurt and Aland, Barbara, *The Text of the New Testament*, Grand Rapids/Leiden: Eerdmans/Brill, 1987.

Alexander, Loveday (C. A.), 'Luke's Preface in the Context of Greek Preface-Writing', *NovT* 28 (1986), 48–74.

'The Living Voice: Scepticism towards the Written Word in Early Christian and in Graeco-Roman Texts' in Clines, David J. A., Fowl, Stephen E. and Porter, Stanley E. (eds.), *The Bible in Three Dimensions: Essays in Celebration of Forty Years of Biblical Studies in the University of Sheffield*, JSOTSup 87, Sheffield: JSOT Press, 1990, pp. 221–47.

The Preface to Luke's Gospel: Literary Convention and Social Context in Luke 1.1–4 and Acts 1.1, SNTSMS 78, Cambridge: Cambridge University Press, 1993.

review of Burridge, Richard A., *What are the Gospels? A Comparison with Graeco-Roman Biography* (Cambridge: Cambridge University Press, 1992) in *EvQ* 66 (1994), 73–6.

'Narrative Maps: Reflections on the Toponymy of Acts' in Carroll R., M. Daniel, Clines, David J. A. and Davies, Philip R. (eds.), *The Bible in Human Society: Essays in Honour of John Rogerson*, JSOTSup 200, Sheffield Academic Press, 1995, pp. 17–57.

'The Preface to Acts and the Historians' in Witherington, Ben, III (ed.), *History, Literature and Society in the Book of Acts*, Cambridge University Press, 1996, pp. 73–103.

Alexander, T. C., 'Paul's Final Exhortation to the Elders from Ephesus: The Rhetoric of Acts 20:17–38', PhD thesis, Emory University, 1990.

Argyle, A. W., 'The Greek of Luke and Acts', *NTS* 20 (1974), 441–5.

Askwith, E. H., '"I" and "We" in the Thessalonian Epistles', *The Expositor* 8 (1911), 149–59.

Aune, David E., *Prophecy in Early Christianity and the Ancient Mediterranean World*, Grand Rapids: Eerdmans, 1983.

The New Testament in its Literary Environment, Cambridge: James Clarke, 1988.

'Prolegomena to the Study of Oral Tradition in the Hellenistic World' in Wansbrough, Henry (ed.), *Jesus and the Oral Gospel Tradition*, JSNTSup 64, Sheffield: JSOT Press, 1991, pp. 59–106.

Bailey, Kenneth E., *Through Peasant Eyes*, Grand Rapids: Eerdmans, 1980.

Barclay, John M. G., 'Mirror-reading a Polemical Letter: Galatians as a Test Case', *JSNT* 31 (1987), 73–93.

'Thessalonica and Corinth: Social Contrasts in Pauline Christianity', *JSNT* 47 (1992), 49–74.

'Conflict in Thessalonica', *CBQ* 55 (1993), 512–30.

Barclay, William, 'A Comparison of Paul's Missionary Preaching and Preaching to the Church' in Gasque, W. W. and Martin, Ralph P. (eds.), *Apostolic History and the Gospel*, Exeter: Paternoster Press, 1970, pp. 165–75.

Barrett, C. K., *Luke the Historian in Recent Study*, London: Epworth Press, 1961.

The Pastoral Epistles, New Clarendon Bible, Oxford: Clarendon Press, 1963.

'Acts and the Pauline Corpus', *ExpTim* LXXVIII (1976–7), 2–5.

'Paul's Address to the Ephesian Elders' in Jervell, Jacob and Meeks, Wayne A. (eds.), *God's Christ and His People: Studies in Honour of Nils Alstrup Dahl*, Oslo/Bergen/Tromsö: Universitetsforlaget, 1977, pp. 107–21.

The Gospel according to St John, 2nd edn, London: SPCK, 1978.

'Theologia Crucis – in Acts?' in Andresen, C. and Klein, Günther (eds.), *Theologia Crucis – Sigum Crucis*, Tübingen: J. C. B. Mohr, 1979, pp. 73–84.

'Apollos and the Twelve Disciples of Ephesus' in Weinrich, William C. (ed.), *The New Testament Age: Essays in Honor of Bo Reicke*, Macon, Ga.: Mercer University Press, 1984, vol. I, pp. 29–39.

'Sayings of Jesus in the Acts of the Apostles' in Refoulé, François (ed.), *A Cause de l'Evangile: Etudes sur les Synoptiques et les Actes offertes au P. Jacques Dupont, OSB à l'occasion de son 70e anniversaire*, LD 123, Paris: Éditions du Cerf, 1985, pp. 681–708.

'Luke-Acts' in Carson, D. A. and Williamson, H. G. M. (eds.), *It is Written: Scripture Citing Scripture. Essays in Honour of Barnabas Lindars, SSF*, Cambridge University Press, 1988, pp. 231–44.

A Critical and Exegetical Commentary on the Acts of the Apostles, vol. I: Preliminary Introduction and Commentary on Acts I–XIV, ICC, Edinburgh: T. & T. Clark, 1994.

A Critical and Exegetical Commentary on the Acts of the Apostles, vol. II: Introduction and Commentary on Acts XV–XXVIII, ICC, Edinburgh: T. & T. Clark, 1998.

Barth, Markus, *Ephesians*, AB 34 and 34A, 2 vols., Garden City, N.Y.: Doubleday, 1974.

Barth, Markus and Blanke, Helmut, *Colossians: A New Translation with Introduction and Commentary*, AB 34B, New York/London: Doubleday, 1994.

Bauckham, Richard, 'Pseudo-Apostolic Letters', *JBL* 107 (1988), 469–94.

Beck, Brian E., 'The Common Authorship of Luke and Acts', *NTS* 23 (1977), 346–52.

Belleville, Linda L., *Reflections of Glory: Paul's Polemical Use of the Moses-Doxa Tradition in 2 Corinthians 3.1–18*, JSNTSup 52, Sheffield: JSOT Press, 1991.

Best, Ernest, *A Commentary on the First and Second Epistles to the Thessalonians*, Black's NT Commentaries, London: A. & C. Black, 1972.

Paul and His Converts, Edinburgh: T. & T. Clark, 1988.

A Critical and Exegetical Commentary on Ephesians, ICC, Edinburgh: T. & T. Clark, 1998.

Bicknell, E. J., *The First and Second Epistles to the Thessalonians*, Westminster Commentaries, London: Methuen, 1932.

Bitzer, Lloyd F., 'The Rhetorical Situation' in Fisher, Walter R. (ed.), *Rhetoric: A Tradition in Transition. In Honor of Donald C. Bryant*, Ann Arbor: Michigan State University Press, 1974, pp. 247–60.

Blight, Richard C., *An Exegetical Summary of 1 and 2 Thessalonians*, Dallas: Summer Institute of Linguistics, 1989.

Blomberg, Craig L., 'Midrash, Chiasmus, and the Outline of Luke's Central Section' in France, R. T. and Wenham, David (eds.), *Gospel Perspectives, vol. III: Studies in Midrash and Historiography*, Sheffield: JSOT Press, 1983, pp. 217–62.

'The Law in Luke-Acts', *JSNT* 22 (1984), 53–80.

Bock, Darrell L., *Luke, vol. 1: 1:1–9:50*, Baker Exegetical Commentary on the NT 3A, Grand Rapids: Baker Book House, 1994.

Luke, vol. 2: 9:51–24:53, Baker Exegetical Commentary on the NT 3B, Grand Rapids: Baker Book House, 1996.

Boers, Hendrikus, 'The Form-Critical Study of Paul's Letters: 1 Thessalonians as a Case Study', *NTS* 22 (1975–6), 140–58.

Boismard, M.-É. and Lamouille, A., *Les Actes des Deux Apôtres III: Analyses Littéraires*, Paris: Librairie Lecoffre, 1990.

Booth, Wayne C., *The Rhetoric of Fiction*, University of Chicago Press, 1961.

Borgen, Peder, 'From Paul to Luke', *CBQ* 31 (1969), 168–82.

Botha, Pieter J. J., 'The Verbal Art of the Pauline Letters: Rhetoric, Performance and Presence' in Porter, Stanley E. and Olbricht, Thomas H. (eds.), *Rhetoric and the New Testament: Essays from the 1992 Heidelberg Conference*, JSNTSup 90, Sheffield: JSOT Press, 1993, pp. 409–28.

Brawley, Robert L., *Luke-Acts and the Jews: Conflict, Apology, and Conciliation*, SBLMS 33, Atlanta: Scholars Press, 1987.

review of Aejmelaeus, Lars, *Die Rezeption der Paulusbriefe in der Miletrede (Apg 20:18–35)* (Helsinki: Suomalainen Tiedeakatemia, 1987) in *JBL* 108 (1989), 532–4.

Centering on God: Method and Message in Luke-Acts, Louisville, Ken.: John Knox Press, 1990.

Bright, John, *Jeremiah*, AB 21, Garden City, N.Y.: Doubleday, 1965.

Bruce, F. F., *The Speeches in the Acts of the Apostles*, London: Tyndale Press, 1943.

The Acts of the Apostles, 2nd edn, Grand Rapids: Eerdmans, 1952.

Commentary on the Book of Acts, NICNT, Grand Rapids: Eerdmans, 1956.

'The Speeches in Acts – Thirty Years After' in Banks, Robert J. (ed.), *Reconciliation and Hope: New Testament Essays on Atonement and Eschatology Presented to L. L. Morris on his 60th Birthday*, Exeter: Paternoster Press, 1974, pp. 53–68.

'Is the Paul of Acts the Real Paul?', *BJRL* 58 (1975–6), 282–305.

Paul: Apostle of the Free Spirit, Exeter: Paternoster Press, 1977.

'The Acts of the Apostles Today', *BJRL* 65 (1982–3), 36–56.

'The Acts of the Apostles: Historical Record or Theological Reconstruction?', *ANRW* II/25.3 (1985), 2569–603.

'Chronological Questions in the Acts of the Apostles', *BJRL* 68 (1985–6), 273–95.

1 and 2 Thessalonians, WBC 45, Waco, Tex.: Word Books, 1986.

The Book of Acts, NICNT, revised edn, Grand Rapids: Eerdmans, 1988.

The Acts of the Apostles, 3rd edn, Leicester: Apollos, 1990.

Budesheim, Thomas L., 'Paul's *Abschiedsrede* in the Acts of the Apostles', *HTR* 69 (1976), 9–30.

Bultmann, Rudolf, *Theology of the New Testament*, vol. I, London: SCM, 1952.

Burridge, Richard A., *What are the Gospels? A Comparison with Græco-Roman Biography*, SNTSMS 70, Cambridge University Press, 1992.

Cadbury, Henry J., *The Making of Luke-Acts*, London: SPCK, 1927, repr. 1958.

'Four Features of Lucan Style' in Keck, Leander E. and Martyn, J. L. (eds.), *Studies in Luke-Acts*, London: SPCK, 1968, pp. 87–102.

Caird, G. B., *Paul's Letters from Prison*, New Clarendon Bible, Oxford University Press, 1976.

Caird, G. B. and Hurst, L. D. (ed.), *New Testament Theology*, Oxford: Clarendon Press, 1994.

Campbell, R. Alastair, 'The Elders of the Jerusalem Church', *JTS* NS 44 (1993), 511–28.

The Elders: Seniority within Earliest Christianity, Studies of the NT and its World, Edinburgh: T. & T. Clark, 1994.

Carroll, John T., Green, Joel B., Van Voort, Robert E., Marcus, Joel and Senior, Donald, CP, *The Death of Jesus in Early Christianity*, Peabody, Mass.: Hendrickson, 1995.

Carson, D. A., Moo, Douglas J. and Morris, Leon L., *An Introduction to the New Testament*, Leicester: IVP, 1992.

Castelli, Elizabeth A., *Imitating Paul: A Discourse of Power*, Louisville, Ken.: Westminster Press/John Knox Press, 1991.

Chadwick, Henry, 'The Shorter Text of Luke XXII.15–20', *HTR* 50 (1957), 249–58.

Clark, Andrew C., 'Parallel Lives: The Relation of Paul to the Apostles in the Lucan Perspective', PhD thesis, Brunel University, 1997.

'The Role of the Apostles' in Marshall, I. Howard and Peterson, David (eds.), *Witness to the Gospel: The Theology of Acts*, Grand Rapids/Cambridge: Eerdmans, 1998, pp. 169–90.

Clarke, Andrew D., '"Be Imitators of Me": Paul's Model of Leadership', *TynBul* 49 (1998), 329–60.

Collins, Raymond F., *Studies on the First Letter to the Thessalonians*, BETL LXVI, Leuven University Press, 1984.

Collins, Raymond F., 'The First Letter to the Thessalonians' in Brown, Raymond E., Fitzmyer, Joseph A. and Murphy, Roland E. (eds.), *The New Jerome Biblical Commentary*, London: Geoffrey Chapman, 1989, pp. 772–9.

Conzelmann, Hans, *The Theology of St Luke*, ET of *Die Mitte der Zeit*, London: Faber & Faber, 1960.

Acts of the Apostles, Hermeneia, Philadelphia: Fortress Press, 1987.

Cosgrove, Charles H., 'The Divine ΔEI in Luke-Acts: Investigations into the Lukan Understanding of God's Providence', *NovT* 26 (1984), 168–90.

Cranfield, C. E. B., *A Critical and Exegetical Commentary on the Epistle to the Romans*, vol. II, ICC, Edinburgh: T. & T. Clark, 1979.

Creed, J. M., *The Gospel according to St Luke*, London: Macmillan, 1942.

Danker, Frederick W., *Benefactor: Epigraphic Study of a Graeco-Roman and New Testament Semantic Field*, St Louis, Mich.: Clayton Publishing House, 1982.

Davies, W. D., *The Gospel and the Land: Early Christian and Jewish Territorial Doctrine*, London/Berkeley/Los Angeles: University of California Press, 1974.

'Paul and the People of Israel', *NTS* 24 (1978), 4–39.

Dawsey, James M., *The Lukan Voice*, Macon, Ga.: Mercer University Press, 1986.

de Boer, Willis P., *The Imitation of Paul: An Exegetical Study*, Kampen: Kok, 1962.

de la Potterie, I., SJ, 'Les deux noms de Jérusalem dans les Actes des Apôtres', *Bib* 63 (1982), 153–87.

De Young, J. C., *Jerusalem in the New Testament*, Kampen: Kok, 1960.

Dean, Margaret E., 'The Grammar of Sound in Greek Texts: Toward a Method for Mapping the Echoes of Speech in Writing', *AusBR* 44 (1996), 53–70.

DeMaris, Richard E., *The Colossian Controversy: Wisdom in Dispute at Colossae*, JSNTSup 96, Sheffield: JSOT Press, 1994.

Denney, James, *Studies in Theology: Lectures Delivered in Chicago Theological Seminary*, London: Hodder & Stoughton, 1895.

DeVine, Charles F., 'The Blood of God in Acts 20:28', *CBQ* 9 (1947), 381–408.

Dibelius, Martin, *A Fresh Approach to the New Testament and Early Christian Literature*, London: Ivor Nicholson & Watson, 1936.

Studies in the Acts of the Apostles, London: SCM, 1956.

Dibelius, Martin and Conzelmann, Hans, *The Pastoral Epistles*, Hermeneia, Philadelphia: Fortress Press, 1972.

Dodd, C. H., *The Apostolic Preaching and its Development*, London: Hodder & Stoughton, 1936.

Dolfe, Karl Gustav, 'The Greek Word of "Blood" and the Interpretation of Acts 20:28', *SEÅ* 55 (1990), 64–70.

Donaldson, T. L., 'Parallels: Use, Misuse and Limitations', *EvQ* 55 (1983), 193–210.

Donaldson, Terence L., 'Israelite, Convert, Apostle to the Gentiles: The Origin of Paul's Gentile Mission' in Longenecker, Richard N. (ed.), *The Road from Damascus: The Impact of Paul's Conversion on His Life, Thought and Ministry*, McMaster NT Studies, Grand Rapids/ Cambridge: Eerdmans, 1997, pp. 62–84.

Donelson, Lewis R., 'Cult Histories and the Sources of Acts', *Bib* 68 (1987), 1–21.

Donfried, Karl P., 'Paul and Judaism: 1 Thessalonians 2:13–16 as a Test Case', *Int* 38 (1984), 242–53.

'The Cults of Thessalonica and the Thessalonian Correspondence', *NTS* 31 (1985), 336–56.

'1 Thessalonians, Acts and the Early Paul' in Collins, Raymond F. (ed.), *The Thessalonian Correspondence*, BETL 87, Leuven University Press, 1990, pp. 3–26.

Donfried, Karl P. and Marshall, I. Howard, *The Theology of the Shorter Pauline Letters*, NT Theology, Cambridge University Press, 1993.

Downing, Gerald F., 'Theophilus's First Reading of Luke-Acts' in Tuckett, Christopher M. (ed.), *Luke's Literary Achievement*, JSNTSup 116, Sheffield Academic Press, 1995, pp. 91–109.

Dunn, James D. G., *Jesus and the Spirit: A Study of the Religious and Charismatic Experience of Jesus and the First Christians as Reflected in the New Testament*, London: SCM, 1975.

Romans, WBC 38A and B, 2 vols., Dallas: Word Books, 1988.

Unity and Diversity in the New Testament, 2nd edn, London: SCM, 1990.

The Acts of the Apostles, Epworth Commentaries, London: Epworth Press, 1996.

The Epistles to the Colossians and to Philemon, NIGTC, Carlisle/Grand Rapids: Paternoster Press/Eerdmans, 1996.

The Theology of Paul the Apostle, Edinburgh: T. & T. Clark, 1998.

Dupont, Jacques, *Le Discours de Milet: Testament Pastoral de Saint Paul (Actes 20,18–36)*, Paris: Editions Cerf, 1962.

'La Construction du Discours de Milet' in Dupont, Jacques (ed.), *Nouvelles Etudes sur les Actes des Apôtres*, Paris: Editions du Cerf, 1984, pp. 424–45.

Ehrhardt, Arnold, *The Framework of the New Testament Stories*, Manchester University Press, 1964.

Elliott, J. Keith, 'The Anointing of Jesus', *ExpTim* 85 (1973–4), 105–7.

'Jerusalem in Acts and the Gospels', *NTS* 23 (1977), 462–9.

Elliott, Keith and Moir, Ian, *Manuscripts and the Text of the New Testament: An Introduction for English Readers*, Edinburgh: T. & T. Clark, 1995.

Ellis, E. Earle, *The Gospel of Luke*, NCB, 2nd edn, London: Marshall Morgan & Scott, 1974.

Enslin, Morton S., '"Luke" and Paul', *JAOS* 58 (1938), 81–91.

'Once Again, Luke and Paul', *ZNW* 61 (1970), 253–71.

'Luke, the Literary Physician' in Aune, David E. (ed.), *Studies in New Testament and Early Christian Literature: Essays in Honor of Allen P. Wikgren*, NovTSup 33, Leiden: Brill, 1972, pp. 135–43.

Reapproaching Paul, Philadelphia: Westminster Press, 1972.

Ernst, Josef, *Das Evangelium nach Lukas*, RNT, 5th edn, Regensburg: Verlag Friedrich Pustet, 1977.

Esler, Philip F., *Community and Gospel in Luke-Acts: The Social and Political Motivations of Lucan Theology*, SNTSMS 57, Cambridge University Press, 1987.

Evans, Craig A., *Luke*, NIBC 3, Peabody, Mass.: Hendrickson, 1990.

'Source, Form and Redaction Criticism: The "Traditional" Methods of Synoptic Interpretation' in Porter, Stanley E. and Tombs, David (eds.), *Approaches to New Testament Interpretation*, JSNTSup 120, Sheffield Academic Press, 1995, pp. 17–45.

Evans, Christopher F., *Saint Luke*, London: SCM, 1990.

Exum, C. and Talbert, Charles H., 'The Structure of Paul's Speech to the Ephesian Elders (Acts 20,18–35)', *CBQ* 29 (1967), 233–6.

Faw, Chalmer E., 'On the Writing of First Thessalonians', *JBL* 71 (1952), 217–25.

Fee, Gordon D., *The First Epistle to the Corinthians*, NICNT, Grand Rapids: Eerdmans, 1987.

1 and 2 Timothy, Titus, NIBC 13, Peabody, Mass.: Hendrickson, 1988.

Paul's Letter to the Philippians, NICNT, Grand Rapids: Eerdmans, 1995.

Filson, Floyd V., 'The Journey Motif in Luke-Acts' in Gasque, W. W. and Martin, Ralph P. (eds.), *Apostolic History and the Gospel: Biblical and Historical Essays Presented to F. F. Bruce on His 60th Birthday*, Exeter: Paternoster Press, 1970, pp. 68–77.

Fitzmyer, Joseph A., *Luke I-IX*, AB 28, Garden City, N.Y.: Doubleday, 1981.

Luke X–XXIV, AB 28A, Garden City, N.Y.: Doubleday, 1985.

'The Pauline Letters and the Lucan Account of Paul's Missionary Journeys', *SBLSP* 1988, 82–9.

Romans: A New Translation with Introduction and Commentary, AB 33, London: Geoffrey Chapman, 1993.

Flender, Helmut, *St Luke, Theologian of Redemptive History*, London: SPCK, 1967.

Foakes Jackson, F. J. and Lake, K. (eds.), *The Beginnings of Christianity, Part I*, 5 vols., London: Macmillan, 1920–33.

Frame, J. E., *The Epistles of Paul to the Thessalonians*, ICC, Edinburgh: T. & T. Clark, 1912.

France, R. T., *Jesus and the Old Testament*, London: Tyndale Press, 1971.

The Gospel according to Matthew: An Introduction and Commentary, Tyndale NT Commentaries, Leicester: IVP, 1985.

Gardner, Percy, 'The Speeches of St Paul in Acts' in Swete, H. B. (ed.), *Cambridge Biblical Essays*, London: Macmillan, 1909, pp. 379–419.

Gärtner, Bertil, *The Areopagus Speech and Natural Revelation*, Uppsala: Gleerup, 1955.

Gasque, W. W., 'The Speeches of Acts: Dibelius Reconsidered' in Longenecker, Richard N. and Tenney, M. C. (eds.), *New Dimensions in New Testament Study*, Grand Rapids: Zondervan, 1974, pp. 232–50.

A History of the Criticism of the Acts of the Apostles, Grand Rapids: Eerdmans, 1975.

'The Book of Acts and History' in Guelich, Robert A. (ed.), *Unity and Diversity in New Testament Theology*, Grand Rapids: Eerdmans, 1978, pp. 54–72.

Gaventa, Beverly R., 'Toward a Theology of Acts: Reading and Re-reading', *Int* 42 (1988), 146–57.

Geldenhuys, Norval, *The Gospel of Luke*, NICNT, London: Marshall Morgan & Scott, 1951, repr. 1977.

Gempf, Conrad H., 'Historical and Literary Appropriateness in the Mission Speeches of Paul in Acts', PhD thesis, Aberdeen University, 1988.

'Athens, Paul at' in Hawthorne, Gerald F., Martin, Ralph P. and Reid, Daniel G. (eds.), *Dictionary of Paul and His Letters*, Downers Grove/ Leicester: IVP, 1993, pp. 51–4.

'Public Speaking and Published Accounts' in Winter, Bruce W. and Clarke, Andrew D. (eds.), *The Book of Acts in its Ancient Literary Setting*, A1CS 1, Carlisle/Grand Rapids: Paternoster Press/Eerdmans, 1993, pp. 259–303.

Giles, Kevin N., 'Luke's Use of the Term ἐκκλησία with Special Reference to Acts 20:28 and 9:31', *NTS* 31 (1985), 135–42.

Gooding, David W., *True to the Faith: A Fresh Approach to the Acts of the Apostles*, London: Hodder & Stoughton, 1990.

Goulder, Michael D., *Type and History in Acts*, London: SPCK, 1964.

Luke: A New Paradigm , JSNTSup 20, 2 vols., Sheffield: JSOT Press, 1989.

Grayston, Kenneth, *Dying, We Live: A New Enquiry into the Death of Christ in the New Testament*, London: Darton Longman & Todd, 1990.

Green, Joel B., *The Death of Jesus: Tradition and Interpretation in the Passion Narrative*, WUNT, 2nd series, 33, Tübingen: J. C. B. Mohr (Paul Siebeck), 1988.

'Internal Repetition in Luke-Acts: Contemporary Narratology and Lucan Historiography' in Witherington, Ben, III (ed.), *History, Literature and Society in the Book of Acts*, Cambridge University Press, 1996, pp. 283–99.

Guthrie, Donald, *New Testament Theology*, Leicester: IVP, 1981.

Haenchen, Ernst, 'The Book of Acts as Source Material for the History of Early Christianity' in Keck, Leander E. and Martyn, J. L. (eds.), *Studies in Luke-Acts*, London: SPCK, 1968, pp. 258–78.

Die Apostelgeschichte, MeyerK, 15th edn, Göttingen: Vandenhoeck & Ruprecht, 1968.

The Acts of the Apostles, ET of *Die Apostelgeschichte* (14th edn) by R. McL. Wilson, Oxford: Blackwell, 1971.

Die Apostelgeschichte, MeyerK, 16th edn, Göttingen: Vandenhoeck & Ruprecht, 1977.

Hafemann, Scott J., *Paul, Moses, and the History of Israel: The Letter/ Spirit Contrast and the Argument from Scripture in 2 Corinthians 3*, WUNT 81, Tübingen: J. C. B. Mohr (Paul Siebeck), 1995.

Hanson, A. T., *The Pastoral Epistles*, NCB, London/Grand Rapids: Marshall Morgan & Scott/Eerdmans, 1982.

Hanson, R. P. C., *The Acts*, New Clarendon Bible, Oxford: Clarendon Press, 1967.

Harnack, Adolf, *The Acts of the Apostles*, London: Williams & Norgate, 1909.

Harris, Murray J., *Jesus as God: The New Testament Use of Theos in Reference to Jesus*, Grand Rapids: Baker Book House, 1992.

Havener, Ivan, 'The Pre-Pauline Christological Credal Formulae of 1 Thessalonians', *SBLSP* 1981, 105–28.

Hemer, Colin J., 'Luke the Historian', *BJRL* 60 (1977), 28–51.

'Observations on Pauline Chronology' in Hagner, Donald A. and Harris, Murray J. (eds.), *Pauline Studies: Essays Presented to Professor F. F. Bruce on his 70th Birthday*, Exeter: Paternoster Press, 1980, pp. 3–18.

'First Person Narrative in Acts 27–28', *TynBul* 36 (1985), 79–109.

'The Speeches in Acts: I. The Ephesian Elders at Miletus', *TynBul* 40 (1989), 77–85.

226   Bibliography

Hemer, Colin J. and Gempf, Conrad H. (ed.), *The Book of Acts in the Setting of Hellenistic History*, WUNT 49, Tübingen: J. C. B. Mohr (Paul Siebeck), 1989.

Hengel, Martin, *Acts and the History of Earliest Christianity*, London: SCM, 1979.

Between Jesus and Paul, London: SCM, 1983.

Hock, Ronald F., *The Social Context of Paul's Ministry: Tentmaking and Apostleship*, Philadelphia: Fortress Press, 1980.

Holtz, Traugott, *Der erste Brief an die Thessalonicher*, EKKNT 13, Zürich: Benzig, 1986.

Hooker, Morna D., 'Were There False Teachers in Colossae?' in Lindars, Barnabas, SSF and Smalley, Stephen S. (eds.), *Christ and Spirit in the New Testament: In Honour of Charles Francis Digby Moule*, Cambridge University Press, 1973, pp. 315–31.

Houlden, J. L., *The Pastoral Epistles: I and II Timothy, Titus*, TPI NT Commentary, London: SCM, 1976, repr. 1989.

Hubbard, Benjamin J., 'Commissioning Stories in Luke-Acts: A Study of Their Antecedents, Form and Content', *Semeia* 8 (1977), 103–26.

Hurd, John C., 'Paul Ahead of his Time: 1 Thess. 2:13–16' in Richardson, Peter and Granskou, David (eds.), *Anti-Judaism in Early Christianity, vol. 1: Paul and the Gospels*, Studies in Christianity and Judaism 2, Waterloo, Ont.: Wilfrid Laurier University Press, 1986, pp. 21–36.

Jeremias, Joachim, *Unknown Sayings of Jesus*, London: SPCK, 1958.

The Eucharistic Words of Jesus, London: SCM, 1966.

Jervell, Jacob, *Luke and the People of God*, Minneapolis: Augsburg, 1972.

The Unknown Paul, Minneapolis: Augsburg, 1984.

Die Apostelgeschichte, MeyerK, 17th edn, Göttingen: Vandenhoeck & Ruprecht, 1998.

Jewett, Robert, *Dating Paul's Life*, London: SCM, 1979.

The Thessalonian Correspondence: Pauline Rhetoric and Millenarian Piety, FFNT, Philadelphia: Fortress Press, 1986.

Johanson, Bruce C., *To All the Brethren: A Text-Linguistic and Rhetorical Approach to 1 Thessalonians*, ConB NT Series 16, Uppsala: Almqvist & Wiksell International, 1987.

Johnson, Luke T., *The Literary Function of Possessions in Luke-Acts*, Missoula: Scholars Press, 1977.

The Acts of the Apostles, Sacra Pagina 5, Collegeville: Liturgical Press, 1992.

The Gospel of Luke, Sacra Pagina 3, Collegeville: Liturgical Press, 1992.

'Luke-Acts, Book of' in Freedman, David N. (ed.), *Anchor Bible Dictionary*, vol. IV, New York: Doubleday, 1992, pp. 403–20.

Letters to Paul's Delegates, The NT in Context, Valley Forge, PA: Trinity Press International, 1996.

The Real Jesus: The Misguided Quest for the Historical Jesus and the Truth of the Traditional Gospels, New York: HarperSanFrancisco, 1996.

Juel, Donald, *Luke-Acts*, London: SCM, 1983.

Kaestli, Jean-Daniel, 'Luke-Acts and the Pastoral Epistles: The Thesis of a Common Authorship' in Tuckett, Christopher M. (ed.), *Luke's Literary Achievement: Collected Essays*, JSNTSup 116, Sheffield Academic Press, 1995, pp. 110–26.

Karris, Robert J., *Luke: Artist and Theologian. Luke's Passion Account as Literature*, Theological Inquires: Studies in Contemporary Biblical and Theological Problems, New York: Paulist Press, 1985.

Käsemann, Ernst, *The Disciples of John the Baptist in Ephesus*, SBT 41, London: SCM Press, 1964.

'Ephesians and Acts' in Keck, Leander E. and Martyn, J. Louis (eds.), *Studies in Luke-Acts: Essays Presented in Honour of Paul Schubert*, London: SPCK, 1968, pp. 288–97.

New Testament Questions of Today, London: SCM, 1969.

Kaye, Bruce N., 'Acts' Portrait of Silas', *NovT* 21 (1979), 13–26.

Keck, Leander E. and Martyn, J. L. (eds.), *Studies in Luke-Acts*, London: SPCK, 1968.

Kee, Howard Clark, *To Every Nation under Heaven: The Acts of the Apostles*, The NT in Context, Harrisburg: Trinity Press International, 1997.

Kelly, J. N. D., *A Commentary on the Pastoral Epistles*, Black's NT Commentaries, London: A. & C. Black, 1963.

Kennedy, George A., *New Testament Interpretation through Rhetorical Criticism*, Chapel Hill: University of North Carolina Press, 1984.

Kenyon, F. G., 'Tachygraphy' in Hammond, N. G. L. and Scullard, H. H. (eds.), *Oxford Classical Dictionary*, 2nd edn, Oxford: Clarendon Press, 1970, pp. 1033–4.

Kenyon, Frederick G. and Legg, S. C. E., 'The Textual Data' in Dunkerley, Roderic (ed.), *The Ministry and the Sacraments: Report of the Theological Commission appointed by the Continuation Committee of the Faith and Order Movement*, London: SCM, 1937, pp. 272–86.

Kilgallen, John J., 'Paul's Speech to the Ephesian Elders: Its Structure', *ETL* 70 (1994), 112–21.

Kim, Seyoon, *The Origin of Paul's Gospel*, WUNT, 2nd series: 4, 2nd edn, Tübingen: J. C. B. Mohr (Paul Siebeck), 1984.

'Jesus, Sayings of' in Hawthorne, Gerald F., Martin, Ralph P. and Reid, Daniel G. (eds.), *Dictionary of Paul and His Letters*, Downers Grove/Leicester: IVP, 1993, pp. 474–92.

Klein, Günther, *Die zwölf Apostel: Ursprung und Gehalt einer Idee*, FRLANT 77, Göttingen: Vandenhoeck & Ruprecht, 1961.

Klostermann, Erich, *Das Lukasevangelium*, HNT 5, 3rd edn, Tübingen: J. C. B. Mohr (Paul Siebeck), 1975.

Knight, George W., III, *The Pastoral Epistles; A Commentary on the Greek Text*, NIGTC, Grand Rapids/Carlisle: Eerdmans/Paternoster Press, 1992.

Knoch, Otto, *Die »Testamente« des Petrus und Paulus: Die Sicherung der apostolischen Überlieferung in der spätneutestamentlichen Zeit*, Stuttgarter Bibelstudien 62, Stuttgart: KBW Verlag, 1973.

Knox, John, 'Acts and the Pauline Letter Corpus' in Keck, Leander E. and Martyn, J. L. (eds.), *Studies in Luke-Acts*, London: SPCK, 1968, pp. 279–87.

Chapters in a Life of Paul, revised edn, Macon, Ga.: Mercer University Press, 1987.

Koester, Helmut, 'I Thessalonians Experiment in Christian Writing' in Church, F. F. and George, T. (eds.), *Continuity and Discontinuity in Church History: Essays Presented to G. H. Williams*, Leiden: Brill, 1979, pp. 33–44.

Kolenkow, Anitra Bingham and Collins, John J., 'Testaments' in Kraft, Robert A. and Nickelsburg, George W. E. (eds.), *Early Judaism and Its Modern Interpreters*, SBLBMI, Atlanta: Scholars Press, 1986, pp. 259–85.

Kümmel, W. G., *Introduction to the New Testament*, revised edn, London: SCM, 1975.

Kurz, William S., 'Luke 22:14–38 and Greco-Roman and Biblical Farewell Addresses', *JBL* (1985), 251–68.

'Narrative Approaches to Luke-Acts', *Bib* 68 (1987), 195–220.

Farewell Addresses in the New Testament, Collegeville: Liturgical Press, 1990.

Reading Luke-Acts: Dynamics of Biblical Narrative, Louisville, Ken.: Westminster Press/John Knox Press, 1993.

Lake, Kirsopp, *The Earlier Epistles of St Paul: Their Motive and Origin*, 2nd edn, London: Rivingtons, 1914.

Lambrecht, Jan, 'Paul's Farewell-address at Miletus (Acts 20,17–38)' in Kremer, J. (ed.), *Les Actes des Apôtres: Tradition, Rédaction, Theologie*, Gembloux et Leuven: 1979, pp. 307–37.

Lampe, G. W. H., '"Grievous Wolves" (Acts 20:29)' in Lindars, Barnabas and Smalley, Stephen S. (eds.), *Christ and Spirit in the New Testament: In Honour of C. F. D. Moule*, Cambridge University Press, 1973, pp. 253–68.

'The Two Swords (Luke 22:35–38)' in Bammel, Ernst and Moule, C. F. D. (eds.), *Jesus and the Politics of His Day*, Cambridge University Press, 1984, pp. 335–51.

Lange, J. P., *Theological and Homiletical Commentary on the Acts of the Apostles*, 2 vols., Edinburgh: T. & T. Clark, 1869.

Lentz, John C., Jr, *Luke's Portrait of Paul*, SNTSMS 77, Cambridge University Press, 1993.

Lightfoot, J. B., *St Paul's Epistle to the Philippians*, 12th edn, Peabody, Mass.: Hendrickson, 1889, repr. 1993.

Notes on the Epistles of St Paul, London/Peabody, Mass.: Macmillan/Hendrickson, 1895, repr. 1993.

Lincoln, Andrew T., *Ephesians*, WBC 42, Dallas, Tex.: Word Books, 1990.

Lindemann, Andreas, *Paulus im ältesten Christentum: Das Bild des Apostels und die Rezeption der paulinischen Theologie in der frühchristlichen Literatur*, BHT 58, Tübingen: J. C. B. Mohr, 1979.

Lock, Walter, *A Critical and Exegetical Commentary on the Pastoral Epistles*, ICC, Edinburgh: T. & T. Clark, 1936.

Longenecker, Richard N., *Paul: Apostle of Liberty*, Grand Rapids: Baker Book House, 1964, repr. 1976.

'The Acts of the Apostles' in Gaebelein, Frank E. (ed.), *The Expositor's Bible Commentary*, vol. 9, Grand Rapids: Zondervan, 1981, pp. 207–573.

Lövestam, Evald, 'Paul's Address at Miletus', *ST* 41 (1987), 1–10.

Lüdemann, Gerd, 'A Chronology of Paul' in Corley, Bruce (ed.), *Colloquy on New Testament Studies: A Time for Reappraisal and Fresh Approaches*, Macon, Ga.: Mercer University Press, 1983, pp. 289–307.

Paul, Apostle to the Gentiles: Studies in Chronology, ET of *Paulus, der Heidenapostel, vol. 1: Studien zur Chronologie*, London: SCM, 1984.

Das frühe Christentum nach den Traditionen der Apostelgeschichte: Ein Kommentar, Göttingen: Vandenhoeck & Ruprecht, 1987.

Early Christianity according to the Traditions in Acts: A Commentary, ET of *Das frühe Christentum nach den Traditionen der Apostelgeschichte: Ein Kommentar*, London: SCM, 1989.

Lull, David J., 'The Servant-Benefactor as a Model of Greatness', *NovT* 28 (1986), 289–305.

Lund, N. W., *Chiasmus in the New Testament*, Peabody, Mass.: Hendrickson, 1942, repr. 1992.

Lyons, George, *Pauline Autobiography: Towards a New Understanding*, SBLDS 73, Atlanta: Scholars Press, 1985.

Maddox, Robert, *The Purpose of Luke-Acts*, Edinburgh: T. & T. Clark, 1982.

Magness, J. Lee, *Sense and Absence: Structure and Suspension in the Ending of Mark's Gospel*, SBLSS, Atlanta, Ga.: Scholars Press, 1986.

Malherbe, Abraham J., 'Exhortation in First Thessalonians', *NovT* 25 (1983), 238–56.

Paul and the Thessalonians, Philadelphia: Fortress Press, 1987.

'Did the Thessalonians Write to Paul?' in Fortna, R. T. and Gaventa, Beverly R. (eds.), *The Conversation Continues: Studies in Paul and John in Honor of J. Louis Martyn*, Nashville: Abingdon Press, 1990, pp. 246–57.

'Hellenistic Moralists and the New Testament', *ANRW* II/26.1 (1992), 267–333.

Marshall, I. Howard, *Luke: Historian and Theologian*, Exeter: Paternoster Press, 1970.

The Gospel of Luke: A Commentary on the Greek Text, NIGTC, Exeter: Paternoster Press, 1978.

The Acts of the Apostles: An Introduction and Commentary, Tyndale NT Commentaries, Leicester: IVP, 1980.

Last Supper and Lord's Supper, Exeter: Paternoster Press, 1980.

'Pauline Theology in the Thesssalonian Correspondence' in Hooker, Morna D. and Wilson, Stephen G. (eds.), *Paul and Paulinism: Essays in Honour of C. K. Barrett*, London: SPCK, 1982, pp. 173–83.

1 and 2 Thessalonians, NCB, London: Marshall Morgan & Scott, 1983.

The Acts of the Apostles, NT Guides, Sheffield: JSOT Press, 1992.

'Acts and the "Former Treatise"' in Winter, Bruce W. and Clarke, Andrew D. (eds.), *The Book of Acts in its Ancient Literary Setting*, A1CS 1, Carlisle/Grand Rapids: Paternoster Press/Eerdmans, 1993, pp. 163–82.

review of Alexander, Loveday, *The Preface to Luke's Gospel: Literary Convention and Social Context in Luke 1.1–4 and Acts 1.1* (Cambridge University Press, 1993) in *EvQ* 66 (1994), 373–6.

'"Israel" and the Story of Salvation: One Theme in Two Parts' in Moessner, David P. (ed.), *Luke the Interpreter of Israel*, 2 vols., Philadelphia: Fortress Press, forthcoming.

Martin, Ralph P., 'An Epistle in Search of a Life-Setting', *ExpTim* 79 (1967–68), 296–302.

New Testament Foundations, vol. 2: Acts-Revelation, Exeter: Paternoster Press, 1978.

Ephesians, Colossians and Philemon, Interpretation, Atlanta: John Knox Press, 1991.

Mattill, Andrew J., Jr, 'The Purpose of Acts: Schneckenburger Reconsidered' in Gasque, W. W. and Martin, Ralph P. (eds.), *Apostolic History and the Gospel: Biblical and Historical Essays Presented to F. F. Bruce on His Sixtieth Birthday*, Exeter: Paternoster Press, 1970, pp. 108–22.

'The Jesus-Paul Parallels and the Purpose of Luke-Acts', *NovT* 17 (1975), 15–46.

'The Value of Acts as a Source for the Study of Paul' in Talbert, Charles H. (ed.), *Perspectives on Luke-Acts*, Edinburgh: T. & T. Clark, 1978, pp. 76–98.

Metzger, Bruce M., *The Text of the New Testament: Its Transmission, Corruption and Restoration*, 2nd edn, Oxford University Press, 1968.

Michel, H.-J., *Die Abschiedsrede des Paulus an die Kirche Apg. 20,17–38: Motivgeschichte und theologische Bedeutung*, SANT 35, München: Kösel-Verlag, 1973.

Milligan, George, *St Paul's Epistles to the Thessalonians*, London: Macmillan, 1908.

Minear, Paul S., 'A Note on Luke xxii 36', *NovT* 7 (1964), 128–34.

review of Talbert, Charles H., *Literary Patterns, Theological Themes, and the Genre of Luke-Acts* (Missoula: Scholars Press, 1974) in *JAAR* 45 (1977), 85–6.

Mitchell, Margaret M., 'Concerning περὶ δέ in 1 Corinthians', *NovT* 31 (1989), 229–56.

Mitton, C. Leslie, *The Epistle to the Ephesians: Its Authorship, Origin and Purpose*, Oxford: Clarendon Press, 1951.

Ephesians, NCB, Grand Rapids/London: Eerdmans/Marshall Morgan & Scott, 1973.

Moberly, Walter, 'Proclaiming Christ Crucified: Some Reflections on the Use and Abuse of the Gospels', *Anvil* 5 (1988), 31–52.

Moessner, David P., '"The Christ Must Suffer": New Light on the Jesus–Peter, Stephen, Paul Parallels in Acts', *NovT* 28 (1986), 220–56.

Moore, Arthur L., *The Parousia in the New Testament*, NovTSup 13, Leiden: Brill, 1966.

1 and 2 Thessalonians, NCB, London: Nelson/Oliphants, 1969.

Morgenthaler, R., *Die lukanische Geschichtsschreibung als Zeugnis: Gestalt und Gehalt der Kunst des Lukas*, 2 vols., ATANT 14, 15, Zürich: Zwingli, 1949.

Morris, Leon L., *The Apostolic Preaching of the Cross*, 3rd edn, Leicester: IVP, 1965.

The Cross in the New Testament, Exeter: Paternoster Press, 1965.

Studies in the Fourth Gospel, Exeter: Paternoster Press, 1969.

The Gospel according to St Luke: An Introduction and Commentary, Tyndale NT Commentaries, Leicester: IVP, 1974.

The First and Second Epistles to the Thessalonians, NICNT, revised edn, Grand Rapids: Eerdmans, 1991.

Moule, C. F. D., 'The Christology of Acts' in Keck, Leander E. and Martyn, J. L. (eds.), *Studies in Luke-Acts*, London: SPCK, 1968, pp. 159–85.

'The Problem of the Pastoral Epistles: A Reappraisal' in Moule, C. F. D. (ed.), *Essays in New Testament Interpretation*, Cambridge University Press, 1982, pp. 113–32.

Muhlack, Gudrun, *Die Parallelen von Lukas-Evangelium und Apostelgeschichte*, Theologie und Wirklichkeit 8, Frankfurt: Lang, 1979.

Munck, Johannes, 'Discours d'adieu dans le Nouveau Testament et dans la littérature biblique' in Cullmann, Oscar and Ménoud, P. (eds.), *Aux Sources de la Tradition Chrétienne: Mélanges offerts à M. Maurice Goguel*, Neuchâtel/Paris: Delachaux & Niestlé, 1950, pp. 155–70.

Paul and the Salvation of Mankind, London: SCM, 1959.

'I Thess. I.9–10 and the Missionary Preaching of Paul: Textual Exegesis and Hermeneutic Reflections', *NTS* 9 (1962), 95–110.

The Acts of the Apostles, AB 31, New York: Doubleday, 1967.

Neil, William, *The Epistle of Paul to the Thessalonians*, MNTC, London: Hodder & Stoughton, 1950.

The Acts of the Apostles, NCB, London: Oliphants, 1973.

Nelson, Peter K., 'Leadership and Discipleship: A Study of Luke 22:24–30', PhD thesis, Trinity College, Bristol/CNAA, 1991.

Neyrey, Jerome, SJ, *The Passion according to Luke: A Redaction Study of Luke's Soteriology*, New York: Paulist Press, 1985.

Nolland, John, *Luke 1–9:20*, WBC 35A, Dallas, Tex.: Word Books, 1989.

Luke 9:21–18:34, WBC 35B, Dallas, Tex.: Word Books, 1993.

Luke 18:35–24:53, WBC 35C, Dallas, Tex.: Word Books, 1993.

Norden, Eduard, *Agnostos Theos: Untersuchungen zur Formengeschichte religiöser Rede*, Darmstadt: Wissenschaftliche Buchgesellschaft, 1912, repr. 1956.

O'Brien, Peter T., 'Prayer in Luke-Acts', *TynBul* 24 (1973), 111–27.

O'Neill, J. C., *The Recovery of Paul's Letter to the Galatians*, London: SPCK, 1972.

Paul's Letter to the Romans, Harmondsworth: Penguin, 1975.

O'Toole, Robert F., 'Parallels between Jesus and His Disciples in Luke-Acts', *BZ* 27 (1983), 195–212.

The Unity of Luke's Theology, GNS 9, Wilmington, Del.: Michael Glazier, 1984.

'Last Supper' in Freedman, David N. (ed.), *Anchor Bible Dictionary*, New York: Doubleday, 1992, vol. IV, pp. 234–41.

Okeke, G. E., '1 Thessalonians 2.13–16: The Fate of the Unbelieving Jews', *NTS* 27 (1980), 127–36.

Orr, W. F. and Walther, J. A., *1 Corinthians*, AB 32, New York: Doubleday, 1976.

Osborne, Grant R., *The Hermeneutical Spiral: A Comprehensive Introduction to Biblical Interpretation*, Downers Grove: IVP, 1991.

Page, Sydney H. T., 'The Authenticity of the Ransom Logion (Mark 10:45b)' in France, R. T. and Wenham, David (eds.), *Gospel Perspectives: Studies of History and Tradition in the Four Gospels*, vol. I, Sheffield: JSOT Press, 1980, pp. 137–61.

Parsons, Mikeal C., *The Departure of Jesus in Luke-Acts: The Ascension Narratives in Context*, JSNTSup 21, Sheffield: JSOT Press, 1987.

Parsons, Mikeal C. and Pervo, Richard I., *Rethinking the Unity of Luke and Acts*, Minneapolis: Fortress Press, 1993.

Pearson, Birger A., '1 Thessalonians 2:13–16: A Deutero-Pauline Interpolation', *HTR* 64 (1971), 79–94.

Pervo, Richard I., *Luke's Story of Paul*, Philadelphia: Fortress Press, 1990.

Pesch, Rudolf, *Das Abendmahl und Jesu Todesverständnis*, QD 80, Freiburg: Herder, 1978.

Die Apostelgeschichte, EKKNT, 2 vols., Zürich/Einsiedeln/Köln/Neunkirchen: Benzinger-Verlag, 1986.

Petersen, N., *Literary Criticism for New Testament Critics*, Philadelphia: Fortress Press, 1978.

Peterson, David, *Engaging with God: A Biblical Theology of Worship*, Leicester: Apollos, 1992.

'The Motif of Fulfilment and the Purpose of Luke-Acts' in Winter, Bruce W. and Clarke, Andrew D. (eds.), *The Book of Acts in its Ancient Literary Setting*, A1CS 1, Carlisle/Grand Rapids: Paternoster Press/Eerdmans, 1993, pp. 83–104.

Pfitzner, Victor C., *Paul and the Agon Motif: Traditional Athletic Imagery in the Pauline Literature*, NovTSup 16, Leiden: Brill, 1967.

Plummer, Alfred, *A Critical and Exegetical Commentary on the Gospel according to S. Luke*, ICC, 4th edn, Edinburgh: T. & T. Clark, 1913.

A Commentary on St Paul's First Epistle to the Thessalonians, London: Robert Scott, 1918.

Porter, Stanley E., 'Thucydides 1.22.1 and Speeches in Acts: Is There a Thucydidean View?', *NovT* 32 (1990), 121–42.

'The "We" Passages' in Gill, David W. J. and Gempf, Conrad H. (eds.), *The Book of Acts in Its Graeco-Roman Setting*, A1CS 2, Carlisle/Grand Rapids: Paternoster Press/Eerdmans, 1994, pp. 545–74.

Powell, Mark Allen, *What is Narrative Criticism?*, London: SPCK, 1993.

Praeder, Susan M., 'Jesus–Paul, Peter–Paul, and Jesus–Peter Parallelisms in Luke-Acts: A History of Reader Response', *SBLSP* 1984, 23–39.

Prast, Franz, *Presbyter und Evangelium in nachapostolischer Zeit*, Stuttgart: Katholisches Bibelwerk, 1979.

Prior, Michael, CM, *Paul the Letter-Writer and the Second Letter to Timothy*, JSNTSup 23, Sheffield: JSOT Press, 1989.

Rackham, R. B., *The Acts of the Apostles*, Westminster Commentaries, 2nd edn, London: Methuen, 1904.

Radl, W., *Paulus und Jesus im lukanischen Doppelwerk: Untersuchungen zu Parallelmotiven im Lukasevangelium und in der Apostelgeschichte*, Europäische Hochschulschriften, 23.49, Frankfurt/Bern: Peter Lang/Herbert Lang, 1975.

Ramsay, William M., *St Paul the Traveller and Roman Citizen*, 17th edn, London: Hodder & Stoughton, 1930.

Rapske, Brian M., 'Pauline Imprisonment and the Lukan Defense of the Missionary Prisoner Paul in the Light of Greco-Roman Sources', PhD thesis, Aberdeen University, 1992.

The Book of Acts and Paul in Roman Custody, A1CS 3, Carlisle/Grand Rapids: Paternoster Press/Eerdmans, 1994.

review of Lentz, John C., Jr, *Luke's Portrait of Paul* (Cambridge University Press, 1993) in *EvQ* 66 (1994), 347–53.

Reiling, J. and Swellengrebel, J. L., *A Translator's Handbook to the Gospel of Luke*, UBS Helps for Translators 10, Leiden: Brill, 1971.

Richard, Earl, 'Jesus' Passion and Death in Acts' in Sylva, Dennis D. (ed.), *Reimaging the Death of the Lukan Jesus*, BBB 73, Frankfurt: Anton Hain, 1990, pp. 125–69.

Richard, Earl J., *First and Second Thessalonians*, Sacra Pagina 11, Collegeville: Liturgical Press, 1995.

Richardson, Peter and Hurd, John C. (eds.), *From Jesus to Paul: Studies in Honour of Francis Wright Beare*, Waterloo, Ont.: Wilfrid Laurier University Press, 1984.

Rienecker, Fritz, *Das Evangelium des Lukas*, Wuppertaler Studienbibel, Wuppertal: Brockhaus Verlag, 1974.

Riesner, Rainer, 'Jesus as Preacher and Teacher' in Wansbrough, Henry (ed.), *Jesus and the Oral Gospel Tradition*, JSNTSup 64, Sheffield: JSOT Press, 1991, pp. 185–210.

Die Frühzeit des Apostels Paulus: Studien zur Chronologie, Missionstrategie und Theologie, WUNT 71, Tübingen: J. C. B. Mohr (Paul Siebeck), 1994.

Rigaux, Béda, OFM, *Saint Paul: Les Épitres aux Thessaloniciens*, Gembloux: Duculot, 1956.

Robbins, Vernon K., 'By Land and by Sea: The We-Passages and Ancient Sea Voyages' in Talbert, Charles H. (ed.), *Perspectives on Luke-Acts*, Edinburgh: T. & T. Clark, 1978, pp. 215–42.

Rohde, Joachim, *Rediscovering the Teaching of the Evangelists*, London: SCM, 1968.

Roloff, Jürgen, *Die Apostelgeschichte*, NTD 5, Göttingen: Vandenhoeck & Ruprecht, 1981.

Ropes, James H., 'An Observation on the Style of St Luke', *HSCP* 12 (1904), 299–305.

Ross, J. M., 'The Spelling of Jerusalem in Acts', *NTS* 38 (1992), 474–6.

Saller, Richard P., *Personal Patronage under the Early Empire*, Cambridge University Press, 1982.

Sanders, E. P., *Paul, the Law, and the Jewish People*, London: SCM, 1983.

Sanders, E. P. and Davies, Margaret, *Studying the Synoptic Gospels*, London: SCM, 1989.

Sanders, Jack T., *The Jews in Luke-Acts*, London: SCM, 1987.

Sandmel, Samuel, 'Parallelomania', *JBL* 81 (1962), 1–13.

Schille, Gottfried, *Die Apostelgeschichte des Lukas*, THKNT, Berlin: Evangelische Verlagsanstalt, 1983.

Schlueter, Carol J., *Filling up the Measure: Polemical Hyperbole in 1 Thessalonians 2.14–16*, JSNTSup 98, Sheffield: JSOT Press, 1994.

Schmeichel, Waldemar, 'Does Luke Make a Soteriological Statement in Acts 20:28?', *SBLSP* 1982, 501–14.

Schmidt, Daryl, '1 Thess 2:13–16: Linguistic Evidence for an Interpolation', *JBL* 102 (1983), 269–79.

Schmiedel, W. G., 'The Book of Acts' in Cheyne, T. K. and Black, J. Sutherland (eds.), *Encyclopaedia Biblica*, vol. 1, London: A. & C. Black, 1899, cols. 37–57.

Schmithals, Walter, *Paul and the Gnostics*, ET of *Paulus und die Gnostiker*, New York: Abingdon Press, 1972.

Das Evangelium nach Lukas, Zürcher Bibelkommentare: Neues Testament 3.1, Zürich: Theologischer Verlag, 1980.

Die Apostelgeschichte des Lukas, Zürcher Bibelkommentare: Neuen Testaments 3.2, Zürich: Theologischer Verlag, 1982.

'Apg 20,17–38 und das Problem einer "Paulusquelle"' in Bussmann, Claus and Radl, Walter (eds.), *Der Treue Gottes Trauen: Beiträge zum Werk des Lukas für Gerhard Schneider*, Freiburg/Basel/Wien: Herder, 1991, pp. 307–22.

Schnackenburg, Rudolf, *Ephesians: A Commentary*, Edinburgh: T. & T. Clark, 1991.

Schneckenburger, M., *Über den Zweck der Apostelgeschichte: Zugleich eine Ergänzung der neueren Kommentare*, Bern: Fisher, 1841.

Schneider, Gerhard, *Das Evangelium nach Lukas*, 2 vols. Ökumenischer Taschenbuchkommentar zum Neuen Testament 3.1 & 2, Gütersloh: Gütersloher Verlaghaus Gerd Mohn, 1977.

'Zur Bedeutung von καθεξῆς im lukanischen Doppelwerk', *ZNW* 68 (1977), 128–31.

Die Apostelgeschichte, 2 vols., HTKNT, Friedburg, Basel, Vienna: Herder, 1980, 1982.

Schulze, H., 'Die Unterlagen für die Abschiedsrede zu Milet in Apostlegesch. 20,18–38', *TSK* 73 (1900), 119–25.

Schürmann, Heinz, *Der Paschamahlbericht: Lk 22,(7–14.) 15–18. I. Teil einer Quellenkritischen Untersuchung des lukanischen Abendmahlberichtes Lk 22,7–38*, NTAbh 19.5, Münster: Aschendorffsche Verlagsbuchhandlung, 1953.

Der Einsetzungsbericht Lk 22,19–20: II. Teil einer Quellenkritischen Untersuchung des lukanischen Abendmahlberichtes Lk 22,7–38, NTAbh 20.4, Münster: Aschendorffsche Verlagsbuchhandlung, 1955.

Jesu Abschiedsrede Lk 22,21–38: III. Teil einer Quellenkritischen Untersuchung des lukanischen Abendmahlsberichtes Lk 22,7–38, NTAbh 20.5, Münster: Aschendorffsche Verlagsbuchhandlung, 1957.

'Das Testament des Paulus für die Kirche, Apg. 20,18–35' in Schürmann, Heinz, *Traditionsgeschichtliche Untersuchungen zu den synoptischen Evangelien*, Düsseldorf: Patmos, 1968, pp. 310–40.

Ursprung und Gehalt: Erörterungen und Besinnungen zum Neuen Testament, Kommentare und Beiträge zum Alten und Neuen Testament, Düsseldorf: Patmos-Verlag, 1970.

Schürmann, Heinz and Egenolf, Hans-Andreas, *The First and Second Epistles to the Thessalonians*, ET of Heinz Schürmann, *Der Erste Brief an die Thessalonicher* (Düsseldorf: Patmos-Verlag, 1964) and Hans-

Andreas Egenolf, *Der Zweite Brief an die Thessalonicher* (Düsseldorf: Patmos-Verlag, 1965), NT for Spiritual Reading, London: Burns & Oates, 1969.

Schweizer, Eduard, *The Good News according to Luke*, Atlanta: John Knox Press, 1984.

Seccombe, David Peter, *Possessions and the Poor in Luke-Acts*, Studien zum Neuen Testament und Seiner Umwelt, B.6, Linz: Studien zum Neuen Testament und Seiner Umwelt, 1982.

Senior, Donald, CP, *The Passion of Jesus in the Gospel of Luke*, Collegeville: Liturgical Press, 1989.

Shepherd, William H., Jr, *The Narrative Function of the Holy Spirit as a Character in Luke-Acts*, SBLDS 147, Atlanta: Scholars Press, 1994.

Sherwin-White, A. N., *Roman Society and Roman Law in the New Testament*, Grand Rapids/Oxford: Baker Book House/Oxford University Press, 1963, repr. 1981.

Smith, Abraham, *Comfort One Another: Reconstructing the Rhetoric and Audience of 1 Thessalonians*, Literary Currents in Biblical Interpretation, Louisville, Ken.: Westminster John Knox Press, 1995.

Smith, Barry D., *Jesus' Last Passover Meal*, Lewiston, N.Y./Lampeter: Edwin Mellen Press, 1993.

Soards, Marion L., *The Passion according to Luke: The Special Material of Luke 22*, JSNTSup 14, Sheffield: JSOT Press, 1987.

The Speeches in Acts: Their Content, Context, and Concerns, Louisville, Ken.: Westminster Press/John Knox Press, 1994.

Soltau, W., 'Die Herkunft der Reden in der Apostelgeschichte', *ZNW* 4 (1903), 128–54.

Spencer, F. Scott, *Acts*, Readings: A New Biblical Commentary, Sheffield: Sheffield Academic Press, 1997.

Squires, John T., *The Plan of God in Luke-Acts*, SNTSMS 76, Cambridge University Press, 1993.

Stanton, Graham N., *Jesus of Nazareth in New Testament Preaching*, SNTSMS 27, Cambridge University Press, 1974.

Stark, Rodney, 'Antioch as the Social Situation for Matthew's Gospel' in Balch, David L. (ed.), *Social History of the Matthean Community: Cross-Disciplinary Approaches*, Minneapolis: Fortress Press, 1991, pp. 189–210.

Stauffer, Ethelbert, *New Testament Theology*, ET of *Die Theologie des neuen Testaments* (5th edn), London: SCM, 1955.

Stein, Robert H., *The Synoptic Problem*, Leicester: IVP, 1988.

Luke, New American Commentary 24, Nashville: Broadman Press, 1992.

Stier, Rudolf, *The Words of the Apostles*, Edinburgh: T. & T. Clark, 1869.

Stolle, Volker, *Der Zeuge als Angeklagter: Untersuchungen zum Paulusbild des Lukas*, Stuttgart: Kohlhammer, 1973.

Strelan, Rick, *Paul, Artemis, and the Jews in Ephesus*, BZNW 80, Berlin: de Gruyter, 1996.

Strobel, August, 'Schreiben des Lukas? Zum sprachliche Problem der Pastoralbriefe', *NTS* 15 (1968–9), 191–210.

Sylva, Dennis D., 'Ierousalēm and Hierosoluma in Luke-Acts', *ZNW* 74 (1983), 207–221.

Sylva, Dennis D. (ed.), *Reimaging the Death of the Lukan Jesus*, BBB 73, Frankfurt am Main: Anton Hain, 1990.

Talbert, Charles H., 'The Redaction Critical Search for Luke the Theologian' in Miller, Donald G. (ed.), *Jesus and Man's Hope*, vol. I, Pittsburgh Theological Seminary, 1970, pp. 171–222.

Literary Patterns, Theological Themes, and the Genre of Luke-Acts, SBLMS 20, Missoula: Scholars Press, 1974.

review of Michel, H.-J., *Die Abschiedsrede des Paulus an die Kirche: Apg. 20,17–38* (München: Kösel-Verlag, 1973) in *JBL* 94 (1975), 145.

Reading Luke: A New Commentary for Preachers, London: SPCK, 1984.

'Discipleship in Luke-Acts' in Segovia, Fernando F. (ed.), *Discipleship in the New Testament*, Philadelphia: Fortress Press, 1985, pp. 62–75.

Talbert, Charles H. (ed.), *Perspectives on Luke-Acts*, Edinburgh: T. & T. Clark, 1978.

Luke-Acts, New York: Crossroad, 1984.

Tannehill, Robert C., *The Narrative Unity of Luke-Acts: A Literary Interpretation, vol. 1: The Gospel according to Luke*, Philadelphia: Fortress Press, 1986.

The Narrative Unity of Luke-Acts: A Literary Interpretation, vol. 2: The Acts of the Apostles, Minneapolis: Fortress Press, 1990.

Luke, Abingdon NT Commentaries, Nashville: Abingdon Press, 1996.

Taylor, Justin, SM, *Les Actes des Deux Apôtres VI: Commentaire Historique (Act. 18,23–23,31)*, Ebib, NS 30, Paris: Librairie Lecoffre, 1996.

Taylor, Nicholas, *Paul, Antioch and Jerusalem: A Study in Relationships and Authority in Earliest Christianity*, JSNTSup 66, Sheffield: JSOT Press, 1992.

Taylor, Vincent, *The Passion Narrative of St Luke*, SNTSMS 19, Cambridge University Press, 1972.

Thiering, Barbara, 'The Acts of the Apostles as Early Christian Art' in Maclaurin, E. C. B. (ed.), *Essays in Honour of Griffithes Wheeler Thatcher 1863–1950*, Sydney University Press, 1967, pp. 139–89.

Tholuck, F. A. G., 'Die Reden des Apostels Paulus in der Apostelgeschichte, mit seinen Briefen verglichen', *TSK* 12 (1839), 305–28.

Thomas, John Christopher, *Footwashing in John 13 and the Johannine Community*, JSNTSup 61, Sheffield: JSOT Press, 1991.

Thompson, J. A., *The Book of Jeremiah*, NICOT, Grand Rapids: Eerdmans, 1980.

Thompson, Michael B., *Clothed with Christ: The Example and Teaching of Jesus in Romans 12.1–15.13*, JSNTSup 53, Sheffield: JSOT Press, 1991.

Thomson, Ian H., *Chiasmus in the Pauline Letters*, JSNTSup 111, Sheffield Academic Press, 1995.

Thrall, Margaret E., *A Critical and Exegetical Commentary on the Second Epistle to the Corinthians*, vol. I, ICC, Edinburgh: T. & T. Clark, 1994.

Tiede, David, *Prophecy and History in Luke-Acts*, Philadelphia: Fortress Press, 1980.

Towner, Philip H., *The Goal of Our Instruction: The Structure of Theology and Ethics in the Pastoral Epistles*, JSNTSup 34, Sheffield: JSOT Press, 1989.

Tragan, Pius-Ramon, 'Les «Destinaires» du Discours de Milet: Une Approche du Cadre Communautaire d'Ac 20,18–35' in Refoulé, François (ed.), *A Cause de l'Evangile: Etudes sur les Synoptiques et les Actes offertes au P. Jacques Dupont, OSB à l'occasion de son 70e anniversaire*, LD 123, Paris: Editions du Cerf, 1985, pp. 779–98.

Trites, A. Allison, *The New Testament Concept of Witness*, SNTSMS 31, Cambridge University Press, 1977.

Trompf, G. W., *The Idea of Historical Recurrence in Western Thought: From Antiquity to the Reformation*, Berkeley/Los Angeles/London: University of California Press, 1979.

Turner, Max, *Power from on High: The Spirit in Israel's Restoration and Witness in Luke-Acts*, JPT Supplement Series 9, Sheffield Academic Press, 1996.

Tyson, Joseph B., *The Death of Jesus in Luke-Acts*, Columbia: University of South Carolina Press, 1986.

Images of Judaism in Luke-Acts, Columbia: University of South Carolina Press, 1992.

van Manen, W. C., 'Paul' in Cheyne, T. K. and Black, J. Sutherland (eds.), *Encyclopaedia Biblica*, vol. III, London: A. & C. Black, 1902, cols. 3603–6, 3620–38.

Vielhauer, Phillip, 'On the Paulinism of Acts' in Keck, Leander E. and Martyn, J. L. (eds.), *Studies in Luke-Acts*, ET of 'Zum Paulinismus der Apostelgeschichte' (1950), London: SPCK, 1968, pp. 33–50.

Wainwright, Allan, 'Where Did Silas Go? (And What Was His Connection with *Galatians*?)', *JSNT* 8 (1980), 66–70.

Walaskay, Paul W., *Acts*, Westminster Bible Companions, Louisville, Ken.: Westminster John Knox Press, 1998.

Walker, W. O., Jr, 'Acts and the Pauline Corpus Reconsidered', *JSNT* 24 (1985), 3–23.

Walton, Steve, 'Sacrifice and Priesthood in Relation to the Christian Life and Church in the New Testament' in Beckwith, R. T. and Selman, Martin J. (eds.), *Sacrifice in the Bible*, Carlisle/Grand Rapids: Paternoster Press/Baker Book House, 1995, pp. 136–56.

'What Has Aristotle to Do with Paul? Rhetorical Criticism and 1 Thessalonians', *TynBul* 46 (1995), 229–50.

'Rhetorical Criticism: An Introduction', *Themelios* 21 (1995–6), 4–9.

Wanamaker, Charles A., *The Epistles to the Thessalonians*, NIGTC, Grand Rapids/Exeter: Eerdmans/Paternoster Press, 1990.

Watson, Duane F., 'Paul's Speech to the Ephesian Elders (Acts 20:17–38): Epideictic Rhetoric of Farewell' in Watson, Duane F. (ed.), *Persuasive Artistry: Studies in New Testament Rhetoric in Honor of George A. Kennedy*, JSNTSup 50, Sheffield: JSOT Press, 1991, pp. 184–208.

Weatherly, Jon A., 'The Jews in Luke-Acts', *TynBul* 40 (1989), 107–17.

'The Authenticity of 1 Thessalonians 2.13–16: Additional Evidence', *JSNT* 42 (1991), 79–98.

238   Bibliography

'Jewish Responsibility for the Cross in Luke-Acts', PhD thesis, Aberdeen University, 1991.

Wedderburn, A. J. M. (ed.), *Paul and Jesus: Collected Essays*, JSNTSup 37, Sheffield: JSOT Press, 1989.

Weiser, Alfons, *Die Apostelgeschichte*, Ökumenischer Taschenbuch-Kommentar zum Neuen Testament, 2 vols., Gütersloh: Gütersloher Verlaghaus Mohn, 1981, 1985.

Wenham, David, 'Paul and the Synoptic Apocalypse' in France, R. T. and Wenham, David (eds.), *Gospel Perspectives: Studies in the History and Tradition in the Four Gospels*, Sheffield: JSOT Press, 1981, vol. II, pp. 345–75.

Paul: Follower of Jesus or Founder of Christianity?, Grand Rapids: Eerdmans, 1995.

Westcott, B. F. and Hort, F. J. A., *The New Testament in the Original Greek: Introduction and Appendix*, 2nd edn, London: Macmillan, 1896.

Whelan, Caroline F., 'Amica Pauli: The Role of Phoebe in the Early Church', *JSNT* 49 (1993), 67–85.

Wilckens, Ulrich, 'Interpreting Luke-Acts in a Period of Existentialist Theology' in Keck, Leander E. and Martyn, J. L. (eds.), *Studies in Luke-Acts*, London: SPCK, 1968, pp. 60–83.

Wilder, Terry L., 'New Testament Pseudonymity and Deception', PhD thesis, Aberdeen University, 1998.

Williams, C. S. C., *A Commentary on the Acts of the Apostles*, Black's NT Commentaries, London: A. & C. Black, 1957.

Williams, David J., *Acts*, Good News Commentaries, San Francisco: Harper & Row, 1985.

Acts, NIBC 5, Peabody, MA: Hendrickson, 1990.

1 and 2 Thessalonians, NIBC 12, Peabody, MA: Hendrickson, 1992.

Wilson, Stephen G., *The Gentiles and the Gentile Mission in Luke-Acts*, SNTSMS 23, Cambridge University Press, 1973.

Luke and the Pastoral Epistles, London: SPCK, 1979.

Winter, Bruce W., 'The Public Honouring of Christian Benefactors: Romans 13.3–4 and 1 Peter 2.14–15', *JSNT* 34 (1988), 87–103.

'Entries and Ethics of the Orators and Paul (1 Thessalonians 2:1–12)', *TynBul* 44 (1993), 55–74.

Seek the Welfare of the City: Christians as Benefactors and Citizens, First-Century Christians in the Graeco-Roman World, Carlisle/Grand Rapids: Paternoster Press/Eerdmans, 1994.

'*Christentum und Antike*: Acts and Paul's *Corpus* as Ancient History' in Hillard, T. W., Kersley, R. A., Nixon, C. E. V. and Nobbs, A. (eds.), *Ancient History in a Modern University, vol. 2: Early Christianity, Late Antiquity and Beyond*, Grand Rapids/Cambridge: Eerdmans, 1997, pp. 121–30.

Witherington, Ben, III, *The Acts of the Apostles: A Socio-Rhetorical Commentary*, Carlisle/Grand Rapids: Paternoster Press/Eerdmans, 1998.

Witherup, Ronald D., SS, 'Cornelius Over and Over and Over Again: "Functional Redundancy" in the Acts of the Apostles', *JSNT* 49 (1993), 45–66.

Wright, N. T., 'The Messiah and the People of God', DPhil thesis, Oxford University, 1980.

Colossians and Philemon, Tyndale NT Commentaries, Leicester/Grand Rapids: IVP/Eerdmans, 1986.

The Climax of the Covenant: Christ and the Law in Pauline Theology, Edinburgh: T. & T. Clark, 1991.

Jesus and the Victory of God, Christian Origins and the Question of God 2, London: SPCK, 1996.

Zahn, Theodor, *Introduction to the New Testament*, vol. III, Edinburgh: T. & T. Clark, 1909.

Zehnle, Richard, 'The Salvific Character of Jesus' Death in Lucan Soteriology', *TS* 30 (1969), 420–44.

Ziesler, John, *Pauline Christianity*, Oxford Bible Series, Oxford University Press, 1990.

INDEX OF ANCIENT TEXTS

References in **bold** indicate a significant discussion.

INDEX OF MODERN AUTHORS

INDEX OF SUBJECTS

New Testament Studies

Published under the auspices of Studiorum Novi Testamenti Societas

Editor
Christopher Tuckett, University of Oxford, UK

New Testament Studies is an international periodical published under the auspices of the Studiorum Novi Testamenti Societas, whose members comprise the leading New Testament scholars writing in the world today. For over forty years the journal has published original articles and short studies on a wide range of issues pertaining to the origins, history and theology of the New Testament. Always well-documented and thoughtfully written, these articles are representative of the 'cutting edge' in a discipline which has witnessed significant new advances in recent years. Ample space is given to exegetical, historical and interpretative treatments alike, as well as to discussion of the variety of methods which can be applied to New Testament study. Contributors come from many different backgrounds and from all parts of the world. Articles are published in English, French or German.

Recent articles include

Two Philonic Prayers and Their Contexts: An analysis of *Who is the Heir of Divine things (Her.)* 24-29 and *Against Flaccus (Flac.)* 170-75, *Peder Borgen*

Sens de l'Écriture. Réexamen á la lumière de l'herméneutique philosophique et des approches littéraires récentes, *Marcel Dumais*

The First Testing of Jesus: A Rereading of Mark 1.12-13, *Jan Willem van Henten*

Kollektenbericht, 'Wir'-Bericht und Itinerar. Neue (?) Überlegungen zu einem alten Problem, *Dietrich-Alex Koch*

The Conversion of the Imagination: Scripture and Eschatology in 1 Corinthians, *Richard B. Hays*

Take a closer look - *free*
book

If you wish to receive a sample copy and further information on **New Testament Studies,**
please photocopy this coupon and send to: Journals Marketing Department,
Cambridge University Press, The Edinburgh Building, Shaftesbury Road, Cambridge, CB2 2RU, UK
or
40 West 20th Street, New York, NY 10011-4211, USA

Name _____

Address _____

_____

_____

_____

New Testament Studies is published quarterly in January, April, July and November. Volume 46 is available in 2000.
For further information on prices please contact the Journals Marketing Department
in Cambridge: tel +44 (0)1223 325806 *fax* +44 (0)1223 315052 *email* journals_marketing@cup.cam.ac.uk
in New York: tel (914) 937 9600 x 154 *fax* (914) 937 4712 *email* journals_marketing@cup.org

CAMBRIDGE
UNIVERSITY PRESS
The Edinburgh Building, Cambridge, cb2 2ru, UK
40 West 20th Street, New York, ny 10011-4211, USA